LEANING INTO THE WIND

WOMEN WRITE FROM THE HEART OF THE WEST

Edited by LINDA HASSELSTROM,
GAYDELL COLLIER, and NANCY CURTIS

A Marc Jaffe Book

A Mariner Book

HOUGHTON MIFFLIN COMPANY

Boston   New York

For information about permission to reproduce selections from this book,
write to Permissions, Houghton Mifflin Company, 215 Park Avenue South,
New York, New York 10003.

Library of Congress Cataloging-in-Publication Data
Leaning into the wind : women write from the heart of the West / edited by
Linda Hasselstrom, Gaydell Collier, and Nancy Curtis.
    p.   cm.
"A Marc Jaffe book."
ISBN 0-395-83738-3   ISBN 0-395-90131-6 (pbk.)
ISBN 978-0-395-90131-1
1. Women pioneers — West (U.S.) — Biography — Anecdotes. 2. Rural women —
West (U.S.) — Biography — Anecdotes. 3. Women Ranchers — West (U.S.) —
Biography — Anecdotes. 4. Farm life — West (U.S.) — Anecdotes.
5. Frontier and pioneer life — West (U.S.) -- Anecdotes. 6. West (U.S.) —
Biography — Anecdotes.   I. Hasselstrom, Linda M. II. Collier, Gaydell M.
III. Curtis, Nancy, date.
F596.L48   1997
978'.02'082 — dc21   96-49271   CIP

Printed in the United States of America

20 19 18 17 16 15 14 13 12 11

Illustrations by Nancy Jellico

Dedicated to all High Plains women,
whose stories, told or untold,
sing like the prairie winds.

Contents

ROSE KREMERS ~ Leaning into the Wind

Flood, drought, wind, hail, tornado, fire, financial trauma —
we suffered them all, each in turn slicing still another sliver
from my heart until I thought my heart was dead, it must
be dead, had to be dead, for survival depends upon courage
and resilience and fortitude and I had none of those. A
hollowness of soul crept in, leaving me bereft and lonely
and alone.

I don't know where it went, that utter despair, that dry-
ness of the soul. It's gone now, disappeared like a shadow
at noon. I misplaced it somewhere in that whispering sea
of grass, somewhere among the bare-root pines, or perhaps
at dusk among the wild lilies in the gray-gumbo prairie. It
was lost in the sinking of roots into the hardsod — a simple
thing after all, to anchor, to stay. It just takes a leaning into
the wind.

Introduction:
Grass Widows and
Wrinklebelly Women

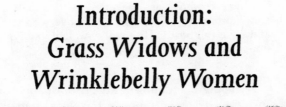

> Pay a holy kind of attention.
> — *Morgan Songi*

Americans seize on symbols for a variety of reasons. Craving a macho look, a New York stockbroker slips on pointy-toed boots in psychedelic colors to dine with a lady in a fringed skirt and moccasins. For instant recognition in international competitions, U.S. Olympic teams wear cowboy hats. From Sacramento to Schenectady, stylish females tote turquoise bracelets and perch on peeled-log furniture, assuring themselves the trees died of natural causes. In some locales, silver-trimmed saddles and fancy spurs cost more than working ranches.

Naturally, some Westerners think our cherished emblems have been corrupted by popularity, so the state's richest rancher wears a seed cap. Sightseeing scriveners in each century have scrawled notes about desolate and godforsaken deserts. If they get home — these days, that means if they backpack enough designer water — they write best-selling books analyzing the bleak Western soul.

The editors of this anthology, all three ranch women, used to joke about the West's perennial popularity, remarking how seldom our instant Western neighbors helped brand calves or shovel manure out of the barn. "He's not a real rancher," we'd say with a spare grin. "He just found the hat." I received rejection slips from publishers with comments about my "boring and brutal" life; why would anyone want to read that? We chuckled at drop-ins, folks who gallop through the plains and scuttle back to a metropolis, abruptly becoming authorities. "Bungee-jump journalists," Nancy calls them. When some honky-tonk cowboy or cowgirl is yahooed by an Eastern magazine as the genuine article, folks who live in the West shake their heads. We commended ourselves on our ability to laugh at such troubles, joking about all this for years before we got grumpy. If we weren't so busy, we'd say, we could tell true stories that would make those phony books curl their pages and tumble away with the next high wind.

The fake cowboys are the ones wearing hats
and Western shirts and are often overweight
and have full beards. The real ones look oddly
unobtrusive.

— *Deirdre Stoelzle*

After all, as Wyoming poet laureate Robert Roripaugh says, Western history was mostly written by "trappers, travellers, traders, transients, tourists and transplants." Historians jumbled legitimate accounts with pure hogwash from cheap Western novels, fostering legends that were accepted as truth. Only a trickle of "the river of stories from this land" flowed into the pages of books, and only a droplet were tales by women.

We've often met city folks who thought all Western women are slim blondes in tight jeans on prancing palominos. Or musclebound heifers who look and smell like old leather. We asked each other how we could change old stereotypes, and wondered why women in other areas consider us "unliberated." Anthologies of Western writing are as plentiful as real estate agents or lice on a sick cow, but they're usually edited by college professors. So we'd shake our heads and go on writing and editing between cow chases.

But we kept thinking. How could we show the world the real women we know, living monuments like those who taught us how to stand on our own feet? Strong Western women who stare down the future, eyes squinting against the glare?

I decided anything worth bitching
about is worth doing myself.

— *Terry L. Schifferns*

None of us can quite pinpoint the moment we decided to create an anthology. We only know it sounded logical at the time. We told ourselves we were as handy with words as with bridle reins and cow remedies — "Western girls who grew up free." We knew we could find a way to show readers how "where we come from shapes who we are."

As a child, Gaydell Collier knew she wanted to live in the West, reminding us in "Wyoming Bound" that one need not be born Western to be a plainswoman. She's lived on and loved a Wyoming ranch most of her life, the last twenty years a small horse ranch near Sundance.

Nancy Curtis grew up on a ranch near Glendo, Wyoming, learning about cows from her father. She helps operate the family ranch; now her daughter is considering coming back when she finishes graduate school. Nancy's award-winning High Plains Press allows her to "mother" writers along with bovines. Once, expecting a call from a New York publisher during calving season, she asked her mother to answer the phone. "Don't say I'm out checking on my first-calf heifers," Nancy instructed. "Say I'm meeting with my production staff." Her staff, she reported, turned out some nice calves that year.

Born in a Texas city, I dreamed of black stallions before moving, at age nine, to a South Dakota ranch. There I learned to ride a skinny sorrel mare and dream of waddling cows. I returned to work for my father and write about environmental issues, expecting to inherit and operate the ranch. When my father told me to stop writing or get out and not come back, I settled in Cheyenne, Wyoming. Now I commute to the ranch, and my name is on the deeds.

Let it begin with the land.

— *Kathleene West*

We followed Western tradition by ignoring custom to create this book. Smart editors write a proposal to several publishers, one of whom might respond with enthusiasm and a cash advance. Contract and expense money in hand, the editors settle into a cozy retreat to collect material. But we skipped the proposal, doubting it would impress a publisher who'd never heard of us and knew nothing of daily life in the West. Besides, we couldn't prove such an anthology would be good; all we had was gut instinct.

Separated by several hundred miles, "joined by location and tradition and love," we conducted most editorial meetings by mail. Blizzards, full-time jobs, and the chores of conducting our own lives — filled with the customary complications brought about by children, parents, spouses, taxes, and weather — kept us from meeting often.

How would contemporary Western women evaluate their lives and their place in modern society? We aimed to find them — scattered between housing developments and sagebrush — and let them tell their own stories in their own words.

First, of course, we thought of women we knew — literally or symbolically — ranch women thriving on hardscrabble places. But we also wanted to hear from women who lived in other relationships with the land. We recognized how quickly the West's population is changing, so we needed the views of women whose heritage, culture, and opinions are exotic to us. If we're all going to live here in cooperation, perhaps even in harmony, we must try to understand each other. We believe this diverse collection of women's voices will function as part of an ongoing dialogue. Included here are women who speak for slaughtered cattle, and vegetarians who might visit with us over coffee, but wouldn't eat a steak from one of our best yearlings. We'd even accept work from animal rights activists if they cared about the West we know. On the other hand, we wouldn't choose writing because its style or its author's lifestyle was politically correct. Content would be our only consideration.

We realized that many readers might be interested in the daily details of our physical labor, but rather than presenting a litany of jobs, we wanted to let Western women tell how they view their lives. We solicited contributions from contemporary women who do, or once did, physical labor connected to the land. What, we asked, do they think of their companions, both animal and human? What conditions — weather? isolation? — affect them most? What do they think when a friend remarks how they're wasting their lives or their educations in a barren land?

> Acres hold them in the cycles of plants, growth, and harvest.
>
> — *Kathleene West*

We'd judge the writing on clarity of expression, with less regard for grammar and writing style. Hunch told us these women would speak clearly and with inspiration. Each piece of writing must be authentic, the writer's personal experience. Conceding we couldn't define authenticity, we insisted we'd recognize it. An out-of-region editor might not understand authentic if she were standing in it.

Most Western women are too busy to join clubs or write letters to the editor. They work hard, but they also enjoy themselves too much to waste energy arguing about politics or analyzing their philosophies on paper. They might flip through a fashion magazine in the grocery store and chuckle later, telling a neighbor fringed blouses and high-heeled orange boots are "in." Then, uncomplaining, they slip into manure-caked galoshes and a four-wheel-drive pickup.

> Living between God and the ground.
>
> — *Barbara M. Smith*

How could we inspire them to deliberate on their lives, reveal their thoughts? After lengthy discussion, we discarded a few more publishing rules. No editor in her right mind takes (shudder) handwritten manuscripts. We did. We set no word limits, inviting essays, articles, reminiscences, diary entries, or poetry. But no fiction; too much fiction has warped the world's view of the West.

We sent information to publications in six Western states — North and South Dakota, Nebraska, Colorado, Montana, and Wyoming. News releases went to agricultural weeklies, stock-raising newsletters, and small-town newspapers, to extension agencies, libraries, and arts councils. We asked rural teachers to give information to farm women, some taking classes so they could get jobs as their families lost their land or homes.

Did they choose this place or
did the land choose them?

— *Kathleene West*

We were unprepared for the chorus of women's voices, the myriad in-
dividual songs we received. Manuscripts from 550 women erected a tower
of submissions twelve feet high.

Several women sent family photo albums, one a mother's tattered
notebook more than seventy years old, with penciled entries about
money spent or eggs gathered. Several sent self-published histories.
Some wrote letter after letter, recalling and reciting more about their lives
every day. Several sent hundreds of handwritten pages. We were horrified
that our correspondents trusted us — and the postal service — with irre-
placeable keepsakes. Many writers thanked us for inspiring them to write
for their children or for themselves, even if we didn't print their stories.
Later, women whose work we could not include in this book wrote again
to thank us for considering their writing, for working to "make this vol-
ume representative of the courage, stamina, and idealism of Western
women."

Squirming, we tried to convince ourselves we didn't have to read it all.
At different times we adopted different traits. I'd growl, "Let's start by
sending the albums back." Gaydell would reply, "But look at what she
wrote about this blizzard. I'll just type that part." Periodically, Nancy
would slam a fist on the table and declare, "We've got to be ruthless." Gay-
dell and I would nod, tears dribbling as we read about the deaths of horses
and children.

Eventually all three of us read everything submitted, typing the parts
we liked best. Several times we heaved boxes of manuscripts into a car and
spent time together, learning to trust each other's judgment and sense of
humor. We spent a couple of weekends in Gaydell's domain, the Crook
County Library in Sundance, Wyoming. When the library was open, we sat
at a table in a back room, looking editorial. After closing we scattered,
sprawling in chairs or on the floor among the stacks. Reading. Sunrise to
midnight. Sometimes we'd gather the others to read aloud, listening to the
rhythm of words, strangling on tears as we deciphered arthritic hand-
writing.

I become water, wind, sky, hills.

— *Phyllis Luman Metal*

Emerging late one Sunday, Nancy and I drove home on flooded high-
ways. We'd noticed a little water seeping in under a door, but didn't know
there had been heavy rains and squalls. Picture it: We're ranchers, trained

to plan each day around weather in a climate so dry even pagans pray for moisture. But we hadn't noticed thirty-six hours of rain.

We've all been toughened by life and we know the Western code: Swallow complaints. Don't talk about trouble. Stress? Headaches? Never heard of them. We expected to, and did, find women as tough as we are. But the manuscripts were startling in ways we hadn't expected. We also met women more patient and angrier than we are, women who have endured pain that struck us dumb and yet kept their hope and faith. And we knew they weren't dusty bones clothed in someone's imagination; these women are alive. Someday we might meet them.

> Wyoming belonged to my real self, not to fiction.
> — *Gaydell Collier*

Gradually, we narrowed the submissions. We'd laugh and enjoy, say, five essays about heifer-watching at midnight, but knew we could choose only one to represent all midnight heifer midwives. Again and again we copied good lines. These women showed us why they lived in the West, with "no other guidance than the familiar sway of the land through their bones." Not all stayed in one plains place for a lifetime, but sharp memories of rain on the canvas of a wagon, the flavor of water in a particular stream, admitted them to this company. One tale of a mother chasing a hired man with a horsewhip stands for similar tales remaining untold, sometimes not even whispered.

Many details defined authenticity for us. A writer might evoke a real blizzard, "chilling us from our centers both ways." The familiar and the unusual began to blend into a portrait of Western women we recognized.

Some women believe that the land, with nightingales and cathedral thunderheads, helped to save them. Some writers startled and informed us, showing how an unusual occupation like running a trap line may impart new purpose. Though the editors' views on sheep differ radically, we all admired the women's fortitude in learning hard lessons about saving bum lambs. We were often intrigued by contrasting views on various subjects.

No matter what their work, most of these writers have discovered pride in themselves and their way of life. Their views into history and the future are as broad and varied as their horizons. One may say, "Seasons on the plains give our lives definition; their abruptness and ferocity breed survivors and pride," while another responds, "This land and its seasons are not friends of mine."

Elk ranchers and wilderness rangers offered us fresh perspectives. Call them pioneers and they politely disagree, saying, "Not when you compare my life to a real pioneer. A mountain mama, maybe." More than one was frustrated by being called a housewife instead of a farmer. While some own the land where they work, others work for landlords, defining themselves not by gender or ownership but by labor — "Ranching is not only what we do, it's who we are." Some say, "The land is our trial, our comfort, and ultimately our identity." Today's Western woman speaks with quiet force, as she always has — even during the last couple of centuries when historians weren't listening. And she may find unique and yet primeval ways to mark her territory.

We chuckled at many demonstrations of the Western woman's essential sense of humor. Western women can joke about labor because they know that the journey to the future may take them in unexpected directions.

> The storms anchored me.
>
> — *Morgan Songi*

Separated by fierce winters and steaming summers, we kept reading, letters flowing back and forth as we considered, edited, retyped. The more we read, the more vehemently we believed in the women whose voices we heard even in our sleep. We never stopped working on the book, though the convolutions in our own lives sometimes left us dizzy as one year passed, two, four. When we started getting letters asking what had happened to the book, we replied and worked harder, telling each other that busy Western women would understand.

Over and over, we debated what to call these women.

Naturally, we wanted a handy collective term, but we agreed on only one thing: it wouldn't be "cowgirls." They don't all like cows, and the term "girl" should embarrass any grownup. Besides, the shiny cowgirl is just another mythical vampire. These real women are not so bland, not so simple to portray.

Descriptive phrases from our neighborhoods tempted us. "Grass widows" used to be unmarried women with children, but today the term suggests a community's puzzlement over a husband's precise location. A snowplow operator we know uses "grass widows" in scorn, meaning women who talk about loving the country but want their road cleared of snow if they haven't been to town for a couple of days. "Wrinklebelly" is no insult, since it implies a woman who's toughened up, lost her easy-living fat to lean muscle. But these terms aren't universal, and certainly not some advertising agency's idea of a marketing plan.

> On the plains, in the mountains, you learn that
> you are as important as the beaver, the hawk,
> the dragonfly — but not more so. You are part
> of the circle.
>
> — *Gaydell Collier*

After five years of work and a collective century and a half of thought, we agree on several traits Western women share. Tough and independent, they live comfortably with contradiction, and wouldn't all agree why. "Plainswomen are realistic and romantic, tender and strong." They are quietly proud of their accomplishments and well informed about a world that is largely ignorant of them.

Sweat-stained, these women wear plains mud on their shoes and under their fingernails. They have scars to prove they belong, that they've dug beneath thin topsoil. Staying makes them part of a unique history and validates their writing. They possess "the power and the dignity that comes from strife and experience and teeth-grinding faith." In fact, the writing by these women clearly demonstrates the contradictions inherent in Western life and people. Her "Home on the Range" may make a woman both "a certified schizophrenic, cowering in dreadful doubt and pain, and just as surely a valiant woman unafraid of dragons and demons and stacks of overdue bills." A Western woman dislikes cattle, sheep, or horses, or believes in "the sheer ecstasy of that moment" of a colt's birth. She may become "death's handmaiden," as well as a lifesaver. She may spend her honeymoon cleaning the barn or shoveling snow in a blizzard and be proud and happy to work the land with her husband.

A woman who thrives here must be able to endure hardship, to bear "long gray winters of isolation." But — and this may be even more important — she must also embrace beauty that may bloom and fade in an hour.

Tough times are, as they have always been, part of the Western woman's experience, and the writings that follow prove it. But observing only the hardships would leave the panorama incomplete. Hearing the "carol of a meadowlark" helps a woman bear "the disappointment of the barren years." Reflecting that "perseverance is part of the genetic code," many of these women learned to "delight in the mud of March, because it means a hay crop is on the way."

What other qualities define an authentic plainswoman? Some castrate lambs with their teeth or saddle their own horses. Many speak of fathers who believed "that his girls could do anything his boy could do." Still, if a man orders a woman to jump in front of five 1,600-pound bulls armed only with a sunflower stalk, she may write about it rather than committing murder. Or not.

Mourning her losses, a Western woman may reflect on the link between birth and death. Women here still dig in their toes to "hang on," and sing when they feel like sobbing.

Knowledge of freedom lies bone-deep in these women, whether it means loping over the countryside on horseback or climbing onto a Quonset roof. But a stern land teaches lessons ruthlessly, and a woman here, as anywhere, may lose much of what she loves. She may help her father roll barbed wire, but she will eventually understand why he'd sell the ranch where she'd hoped to make a life. She may use anger sparked by injustice to forge a new life, or she may learn a harsh lesson, as does a widow who has bought into the family ranch corporation to provide security for her children: "I've been taking pride in something they don't consider mine." Still, plainswomen go on, becoming part of history.

> Walking easily from milking to baking, from mucking to hugging; walking easily, walking slowly, walking wisely, walking well. (It's a prairie walk, you know?)
> — *Ruth Schubarth*

"I become one of the gullies carrying these stories down to the children," writes one. Each woman, each story, each reader is a rivulet, part of the stream, the river, the plains.

When Sue Chalk wrote, "This place is inherited through women's blood," she referred to a particular ranch. I embrace her line as a fitting aphorism for the history of the High Plains, a testimony to the women who have written *Leaning into the Wind*.

LINDA HASSELSTROM
Cheyenne, Wyoming, 1997

ONE

Growing into the Land

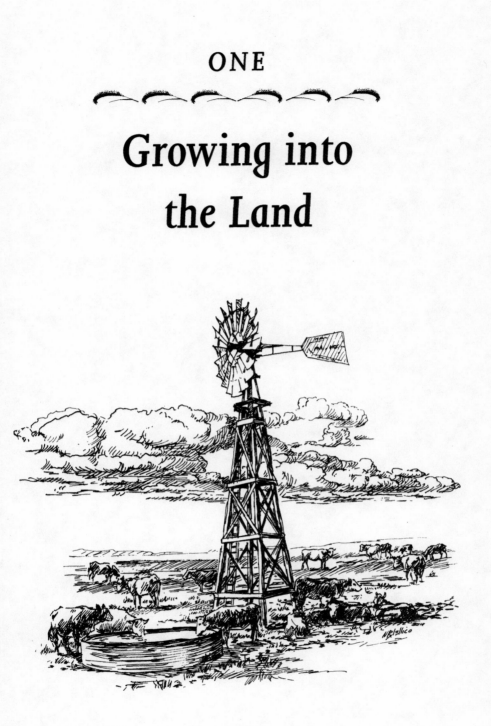

This Soil, My Body

GAYDELL COLLIER Wyoming Bound

I wasn't born here on the High Plains. I'm here because, even as a child, I knew I had to come home. Raised in the suburbs of New York City — amid neat houses, each centered in its patch of lawn bordered by concrete sidewalks — I sought the untenanted fields beyond. I'd walk to school singing, "Afoot and light-hearted, I take to the open road . . . the long brown path before me leading wherever I choose . . ." but with heavy heart I'd trudge along gray asphalt. Riding in the back seat of our old Dodge, I observed from the Whitestone Bridge a sea of rooftops as far as the eye could make out in the haze, not amber waves of grain but gray, cracked, dried fields of tar and slate. And I knew — even before I was twelve — that I would come to Wyoming.

I loved books, and I read horse and dog stories set in Wyoming, *My Friend Flicka* and *Thunderhead* among them. I sat in my room with the door closed and drew wonderfully detailed maps of Wyoming while my brother played with other children outside. I listened to *The Lone Ranger* (because of Silver and Scout) and *Sergeant Preston of the Yukon* ("Good boy, King!") and peopled the Wyoming mountain ranges and river basins with myself — a dozen myselfs — all riding horses into the wind, free and exultant, or else — afoot and light-hearted — striding down and beyond the open road.

I knew Wyoming very well, yet I knew nothing. I knew I had to go there, had to live there, that Wyoming was my home no matter how misguided and misplaced my parents might be. I spoke to them about it. I explained the desperate importance of going to Wyoming in words that were clear to me, but apparently unconvincing to them. My father was the building manager of Bowling Green Offices at 11 Broadway. What does real estate by the square foot have to do with the vastness of Wyoming? But my father, when not forced to be a realist, was a reader and a dreamer — a romantic.

I remember, the year I was twelve, when we discussed his upcoming summer vacation. I begged to go to Wyoming and he finally countered with an exasperated "Well, if you want to go to Wyoming so much, why don't *you* make the money to take us there!" That year we went to Cutchogue and rented a sea-smelly cabin and dug clams. And I read my books.

He never remembered saying it. I never forgot. Up in my room, among my Wyoming maps, among my books, I began my secret campaign. I bought a gray metal strongbox where I could lock away every quarter saved from my dollar-a-week allowance, every wage earned from baby-sitting at fifty cents an hour. Slowly my little hoard grew. No one suspected. I still bought a few favorite comics and an occasional ice cream cone — who would notice the ones I didn't buy?

Birthdays passed. I took riding lessons and guitar lessons, did well in school, and lived a more or less normal adolescent life. I wrote poems and stories — entirely fictional works set here, there, and anywhere, but never in Wyoming. Wyoming belonged to my real self, not to fiction.

Early in the spring when I was going on sixteen, the subject of summer vacation came up, and again I mentioned Wyoming — this time with just a faint touch of optimism. The time had come.

"Wait," I told my parents. "We *can* go to Wyoming!" I dashed upstairs for my strongbox. I hadn't counted the money lately but the box was heavy and I'd worked hard. They said nothing as I unlocked the box. With pride and melodrama, I opened it and dumped it into the middle of the dining room table, dollar bills and coins tumbling and rolling. My parents were as bewildered as they were astonished. Where had it come from? What in the world was it all about?

"Don't you *remember?*" I asked my father. "Don't you *remember* you said I should make enough money to take us to Wyoming?"

Well, of course he didn't remember. But I went to bed in triumph. Nearly two hundred dollars! My parents stayed up very late afterwards.

It was many years before I really understood what had happened that night — and when I did understand I could hardly believe how much love and sacrifice had been exchanged for a pitiful pile of coins and bills.

My father mortgaged the house. He bought a new car. He must also have mortgaged his life for years to come — he somehow bargained for eight weeks of vacation all in one summer — an unheard-of extravagance at that time. And once these monumental acts were accomplished, it was announced that in that summer of 1951, we would take our trip — a magnificent family odyssey that would go to national parks and the Pacific coast, that would cover the West, and that would climax with a whole week in Wyoming.

The planning was glorious. My father and I spent weekends crawling around the living room floor poring over spread-out maps, adding mileages, deciding what had to be seen at all costs, what could be missed. My mother left it to us except for one stipulation. Wyoming had to be last. How could the reality ever match up to these incredible expectations? The disappointment that was bound to be Wyoming could never be allowed to taint the rest of the trip. I had no such apprehensions and agreed happily — I had always been one to save the best for last. And I was to plan the Wyoming part myself. I selected several dude ranches on the basis of my own formula — a ratio of the most horses to the fewest people.

And at last we were on our way, heading north into Canada, through the Soo, back into the States, through Glacier Park up to Banff and Lake Louise, over the mountains into British Columbia and down the redwood coast to Santa Barbara, across the desert to Las Vegas and the Grand Canyon, up through Utah, and finally — finally — entering Wyoming's southwest corner and sliding up to Teton and Yellowstone.

What more need I tell you? We stayed a short time at Wapiti and then settled in at the H Bar V, south of Douglas, a piece of paradise on earth.

Wyoming a disappointment? No, I had come home; the only disappointment was in leaving — at the very last minute, so that my father, exhaustion showing in dark smudges under his eyes, had to drive home nonstop in order to make it to work Monday morning.

My heart stayed in Wyoming. I mourned the distance, but had no doubts that whatever destiny was mine would be found or made in my state.

Within four years I returned for good — this time on my own. I married and we raised our children beside the Laramie River, where they could walk or ride a horse through sagebrush and native grasses beyond the open road, where they had to walk to the privy and haul in wood for heating and cooking, where they could climb Jelm Mountain and look out over a hundred miles and see only an occasional rooftop because the sun glinted off its metal.

The important thing is to touch the earth and stand in the wind, to know you are part of a whole — not superimposed like asphalt. On the plains, in the mountains, you learn that you are as important as the beaver, the hawk, the dragonfly — but not more so. You are part of the circle.

Does the land mold you into this acceptance?

Or are you drawn to the land because of who you are?

CINDY FRENCH ~\ Child of the Land

Ever since I was a small child, I realized that there were two kinds of people. I used to pretend that some were children of the land and some were children of the sky. And even as an adult, I sometimes think it might be true. I think children of the land have a close, almost spiritual feeling toward the land, a oneness with nature that manifests itself in awe of nature's beauty and quiet dignity and strength. A simple thankfulness to be allowed to be there and observe it. Children of the sky feel a mystical pull away from the land, a challenge to see beyond their pastures and animal friends, a desire to drive toward the man-made wonders of the world. I was and still am a child of the land.

My parents lost their ranch when I was twelve, and I can still remember sitting on the top rail of the corral, trying hard not to cry as the semis loaded up our cattle. The mammas called their babies with mournful cries, dust circling the corral as they climbed the ramp. We were all saying good-bye to a way of life. I think it was then that I realized what a gift rural life is, and that it should be appreciated, preserved, and enjoyed to the fullest while in our possession, because life moves on and we are never quite sure what paths it will follow.

Country life is a dream, a moment's observance of nature's wonders, the beauty of freedom, and the struggles of hard work. It's a sense of life I don't think you can capture completely in town; it's a way of life I hope my children will experience one day. I hope they'll taste a jar of wild plum jam or see a newborn calf and be able to picture pleasant memories. And who knows, one day maybe they'll begin to sense something special about the land. Maybe they'll feel the call to pick up a pair of reins, dust off a second-hand saddle, and feel the power of twelve hundred pounds of horse beneath them. Maybe they'll smell the sweat, see the indescribable beauty, and feel the love and quiet companionship these animals can share, discovering that they too have a legacy as children of the land.

BARBARA M. SMITH   Transplant

Trailer once battened down
skirted against the blow sand
construction, she laid sod.

Sent for a tree from home
where water fell unplanned
dogwood transplant against sagebrush.

Dug a garden from cracked clay
they watched behind thin curtains
she tilled the rows ready.

What grows here? Tomatoes, zucchini,
strawberries if you water good. Season
doesn't hold for melons much.

She staked them high, thinking of

crowders little ladies field peas

muscadine fig preserves mimosa shade.

Around the plot she laid ground cover
gold red surprise across the baked
edge sucking leftovers from the hose.

It grew not near so tall but green
fierce fruit clung in the gusts
ripening against the odds.

Taste this, she gave to her neighbor.
Brushing dust she bit red juice.
It's hard to get but worth more.

Next year I'll help you if
you like. I'm planting potentilla
perennials all along the west.

If that dogwood dies, I'll get
a cottonwood; it's native
to this place and thrives.

MARTHA THOMPSON ⟶ A New Life on a Dryland Farm

I was a writer when I came to a "dry" farm in the southeastern corner of Laramie County as a bride in October 1941. I knew it would be a lonely place, but I found it was a far more desolate life than I had even imagined.

The one-room homestead shack had been updated about 1915 with the addition of a parlor, impossible to heat or use during the cold Wyoming winters; a bedroom that would freeze ice in below-zero temperatures; a dining room where we ate, read, and listened to our Delco-battery-operated radio during winter nights; and a large, musty, unfinished room upstairs.

There was no central heating, only two wood and coal stoves, plus an oil stove to cook on during the summer. There was no running water, therefore no sink or plumbing.

I had no transportation to leave the farm since my groom, blissfully unaware of my gnawing loneliness, went off in his father's pickup every day but Sunday, and remained working and visiting all day with his parents at their farm, much as he had done when he was single. I walked the lonely, deserted country path near our home, crying with loneliness and frustration — I had no friends; they were back in "civilization" where my life had revolved around my newspaper work.

A fanatic for organization, I spent my days cleaning the old farmhouse, then started on the yard, carrying away pecks of rubble.

My accumulation of books was very meager, my reading appetite voracious, as it had been ever since my first day of school when phonics opened the magic door to reading. As I started on the attic cleaning, I uncovered a mountain of old magazines, sorted them, and kept what appealed to me.

Our cash was limited. When Gerry and I were married, I had some hope chest linens, a trousseau of sorts, and $70. My new husband didn't have any money. In an arrangement I never understood, he worked full time in the spring, summer, and fall during farming season, and less in the winter with the cattle — but his total salary for the five years he was employed on his parents' farm after graduating from high school was $1 on Saturday night, a minimum of clothing, and his board and room.

In view of our limited finances, I was outraged to find after returning home from one of my infrequent trips to the nearby hamlet that Gerry had ransacked the house, his pockets, and my dresser drawers to pay a magazine salesman $5 for a five-year subscription to a magazine. I was more subdued and touched when I found the name of the magazine was *Mother's Home Life,* as I wasn't even a mother yet.

The magazine added a new dimension to my life. It was about homemaking and housekeeping — something I knew little about. The writing I had done was newswriting and occasional feature stories. The little magazine had feature stories and human interest stories about women and their lives.

Except for cleaning and reading and, in a year, my new baby, there was not much else for me to think about since the absence of car and telephone hampered my contact with the outside world. One day I asked my husband, "Who used to live here?"

Gerry told me about the pioneers coming to settle what had been vast cattle ranges when homesteading opened up this area in Laramie County in 1907, and I learned history I had not dreamed about. Once I knew about the homesteaders and why they came and what they did and how they lived, I could not stop exploring the stories of their lives. It led me to a search for places to put my stories. It was too important and too exciting to keep to myself.

At first, the stories were published in newspapers. Then the first collection of them was assembled in a book, *Pioneer Parade,* in 1967. I would like to think that it influenced others to begin collecting stories of pioneers and to enter into the spirit of preserving their history.

I feel kinship with them. I might never have become so conscious of their lives and happenings if I had had more creature comforts my first five years on the plains.

SHELAGH WISDOM ✐ Magic and Miracles

My feet sweep through the dew-soaked grass. I can hear my breath coming in short and hurried bursts; I can see the frozen moisture as I exhale in the early morning air. It's 3:15 A.M. and the moon is my lantern; it lights my way through the quiet pasture. Tiny, dark, wispy clouds fleet across the face of the creamy moon as it suspends lazily in the purple sky.

I search the horizon for the outline of a black mare that's due to foal. I've waited for a week now; she's waxed and has been dripping milk that clings to her black legs and muddies up her white stockings. I am scanning in the black night for a black mare.

The night stands quiet except for the sweeping, air-rushed sounds of a few bats as they scoop up their insect meals; I catch the distant, lonely cooing of a nighthawk.

I stop to listen for the peaceful munching of a grazing mare or a snort of acknowledgment from her. The pasture is small and she's used to my numerous nightly visits, which produce sliced apple treats for her. I know that she knows I'm here, but I don't have her senses. I cannot find her.

I walk slowly to a small rocky rise that swells almost in the center of the pasture, wondering if the black mare is well aware of my presence or if she is enthralled, giving birth.

My heart leaps as I hear a distant, throaty moan, followed by a long, drawn-out grunt. I am momentarily paralyzed, trying to determine the location of the black mare. The sound repeats to my left, down in the deepest cleft of the pasture, just below the small swell on which I'm standing. My skin prickles with excitement.

I speak her name softly, over and over again. I don't want to startle her or disturb her. She doesn't answer; she is enveloped in an animal's silent, courageous world of birth.

I hear her grunt again; louder this time. I hear a movement on the soft earth; a swishing of grass; another moan. I walk slowly in the direction of the sounds, speaking her name softly, approaching cautiously, as quietly as my excitement will allow. It's up to me to find her; it is my option to be here and not hers. I am hoping that she doesn't feel I am imposing on her privacy; I've been with her before when she's foaled and in the past she's acted like she was glad to have some company.

I finally see a thin, dissipating cloud of steam rise from the mare's nostrils toward the sky. I hear the mare's heavy breathing, hear her sniffing and exploring something new. I can hear her tongue licking at a new life, and I utter a muffled cry of joy at the tiny peal of a new foal's first nicker.

I dare not move for fear of shattering the sheer ecstasy of that moment and miracle in time.

I finally calm myself down enough to come closer to the mare. I see the outline of her head as she raises it quickly as I approach. I speak softly to her again and she nickers. Her head drops back to her baby. I am close enough now to see very faintly the outline of the mare's back against the sky. I can smell the incomparable smell of horses, green grass, and birth. I talk to the mare soothingly, telling her what a good mare she is; what a good mother she will be. The foal nickers again; I strain to see it but see only darkness against the grass. I will have to wait.

I sit down in the tall grass about fifteen feet from the mare and her new foal. I patiently wait as she cleans her baby and encourages it to stand. He's unsteady but strong — he maintains his balance for a few seconds and then crashes to the ground.

The black mare lies down beside her baby to rest, and all is quiet for half an hour or more. The moon has been sliding liquidly down the graying sky, making way for the arrival of morning. A few clouds reveal a hint of pink on their undersides; it's calm and peaceful. More birds are stirring; quietly chirping, anxiously waiting for the first rays of the sun to stretch warming beams across the sky, the mountains, and the fields.

It's lighter now, and I can see that the foal has a bald face. I can't tell if it's brown, black, or bay. The mare has risen and encouraged the foal to get up again, and after a number of attempts it finds balance and seems stronger. It probes and prods in all the wrong places for its mother's udder, and finally finds it quite by accident. She is patient; she nickers, licks and nuzzles her foal, and looks proudly at me several times to see if I am watching. I talk quietly to her off and on, unaware until much later that the dampness of the night and early morning has soaked my clothes, my hair, and chilled me to the bone. I am stiff from sitting in the cold, but elated with the new arrival. I wait and watch the morning descend on the pasture and this miracle of birth; bewitched by the magic and enthralled with having been blessed in sharing with the mare.

As the dawn creeps slowly across the fields and grasslands, I discover that the foal is black, and it is a horse colt. He's never noticed me, the idiot sitting in the wet grass.

TERRILL FOSTER ⟍ *A Lady of the Night*

I became a 2 A.M. "lady of the night" starting in January and quit my job on April Fool's Day. I live on a cattle ranch and when our cows and heifers have their calves they must be checked every four hours, at 2, 6, and 10 P.M., and 2, 6, and 10 A.M.

My husband, Ralph, or a live-in hired hand had always done the night check, but this year we didn't have a live-in hired hand and Ralph was facing thirty-five radiation treatments for prostate cancer, requiring him to drive one hundred miles five days a week for seven weeks. He got Saturdays and Sundays off. I wanted him to sleep uninterrupted all night, so I became a lady of the night, wondering if I'd be able to stay awake to teach kindergarten three full days each week.

We fed the heifers and cows in corrals during the day and put them into divided pens in the barn at night. At ten each night I'd herd the heifers and cows into shelter. One heifer refused to go; I prayed she would not have her calf some night when I was home alone.

I enjoyed the 2 A.M. check, discovering the night was full of sounds, sights, and weather. I had never noticed in all my forty-two years of marriage this totally different night life. The weather and I became good friends; some nights I dressed in double sweat suits, snowboots with extra socks, warm jacket, gloves inside mittens, and a stocking hat tied down with a scarf. Some nights I found the night air invigorating and full of energy.

My farsighted glasses steamed over with warm air escaping from the scarf tied around my nose and mouth. Steam came off the frost on the cows' and heifers' backs and out of their mouths and through the crystals on their nose hairs. I rubbed off as much frost as the animals would allow me to.

Some nights were crunchy cold, with frost crystals glittering on the bare branches of the only tree in the yard, a Russian olive. Thousands of stars pinned the black velvet sky, but in all the nights outside I didn't see a falling star. Sometimes clouds covered the stars like comforters.

Some nights the wind gently blew the pipe chimes a Pennsylvania friend made to hang in the tree. When the wind blew stinging sleet into my face, I would walk backwards to the sheds. Some nights the wind blew soft snowflakes or rain into my face. Later in March, I was kissed by fifty-four degrees of warmth. My face felt so alive; when I returned to the house, I scrubbed it and put on toner, moisturizer, and makeup, so my face was ready for school at four.

Many nights the coyotes yowled. They kill forty to sixty of our lambs every year. I haven't had a new car since 1972 because of the "money" these coyotes ate. I don't like to hear coyotes. They sound like they're planning the morning raid or telling about yesterday's. Our two Great Pyrenees dogs, White Fang and Buck, protected our sheep in the hills for a few summers, but now the coyotes are used to them and no longer afraid.

Hearing the Canada Geese fly north over the corrals, I'd look up to see black silhouettes going across the sky under the stars. The sound of trains on tracks traveled four miles coming up Black Stump Draw. Hooty owls talked to each other. At 2 on March 25, I heard dozens of frogs singing, getting ready for the spring concert.

During February, everything went okay. Then Ralph decided to go for a treatment at 4:30 one afternoon, stay all night and get another treatment at 8:30 the next morning. By that time, about sixty calves had been born with *no problems*.

March First: When I checked the cows at 6 A.M., they were all out of the feeding corral, in the yard, and in the haystack. I called our dog, Tim, but he did not come. Alone I herded them back to their pens. At 10 P.M., a heifer was having a problem, and another heifer was getting started. A huffy cow had calved; she stomped toward me a couple of times until I was too nervous to put her in the "maternity ward." I called our daytime hired hand, Rick, only seven miles away, for help.

We put the heifer having trouble into a stanchion; the other heifer was doing fine. In the barn with an equalizer, Rick put the huffy cow and her calf into a pen of their own.

When we went back to the shed, the heifer that had been doing fine had a dead calf, smothered when the birth sac stayed on its nose. It wasn't anyone's fault, but I felt guilty. We had trouble pulling the other calf. I felt depressed, even though things were straightened out and we had gotten one live calf. What a waste. A cow carries her baby nine months and then loses it.

The next night, March 2, Ralph went to Buffalo to play in a pool tournament, expecting to be home at midnight. At 10 P.M., a heifer was having trouble so I called Rick again. We were making no progress with this big calf when Ralph came. With his help, we pulled the calf, but it was a dodo head. It never learned to suck, and five days later it was dead.

The next week Monday, with Ralph gone and a heifer having problems, I called our daughter Brenda, who lives a half-mile away. With help from my 14-year-old grandson, we got the calf pulled. On Tuesday again, while Brenda and I were having a terrible time trying to pull a calf, Ralph came home to help, but the calf was so big we did not get it out alive. Thereafter, we set up a trailer, ready to load a heifer as soon as we saw huge feet again, so we could take her thirty-six miles to a vet.

From then until Wednesday, March 17, when Ralph had his last treatment, I was a nervous wreck on the nights he was gone.

Many mornings I was fully awake by the time I got back into the house, so I practiced the piano for my weekly lessons or worked on writing assignments. Thursday nights I watched videos between check times because I didn't have to teach school on Friday. I didn't feel I was wasting time, since ordinarily I would be sleeping. Sometimes I read or, if I was really awake and full of energy, I'd shower to warm up and do aerobics.

Being a lady of the night changed me and made me more aware of night life and of ranch reality.

SUSANNE K. GEORGE Birth

the bay mare
lay in the fresh straw
sides heaving
neck wet with sweat
muscles straining

one push —
two pale hooves appear —
another —
a pink nose —
then chest, back, hips and legs
slip onto the straw

weak from pain and labor
the mare
raises her head
toward her firstborn
still linked by nature
and something stirs
within her
something stored
for centuries

she calls to him
and he
still swimming in her waters
hears
surfaces to life

and finds her eyes

KALLI DESCHAMPS ⌒ *What's in a Smell?*

Have you ever had the memory of a smell buried so deep in the well of your subconscious that its slightest essence can bring to mind vivid pictures from a chain of events years past? For me, the aroma of a bale of sweet hay brings back memories of our first snow-coated winter and a barn full of dairy cows.

We all looked forward to the evening milking, for then our small world reached its zenith. Ed was home, his work in town complete for the day. Richard at four and Joey at four months — each had a place in our family barn. Surcingles encircled the cows. Stainless steel buckets were attached to the waiting hooks. Four nozzles sucked onto the teats and the process began. While the cows were milking, two at a time, Richard entertained his sister as she peeked, grinning from the depths of her blanketed stroller. When a bucket was lifted onto the scales, while the cow waited to be stripped, Richard ran to help his dad — to squeeze a teat, to feel that he was part of the daily process. Milk was poured, cream separated, animals fed. It was over — but not quite. We would open the double doors, emerge from the warmth of the barn into a star-studded night, clear and cold. There above us rose the beauty of snow-blazed Lolo Peak, silhouetted in all its majesty, against the thick onyx sky. We would walk slowly toward the house, carrying our buckets of cream, silent in our joy. Sometimes we would stop and talk. It was then that our life seemed complete, as we shared the fulfillment of these simple pleasures.

Thirty-five years have passed. The climax of my story has yet to be reached. We are the ranchers of today, but the philosophy of our life was set in a barn on Lolo Creek during a long cold winter at the onset of our youth.

SANDRA KNOX ⌒ *Maybe*

My heart is racing, my breath is a struggle of short gasps. I chop at the layer of ice separating me from the baby calf that bawls for help, eyes pleading as he sinks into dark water.

My eyes pop open as I hear the calf bawl again. Cuddled under the electric blanket, I'm happy to realize I was dreaming. When the calf bawls again, it's not a dream.

Rolling over, I find my nose inches from the face of a baby calf I rescued on my midnight check. He was nearly frozen, legs stiff, only a weak breath away from death. Grabbing a back leg, I swung up on my horse and pulled him into the saddle with me. The quarter-mile to the barn seemed longer. Bitter wind whipped the snow into my face. My horse tried to turn aside and put his tail to the wind. By the time I reached the barn, my glove was frozen to the calf's wet leg, and he bellowed the long, drawn-out bawl meaning death is near.

I slid the barn door open to get relief from the cutting wind. Pal followed me inside to his stall, shook the saddle, and began munching hay. I loosened his cinch. It was 1:15 A.M.

Loading the calf into the sled, I tucked my heavy overcoat around him and headed for the house. He would be the fourth baby in two days to bathe in my newly decorated mauve and gray bathroom. Spreading the plastic sheet over the new carpet, I noticed a hole the sharp hooves of the last visitor left in his struggle to get up.

When my clock chimed three times, the baby was finally warm and dry, content to sleep by the floor heater. I untangled the hair dryer cord from the four long legs, and added my wet, filthy clothes to the mess in the tub, another job that can wait for morning. Scrubbing my hands and arms, I wondered if my skin would ever stop feeling like sandpaper. I turned over two chairs to guard the bathroom door and lay down for a few hours' sleep.

My bright-eyed alarm clock is now sucking the knob of my dresser. How did he get past the barricade and into my room next door? I pull the robe over my arms and let him suck my fingers; he follows me to the porch for safekeeping until his mother can take over his care and feeding.

Maybe the snow will stop this morning.

Maybe the wind will let up.

Maybe the sun will shine.

Boy, do I need a cup of coffee.

PHYLLIS M. LETELLIER 🖊 **Night Lambing**

Blowing snow immediately plasters my glasses and all the cold-weather clothing I own isn't enough to deter twenty-five-mile-an-hour wind at twenty below.

"You couldn't pay me enough to do this!" I leave the old Wagoneer and struggle through the blizzard toward the lambing sheds, more than a mile from the house. For the last couple hundred yards the road is drifted full. My husband checked the drop herd at midnight. It's now 1 A.M., and the herd is mine for the rest of the night. I've had three blissful hours of uninterrupted sleep.

A good ear and a gentle step (both badly hampered by the frigid gale) are my best allies. I can often hear a problem long before I spot it, and the fewer sheep I disturb, the easier my job.

I reach inside the shed to flip the light switch. Many of the ewes are huddled along the shed out of the wind. Still listening, I aim my flashlight at rear ends, checking for lambing problems. A stumble or quick move would have most of the herd on their feet, facing me, and I can't check rear ends when all I can see are startled eyes.

I swing the light into dark corners, about to decide I've lucked out, when I hear a faint *baa* from the farthest corner of the corral — at the bottom of the hill. An ideal corral wouldn't have a bottom of the hill, but this corral just grew by what was expedient, not by what the night lamber would have chosen.

Only minutes old, the new lamb is barely on his feet and already covered with ice. "I'm too tired for this." I edge up to the pair, crossing mental fingers that this isn't one of the wild old girls I'll have to run down and drag to the shed.

I grab the lamb by a hind leg and, half dragging, half carrying him, start the slow trip to the shed. His mother follows! I only have to put him down a couple times for her to smell and lick to keep her with us until I get her into the shed and slam the door behind us (whew!) and next into a dry, freshly strawed jug. I position one heat lamp over the baby, another on the side, and iodine his navel. Then I throw the ewe to check her bag and to milk the wax plug out of each tit.

Then I finish my sweep of the corrals. In the twin and singles pens, several lambs are resting on the warmest thing they can find on a cold night: mother's woolly back. Lambs have done that through the ages, but I always wonder how each new generation figures it out.

Back in the shed, operating on automatic pilot, I feed and water the new ewe, break ice on water pans, and reposition a few heat lamps down the row of sheep jugs. Even in the closed shed, with the heat lamps glowing in a row, the cold penetrates everywhere.

When I've done the best I can, I head for the little travel trailer. Though the trailer is protected on two sides by stacked bales of straw, its little propane furnace is no match for the fury outside. I step out of my boots and drop my parka where it will get warm before I set the kitchen timer on the table for 40 minutes and collapse onto the bed. This is my season for sleeping in stolen moments, always just one nap away from complete exhaustion.

The calm, bright moonlit nights are the ones I want to bottle and remember, to savor later, but seldom those I tell about in war stories. I tell of the night I found five new lambs and three ewes within a few feet of each other and what I went through before getting everyone with the right mother. I remember the chilled lamb I couldn't save, no matter what I tried, or the one abandoned, no mother ever identified.

What the average night lambing hand — who is also a busy ranch wife and mother in the daytime — is most inclined to remember, though, can be summed up by the same couple words year after year: total exhaustion.

JANELLE MASTERS 　　 **Display Grounds**

It's six o'clock and sunrise
and somewhere the grouse are dancing.
On some eternal ground
in some eternal spring.

They are prancing now and bowing,
strutting to sounds deep in the earth
as I lie in bed and watch
the shadows overhead
of cracks that splint and shatter.
And words that weigh
and fester deep.
They are shuffling now and rattling
their quills, leaping and whirling
in the emerging sun.
Their white tails are peaked to the sky
as they skitter across their part of the earth,
booming and cackling to paradise.
I arise and walk through rooms
of promises in company of cats,
caught in a cool web
of sorrow.

It's six o'clock and sunrise
and somewhere the grouse are dancing,
their wings curved over the bent world.
A meadowlark is singing to them now,
its words flowing yellow into the red sun:
Dance on, it urges. *Prance on,*
on this our eternal ground
in this our eternal spring.

PAGE LAMBERT 　　 *Redy's Foal*

It seems to be about mothers and daughters. Some women would have it
differently. But there is an intrinsic fact that cannot be altered. The womb
belongs to the woman. I came from my mother's womb, my daughter came
from my womb. No test tube, no alternative lifestyle, no tampering of
humankind will make the womb obsolete. With each menses, with each

waning and waxing moon, with each ocean tide that comes in and goes out, the cycle is perpetuated.

We knew Redy was young when we bought her. Mark had said, "No more mares. They're too much trouble." I parleyed, "The mares are no trouble when the geldings aren't around." The half-earnest sparring continued. Then Redy was ridden into the sale ring, a pastel gray and white paint horse possibly bred to a black and white stallion.

"Look how she handles, folks," the auctioneer crooned. "Not bad for a greenbroke horse. With a little work she'll be smooth as silk. See how gentle — works from either side. Why you can climb all over her and she doesn't mind a bit. Now that's a gentle mare. And pasture-exposed, it says. Why, folks, there's probably a little paint foal in there just waiting for spring. Who'll start the bidding? Do I hear six hundred dollars?"

She reminded me of Romie. Small head, kind brown eyes, petite build. I nudged Mark. "Bid on her, bid on her," I whispered. The program in Mark's hand moved slightly and the ring man caught the motion. Mark nodded his head.

Miss Redy Cash, a blue roan, tobiano paint mare, sired by Par for Cash and out of Miss Redy Cube, a coming three-year-old; she needs a lot of work, but she's gentle and kind and small — she'll make a great horse for Matt or Sarah. And a foal besides. A foal. Wobbling to its feet. Curious, prancing, mischievous, ornery. A dream come true.

But nature doesn't agree. Too young to be a mother, Redy doesn't carry full-term. The unexpected labor pains, three months premature, come during the night, while she's alone in the corral. In the morning, the dirt shows signs of her struggle, the frightened thrashing. Her first breeding, her first colt, a late-term miscarriage. She's only two herself, still a filly. "Pasture-exposed" the sale papers said. Three more months and the foal would have been resting on young spring grass. It's for the best, we console. Gives Redy a chance to grow a little more. Pretty hard on a young horse like that to be bred so young. We'll keep her in with Romie for the rest of the winter, close to the barn, where we can hay them and grain them each day, let her put a little weight on. Keep Romie company. We can always breed her again. Work with her this spring, ride her a lot. Then maybe next year we can think about breeding her again. After that, who knows?

The image of Redy's aborted foal will not leave me. I see the fetus over and over again, lying on the cold ground, a stud colt. His hooves are soft, like fingernails after a long bath. His translucent skin is pink and gray, already mapping out where the hair will grow black or white. His face is well-marked, the pigment around his nose and eyes dark. Whiskers already sprouting from his muzzle are soft and delicate. I want them to twitch, to move. But he lies still. The membrane is gone from around his body. How long did Redy lick and clean him before she accepted his inertia?

When I get home from work at noon, the dogs have carried the dead foal up on the lawn. Burying him would have done no good. By evening the immature head is all that is left.

That same day a local high school girl, blond and blue-eyed, pretty and athletic, gave birth to a baby boy three weeks premature. The girl's parents were not happy. She was unmarried, too young to be forced to settle down. The father was several years older. And darker — a tall, long-limbed Native American man. At 5 A.M., during the early morning hours, while others slept — while Redy struggled in the corral — a baby boy was born.

I see the baby often. He has a wonderful head of thick black hair and perfectly formed fingers, tipped with tiny nails still soft. I watch the young mother nestle this child in the crook of her neck. He buries his dark head against her long blond hair and nuzzles. The mother is proud, a survivor. The father is proud too, eager to provide. They are becoming a threesome.

On my walks, I stop by the barn before heading into the hills. I stroke Romie's nose and rub her ears. She hangs her head down and rests it against my thigh. We have hugged like this for twenty-five years. I touch the deep hollows above her eyes and try not to notice the gauntness of her hips. Then I walk over to Redy.

She stops chewing her hay and greets me. I think of the black and white paint stallion and imagine him sniffing her, his nostrils flaring and snorting at the scent of her first heat. The odor would have caused him to arch his muscled neck and let loose his great phallus. Or maybe Redy, in her restlessness, jumped the fence and approached him, tail held high and quivering.

I stroke her belly. For several days it remains swollen and I harbor a secret wish that a foal, perhaps a twin to the aborted colt, still grows safely within her.

Childhood dreams metamorphose. Only a hint of the young girl remains. My womanness spirals around me, sometimes like a cocoon, sequestering; sometimes like a spinning top that breaks the bonds of gravity, flying off into space on a solitary journey — only to return, earthbound, wombbound, the spinning slowed to a pregnant pace.

DELCIE D. LIGHT ⌁ March Communion

My son and I stomp fat boot prints
into the squishy road. Winter's last wind
drives drizzle and lifts our laughter
over the hill like a tossing kite.

A trickle swirls down the road,
polishing pebbles into gems.
Poking with his muddy mitt, he pries a pretty
from the rimy road, and gifts me with the jewel.

Following the sparkling spring,
bundled and silly as scarecrows, we slosh
to a golden stubble field splotched white,
and framed black by barren oak.

A doe and yearling buck cease foraging.
Still as stone monoliths we stand
mesmerized in a misty, sacred setting.
Dusk deepens and vespers end.

The deer break the spell, fading
between black trunks into the fog.
Did we see druids from timeless time?
Blue eyes smile at me over pink cheeks.

With this silent benediction
my son and I turn toward home,
The wind lifts our laughter into Spring.

ANITA LORENTZEN-WELLS ⌁ Runt

She's still here
alone,
curled under the infrared light,
shivering.

I lift her up
in my gloved hands,
cradling the tiny frame,
watching her protruding ribs
undulate with each breath.

Half opening her glazed-over eyes,
she peeks at me.
Content, they close as she
snuggles closer to my warmth.

It's become a ritual.

My father walks in,
so I lay her next to her mother
and tend to my chores.

SMACK!

My body freezes
at the familiar sound.
I turn and run.

She's lying on the cold concrete
at my father's feet —
blood trickling from the snout,
a body stone-still,
eyes frozen open in shock.

Biting my tongue, I look up . . .
"Dad,
what if I'd been a runt?"

LOIS J. MOORE   *Porky's Hard Labor*

One January when I was eleven, the temperature hovered around zero, with snow sweeping across the corral, stinging my face as it hit. When a big Hampshire sow decided this was the night to deliver her litter, we wrapped eight little pigs in a blanket, carried them to the house, and put them in a tub of straw near the stove so they wouldn't freeze to death. Their lives provided our food; they must survive.

Still the sow lay there, and labor continued. I sat beside her on an upside-down feed bucket with a lantern beside me. "Come on, mama, let's have that last one so I can go to bed." I waited and waited. Nothing happened. No afterbirth appeared, and the sow kept straining. I knew something was wrong and made up my mind to investigate. I threw my coat over the manger and rolled my sleeve up past my elbow.

When I inserted my hand into the sow's slimy vagina, I could feel nothing. Further. My whole arm was in the sow when I felt a hard object and ran my hand over it: a dead pig lying crossways. I turned the pig and pulled on it. Out it came. In a few minutes the sow rose up on her front legs and grunted twice. This was her "Thank you." Our meat supply for the year was saved.

TAMMI LITTREL   *The Surrogate*

On a cold night in March I was making a late-night check of the "heavies" in the calving lot. The wind was whipping snow around and each cow wore a white blanket of snow and ice on her back. As usual, the yellow heifer met me at the gate and followed me on my rounds.

When we were just starting out, the pickings were pretty slim when it came to selecting and keeping replacement heifers, and that's how she ended up in the herd. She turned out to be one of those cows who took it upon herself to check into everybody's business. The older cows in the lot stayed still while I walked around them, with Old Yellow shadowing my every step.

Dawn was just a pink hint in the east as I hurried into my coveralls and boots to make my next check. Most of the cows were at the gate, waiting to be turned out for the day. One cow was on her side and her eyes were glazed over. An old cow, she had calved, prolapsed, and died instantly. Quickly, I looked around, expecting to see a frozen calf, as I knew no baby calf could have survived the cold without a mother cleaning him up or giving him warm milk.

Oddly, Old Yellow lay in one corner. She was about ten to fourteen days away from calving. As I marched over, she stood up and there behind her was a frosty baby calf! Old Yellow mooed softly to the calf, which had been cleaned up, and it stood and started to nurse.

If the yellow cow had been closer to calving, I could have understood it. Sometimes while a cow is calving she gets confused and claims another cow's new baby as her own, but Old Yellow had saved that calf's life! The orphaned calf was put on the milk cow and about two weeks later, Yellow had her own baby.

As years went by, she became more and more bossy. We were always happy when she calved and was turned out and out of our hair. As with all of us, though, time caught up with her and we had to sell her, but I will never forget the bitterly cold night that she saved another cow's calf.

JEANNE ROGERS ⟋ Ninety Degrees and Rising

I lean back
into the shady side of the haystack
and let the wind
dry the sweat on my face.
Other things dry there as well —
bits of hay, dirt, dead bugs.
Large, round, yellow spiders are prolific
in this field. The kids asked
What are they? I said, They're gross.
I'll probably dream
about monstrous yellow spiders dragging me off
to their nests of hay.

I pray the farm hand
stays together one more year.
Old equipment, new hay.
Yesterday a rim on the front end
of the old M tractor busted. Thank goodness
for nephews who weld.

I pray Johnnie's back holds out
one more season. Stacking small square
bales (called idiot cubes in some
circles) is WORK (in capital letters).
Frustration threatens to win out —
equipment repairs, weather,
and demands on his time
that are out of his control. That
and the fact that his wife and children
don't always work
along the same lines he is thinking.

I pray the strings
quit breaking. We got a bad batch
of twine and bales
are breaking apart as they are lifted.
Retying bales is NO FUN (in capital letters)
and is one more
frustration between us
and a done deal.

I hear the tractor make the turn
at the gate, bringing another load

to the stackyard.
I will survive, if only by not thinking
about the hay caught under my shirt,
in my bra, in my jeans,
the scratches on my legs, the stickers
in my shoes and socks.
That and the fact that, as I pull
on worn gloves and grab my hayhook,
forgive me, hon,
I pray for rain.

AUDREY A. KEITH ⟍ Spring Calving

The cow pivoted in the center of the corral, refusing to let me get behind her. The last thing I needed right now was a modest cow.

I could have used a warm breeze instead of the icy wind. Or grass underfoot — that would have been easier to walk over than powdery snow and frozen manure. But most of all, I could have used a glimpse into the future the day we decided to double our beef herd.

Beef prices were high in '72. We had two hundred acres of native pasture, hay, a barn, and corrals. Our son wanted to get a start in farming. Beef seemed the logical way to start.

In November we bought sixty-five head of bred heifers at $365 each, due to start calving in mid-March. We planned to feed them during the winter, then pick out the best ones to keep and sell the rest. A lot of television time was being devoted to the high price of beef, but we were too busy to pay much attention. Beef was still cheaper than fish.

Those heifers gobbled up a lot of hay and grain, but they hadn't grown a bit by February when the first calves arrived, a full month early. We had expected tiny black Angus calves. We got huge Simmental-Hereford crosses.

We lost the first cow and her calf because she had trouble in the middle of the night. After that we checked the herd every two hours, day and night. My husband, Oran, decided that as long as I stayed up late to read I could just as well do something more useful than waking him to check the cows. So I was stumbling around in the icy barnyard with wind and snow blowing down my neck. He checked them at ten and went to bed. I checked them at midnight and two and he got up at four. Our nephew Jim checked them at six before he went to school. I was to sleep in mornings, and once in a while the phone did not ring by seven.

The immaculate women complaining about beef prices on television were frequently on my mind, especially on the most miserable nights. I would have given a lot to have them with me.

After out-maneuvering the cow, I climbed the fence and went to check #19 in the north lean-to. Then I could go in to my warm bed. I swept the cavernous interior quickly with my flashlight before I entered. A few cows turned their heads to look at me, never missing a beat in the calm mastication of their cuds. When I was halfway across I heard a soft *hoohf!* at my left elbow. I didn't need the light to know it was the Angus cow that had calved that afternoon. I used the light anyway. There she stood, between me and the only exit, looking like a belligerent musk ox.

Decisiveness is highly overrated. The cow walked away while I was still trying to decide: up through the roof or down into the ground?

While most of the cows needed help, they also distrusted our motives. We had to rope them, then snub them to a post. I learned to prepare the calf-puller while Oran slipped the chain over the calf's feet.

Hold it close to the heavy top. Do not catch the winch handle on your pant leg. Do not set handle on toe. Pull cable from winch with right hand.

When he took the calf-puller from me, he handed me the rope to clutch. Tightly.

Along with this crash course in bovine obstetrics, I picked up a little knowledge in related subjects. The red white-face we warmed up in the bathtub had a faulty navel, and the warm water merely hastened his demise. While I scrubbed the tub I told myself that at least we hadn't wasted two weeks and $38.50 on him before he died. It didn't help much.

The method worked better on a little black calf. At first I would have sold him for a nickel, if I could have found a sucker, but then he dried out and we had trouble keeping him confined.

The next day a calf was born dead. We took the shiny clean calf, rolled him around on top of the wet, bloody, dead one, and then grabbed the dead calf and left before the cow could get up. When we checked later she had claimed the new calf.

Most of my encouragement came from smaller incidents. Like the first night the cows didn't leap to their feet the minute I climbed the fence. Or the night I found my way out of the pitch-black barn after the flashlight dimmed out in two seconds. I didn't even pass out watching my first cesarean, although it was close. It had never occurred to me that only a local anesthetic was used.

While Oran was hauling cows sixty-five miles to the vet for cesareans, a neighbor would come to help, if needed. One day he caught this wild little cow and couldn't hold her. So after he snubbed the rope around a post, Jim dallied it around a second post. I took the end of the rope and wrapped it around a post, too. She continued fighting until the rope was so tight her eyes bulged and her tongue protruded like a water balloon. Then she collapsed on the ground. We started playing all the rope back out. As soon as we had completed this she jumped up and went for Jim. We went through the routine once more, only faster. This time, when she hit the ground we pulled the calf, in spite of the horrid gasping sounds. Then we grabbed the calf-puller and rope and disappeared over the fence.

I got lots of practice at climbing fences. Jim opened a gate while I was crossing a pen. A little Charolais calf came through, closely followed by his overprotective mother. I know I don't look my best while wading around in six inches of organic fertilizer and melted snow, in dirty clothes and with dark circles under my eyes, but I find it hard to believe that I looked dangerous enough to justify her reaction. Even handicapped by size ten overshoes over my size seven moccasins, I beat her to the fence.

That afternoon we wanted her calf in the barn, out of the wet snow. We took a loader-tractor out to the calf, and my husband threw the calf in the bucket with me. We all hated this arrangement, except Oran. The calf wanted out and the cow wanted in. I sat on the calf, pounded the cow in the face with a club, and aged ten years. Oran leisurely strolled back to get on the tractor and lifted the bucket very slowly.

At last, one glorious day in late April, we sold the twelve cows that hadn't calved yet. One of them sold for $165 — exactly $200 less than we had paid for the privilege of feeding her for five months. And it was worth every cent. That was the first good night's sleep we'd had in nine weeks.

TWYLA HANSEN   **Planting Trees**

Humming an old hymn,
I shove my spade deep
and turn over rich earth.
Good soil, good ground for
growing trees that alone
I'm planting this Good Friday.

As did my grandfather, who,
looking over the homestead,
uttered in Dane: *Augk! No trees!*
and set out to correct the
godless plains. And my young
father planting oak, elm, pine,
and cedar, maple, spruce, and
hackberry. I learned those

stories later, worshipped among
the limbs of their labor.

Now these hands and feet
tire, wish they were finished,
yet never quit. Like my
father and grandfather before me,
I pray to the soil, to the sky
for strength, for good planting
weather, to continue. Each
shovelful now a sacrament:
Take, eat, this soil my body
crumbled for your roots; drink
of this water, my blood, shed
for you now, and ever more.

And I sing the hymn
again and again,
knowing there is no end,
knowing no end.

C. J. PRINCE ✎ Bill, the Comeback Kid

As a greenhorn shepherdess I have learned by doing until I got goats:
angora, cashmere, and one lovely Alpine/Nubian cross.

I am an actress and writer by profession but often my heart is in the
pasture. Without a barn, I use the garage for a nursery; three lambing jugs
entirely fill the space, while two cars collect ice and snow outside.

One night I return from the TV studio in the dark after a long day of
shooting delays. The full moon plays hide and seek among the massive
clouds that canopy the Bijou Valley. As I walk up the path to the shed, I hear
a tiny sound amidst the cacophony of donkey bray, geese squawk, and
goats and sheep bellowing their hunger. It is a sound like a human crying.

I almost spill the bucket of water as I drop it alongside the grain bucket.
Speed feeding, I hurl an armload of grass and alfalfa hay over the fence and
enter the paddock, pausing to switch on the light in the shed. The animals
stampede toward the hay as I run toward the continuing cry.

Dollie, a white angora doe, stands guard over a curly white kid, still
alive because this was an unseasonable sixty-five-degree March day. I scoop
him into my arms, feeling him quiver in the night chill.

"Put the dogs in the house," I shout, hoping my husband, Michael, will hear. "And bring the flashlight." I feel shrouded in ignorance, though I've read stacks of books on kidding, even viewed videos.

Mama Dollie follows as I carry the wee kid down the path. Michael opens the lambing jug and brings me a china cup. I know I must get colostrum into the tiny goat but he seems too weak to nurse. I express milk into the cup and, holding the kid like a baby, let him sip.

I call my friend Jeanne who raises angora goats. "Fill a baby bottle with hot water," she says. "Empty all but a tablespoon into the doe's water, and milk her right into the bottle. The water on the sides will keep the colostrum from sticking. Cover his eyes when you feed him; he's looking for a dark place to suckle between two vertical lines."

It is now past nine P.M. and I live an hour and a half from an all-night supermarket. But my neighbor's baby is over a year old and she has plenty of bottles. I drive the dirt road to her house like the Indianapolis speedway.

Beside a roaring fire in the wood-burning stove, I hold the wee goat in my arms to feed him. I put him in the kidding pen on a hot water bottle wrapped in an old towel. Dollie murmurs and licks his face.

Before dinner for the humans, I have another chore: trudging up the hill to find the small dead body of the second kid, another male. This year I wanted females to increase my herd. I am sad in that detached way I've noted in old-timers, with too much work for the living to spend time grieving for the dead. I pick up the cold, woolly body and shout into the night for my husband to dig a grave.

The full moon glimmers through the ponderosa pines as we dig deep in frozen soil to discourage dogs and coyotes. I place the baby angora goat in the grave and ask the spirit of Edgar Rice Burro, a donkey buried close by, to watch over this innocent animal.

After we eat leftovers, I feed the tiny goat again, calling on the unknown spirit-keepers of baby goats; on the great goat goddess if there is one; on St. Francis, who helps all critters; on St. Jude, patron saint of miracles; and anyone else who might send healing energy to this little one. I feel responsible. If I'd put Dollie in a kidding pen earlier, he would have been protected from the weather and the other animals milling around the paddock. Every two hours I hold him to the teat or express milk and warm the hot water bottle.

"I've named him Bill," I announce to Michael, who likes ordinary names for animals. The ram is Aristotle, other animals include Mozart, Othello, and Lewis Carroll. This year, since I'm a *Next Generation* Trekkie, there will be Worf, Dr. Beverly Crusher, Deeana Troy, and Kira. "I named him for Bill Clinton. I want him to be the comeback kid."

Bill doesn't stand up. He drinks from the bottle but makes no attempt to get on his feet. I can't get my hands around Dollie's teats — like long pink milk bombs — to milk her out. My fingers ache from relieving her. She is protective, nibbling at the red hair falling into my eyes. She never butts, just pushes me until I pat her, rub her neck, and give her a kiss.

Other lambs and kids, newly born, struggle to their feet in minutes; Bill finally pushes up his front feet and falls. He suffered in those first few hours of life. A few scabs are healing on the left side of his body, but his left legs can't support his weight and his tail is smashed.

Days pass; I think he's getting stronger until he gets scours. With warm water I wash his hind legs and bottom. More phone calls to Elizabeth, Mary Sue, and Jeanne, my hotline to goat health. Mary Sue advises electrolytes for four days; the scours vanish.

At two weeks, Bill cannot walk but shows great energy and strength. His left hind leg is pronated — turned backward. A vet agrees his tail is dead, cuts it off, and splints his left hind leg. At last Bill struggles to his feet, hobbling precariously. Visitors oooh and aaah over the pathetic little goat. He basks in all the attention. Weariness weighs on me even though I'm down to feeding him four times a day. Hearing my voice, Bill runs to me, peg-legged.

When the splint is removed, muscle tissue has atrophied; once again, Bill has a hard time standing up. But he's determined, and the hind leg begins to hold his weight.

Obviously I will not use Bill as breeding stock but hesitate to castrate him after so much stress. I wait until he is a month old, castrating during the dark of the moon. He is weak for three days, eating little.

I wait also to disbud, recommended at three to five days, before the horn grows too long. Elizabeth, who's raised dairy goats for twenty years, helps nipping off the tips of his horns and restraining him while she applies the searing hot iron to stop horn growth. After initial impact, Bill stops screaming, and survives.

Bill and Dollie occupy a special pen since he isn't steady enough to be in the paddock with the rowdy lambs and frolicking kids and their head-butting mothers.

A goose sets on her nest, the irises bloom; Bill consumes two sixteen-ounce bottles a day. By the new moon in May I've weaned all the lambs. Hay is short this late spring, but pastures are green when Bill and Dollie join the lambs in the Findhorn pasture. Each day Bill is more sure-footed, a symbol of hope and determination. His curly white locks grow in tight mohair ringlets.

DECK HUNTER ⌒ *Wilderness Ranger*

This time the middle-aged man I'd seen two weeks earlier brought his wife with him. Both were on horseback as they approached me near the first of the Seven Brothers' lakes. He called, "I hope you don't mind but I told my wife there was a lady ranger up here who was older than I was, and she wouldn't believe me!"

We both laughed and I assured him I was happy to see both of them. She was curious about how I became a wilderness ranger for the U.S. Forest Service.

In 1970, I made my first backpacking trip, leading my Ohio Girl Scout troop to the Bighorn Mountains in Wyoming. Later as a backpacking instructor, I led groups annually to those mountains. After years of enjoying the national forests, I wanted to thank the Forest Service by doing volunteer work one summer. Since I'd climbed both Cloud Peak and Bomber Mountain and backpacked on both sides of the Big Horn range, I applied to the Buffalo District of the Bighorn National Forest.

Bill Bailey and his wife weren't the first to be surprised. A schoolteacher from Gillette asked, "Would you mind if I asked how old you are?"

"I'm going on fifty-seven," was my reply. He shook his head, telling me he was going on forty.

My job as a wilderness ranger covered a wide variety of responsibilities. First, since I was probably the only Forest Service person most mountain visitors would meet, public relations were important. I listened to their gripes and answered questions, hoping they had a good time.

In my years of backpacking and climbing, I saw many people who were poorly prepared for the mountains, so safety was primary to me. I regularly suggested safety tips.

Others arrived without knowing where they were. Most were not skilled in map reading and had no topographical map and no concept of distance and time. I advised such folks about places to camp and how to shorten their day-hikes, selecting places they could reach without overextending themselves.

The part of the job I disliked was picking up trash left by careless visitors. Wilderness rangers carried large black trash bags and cleaned up as we hiked from area to area and lake to lake. We lugged these bags to a central location to be taken out on horseback in the fall. I gathered thirteen bags at one location that summer.

Disgusted with this cleanup, I still found satisfaction in discarding the scorched rock ring, scattering cold ashes in the woods, and finally tossing twigs and pine needles so each campsite looked natural once again.

Only five feet two-and-a-half inches tall and at an age when some considered me a senior citizen, I wasn't anyone's first thought of a wilderness ranger. I greeted visitors with a cheery, "Hello there! I'm your wilderness ranger and if I can be of any help to you, just let me know!"

A bit startled, they frequently asked, "Are you up here all alone? Aren't you afraid? Where do you stay? What about the bears?" I explained that I was alone, but I carried a radio and checked in every day or two with the district office in Buffalo. This radio would also be an asset if they required emergency assistance, and I always informed group leaders where I would be camped.

No, I wasn't afraid. I had backpacked alone on numerous occasions, but not until I was *very* experienced and confident of my skills and safety. I paid attention to every little detail. When opening or closing my pocketknife, my total concentration was on that simple act I'd done a hundred times. I knew I couldn't afford any cuts or injuries, so I took no chances. I think being a little older also made me a little wiser.

The Forest Service had placed two base camps in the wilderness area, and I swapped tents with another ranger each week to avoid hiking the same trails. Each canvas tent contained a sheepherder's stove, two cots, and tools like shovels, saws, axes, and the ever-necessary trash bags. In addition, I backpacked to remote areas, carrying a full backpack with tent, sleeping bag, food, and other necessities.

One night I returned to my little backpack tent to find four men camped not far away. I ambled over and introduced myself. They were from Omaha, Nebraska, and asked if I minded if they camped so close. They'd hiked seven miles, including two thousand feet of elevation, and were plumb tuckered.

The next day they took a day-hike and when they returned they invited me to join them for dinner. What a feast! They served a canned ham, scalloped potatoes, dehydrated corn, and pineapple cheesecake! As I crawled into my sleeping bag later, I heard soft harmonica music. In my two summers as a ranger, these were the only campers to invite me to dinner. We still keep in touch and have visited each other's homes.

Many campers were unprepared for the unpredictable weather in the high mountains. In the morning, hikers left lower-elevation trailheads in shorts, T-shirts, and sneakers. But by early afternoon, clear blue skies grew cloudy and severe hailstorms came often. I felt sorry for a little girl in her sunsuit and short cotton socks and sneakers, shivering as rain dripped down her bare arms. Her father was no better off in soaking wet blue jeans. They had to hike seven miles back to their vehicle.

During the summer, I experienced the full range of weather. The blizzard of April 1984 left streams overflowing from melting snow in July. While hiking out of the mountains one day, I encountered a swollen creek. Wading, I soon was nearly thigh-deep and not yet in midstream. I saw trees jammed downstream and knew if I fell I would be swept against them. Turning back, I looked upstream and found a log across the water. Still wearing my backpack, I was not confident of balance for such a crossing.

I was only a mile from the trailhead, and I didn't want to turn around and hike fourteen miles via another trail. So I used my radio to call the Forest Service for assistance. A knight in shining green Forest Service armor extended a pole to give me added balance while I crossed on the log. I took some ribbing, but a news item later that week reported a backpacker in the Tetons had fallen in a similar stream and drowned, pinned against the rocks. Mountains are unforgiving.

Our work schedule was a five-day week starting on Thursday and ending on Monday. Weekends were always busy with lots of backpacking groups, horseback campers, and fishermen. On quiet evenings I found a site off to myself and enjoyed time alone. That summer I hiked 267 miles with time to really see the forest's beauty.

The following summer I was delighted to return to the Buffalo District as a paid wilderness ranger. I later learned that, at 58, I was the oldest wilderness ranger in the region.

NOREEN McCONNELL ~~~ **American Dream
on an Elk Ranch**

My family tells the story of my great-grandmother Minnie Craig, who moved out to this place to homestead with her husband. She was so lonesome that sometimes she would go outside and yell just to hear noise in this desolate place! Yet she endured.

Years later, Minnie's daughter, my Grandma Fannie, with my grandfather, John Dunning, Sr., met the challenge. She taught school to supplement the ranch income; one year she taught so far away she could only come home on weekends to be with her husband and little boy, my dad. She endured. She used to tell how lonesome it became when many people moved from their homestead places in the thirties. Yet they endured. Grandma kept on teaching when Grandpa's stroke left him partially paralyzed; then she taught for several years as a widow, living on this ranch for all but the last couple of years of her life. My dad went to college and became a teacher because he had seen that you couldn't count on this farm making a complete living for a family.

My dad, John Dunning, Jr., juggled teaching, farming, and ranching for thirty-one years with my mom, Karen's, help.

My husband Craig and I found running a beef cow/calf operation on this ranch today just as challenging as it was for the first homesteading families many years ago. But we found a new occupation that has become our dream come true: creating Elk Echo Ranch. Raising elk as an alternative to livestock is so pleasurable and rewarding that it never seems like a job!

We started with one bull and five cows; in under a year we had forty-eight elk of our own. We had run a beef cow/calf operation for many years and a lot of the concepts in beef and elk care overlap.

We have no problems keeping them in; they love to see us coming with their feed. An old cowboy in Wyoming once said "It don't take much fence to keep in a happy horse!" The same is true with elk.

Elk are profitable; you can run four elk to one beef cow on pasture, or by supplementary feeding, six to one. At present, a weaned elk heifer sells for an average of four thousand dollars; a weaned bull calf for two thousand. But even if the selling price goes down, their feed maintenance is so low that we'd still be ahead.

Each elk has its own temperament and personality; the more time you spend with them, the easier it is to recognize. Many of our names for our animals develop from being with them for a while. We have a Lazy Susan, who likes to graze on nice green grass while lying down; Bathsheba, an especially beautiful heifer who has enticed many a visitor; Windy Racer, who loves to toss back her head and run.

Calving season begins the middle of May. In the wild, the survival rate of calves is only about forty percent; tame elk have around an eighty-five to ninety-five percent survival rate. It is wonderful to watch them grow from taking their first awkward steps to gracefully playing king of the mountain over a patch of cornstalk bales. Calves talk to each other and their moms in an array of cries, whines, barks, and chirps.

If we need to bottle-feed a heifer calf, she bonds very closely with us and will be a special pet, and have a calming effect on the rest of the herd. If a bull calf needs supplementary feeding, we buy a goat to be a surrogate mother. If we feed him ourselves, when he is in his third season he can become dangerous. We know the temperament of each bull and feed them grain each day. In mating season, when the bulls are with the cows, we are respectful of their different natures.

During the fall a bull keeps his herd together and works hard at over-seeing them night and day. A mature bull will lose twenty percent of his body weight because Mother Nature tells him that he only has seventy to eighty days to service his harem.

In March and April bulls shed antlers or buttons and start new growth. An elk rancher can either let the magnificent horns grow out and calcify, or harvest the velvet, which is comparable to trimming a toenail or fingernail on a human. Velvet demands vary from year to year; the price fluctuates from forty to one hundred dollars per pound. The product has been used for thousands of years in the Orient to build up the body's natural resources against disease, like vitamins and health foods are used here, and now it's catching on in the U.S.

Statistics show that many unusually successful people come from little communities — the smaller the better. People who thrive in a rural community are resourceful individuals who set goals and pursue them on their own. The most successful people in life are those who are doing what they most enjoy. We want to continue the tradition of doing what it takes to make the dream of staying on the family land come true.

GENEVIEVE EPPICH ⟶ Elk Make Me Boil

Play time in summer. My three sisters and I hiked a lot up on the mountain. Once we decided to make us some stilts out of quakey trees. So we went up on the forest and we had a ball. Had to take tools with us to build the stilts. In the 1930s we never saw any deer or elk.

Yes, now it really makes me boil, the deer and elk just taking over your ranch. That I believe makes me the maddest of anything. The past four summers I spend my time every night down in the fields running the darn deer out so I can get enough second hay for my sheep. This is not right. Seems anymore you have to fight for what is yours.

The year 1944 I was on the mountain by a spring. Saw this animal coming up the drift fence. Moved slowly toward it. That was the first elk I ever saw in the wild. Now they steal your crops from you.

PATRICIA MIDGE FARMER ⟶ Transplanted

If I had not come to these high plains,
my heart would have missed
the beat of this love of place,
my guts would have yearned for
some unknown fulfillment,
my mind would have shrunk
to a small, civilized size,
and my soul would have tentacles,
searching, always reaching out
for what I found here.

But I am now like the tenacious sage
wide roots forced into

this seldom yielding ground
to make a place for me
to hold on tight
to nurture and be nourished
and, oh this land does feed me.

LEE HELVEY   New York Versus Kirby

For the first few years I lived on our ranch I cannot honestly say I was happy. I had grown up in New York City, had gone to school in Paris, which I loved, and had worked for Radio Free Europe in New York. I definitely felt isolated in the hills of this narrow mountain valley and was very lonely. I'd come from a totally dysfunctional family in the East so I had no support from that quarter. In Montana we were poor, a new experience for me, and I had to learn cooking, cleaning, and child rearing from the ground up. However, we had four children in very short order so I was too busy learning to exist to dwell much on my state of mind.

As an example of the humor and tolerance I found here, I recall a long-time inhabitant who was being annoyed by a zealous religious acquaintance who wanted him to at'end church regularly. The man endured this nagging for quite a while and finally said firmly to the zealot, "I believe in God." There was a pregnant pause and then he continued. "And I know her name, too." Of course the zealot asked what it was and the man said with finality, "Mother Nature."

In 1965 I became the rural mail carrier between Kirby and Busby, which was a great adventure for me and gave me my first spending money. Three times a week I'd meet the Sheridan, Wyoming, rural carrier a few miles up the road and take that mail to Kirby, a post office the size of a closet with a potbellied stove and an outhouse out back. The postmistress would hand me more mail, which I took to Busby, about eighteen more miles north, all on the Cheyenne reservation. I'd collect more mail from there and from mailboxes all the way back to Kirby. Often my one-year-old daughter, Elizabeth, would accompany me. In those days rural carriers picked up passengers, distributed shared magazines, and carried supplies to the one local store (which burned down in the '70s and was replaced by a saloon — the only building left in Kirby). Cheyennes often caught rides with me to Busby and our very blonde baby was the subject of much laughter, finger pointing, and discussion. Willie Fighting Bear and his wife occasionally rode with me and used that time to lecture me on the evils of smoking. Only once did my pickup quit me while carrying the mail — at the Busby Store. Kenneth LaFever gave me a lift to the reservation line, where a local rancher who had been sent by the postmistress to look for me met me on his snow machine. We transferred all the mail sacks and were off in a cloud of snow to the Kirby post office with me sitting behind him. The first thing I bought with my paycheck was a secondhand piano.

When our children reached the age to attend high school, the children and I lived in Sheridan. I substitute taught in all the town schools, but especially in the high school, as I discovered teenagers were my preference. I'd had three years at Smith College in the early '50s but had never been trained as a teacher. The realization that I was fairly successful at it brought me out of my shell and gave me some much-needed self-esteem. Every Friday after school we'd load up the dog, the Mixmaster, the vacuum cleaner, clothes, and groceries and head for the ranch, only to perform that routine in reverse on Sunday nights.

In October 1992 I returned to New York City to visit friends and room-mates from my boarding school and college days. Three of my closest friends are psychoanalysts who work very hard at their profession. They proudly showed me their couches, their elegant offices and waiting rooms, and even took me to evening seminars given by learned professors. They pointed out what was beginning to dawn on me anyway — everyone in New York City (who can afford seventy-five to a hundred dollars an hour) is either being psychoanalyzed or is doing the psychoanalyzing. If this state of affairs had not been so sad, it would have been amusing. I feel so blessed to have lived the life of a rancher, to be able to enjoy nature, work alongside my husband, and appreciate the environment that has so well nurtured all our children. I hope there will always be a place for the family ranch in this country.

LOUISE STENECK ～ The Handmaiden

This is how I helped him die.

He was a tiny piglet, no larger than my hand, born with a gaping hole in his skull. His few allotted hours of life would be hours of suffering. I lifted him from his mother's side and held him for a moment against the warmth of my beating heart. I stroked his underbelly, as smooth and soft as a baby's bottom, and hummed a quiet melody to still his fear. Then I placed him gently on the concrete floor and smashed his fragile little head with a hammer. I dropped his body into a bucket and went back to my chores.

I am death's handmaiden. I am there when the old sow with pneumonia rattles her last breath and, with a great shuddering of her massive body, leaves this time and place. I am there when the blizzard comes roaring through the night like a mighty freight train, smothering pigs huddled in their sheds, freezing piglets solid in an hour. I am there when the dog is run over in the road, when hail batters the garden to a memory, when baby sparrows fall from their nests and are eaten by the cat.

I can't talk to anyone I know about this. My friends are town people and death is not as real for them. Death is something they see on television or read about in the newspapers. Death is the painted imitation of life displayed in open coffins at funerals. Death is an unidentifiable road kill at sixty miles an hour.

I feel sorry for them, and for millions in this country who are so far removed from the natural order of things that death does not seem real. They rise to the ring of alarm clocks in houses shuttered against the world. Their days are spent in cars and offices and stores. They eat food from packages printed with unpronounceable ingredients. They fall asleep in the blue glow of the television. They believe their lives will last forever.

They don't see how the sun rises with all the fanfare of a circus coming to town. The trumpets blare, the lions roar, the clowns turn somersaults and shout, "Get up, get going! Smell that bacon frying! Feel that soft breeze blowing! Hear those birds singing! Life is short! Enjoy! Enjoy!"

They've never watched a lamb plop wet and shining from his mother's womb or stooped to smell the endless promise of freshly turned soil or stood out in their nightgowns under a chill October moon to hear the coyotes singing life's haunting song.

Do they know what they are missing? I sometimes see them as little balloons, adrift above the wondrous flow of life and death, the harshness and all the beauty.

This is how I helped him live.

He was too long in coming, wrapped in the glistening red afterbirth, his little body still and lifeless. I reached down and pulled him from the smothering pile, felt the faintest flicker of a heartbeat. I lifted him to my face and placed my lips over his nostrils and blew the tiniest puff of air into his lungs. I turned him over and massaged his chest, then blew again. He sensed life, and with a great shake and shudder, opened his eyes and breathed on his own. I dried his wet body, placed him at his mother's nipple, and went on with my chores.

I am there when the boar mounts his quivering partner and creates the future with his seed. I am there when the first pale green shoots of corn crack the earth's hard crust and stretch for the sun. I am there when the puppies wriggle blindly to their mother's breast, when the prairie bursts into bloom, when the springtime morning is a symphony of birds heralding a new day.

I am life's handmaiden.

MARY KATHRYN STILLWELL

Winter Song

A coyote wakes me —
a hoot, a howl in early morning
snow light —
from the next room
where our son, the Colombian hooter
begins his ascent,
rising from the night
toward warm soy
that he will guzzle
then fall back
into sleep again.

We must all wake to coyotes
every now and then,
listen to their singular song,
their collective chorus,
in early morning snow light.
What will we do when the hunter
cuts the last song short?

This day is coming,
and we make plans
to move to coyote country,
post No Hunting signs,
to tuck our son into bed
certain that some morning
he will wake to their hoot,
their howl, the first song
of distance
in early snow light.

I Carry the Ranch Inside Me

ANITA LORENTZEN-WELLS
Irrigating with Grandpa

Dawn cracks, and the sun's yolk glows on the horizon.
Grandpa's red Ford glides in the gravel drive,
pausing at the sidewalk's edge.
My sister and I yank on our shorts and mud-caked shoes
and clomp our way into the pickup
with its jug of stale water, weather reports and farm markets.
Grandpa shifts the power-less steering into gear,
his taut, sinewy hands wrestling
with the wheel, coaxing the accelerator into motion.

The cornstalks wipe their morning dew on our thighs
as one on a side
we trail the ditch, starting the tubes in rows
whose mouths were groomed into smooth furrows
by Grandpa's shovel, his seasoned companion.
He consults his penciled notes,
pairing each dry row with a black faucet,
patching any footprints
on the fragile embankment.

He was the master, and we, his disciples —
our summer ritual a communion with the soil
that would, in time, summon him home.

JANEEN JACKSON ✎ Country Seedling

I remember a time when we were privileged to live in an old, broken-down, secluded house in the pines. We didn't have much in the way of furniture or toys, but that didn't matter because we had the whole outdoors. We slept on mattresses on the floor and even the granddaddy longlegs crawling over us at night didn't spoil the peace and solitude we loved there. We had to go into town to bathe in a friend's tub, but in between my mother took the water we hauled in, filled a tin washtub, and we got a scrubbing.

I remember pine cone fights. Ouch, did they sting! I remember my stepdad bringing home a barrel, and we stood on it barefooted and rolled it over every kind of terrain for hours. We climbed on huge rocks, building great rock forts. I'd pretend I was the wild stallion with flowing mane, standing on top of a hill or rock, sounding out a whinny to tell the world how much I loved the freedom. I remember catching baby horned toads and looking them all over before turning them loose on the forest floor.

That was the start in me of a burning love for critters and the out-of-doors. Yes, I am convinced it was the beginning of the feeling that would mold me into what I am today — a rancher.

Ranching is a pleasure to us where it might be poison to another. I see eighty- and ninety-year-old ranchers still plugging along and I talk to them at sales. I hope we can spend the rest of our days here, and when we die they can plant us right here on the ranch and plant wildflowers on top of our graves and let the cattle, elk, deer, and wild turkeys feed over us. Good enough for me.

MAVIS BUCHOLZ ✎ Ranger and Me

I grew up on a farm in the center of North Dakota. I was an only child until I was eleven years old. Therefore I spent most of my time alone or with my many pets. Horses were my great love.

I was nine years old the first time I saw Ranger. He was a brown and white horse, a little smaller than the average quarter horse of today. My dad bought him from a farmer some fifty miles away, and I was given orders never to take this horse out of the barn or to ride him, because he loved to run and would possibly get away from me. I spent many hours getting to know Ranger, and he in turn learned to trust me.

The day finally came when Ranger and I ventured out onto the prairies — and we became inseparable. One of my chores every day was to bring the dairy cows home from the big pasture. This consisted of 320 acres of prairie. My dad always insisted that I not ride with a saddle; I had to ride bareback. In case I fell or was thrown from the horse, I would fall free and not become tangled in the stirrups and dragged.

The summer I was eleven, a friend of my dad's who bought horses from the farmers in the area asked my dad to accompany him to a vacant farm six miles from our place to catch and load some untamed horses. I was so excited, I begged and begged to go along and bring my horse, too. My mother was not too happy with me, but I just had to be there for all the excitement of loading "wild" horses. My dad finally weakened and loaded Ranger onto the truck for the journey. Once we arrived at the vacant farm, my dad was reluctant to unload my horse, since the horses to be caught were already in the corral, and he felt there was no need for him. I insisted. I came to ride and I wanted my horse off the truck! So Dad put Ranger into the barn, tied, with his bridle on. Dad and his friend began to load the horses.

One of the last horses became difficult to handle, so the men harnessed a tame horse and planned to snub the wild horse to the harness and drag the renegade onto the truck. In the process of securing one horse to the other, the rope that was looped around the wild horse's neck and through the harness collar dropped to the ground, and in the struggle, my dad stepped onto the coiled rope.

There was so much dust churned up by both horses that it was impossible to see clearly. Then, in a blink of an eye, both horses started to run. In that cloud of dust, neither the truck driver nor I could see Dad. We both thought he was hanging on to the rope trying to stop the two horses. But as they came to the edge of the dusty yard and galloped onto the prairie, we saw that my dad's hands were free and in the air. He wasn't holding the rope, he was being dragged by those two horses. The truck driver started to run after the horses, but I just stood there — and in a second I remembered my horse in the barn.

Ranger was excited by all the commotion, but I was able to climb onto the side of the stall and jump on, and then untie him. We left that barn door at a full gallop. By this time my dad was some distance from the yard. By the time I was near enough to see him, and for him to see us, he had been dragged a quarter of a mile over grass and rocks. He stretched toward the rope in an attempt to reach his ankle but he couldn't. By then the pain was so intense he turned over onto his stomach — and all the while those two horses were at a full gallop.

Dad saw me come up alongside of him, and he yelled for me to stop those horses. I knew that Ranger usually shied, but for some unbelievable reason he never even turned an ear in my dad's direction. Bouncing alongside, he just headed for those two horses. As I came up to the harnessed horse, I knew that the only way I could possibly stop them was to grab that horse around his neck, and since I didn't have a saddle, there was nothing for me to hang on to except Ranger's neck. So there I hung between two horses! I hung on for dear life; and the horses stopped.

My dad was able to sit up and unwind the rope from his ankle, telling me, "Don't let go." Once he was free I dropped to the ground, still holding on to my pony's reins. The other two horses ran to the end of the pasture.

The realization of what had happened didn't really register in my mind. I thought my dad would just get up, dust himself off, and we would get those horses and put them in the truck. When I turned to look at Dad, I could not believe what I saw. He was covered with dirt and blood. The overalls that he had been wearing were completely torn away on the back-side from the waist down. The flesh from the buttocks area was torn away, exposing bone. To this day I don't know how my dad stood the pain. He stood out there on the prairie as pale as death and said, "Good thing we brought your horse."

The truck driver drove the truck out to where we were and helped Dad into the cab. They then headed back home. I rode the six miles home on Ranger as fast as he could carry me. By the time I arrived, Mom had Dad in the car and was heading for the Harvey Hospital, which was fifty miles away.

My dad spent two weeks in the hospital. He came home for a week but had to go back due to blood poisoning. He did get well and lived to farm and ranch for many more years. The rope burn on his ankle never disappeared.

ANN VONTZ   From the Ukraine to the Plains

My father, mother, and year-old sister arrived in North Dakota in the spring of 1910 from Kiev, Ukraine.

My mother yearned for the companionship of the sisters, brothers, and parents she left behind. My father, who had nearby relatives, could not accept this. He told her, "The plains are like the steppes in the Ukraine; you will learn to love your new home."

Dad preferred to use horses on his land and put in long hours. Mother had no adult companionship from early morning until late at night. No one spoke her native language.

After four years, my mother rebelled by leaving the farm on many occasions. Leaving meant walking. She'd start to walk back to Kiev with three little ones at her side, one in her arms, and pregnant with another.

I was told later that once, when I was three, I either strayed or lagged behind as we walked to Kiev. I was lost on the green prairie for three days. When the search party found me, I was nine miles from home and my tears had washed rivulets in the dust on my cheeks. The feeling of abandonment persisted in me for many years. Nightmares were common, even into my adult years.

I remember little about my mother. My Aunt Mary told me that she never saw my mother sit down unless she was breast-feeding one of us. She did not have the time or energy to care for so many children. Her sixth child was a son, which made my father happy; the baby lived only eight months.

After five years on the North Dakota homestead my mother was committed to an asylum in Jamestown, where she died three years later. Loneliness, hardship, and despair caused many settlers to go crazy. The winters, for women, were more difficult to bear than the summers. In the asylum my mother gave birth to her seventh child, a daughter. Friends of the family adopted her.

My mother's absence was not clear to me. I felt she would be in our presence any minute.

My sister and I now recall happenings that we didn't understand at the time, but we surely do now. I asked Nellie, "I remember playing with some copper pipe, glass jars, and water, but can't figure out what Dad used them for." Nellie, who was older, knew. Dad and his cohorts found a way to break the monotony. Liquor was prohibited, so to have it meant to make it. The men moved the still from one farm to another to keep the feds guessing. The jugs were filled with whiskey and divided among those involved.

Sometimes Dad put me in a buggy, ten years old, driving a reliable old nag, and said, "Take these tools to John. If anyone stops you, don't talk to them." Now I see that I was part of the distribution system. Why did my father risk doing such things?

I can only speculate on how it would have been to grow up on the prairie with a mother. I believe Father gave us a good upbringing. He taught us self-reliance and instilled in us love for the land and animals. His insistence on education certainly shaped my character. He seldom raised his voice with us. But I still have no answer for how he could have seven children with his wife, my mother, and yet couldn't find *any* time to keep her smiling.

DIANNE ROOD KIESZ   Morrill County Soddy: 1990

hard to believe
she raised 13 children
here
the last still living
in our community

no older than my mother;
while the world fought
two Great wars and
"kept peace" in Korea
she whitewashed
earthen walls to
mimic light;
the nation elected its first
Catholic president while she
scrubbed planked floors
hauled water buckets
and slop.

neighbors took showers
installed propane heat
watched TV;
she and hers canned dills
over wood
churned by hand
shared a tubful on
Saturday night.

the thatched roof
harbored dignity
cleanliness and love
now buried beneath
twenty-six abandoned years;
dubious tourists focus cameras
and call it "quaint."
we knew it as
Grandma's house.

CORA ESCH 　 *Horse Trader's Daughter*

Until I was fourteen I spent every summer traveling Nebraska in a covered wagon. My father was a horse trader. When school was out in the spring, we'd leave our winter headquarters in Walthill, Nebraska, to "go on the road." I can recall it all and make it as real as if I was in the wagon bumping along the unimproved country roads.

I'm sure the life of a road trader was not very pleasant for my mother, as our living quarters was the wagon, a structure about seven feet wide and nine feet in length. A small gas stove, cupboards for dishes and pans, a bed in the back of the wagon with a trundle bed underneath and storage overhead — it was adequate. In my memory's eye I see Mother as she cooked over an open fire when it was too hot to use the gas stove in the wagon. I remember her, quite often with a baby in her arms, as she drove a team of horses that pulled the covered wagon while my father and brother each drove another wagon. I can still feel her work-worn hands as they stroked my hair, comforting me in times of distress.

I can see Papa as he sat on a fallen log or a camp stool, whittling and whistling, as he waited for a local farmer who wanted to buy, sell, or trade horses. I recall the friendly arguing, the sometimes not so friendly bickering, the final settlement of the deal, and I can feel the sense of complete happiness of my father at that time in his life. I recall the not so happy days when the tractor replaced the horse for field work, and the need for work horses ceased to exist. I still feel the frustration and anguish suffered by my father when the good horses were sold for slaughter, to be used in dog food or for overseas shipments.

But for my siblings and me, the life was savored. I see my sister as she played with corn silk dolls made from the corn that grew in fields along the shady lane where we camped. I hear the laughter of two small girls as we chased multicolored butterflies and tiny fireflies that seemed to hover just beyond our reach. I see the two of us in the shade of the giant oak trees that grew in abundance along the roadways, cutting paper dolls from the Sears, Roebuck catalog. I smell the perfumed aroma of the wild roses that grew in profusion along the fence row. I see it all as if it was yesterday instead of sixty years ago.

I close my eyes and my brother, in his suspendered overalls, his straw hat pushed back on his head, is again herding horses along the grassy roadsides of our campsite. I remember his kindness, his gentle teasing, and I remember well how he would tie a rope to a bucket handle and drop the bucket into one of the many creeks that flow throughout Nebraska to fill the water barrels for the horses to drink. I still shiver with anticipation as I remember the thrill of having the rope tied about my waist to slowly descend into the creek. A sense of excitement runs through me yet as I feel the clear cool water flow over my hot sweaty body.

Tears fill my eyes as I realize that most of those things I remember are gone.

I can hear the rain that fell against the canvas top of the wagon, making music only I could appreciate; I also remember the more violent storms when the men hurriedly anchored the wagon with ropes fastened to iron stakes pounded into the ground to keep the wagon from blowing over. I hear the howling wind and feel the wagon swaying with its blasts.

I remember one of the most pleasant parts of our summer trip was seeing our old friends, people we visited each year. Our schedule was always planned so we would be with special friends for the big Fourth of July celebration in Shelton, Nebraska.

I remember how great it was to sleep in a soft bed, while my friend was thrilled to sleep in the camping buggy; eating a meal, in a house once again, and in return our friends sharing a meal with us in the camp area. I recall the love and appreciation I felt for these kind and beautiful people. I have felt, too, the lack of understanding by some. We were occasionally called Gypsies, some farmers refused us permission to camp on their land. As Papa said, "I don't blame them. They've probably been cheated by some trader going through the country. We'll move on to the next place where we are welcome."

While our living standards have changed and there is no way to compare, I often wonder if I could be as charitable to a group of weary travelers as most people were to us. I sincerely hope that, should a group present themselves at the door of my bed and breakfast, I will remember the kindness shown to us many years ago and reciprocate with that same treatment.

BERTHA HOLSINGER   *All for a Box of Crayons*

About seventy-six years ago, when I was rather young, I was riding on a spring wagon, perched on the seat beside my aunt who was taking the kids to school. The horses were trotting along when I spotted a box of crayons on the ground. I hollered for my aunt to stop as I leaned over the side to show her. I leaned too far and fell out. The back wheel of the wagon went over my leg and broke it. My aunt took me home, where my grandpa wrapped it. First he put rags, then put a piece of lathe on each side, then wrapped it again. He then stretched an old stocking over it. I do not remember how long it took to heal, but I do remember that I couldn't walk at the Fourth of July picnic. I had to sit with the little kids that crawled rather than walked.

That was also the first time that I ever had an ice cream cone. It was strawberry, and ooh how good it was! My leg healed and has served me many years. I've worked all my life, and danced when I was younger. I still go for long walks, so I guess Grandpa did a good job, and I'm glad he was able to.

ANN GORZALKA   *Legacy of Strength*

One doctor practiced in Moorcroft when we lived there. His office was in the hotel lobby, and I had occasion to visit it once. While playing I nearly cut my leg off in an accident with broken glass. If there was anesthetic in the early 1930s, I wasn't given any that day. A nurse neighbor and Mom held me down while the doctor cleaned my wound with something that felt like liquid fire before he sutured my leg with some thirty stitches.

The office door was open a crack, and while I was screaming and trying to kick loose I saw a very wide-open eye belonging to a small boy peeking through the crack.

I couldn't use my leg for six weeks, but Mom changed the bandages and nursed me back to health.

Some time later the doctor left Moorcroft and Mom was on her own nursing my younger brother through his annual bouts of pneumonia using mustard plasters and prayers.

One November I came down with a nearly fatal case of typhoid fever. Mom sat up with me night after night, reassuring me after attacks of high fever and terrifying hallucinations.

My mother, as did countless other pioneer women of her era, faced hard work, disappointment, illness, and death with a strength that was bred in them. But this legacy didn't make their lives any easier.

It seemed Mom had experienced it all, the cycle of love and death repeating itself at intervals throughout her life. Once again she was called upon to fight the battle, this time it was for her firstborn.

The tragic events began when my sister, brother, and I were playing house in a partially burned government trapper's cabin. Three sides and part of the roof of the log structure were standing. Inside was a rickety table, rusty stove, and broken cabinet. My sister went through the cabinet looking for things to play with. She found a container of white powder and some burned raisins scattered about. She took them to the table and mixed them with a stick, offering each of us a taste. We refused, she tasted it.

It made her sick a short time later. Mom nursed her for two days before my parents took her to Gillette, a larger town some seventeen miles from Moorcroft. There she was admitted to the hospital where she died a few days later.

The white powder she had mixed with the raisins and tasted was strychnine. The poison was used in bait by government trappers to kill coyotes. Age had weakened it, otherwise she would have died within minutes.

I stood at the foot of her casket and looked at her white anklets while Dad consoled Mom. I didn't cry but I was lonely and wanted her back. That was my last memory of Moorcroft, that and the haunting strains of "Red Wing," the song Mom hummed to herself during those long nights she sat by our bedside, keeping vigil.

MARGARET TRAUTMAN ~~~ **Mother Left a
Light Burning**

The winter of 1920 was a cruel one, with lots of snow and bitter cold. The doctor was forced to hire a driver and a team of strong horses to take him on the many calls he got each day.

That night, the driver, Gust, turned in the gateway of our farm. The horses were spirited and anxious to get home after a long trip. They were only two miles from their warm stable. Our family dog barked, the horses plunged and were hard to control. It was very late, so the doctor said to his driver, "Looks like everybody is asleep, so just go on home."

Mother had left a light burning, waiting for the doctor, because my oldest sister, Vivian, was running a high fever.

As the team drove away, she ran out in her night clothes and bare feet to catch the doctor. And so the deadly "flu" set in, turning quickly into pneumonia.

Each day neighbor ladies came from Cleveland, doing everything they could to help my young mother — bathing, cooking special broth, sitting with her all night — and then they too contracted the flu. (Three other mothers in the community died in one week.)

The evening of Mother's death, my father called John, my brother, age nine. He was to go on horseback in the dark and cold to get the doctor. He was a sturdy youngster, and yet so afraid. When he reached the doctor's home, he pounded on the door, telling him Mother was very ill.

My oldest sister, lying in bed in the next room, could hear our mother gasping for breath, and then all was still.

I remember my father coming downstairs. My brother and I were lying on a bed, half asleep, and he said, "Mother is dead." John cried and cried. He had tried so hard to get the doctor in time.

The casket was brought by train from Jamestown, then by bobsled to the farm home.

Neighbor ladies washed and dressed the body. Uncle Charlie and my father brought the body down the stairs and laid it in the casket by the north wall of the living room. The doors were closed to keep the room cold.

The minister came and two teachers from the school. They sang for the funeral. One was my first grade teacher; later she held me on her lap. Then Uncle Charlie backed his team and bobsled to the door. The casket was loaded for the trip to the cemetery. None of us children could go, but we watched from the window as the horses drove away.

My mother, thirty-three years old, was mother to five children, ages one and one-half to fourteen.

PHYLLIS LUMAN METAL ⟍ I Carry the Ranch Inside Me

I carry the ranch inside me. I can close my eyes and see every sticky weed around our house, the gopher holes, the path to the coal house and the privy. And I can feel my feet on the path as I run barefoot from our house to the ranch house where the corrals wedge against the cottonwoods that line the river. I pass the garden where only weeds grow, for the gophers have eaten the young vegetables and the garden has been abandoned to the weeds. I go down under the barbed wire fence, into the creek. I love the rich black mud that my feet sink into, the school of tiny minnows darting away like a thousand scattered pins flashing their silver to the sun. Sometimes I take my net and catch them, fill jars with water and line the front porch with silver sparkles until the minnows turn belly up and begin to smell.

I go up the creek bank to the prairie dog town and watch the dogs stand up and bark at me for invading their village. Then I walk through the grass to where the still fresh cow pies lure my bare feet, and I squish the dung between my toes.

Finally I lift the horseshoe off the tall pole gate and slide through the opening. The gate squeaks like an old joint as I go see Rosie, the ranch cook.

"Don't you come into my clean kitchen with that shit on your feet," she says. "The pump's outside the door." After I pump icy water over my feet, she says, "Peel these spuds, half-pint." When dinner is ready, she bangs on the metal triangle and the cowboys stroll up from the bunkhouse, joshing each other. I go back to our house to eat in silence with my mother and father.

After dinner I cross the meadows and climb to the top of the first sage-covered foothill. I sit cross-legged on the hard ground and watch the sun set behind the foothills on the other side of the river. Then the sky darkens and millions of stars appear. I become water, wind, sky, hills — each in turn. And I sit there with always the same mystery. Does it end up there in some absolute emptiness? And if it ends, does something else begin?

And then I go down into the valley, across the meadows, back home. We always sit in candlelight. My mother says it is so much softer. We sit in silence, my mother, my father and me. Conversation's just a waste of time, he says. But my mother is restless with the silence.

Could there have been any other kind of childhood? There would have been no frontier in my mind, no wide open space that led on and on. From my childhood on the frontier I got the soul of an adventurer, and I spent the rest of my life finding ways to move into new directions. From my parents I received a contradiction of lifestyles — the ranch where my father was raised and that I loved, and the city, the seductress, my civilized mother's answer to life's problems.

My grandfather's ambitions led him to marry a sophisticated lady, the product of a romantic fantasy. The idea of marrying a lady was firm in my father, and he repeated history. The Cowboy married a Lady.

They fell in love at a party, he in a tuxedo and she in an evening gown. She didn't see him in a cowboy hat and boots until after the wedding.

When my father and mother decided to get married, Grandpa was laid up from being struck by lightning. He wanted Dad to run the outfit, so he built the city house that we lived in at the ranch and gave my parents a Pierce Arrow for a wedding present. The house was designed by an architect, and every stick of wood was brought in by wagon. My grandmother's summer house was then moved down the river to become the ranch house where the cook and maid my father had promised my mother lived. The cowboys lived at the bunkhouse, and they ate at the ranch house. No cowboy ate a meal at our house.

Father worshipped Mother as something precious and superior to the other hard-working ranch women. He teased her about her aristocratic ways, yet he was proud of her, and she somehow elevated him above the hard life. His beautiful lady made it worthwhile.

I knew there was seduction in my mother's ways. The world of the beautiful fairy princess was seductive and ephemeral. She had a degree in music from the College of the Pacific, yet there was no musical instrument in our house — only that Victrola where she played her Caruso records when my father was away. He made fun of them, imitating Caruso purposefully off key and poking at her city slicker ways until she ran crying into the bedroom. And then he put his arm around her, bringing her out. "There, there, little girl," he said, and held her tight and squeezed her buttocks.

I remember the Blizzard of 1922; it lasted for days. This was the first winter that my mother had stayed on the ranch. My father had promised her that she would never have to spend a winter on the ranch. Our house was built to be a summer house. It got so cold that the tacks popped out of the linoleum in the kitchen. We stayed inside near the kitchen stove while the wind howled around the house. My mother didn't go outside except to go to the privy. The snow kept falling and the thermometer hung around sixty below. We had to cover our faces to go outside. My mother cried a lot. She tried to wipe away the thick frost from the windows. I looked at the windows and saw creatures I never talked about. My mother read me fairy tales. It was very quiet. The phone did not ring. Nobody came to our house. We stayed in a little part of the house and fed coal to the stove all day long. My mother cried and said, "If only I could hear from my friends."

My mother did not sleep with my father because he always slept with his six-shooter under his pillow, and he had wild nightmares. In the summer, she and I slept on the big screened-in porch. Mother undressed in the bathroom. Nothing worked in the bathroom, but the fixtures were there. We had the only bathroom in the valley. Folks up and down the valley came to our house to see the modern conveniences. "Well, ain't that something," they said. "Ain't it grand."

A plumber came out from Rock Springs to fix the plumbing once, but he got mad at my father and stuffed the pipes with grain, so we used a privy like all the other ranchers. But at least we had a bathroom, and it set us apart.

Most evenings, my mother came out of the bathroom in her nightie, and when my father called her she giggled and went to his bedroom. I heard noises, and then she would come back to the porch. In the morning, he came out to the porch and pulled down her nightie and played with her breasts. He called them her little tummies. I pretended to be asleep, but I was watching. Then he went into the kitchen and on to work, while she lay in bed.

My mother picked a fresh bouquet of wildflowers for the center of the table every night in the summer. We ate in silence. Eating is serious business, my father said. Sometimes after supper, my father disappeared and my mother sat on the back steps dabbing her eyes with a white handkerchief. "What's wrong," I asked. "Go away," she said. "You would not understand. You are just like him. I have tried so hard to make a lady out of you." But then here came my father up the path from the bunkhouse. He'd been playing cards with the cowboys and was a bit drunk. She stood up when she saw him in front of her, and he grabbed her and held her close. He kissed her and she snuggled into his arms. It was always like this. She took it out on me, and then when he came around she just settled into his arms.

One day Dad roped a coyote and dragged it home to Mother. He called out to her to come see it, but she was busy arranging flowers. So he dragged the coyote into the room where she was and cut the rope. The coyote raced through the house. Mother jumped up on the dining table and screamed, "Get that beast out of here!" Dad lay on the floor laughing and I chased the coyote. Finally the coyote jumped out the window, upsetting Mother's silver tea set. Father was always joking that way, and she didn't understand.

She always held herself apart from the other ranchers and their wives. She'd scrub the water dipper after my father's friends drank from it. She even boiled it after Injun Bill drank from it. Grandpa had traded a pinto pony for Bill when he was twelve years old. He became Grandpa's top hand. My dad always said that Bill ran the outfit, and he was just Bill's errand boy. When I thought about it I got things all mixed up. I thought the Indians would not give up one of their own children, so I figured that Bill was Grandpa's child by one of the Indian women. So to me Bill was my uncle, or at least a family member of some kind. We called him Injun Bill, but not to his face. So I could never understand it when mother boiled the dipper after Injun Bill had taken a drink with from it. This annoyed my father. "What in the hell do you think Bill has got?" he'd ask.

My mother and I went to California for the first five winters of my life. Then, in my sixth year, I began going off to boarding school. At boarding school I was like a wild animal in hibernation. I went through the motions, waiting for the summers, and going home.

Then I was on the train back to the ranch and I'd smell the sage when I was still on the observation platform. And there was Dad waiting for me. "Did they make a city slicker out of you?" he asked. "No, no, I'm a ranch kid," I said.

We'd go to the Park Hotel and I'd change into my overalls and throw the hated dress on the floor. My mother would pick it up and fold it neatly.

I used to think that I was not my parent's real child because they sent me away to boarding school at age six. Now I think my mother sent me because she realized that she had made her bed, and there she must stay all of her life. I think she thought of leaving my father but didn't know how. Divorce was such a disgrace in those days. There was no way out. So she sent me away to school to keep in touch with the world she had given up. I was the pawn.

I never fit in anywhere. When I was young I was my father's little helper. He told the cowboys he could not run the outfit without me. I followed him about with a Prince Albert can in my hip pocket, just like his — except mine was filled with grasshoppers to use as bait when we went fishing.

I memorized every inch of the ranch. I knew the birds and the flowers and the insects. I can still hear wind swaying the creaking old cottonwood trees. Each summer I raised between thirty and forty lambs on cow's milk. I fed the lambs with beer bottles topped with black nipples. Each fall they were shipped and Dad put the money in the bank for me. But my dad and I played a game, pretending my lambs were still mixed in with his big band of sheep. "See Spots over there?" he'd say. I'd named every one of them. And I'd say "Yes." Both of us knew that Spots had long since become lamb chops.

I had my black pony, Cheivo, a little pacer with a blaze face. I curried her every day. I held the bridle behind my back and held a can of grain out front to catch her. She arched her neck and sidled toward me. I slipped the bit in her mouth and climbed aboard. We roamed the ranch together, farther and farther as I learned to open the gates cowboy style while still mounted.

One of the headmistresses at boarding school said that I was a combination aristocrat and barbarian. I think she was right, and these two sides of me had a burning warfare that I didn't understand. The ranch was the bedrock of me. And yet later I was ashamed to admit that I came from a ranch near Pinedale, Wyoming. It seemed all the important people came from big cities.

My dad used to say that civilization was coming to get us. When I was young, I thought civilization was an enormous black bug that would gobble up everything in its path. But my dad was right. It began to reach even Pinedale, Wyoming. Later he'd say, "Civilization has come. Things will never be the same." And one year when they took me to Rock Springs to catch the train to boarding school, we passed a couple of cars. That had never happened before. "The country's getting filled up and ruined," my dad said.

We had a cook we called Aunt Pete. Pete was probably my mother's only friend on the ranch. Pete had been my grandmother's cook for years, and then she gave him to my mother because she knew Mother couldn't boil water. Pete stayed with us during the summers until he decided that ranch life was too hard. He was a fine chef. He wore a chef's hat when he cooked at our house.

He was a hermaphrodite; I heard Rosie talking about it. When he moved on he left a trunk behind, and it was full of ladies' undergarments and makeup. The whole family loved Pete and was sad when he left to be a cook for Douglas Fairbanks in Hollywood. There definitely was a code of the West and if a person did a good job, he was accepted.

My mother was an elegant lady who loved the beauty of the land and was shocked by the lifestyle. She was never part of it all, even after the Depression leveled her and she settled for what she had become, a ranch wife, she still dreamed of the city. Finally, when the doctors ordered my father to move to a lower altitude, they moved to a beautiful area outside Salt Lake City. And the strange thing was that after my father died at age forty-eight, she said that his death ended her life.

By then, my life had gone in other directions. But I love to return to the ranch. When people ask me where I'm from, I say Pinedale, Wyoming. The ranch is a part of me that I carry with me always.

DIANNA TORSON   Miss Top Cat

we rode those idaho roads you and me
waiting for kids to return from grade school waiting for
spouse to return from grad school and when you were pregnant
with a foal you should not have we gave ourselves plenty of
dreams

we dream snowy owls camped in winter trees the green
hummingbird that circles the house and looks in my eyes four

times and the sparrow hawk nest in the house near scott's
window but most of all we dream the flicker that falls from a
tree as we ride by and stop to pick it off the gravel its
eyes closing and long tongue limp as the pesticide plane
disappears down the valley my tears falling on its white
breast covered with brown hearts and the magpie kim feeds in
her room til it dies and the great horned owl sitting on one
telephone pole and the next telephone pole for one mile
snatching birds out of the air and watching us in the foggy
rain and we dream the wild killdeer baby i pick up near cow
creek

we ride through cherry picking and apple picking and
cider making and lamb and pig butchering and bear
sausage making we ride through bear hide tanning and
clothes hanging on lines under flocks of top notched
quail while your foal nickers comfortable in your warm
appaloosa womb and duchess and puppin come home full of
porcupine quills and coyotes run laughing under pumpkin
moons

we ride while pat suffers school and stands with
her nose in circles on blackboards with migraines from
misguided fools we ride while scott sits strapped in his desk
miscreant for not knowing math

and brings warm eggs in from the hen house

in our dreams topper, we ride, after your foal falls and dies
in cow creek your anguished eyes bleeding your nicker to dead
ears and my miscarried marriage past the long needled night —
mare when i was not there and you were defenseless alone

JULIA BROWN TOBIAS ⌒ Justice

In 1908 almost every little girl had a playhouse, and why not? We expected
to grow up to be housewives. I loved creating my playhouse, assembling
my chipped dishes, leaky pans, and boxes and arranging them. My interest
lagged after the playhouse was complete, and I'd become discontent. I
moved often. I had a playhouse on the end of the back porch, one in the
granary, another under the apple tree, and finally, a playhouse in an empty
space of the haymow.

I decided to make mud pies and carried a can of water and another
can of dry dirt. I climbed up the ladder from the feed space in the barn into

the haymow. When I got into the haymow, I saw a man lying on the hay. It was Mike. Mike was the water boy or errand boy for Papa and Uncle Ed when they planted wheat. They used the big Case steam tractor pulling three six-foot drills behind it. Mike's job was to haul coal out to fuel the tractor and to drive the horse-drawn water tank, getting water from the windmill and hauling it out to the tractor. He also brought out the seed wheat or did anything else that was needed to help keep the rig going.

I asked, "Why aren't you out in the field?"

"Oh, I got sick and your uncle told me to come in and lie down on the hay. He'll take me home after a while."

I was so surprised to have someone in the haymow that I didn't pay any attention to where I was going. I stumbled and fell down but managed not to spill my cans. I climbed up and Mike said, "Do that again."

"Do what again?" I asked.

"Fall down."

Believing I'd done some very comical, circus-like act, I promptly made an elaborate fall onto the hay, and then he said to me, "Now unbutton your panties."

"What?" I said.

"Unbutton your panties."

I jumped up, ran over to the ladder, down the ladder, across the yard, into the house as fast as I could go. Mama had her back turned to me and was working at the cook stove. She didn't pay any attention to me. I wanted to tell her what had happened but I didn't know how to begin. I fidgeted around the kitchen from chair to chair. Finally I blurted out, "I don't think Mike will go to heaven when he dies."

"Why?" Mama asked, looking at me strangely.

"Because he talks bad."

"What do you mean he talks bad?"

I told her what happened. She took me by the shoulders and said, "Did he touch you?"

"No."

"Did he touch your panties?"

"No."

"Are you sure he didn't touch your panties?"

"No, he didn't have a chance. I ran down the ladder and came to the house."

She said, "You did exactly right and I'm very proud of you. He's a very bad man. I don't want you to ever go near him again. In fact, don't ever go into the barn again when there're any men there unless Papa or Uncle Ed are with you."

"But Mama, I didn't know he was there. I thought he was out in the field."

"I know you did and you did exactly right." Then with her usual cure-all she said, "Would you like a piece of bread with butter and sugar?"

While I was eating my bread and butter and sugar, she stepped out the door and came back a few minutes later and set something down on the porch. Then she got out a pan of potatoes and sat down to peel them, but situated herself where she could look out the back door. A few minutes later she set the pan down, jumped up, and said, "You stay here."

She ran out the back door and picked up a horsewhip, which she evidently had left there a few minutes earlier. I looked and saw Mike coming out of the barn. Mama ran toward him. He saw her coming and tried to dodge, but she was too quick for him. She lashed him across the back and shoulders with the whip. He ran down the long driveway toward the road with her behind him, whipping him with every step. When he got to the road, he turned toward town. She followed him an eighth of a mile, beating him unmercifully. His back must have been a mass of welts and blood because a whip applied harshly can raise a welt on the skin of a horse, let alone on a man.

She came back to the house and didn't say a word. Neither did I, for some reason. A little later, Papa and Uncle Ed came in from the field and Mama went out to meet them. I waited a minute or two and then slowly followed. I knew she was telling them what had happened and, as I drew near, I heard Papa say, "If I'd been here I'da killed him."

And then Uncle Ed looked at Mama and said, "Ermie, you're a wonder. Imagine a woman being able to do that. Next to tar and feathers, the worst thing that can happen to a man is to be horsewhipped, let alone by a woman."

As I came nearer, they changed the subject, and I never heard it mentioned again. I forgot all about it until after I was grown and something brought it to my mind one day so I asked my mother, "Mama, do you remember the time you horsewhipped Mike?"

She said, "Yes. Do you remember that? I didn't think you did."

"It just came back to me. What happened after that?"

She said, "Well, the next day your father went to see the sheriff to swear out a warrant for Mike's arrest. The sheriff said to him, 'Charley, I'll do it if you really want me to, but I advise against it. The story'll get out all over the county and first thing you know, they'll say that your little girl was really harmed and then they'll say things about your wife. I'll tell you what I'd like to do, since your wife has already given him more punishment than the court would. I'll go see him. I won't go to his house because I don't want to hurt his mother. I'll tell him that you're ready to swear out a warrant for his arrest, and I'll advise him to leave town and never come back.'"

And then Mama added, "I guess that's what happened, because a few days later, Mike was gone, and as far as I know, he never returned."

NELLIE A. O'BRIEN ~~~ *The Muskrat Trapper*

Before farm subsidies, soil banks, social security, and welfare payments came the age of survival, maybe even survival of the fittest. Nature was to be conquered, a living wrested from her. Every predator was an enemy to be shot on sight. Wild animals fell into two categories: those that could be used for food or profit, and competitors.

Teenaged boys living on the edge of cities or in the country trapped beaver and other water dwellers to earn money.

But I was only a girl. My two brothers had first claim on any trapping rights on our Wyoming ranch, no one questioned that. But one year some beaver made a dam in our irrigation ditch where they could be legally trapped. After selling a few beaver furs for fabulous prices, my older brother, Tommy, disdained trapping muskrat. "That's for kids," he said. "I'm big enough to handle beaver trapping. Walter can trap the muskrats when he gets a little bigger."

When Tommy bought himself a new saddle with his fur proceeds, I really became envious of him. Our friend Katherine, who lived on the next ranch and had her own saddle, made snide remarks like, "How can you stand to ride bareback all the time?"

The fall I was ten years old the muskrat were plentiful in the streams flowing through the pasture where we kept the milk cows. One family even bravely moved into the bank of the round pool we called the swimmin' hole, less than two hundred yards from the house. I tore into the house yelling, "Mama, I saw a muskrat in the swimmin' hole. I'm going to set a trap!"

"You don't know how to trap." Walter sneered.

Walter was just enough younger than me to feel I was a rival, even if he was a boy. He was a rather frail child, and Mama probably encouraged him not to be too aggressive; I was far more venturesome.

"You just wait and see," I said, heading for the blacksmith shop where the small steel muskrat traps hung by long chains on a spike. With three traps, I went back to the house, heading for the cellar where the garden vegetables were stored for the winter. "I guess I'd better get a carrot for bait," I said.

Seeing I was serious, Mama said, "We'd better all go with you." Of course she couldn't go off and leave the younger children alone, but she was afraid I might fall into the pool.

Deeply eroded by the little stream that fed it, the pool was about fifty feet in diameter.

The muskrats had moved into the roots of an enormous willow tree overhanging the pool. Fresh grass was strewn around the muddy slide that led up to the hole, an ideal place to set a trap. But I couldn't reach it as the giant tree hung out over the water on either side of the hole, and there were no banks. Mama and I studied the situation.

"There's no way we can get near that hole to set a trap," she said. I know she breathed a prayer of thanks that she had insisted on coming with me; alone I might have been daredevil enough to try.

"We'll have to find another set," I said.

We walked up and down the bank and finally set traps in the shallow ripple leading into the pool. Both sets were baited with a carrot stuck on a stick just beyond the trap.

Mama let me run the trap line by myself. Early in the morning I hastened through the dew-damp, sweet-smelling grass to where the traps were set. As I approached the first one I saw a round ball of fur sitting dejectedly on the bank, fur fluffed out as a bird puffs its feathers. It looked twice its real size, beady golden eyes looking at me balefully, but with no plea for pity.

I knew the moment of truth had arrived. Was I a trapper or not? It all depended on whether I could kill the muskrat. I'd witnessed the killing of chickens, held them firmly by their feet and wings with their necks stretched out on the chopping block. I knew if you had to kill, you must do it quickly and with the very first blow, to crush the skull instantly, preventing suffering for the animal and the trapper. I hesitated, but knew I had to be a trapper. I made sure I had a stick big enough and that my blow was well aimed.

When I tore back to the house, carrying my prize by its snakelike tail, everyone gathered around. "Now you'll have to skin it and stretch its hide," Mama said. Evidently, if I was going to be a trapper, there were a lot of things I'd learn to do alone. "I think there's some stretching boards in the shop," Mama said.

Before long I was trudging farther afield in search of favorable muskrat sets. I learned that they preferred to live near moving streams rather than in stagnant swamps of the sloughs. They liked a certain tall, sweet-smelling grass, young willow shoots, and aspen bark. I learned to make sets close to deep water so the muskrat would dive in and drown. In a couple of years my trap line was two miles long. Very early every morning, I rode my pony to cover it, earning a great deal of money for those hard times. Told I had to share either my profits or my trapping territory with my younger sibling, I shared my earnings since I loved the excitement of seeing what would be in my traps each morning.

We shipped our furs to Sears and Roebuck and spent our money on school clothes ordered out of the catalog. Store-bought clothes were a rare treat. Mama was a good seamstress and hand-me-downs from our older siblings were always available. I didn't buy myself a saddle as I had originally intended, but I remember buying a dark green and black checked jacket. When I looked in the mirror and saw how nice it looked with my red hair, I decided it wasn't so bad to be only a girl after all.

BERNIE KOLLER 〜 Mulberries

My country cousins and I worked for hours in August shaking the limbs of mulberry trees with rakes so the deep black and velvet purple berries would fall on old blankets. Our fingers, teeth, and lips were soon inky-stained from picking and scooping them into buckets. On picking day we could eat as many as we wanted; we had no freezers to preserve them.

At mealtime we poured thick, fresh, sweet cream on these plump purple fruits. Occasionally a bit of leaf or bug wing would float to the top. Without comment we removed the flotsam and relished those royal berries, along with plenty of undetected residue, no doubt.

The prairie is in me like the dirt is in the earth — or in the mulberries.

A. ROSE HILL 〜 Chokecherry Jelly

On the tongue a purple musk, sweet, elusive,
Harmonizes with the butter's salt
On toast, tender, crisp, satisfying to the bite.
A simple breakfast, toast with jelly
From shelves stocked in summer and autumn.
Lime pickles, dills, chokecherry jelly,
I packed memories against the winter's chill.

Lush and tall in spring when these bushes,
New-leafed, bloomed white amidst the green,
Grasses now lie flattened, dusty,
A puffy throne for a baby girl.

Her black cap curls on neck and forehead
From insistent August heat,
Her bright pink dress, her hands
Blued by fruit from branches
Carelessly broken and handed to her.

She plucks each berry with tiny plump fingers,
Brown eyes serious, lips just so,
Stretching for a distant cluster.

Nearby, sweaty, dirty,
Brushing cobwebs from my face,
Along with the chokecherries
I pick a mother's treasured moment
For sealing with the jelly.

JUANITA KILLOUGH URBACH Love and Christmas

We moved into the new farmhouse in the fall of 1925. The kitchen and one bedroom were finished but the other rooms still needed work. Winter was on schedule, unmindful of building plans that were delayed by harvest priorities.

Later I would have a room of my own, but for now my bed occupied one corner of my parents' bedroom.

Early in the morning of this fall day, Dad hitched the big black Percherons, Chief and Tony, to the farm wagon for the twenty-mile trip into Brush for the last load of finishing lumber and interior doors.

My uncle, a carpenter, came and the sound of his hammer and saw reverberated through the house. I liked seeing the progress he made and I queried him about each tool. Already my growing vocabulary was extensive for a three-year-old.

In the afternoon it began to rain. A slow drizzle out of battleship gray clouds. The temperature fell. Mama built a fire in the cook stove, and we huddled close to it.

Mama and I gathered the eggs, and she fed chickens and livestock. On the way to the house she scanned the skies with a worried frown. "I hope your dad gets home before it turns into snow," she said.

We went inside and took off our wet coats. Mama opened the oven door to get the maximum heat into the kitchen. "I'm glad we have plenty of coal," she said, "because we will have to put the heater up tomorrow."

"When will Dad get home?" I asked.

"Not for a while yet. It takes five hours each way besides time to get the wagon loaded."

"Will he be here in time for supper?" I asked, as I was getting hungry.

"No," Mama said, "we'll have to eat and save some for him."

She went to the cupboard and began meal preparations. I watched while she peeled potatoes and sliced ham. Then she opened my favorite Campbell's soup. After we finished eating, I was sleepy so she put me to bed. She laid down on the big bed, and we listened to the muffled drumbeat of rain as it hit the roof and gurgled through the gutter pipes. The monotony of the rain lulled me to sleep.

I awoke when I heard voices. Mama's was in her scolding tone, "You should have worn your coat anyway. Look at you. You're wet to the skin. You'll be sick."

Dad murmured something I couldn't hear and then they lapsed into whispers. I sat up in bed. Dad sure was a sight. His wet clothes clung to his body and water dripped from his overalls onto the new flooring around his feet. His teeth were chattering and his face had a bluish tinge.

Mama hurried to find him dry clothes and sent him into the kitchen to change by the stove. I went back to sleep.

In the days that followed, Dad helped Uncle Andy complete the other rooms. As soon as a room was finished, Mom kalsomined walls and hung curtains. Gradually, our living quarters expanded. I was thrilled with my room and was counting the days until Christmas.

Among my gifts on Christmas morning was a big doll, almost my size. She had long brown curls and blue eyes that opened and closed. She was perfect except for a small blisterlike blemish on her forehead. Mama said it was a birthmark.

A few years passed before I learned the details of that stormy night. Dad had another errand besides getting the lumber. The Golden Rule store, where we bought our groceries, was giving coupons with every ten-dollar purchase. These coupons were redeemable for premiums, one of which was the big doll. Since it was only a few weeks until Christmas, Mama had sent the coupons along with Dad.

Everything went fine until he was about halfway home and it began to rain. Afraid the doll would be ruined, Dad took off his heavy sheepskin-lined coat and wrapped it around the already damp box. The rain continued and the temperature dropped. Dad was not only soaked but nearly frozen by the time he got home. It was all he could do to put the horses in the barn and get to the house with the doll.

Mama had cause for concern because Dad was asthmatic and susceptible to pneumonia.

Disregarding his condition, Dad was willing to take the risk so that I would have a special gift from Santa at Christmas. You don't forget love like that!

JEAN McKENZIE SWEEM ⟋ 1936

No vehicle had been over the three-quarters of a mile to the main road to break a path in the huge snowdrifts that Sunday, the fifth of January, 1936. The fierce wind would have immediately closed the path anyway.

My brother, Bruce, dug us out after going off into the pasture in several places as he tried to skirt the largest drifts. We were nearly to the highway when the car stuck in the largest drift of all. The howling wind made the thirteen degrees below zero seem much colder, but in 1936 we didn't know anything about wind chill factors. Bruce was trying to get me, his fourteen-year-old sister, to Gillette to attend school that week. For seven years I boarded in town, four miles from home, because of winters like this one in northern Wyoming, and because each spring, when everyone at the ranch was busy, the roads were impassable because of mud.

That Sunday afternoon Bruce said we'd have to walk home; we were nearly frozen, but what else could we do? Leading me, Bruce took off his outer coat and put it over my head. We couldn't see the house most of the time. After a while, I began to be afraid we'd passed it, so when the wind shifted, I pulled the coat aside. We were walking toward the house, but it still seemed far away. The wind was strong enough to stop a person in his tracks; I'd have given up if Bruce hadn't kept pulling me, lifting me up when I fell. My mother watched from a window and was a nervous wreck when we got to the house; we had frosted noses, ears, fingers, and toes.

Early the next morning, Bruce dug out the car and we went on to town. The same afternoon we plodded through those drifts in the wind and cold, four people we knew — two of them our best friends — tried to walk home from stalled cars. They all froze to death. The next Saturday night, eating a late supper, we were discussing our friends' tragic deaths when my mother said she didn't feel well. She lay down on her bed, closed her eyes, and never opened them again. It was a massive stroke; she died a few hours later. Our lives were forever changed.

Do I remember 1936?

VIRGINIA A. CASSELLS ⟡ Sandhill Ranch Memories

It seems to me that winters were worse in the old days or else the bad times just stick in your memory.

Easter weekend of 1927 brought a storm that I will never forget. My mother, my teacher, and I traveled to Scottsbluff to spend time with my mother's sister and her family. Sunday morning the wind had picked up, and before noon my mother decided we should head home.

It started snowing and snowing as we crossed the tri-state ditch and headed into the prairie country. Soon we could not see anything, but the ruts kept us from straying, though we were thrown back and forth a lot.

The storm had hit at the ranch earlier. My father went to his brother's house and borrowed his car and came to meet us. He could see better as he was not facing the storm, so when we met he pulled out of the rut and did not hit us.

We traveled together about five miles into the Spoon Butte area when one of the cars stalled from the snow blowing onto the spark plugs. We transferred to the other car, taking the old army blankets from the back seat, since we had only spring coats.

By this time it was four o'clock and almost pitch dark from the storm. We were about one and a half miles from the only house within twelve miles of our ranch. My father knew there was a cross fence that would lead right to the neighbor's house, and if we drifted with the northwest wind, we would find the fence, so we got out and walked, stumbling in the cow trails in the ever deepening snow.

Since I had taken off my long underwear, the snow felt like needles hitting my legs and I kept falling in the ruts. We had wrapped the old army blankets around us. My father picked me up and carried me and did his best to keep my mother and teacher from getting caught in the barbed wire fence as the wind was so strong it would take your breath away.

It seemed an eternity before we hit the corner of the fence at the corrals of the old Sturdivant place, which had been built in 1891. The old sod house was used by the new owners only in the summer.

What a wonderful feeling it was to go through the door of the soddy and shut out the raging storm. The three-foot-thick walls provided insulation, and even before the fire was built in the old potbellied stove, we'd stopped shivering.

There was no food in the house, but my mother had brought two baskets of strawberries and cream with her from the car and that was our supper. After our clothes were dry and we had eaten, my mother found sheets and blankets and made up the beds into which we fell exhausted. The only sound was the noise of the branches of a big tree scraping on the tin roof with every gust of wind. I remember snuggling down and pulling the covers up over me and putting my feet on a sadiron my mother had heated and wrapped in a towel.

The storm was still raging in the morning, so we wrapped ourselves in blankets and faced the storm over to the bunkhouse where the hired man lived, hoping to find him and some food. He wasn't there and about the only food was a large sack of potatoes, lard, and a few eggs. My father fed what cattle were in the barn and milked the cow and gathered the frozen eggs from the hen house. The chickens were all dead in the yard with their feathers sticking up.

Three times a day we struggled to the bunkhouse to eat potatoes. I did not think I could ever eat another one. The hired man did not return.

The storm was still raging the second night when we went to bed. I enjoyed sitting in the three-foot-deep window ledges and watching the storm, but I felt sorry for the dead cattle outside the fence and the chickens in mounds with their feathers sticking up through the snow.

The third day, the storm had slackened off and my father and brother went to the cars, got one of them started, and came after us. My father fed as much stock as was still alive and we started home. It was an exhausting twelve-hour drive. We had to shovel out every hollow, even though we drove on the ridges as much as possible. At home, we faced a snow bank so high we had to make a tunnel to get to the back porch, which was completely packed with snow also.

Years later as we discussed this ordeal, I asked my mother why we and our neighbors never locked our doors. She said, "Because someone might need to get in." That was the philosophy in those days, thank goodness.

CORA MADSEN STEFFES ~~~ Storming, Whole Hog

In Eastern Montana, where I grew up on a ranch, rural children were often called upon to contend with emergencies, such as those caused by violent weather. On a hot, muggy summer day in the late thirties, when I was eleven years old, my brother and I faced a farm crisis.

The screen door slammed behind Dad as he hurried in and announced, "I have to run in to Baker and pick up a mower pitman." He glanced at my brother, who sat reading a dime Western, and added, "Can you take your nose out of that book long enough to check the white sow? Every half-hour or so? Looks like she's ready to pig."

Lee looked up and nodded.

"I can help check," I volunteered.

Dad replied that Lee, being older, had better do the sow-watching. I was disappointed. Seemed like I never landed a responsible job. I was in charge of the setting hens, but chickens were not a big money crop. Not like pigs.

My brother chose to continue reading, even though I begged him to play Chinese checkers. I sat down at the library table, flipped open a copy of *The American Girl*, and found an exciting story about a pioneer girl. How I wished I had lived on the frontier!

"Better stick around. A storm's brewing," said Lee.

Just after he spoke I looked out. A dust cloud billowed over the hill. Leaves, sticks, and paper whirled. Our old two-story house shook and groaned as the wind whacked it full force. I felt the boards tremble under my feet. I nearly choked on dust. It hung heavy in the air. Hearing a loud crash — breaking glass — I spun around. The north living room window lay in jagged pieces on the floor. Swooping and howling like a live thing, wind rushed through the room and pushed the south window out. It smashed on the ground. "The windows!" I screamed. I clamped my hands over my head.

Lee ran in and grabbed my hand. We raced back to the kitchen just as the east window shattered and crashed. From the yawning window frame we looked out at the raging storm. It sucked up a mop and a coal bucket from the porch. A doormat flew from the step. Wind whirled and ripped Dad's overalls from the clothesline. They disappeared in dust and debris.

Our feeble old garage swayed and creaked. Suddenly its rotten timbers gave way and it buckled, folding like an accordion, with each wall in one piece. Its roof landed on top of the heap. Lee sucked in his breath. We turned and looked out south where the toolshed bent in harsh, wild gusts. Another blast and it crumbled in a pile, like a matchstick house.

The hog house roof whirled by!

"Good gosh, the sow!" Lee flew out. Seeing me in hot pursuit, he yelled, "Stay here, it's too rough!"

"No! I can't. I'm scared!" Afraid the house would crash down on me, I ran out after him in the raging wind.

Savage, rough blasts lifted us, whipped us across the yard. At times my feet didn't touch ground. Dirt gritted between my teeth and stung my eyes. Lee, choking on dust, coughed and spit as he ran. Wind blew my eyelids shut! I could barely see. Wind swept us past the chicken coop and on to the pigpen.

No roof on the hog house! Two walls gone. Enclosed in the pen, the white sow thrashed and snapped at baby pigs strewn about. Storm maddened, she had killed one pig. Biting viciously, she tried to devour another.

"She's crazy! She's eating her pigs!" I leaped back.

"Let's get them out!" Lee jumped in the pen. The sow rushed him, gnashing her jaws. Quickly he hopped out. He picked up a heavy stick and swung at her. She charged the stick.

My brother thrust a stout club in my hand. "Stand on the fence. Lean in as far as you dare. Strike each time I dash in. Keep on hitting her."

"I'm scared! I can't!" I squealed.

Lee looked at me levelly. "Shut up! Hit her like I said." He stared at me a moment longer. "Damn it, bash her!"

Scared stiff, I climbed up on the rickety wooden fence and anchored my boots between worn planks. Grasping a fence post with my left hand, I leaned into the pen. Just as I took a practice swing at the sow, I felt rotten planks underfoot give way.

"Sis, look out!"

I fell, throwing myself backward outside the pen, flat on the ground. Lee raced to me.

He set me up and ran his hands across my back. "That was close. You hurt?"

"I don't know." I started to cry.

"No time for that. You're okay." He grasped my arms and pulled me to my feet. "Now get back up there. Be quick."

I jumped up on the fence. It held. As Lee darted close to the sow I struck mightily, bashing her snout. Her nose ran red — how I hated this. She squealed and lunged at the club, her eyes maddened. But she didn't catch

Lee. Swinging on him, her jaws clamped on air. He leaped the fence, a baby pig clutched under his arm. He laid the pig safely on the grass.

Wildly, again and again, Lee dashed in and out of the pigpen. I beat frantically at the sow, sometimes hitting her, sometimes not. She slashed violently at my brother, then at my swinging stick.

At last we had rescued seven little pigs. They huddled together on the grass, out of danger.

We were surprised the wind had stopped.

Later that afternoon when Dad got home, he looked anxiously at us. "You kids all right? In town people talked about a tornado headed this way."

Tight-lipped, he looked at gaping windows, flattened garage, and the crumbled heap of boards where the toolshed had stood.

He jammed his hands in his overall pockets. "By the looks of things, it sure as hell hit here."

Lee told Dad that the white sow had her pigs. And how the storm drove her berserk and she started eating them, but we saved seven. He told Dad that he couldn't have done it alone.

"I hit her with a club," I said.

Then Dad smiled. "Guess you weren't too young for the sow watch, after all."

MAXINE BRIDGMAN ISACKSON
Nothing Worthwhile Is Easy

The fall of 1941, when I was eight, I moved with my parents and baby sister to a sandhills ranch in Nebraska. I was the only school-age child in our district. The nearest school was about ten miles east of the ranch. Our roads were little more than trails, and with the threat of winter weather my parents realized there could be days and even weeks of missed school.

"It would be best if she stayed down there near the school," my dad said.

"But she's only eight!" My mother was worried.

"That's old enough to learn that nothing worthwhile comes easy," Dad persisted.

The Scherzbergs lived a short half-mile from the school and proved to be a hospitable family for me to stay with. I suffered little from homesickness, though at times it did seem a long stretch between weekends. However, on the slow-footed Fridays I was happy when Dad faithfully appeared at four o'clock.

The weather cooperated all that fall and early winter. But one Saturday when I was at home, huge flakes began to fall toward evening. By Sunday morning a foot of snow lay on the ground and more sifted down.

Dad fed the cattle, and after an early dinner he went out again to assess the situation. "The car'll never get us out, but we could make it on horseback." He stamped the snow from his overshoes out on the porch.

"What if the wind comes up and it begins to drift?" My mother worried.

"We'll take two horses and travel right along. I'll have her there and be back by evening," Dad assured.

My mother packed clean clothes in a bag that could be carried behind the saddle while Dad saddled the horses. I pulled on extra stockings and jeans as well as layers of sweaters and heavy outerwear. I gave a hasty good-bye to my mother and little sister, then went out into the cold.

The horses, a long-legged bay and a sturdy roan, were waiting at the gate. Dad tossed me into the chilly saddle atop the roan, for I was too bundled up to climb up there myself. We started at a brisk pace, the horses eager for exercise after confinement in their stalls. They carried us out into the stark whiteness of the valley, the familiar hills looming ghostly through the blur of falling snow. It was a silent world disturbed only by the creak of cold leather and the huffy breathing of the horses as their hooves made soft thuds in the loose snow.

We had just passed the halfway mark, a dead cottonwood with a snow-heaped crow's nest high in its skeletal branches, when the wind hit without warning. Its icy fingers jerked at my scarf and poked at the back of my neck. Brittle crystals smacked my cheeks as the wind whipped the lightly piled snow across our path. Where once we had easily followed the snowy outlines of the trail, visibility became nearly zero.

I tucked my face down into my scarf turtle-style, trying to breathe warmer air. Dad and the bay were a gray shadow ahead. I lost all sense of direction. What if Dad had, too? Would we go in circles out here in the prairie until the horses gave out? Would they find us next spring frozen stiff beneath a drift like a cow that wandered off in a blizzard?

Dad stopped his horse and waited for me to draw up beside him, then leaned down to yell above the wind. "Hang on, Max! It's not much farther!"

At times Dad helped me down from the roan and we walked, floundering along through the blowing snow. When I had regained some feeling in my hands and feet, he loaded me up to ride on. This pattern continued, riding and walking then riding again. I felt worn out and cold to my bones.

"Let's stop and rest," I begged.

Dad shook his head, put me back on my horse and we went on. He told me later that the fence line running along the drifted trail guided him the last few miles. His hallo at the gate brought the family hurrying out. Dad stepped down stiffly from his snow-crusted mount, then came to lift me down from mine.

I was unwrapped in the big, warm kitchen amid a great deal of clucking and my hands and feet were placed in pans of tepid water. Oh, how it smarted as the blood seeped back into those numb members.

Dad gratefully drank the cups of hot coffee and ate the big bowl of soup set before him. He declined the invitation to stay overnight.

"The wind's letting up some," he reassured me as he slid into his old sheepskin coat. "I'll be home by dark."

Dad started on the return trip with the horses that had rested in the warmth of Scherzberg's snug barn. I watched from the kitchen window as Dad, riding the bay and leading the roan, disappeared into the snowy haze. That was the last I was to see him or home for nearly a month. But on Monday morning I was in school, and I was on time! Nothing worthwhile comes easy.

LOIS J. MOORE ~ *The Teacher Rode a Mule*

The salary was low. There were fires to build, floors to clean, supplies to order, storms to brave, lovers to ignore, and superintendents' visits to contend with, but how I would love to do it all over again.

Getting to school was my first problem. I boarded with my parents, who lived two and one-half miles from the school. They owned a white mule named Jenny, which they graciously loaned to me for transportation. Jenny was a challenge. She hated to go to school and stubbornly refused many mornings. Only the reins across her rear end would budge her.

Coming home was a different story. With the bridle on, the halter rope untied, and me mounting by standing on the merry-go-round and jumping on, Jenny knew she was headed home. We began at a slow trot. The closer we came to home, the faster she galloped. Her brays could be heard for miles around. She sucked in so much air to *hee-haw* that her ribs must have come together under her belly when she brayed.

Jenny played tricks on me many times. Her favorite was putting the bridle bit between her back teeth, lowering her head till her nose barely cleared the ground, and chasing rabbits. How angry and frustrated I became when it was time for me to be at school and my mule was taking me in the wrong direction. If I was a little late, the patrons would say, "Jenny is chasing a rabbit again."

JEAN GOEDICKE ～ *Range Wars on the Playground*

Shortly after I began teaching at a country school in Wyoming in 1931, I became aware that Kentucky was not the only state where there were Hatfields and McCoys. I landed right smack-dab into a community where parents and children all along the river were carrying on the wars of the cattlemen and sheepmen of long ago with real intent to do bodily harm to one another. I could not believe that the children took sides.

Because the schoolchildren were continuing the family feuds, I felt that I had to watch over the school grounds each noon and evening to see that no one got himself maimed or killed. Each evening, I gave one little girl, Helen, the daughter of a sheepman, a head start so none of the cattlemen's children could catch up with her and hurt her before she got home. Also, she had to arrive early each morning.

Even during noon hours their play was dangerous. One noon hour I stayed in to finish some school reports. When I went out to call the children in, I found the big boys swinging two little second-grade girls on ropes between forty-foot sandstone cliffs back of the schoolhouse and below Crowheart Butte. My knees shook until I could see that the little girls were safely down.

Helen was a quiet, reserved little girl whose father was in the penitentiary for stealing horses. Her mother was looked down upon by the community because she was living with another man. She could not divorce her husband as long as he was in prison.

During one recess, I overheard the two little second-grade girls talking about Helen's pen being put in the stove. Helen had been absent for several days. I said nothing, but sifted the ashes after school. There was the pen point. The next morning, because it was Lester's job to keep the fires going, I questioned him. He neither admitted nor denied putting the pen in the stove. After a couple of days of indirectly accusing him, his friend Bob, also the son of a cattleman, admitted that he had done it. I told Bob that he would have to apologize to Helen and bring a dollar to school the next day for Helen to buy a new pen. (It would be punishment enough for the son of a cattleman to apologize to the daughter of a sheepman.) He said he didn't have any money and his dad would whip him if he knew. I told him, regardless, he had to bring the dollar. Even though it was during Depression times and no one had much money, he brought a silver dollar to school, apologized to Helen, and gave the dollar to her. The following day, Helen brought the dollar back. Her family would not accept a dollar from a cattleman's family. I had to use the dollar to order a new pen for Helen.

There were other incidents that followed the built-in feud between the families of the cattlemen and sheepmen. On one occasion I planned with the pupils to take their pictures the following morning. Viola, the daughter of a sheepman, a big strong girl who had entered school at midterm, showed up with her face cut, eyes swollen, and some of her hair pulled out. Her white blouse was bloody. She had been in a fight with the cattlemen's sons along the river on the way to school. I felt that as long as fights occurred off the school grounds, I should not get involved. I took pictures anyway, then sent her home to put on a clean blouse and Lester to change his shirt.

VIVIAN HAMBURG ⬩ Just One Dress

When Alice and I were in grade school, we each wore one dress every day for five days a week. We washed our dresses on the weekend so we could wear them the next week. The dresses were made of lightweight material that Grandma Franky dyed a dark blue so that they would not show the dirt. The style was straight and hung loose with a few gathers on each side below the waist. A flap was over the gathers. Grandma Franky also dyed our underwear black, probably for the same reason, or maybe to be closer to the dress color. I had a dress in high school that I just despised. It was a dirty green color. I don't remember how it was made. I never chose a green dress or coat again.

What kind of shoes did I wear in the field? Anybody's shoes. I don't think we ever had a pair of shoes to fit us. Mom and Daddy would go to town and bring shoes to us — too little or too big, we wore them.

JENNIE S. HUTTON ⬩ Gifts from the Heart

my heart dressed you in ruffley pink dresses
as you skipped off to school in rough hand-me-downs
(you remembered washdays, beans and hot biscuits
and the warm steamy kitchen welcoming you home)
I yearned for slippers to dance your wee feet in
but cactus and mud made them quite out of style
(you remember tripping to the late summer breezes
and waltzing with me as we sang all the while)
I loved to dream of the things I would buy you
play house, big doll and piano so grand
(you picked me a blossom of radiant beauty
and said "to the best Mother in all of the land")
I loved to travel to faraway places

with you beside me in the old rocking chair
(you said the best trip was home to the heartstead
and oh how you loved your childhood there)

BEULAH G. DONNELL 〰 Prayer and Fudge

I remember a balmy spring day when my mother, father, and we kids set up our tent in a campground at Whitewood, South Dakota. There we would live while my father worked in the sugar beet plant in Belle Fourche. One of the large oak trees held a big swing. Under it, the ground was covered with acorns I could use for cute little cups, saucers, and dishes.

I loved living outside until the snow started; it snowed and snowed. My father found some old stovepipe and big pieces of tin to build into a sort of stove. We gathered wood and huddled close to keep warm. Mother cooked over a gas burner and our sleeping palettes crowded the floor. The only place my folks could stand was in the middle of the tent.

There were no other people in the park. The snow kept falling and finally covered our tent and my dad's little coupe. Finally a man investigated the smoke coming from the biggest drift and was surprised to find our little family inside. He took us to his home to stay until the snow melted and my father found better living quarters.

At Christmas, we moved to Hot Springs, South Dakota, where I attended first grade. My dad was hired to operate an electric shop, but Mother ran the shop while Dad ran around, fixing and selling appliances. We lived above the store. My little sister, Violet, and I played with other kids on the street behind the shop. We'd go along behind the stores looking in the trash boxes and find crepe paper used for window decorating. We soaked the paper in water and pretended jars of colored water were canned jelly. We sifted dirt and made pies. Since our dad did not want us in the store, we spent lots of time outside. One day I saw my father sneak in the back door and rummage around in a dresser drawer to find his swimsuit. He motioned for me to be quiet and left. With my sister, I went up the street to the Plunge, where I was sure my dad was. We went inside and ran around the pool yelling, "Hi, Daddy!" He was furious; he didn't want the girl he was with to know that he was married, much less the father of two kids!

The Christmases went by as a blur during the terrible, dry thirties. When Mother became ill and had surgery, we spent one summer and winter with my aunt and uncle on their farm near Marsland, Nebraska. My uncle had borrowed money from the bank to buy a new truck so he could plant potatoes he was sure would bring in lots of money. Spelling out the name, rolling the syllables around in my mouth — "Chev-ro-lay" — I marveled at the shiny finish. Spring was nice until the potatoes were cut and planted, but the sun came out and baked everything. With no rain, everything dried up. The wind, like the blast from an oven, got hotter and hotter. Then the grasshoppers came and ate any green stuff left. The wind blew the sandy soil in great heaps so the cows could walk over fences. Of course, since my uncle couldn't make the payments, the Chev-ro-lay had to go back. I felt so bad about that wonderful truck.

We separated milk and saved the cream to ship for sale so we could buy flour and other staples. As Christmas neared, Aunt Myrtle and Uncle Clifford explained that Santa would probably not find us out on the farm, and he wouldn't have much to give us anyway because of the poor conditions of the country.

On Christmas Eve we went to town for the school Christmas program and got home to find Santa had been there. On the dining room table was a pile of candy, gum, a jigsaw puzzle, and a new pair of shoes for each of us! I can see those shoes yet — little oxfords with three creases across the instep. Aunt Myrtle said that we each should have a piece or two of candy and then put the rest in a small paper sack.

Then such a game we had — Uncle Clifford and Violet versus Aunt Myrtle and myself. First they hid the sack of candy and our team hunted and hunted. When we found it, we hid it and they hunted and hunted. This continued for an entire week and on New Year's Day we ate the candy! One time we hung the sack of candy out of an upstairs window on the outside of the house on a long string. The best hiding place of the other team was down deep in the flour bin! No simple sack of candy ever provided so much fun and adventure for four people.

After Christmas we worked one jigsaw puzzle so many times that we were tired of it, so my uncle found a calendar picture, and we carefully turned each puzzle piece over and glued the back side to the picture. After it was dry, my uncle cut the puzzle apart with a thread, see-sawing between each piece. We then had two puzzles, one on the front and one on the back.

I went to live with Grandma and Grandpa for a while when I was in the second grade. The kids at the school didn't seem to be much interested in having a new little girl there. They thought that my name — Beulah Pritchett — was odd, and they teased me. When I cried, they called me "Puke Up Pig Shit," which they thought sounded like Beulah Pritchett. Upset, I went home and told Grandma. My grandparents were quite religious, and Grandma said God would make it right if we prayed. I wondered if God would be concerned about name-calling, and decided not to depend on God entirely. So I talked to a couple of girls at recess time, telling them that when my mother came before Christmas, she'd bring homemade fudge for me to pass out to my friends at school. Right away, some kids got friendly and sidled up to me.

Grandma said, "Just see what a little prayer can do!"

I thought, "I helped, too!"

BONNIE RAE NORDBERG ⟋ Fueling the Fire

Turning twelve or thirteen years old meant more responsibilities, like doing the housework and starting the fire that heated the house. Because I was impatient, I made life harder for myself. It was hard to start a fire without kindling, so I asked my folks about using gasoline to do it. They said, "Absolutely not!"

So I went and got a pint canning jar out of the root cellar and filled it with diesel fuel. The blaze was struggling to survive. I thought the diesel fuel would work great. I slowly poured it on the fledgling fire and of course it immediately blew up. I dropped the jar and thank God it spilled away from me. The fuel ran rapidly toward the wall. I rushed to the sink and quickly filled Mom's roasting pan with water. I poured it on the fire and it spread, going rapidly up the wall. I threw a rug on it, but it didn't smother. Then I picked up the flaming rug and threw it in the kitchen sink. The curtains above caught flame.

My parents and brother were doing chores. I knew they wouldn't hear me if I yelled for help, since the corrals were some distance under the hill. All I could do was call Sarah, our neighbor, for help. They lived about five miles away. She told me to pour soda on the fire, but the box was almost empty, so there wasn't enough to relieve the situation.

I felt helpless; things were out of control. I stayed in the house thinking I might as well die in the fire trying to put it out, I would be in so much trouble. Better dead than alive. I heard the truck coming from the corral and hoped it was my dad. I ran outside and it was Guy coming up the hill to feed milk to the pigs. I yelled at him, "The house is on fire!" He was ten and I was twelve. He saw no smoke and was unaffected. He just yelled at me to take his ice cream bar out of the freezer. I could've killed him.

I returned to fight the fire and probably die. The consequences of my impatience scared me more than the possibility of death. I was saved when my dad came up from the barn and our neighbor Donnie helped him put out the fire. Two of the walls were badly burned. The house was full of smoke and had to be completely repainted. The floor had to be replaced.

My parents weren't upset with me. They were glad I was okay.

ARLYS M. WINKLER ⌒ Outhouse of Memories

The outhouse was built not far from our farmhouse in a small grove of trees, which provided some privacy. It was a "deluxe model two-holer," complete with covers over the holes and handles to lift them off and on. Haphazardly piled in one corner tilted a stack of outdated catalogs. A slippery, torn-out page provided the only toilet paper we knew. Except — Hooray! — except during fall fruit canning time. Mother would purchase lugs of peaches to preserve for winter consumption. Each peach was individually wrapped in soft-to-the-touch pink tissue paper. We'd carefully smooth out every wrinkle, then neatly fold each luxurious square of tissue; we'd push aside the catalogs.

During spring, summer, and fall, in addition to its usual function, our outhouse was a wonderful place to meditate. Some mornings, if I opened the door just a crack, rays of sunlight would sneak in. I could sit forever, mesmerized by dust motes floating in the sunbeams.

Sometimes I'd look through one of the old catalogs, studying the beautiful models on the pages. Looking not so much at what they wore, but how their hair was styled and how they stood. I would practice holding my head and hands the same way, imagining a camera held by a handsome photographer. Yes, I vowed, someday I would be a famous model.

Sometimes my daydreams were sad reflections on punishments from Mom or Dad. Punishments I knew I deserved. Nonetheless, my mind would replay the scene over and over, hoping for a different verdict. Tears would eventually help heal the hurt and I was glad in a different way for the privacy of the outhouse walls while I was crying.

I daydreamed about Jerry or Bernard or Tony, whoever my love was on that particular day, until my daydreaming would be interrupted by footsteps coming up the dirt path.

In winter months our visits to the outhouse were less frequent because we kept a community chamber pot upstairs in a large hallway. Three bedrooms adjoined the hall so someone always had to stand guard when someone else was using "The Pot." The Pot needed to be emptied, and we all took turns with the dreaded chore. We'd *always* procrastinate until its contents were just inches from the top, then we'd slowly slide the pot along the linoleum floor to the edge of the stairs. Cautiously, we'd pick it up by the handle and carefully balance it so we wouldn't spill a drop as we inched down one step at a time. Slowly, ever so slowly, we'd slip out the kitchen door and down the wooded path to the outhouse, where we would finally empty it. Mother always kept a watchful eye and a pail of bleach and water close at hand.

Our outhouse wasn't just any old outhouse. It was a great place to hide when we'd play moonlight, starlight, or hide-and-go-seek. It was just the right height to play ante-I-over.

One day, because I delighted in teasing my brother, who had — conveniently for me — fallen in love, I penciled, "Ralph loves Ann" on the outside of the outhouse. That started something. I recorded and initialed other events: "Arithmetic test, A+" or "nine years old" and the dates. Others in my family began writing on the walls, both inside and out. Dad recorded things like: "Finished seeding early, 4-20-1947," or "Got 40 bu./A-N 40, 8-20-49."

SHARON BOEHMER Four-Holer

I don't think there is any experience for our children to compare to the outhouse. Our children will never experience the refreshing cool feeling of brushing the snow away to set your bottom down. My older brother insisted I swish away the spiders out of the hole before he would go. We had a two-holer.

My aunt and uncle had the best outhouse. They had a four-holer. Each hole was a different size. One hole was so big we worried about falling in. They had their walls wallpapered with comics and Donald O'Connor magazine pictures. A few years ago their son built them a new outhouse for a Christmas gift. This one has lids on the holes, a radio, toilet paper dispenser, and a heater. The walls are paneled.

But there is more to an outhouse. I could dream dreams, hide from my brother, take a quick nap, watch the birds, listen to all the sounds of nature, and run screaming from the outhouse, "There's a wasp!"

My kids don't know what they're missing.

BONNIE LARSON STAIGER *Varmint Eradication*

Must be that I come
from Homestead stock
that makes me such a good shot

Been five, maybe six years
since I picked up that rifle
but Annie Oakley strikes again!

That gopher should'a known
not to mess around on the place
that's sure to get my dander up

Second shot was the one that pulled
him right up out'a his hole and left him
floppin' around the yard for a good minute
till he finally gave up and died

Tough ol' broad, now ya gotta dispose of the body
so I picked 'im up by the tail to haul off
shot right through the head, I see
God, I'm good. Or am I?

The fur on its back
had seven precision stripes
with rows of arrowheads all lined up
between each one

What a perfectly painted little creature
Sleek
   and
      lean
         and
            dead

ERLA K. WERNER ✎ First-Name Relationships

I remember the first calf Dad gave me. I was about ten years old. He had gone to an auction and got home late. He had chores to do, too. So he woke me up and asked if I would help him milk the cows. I did, and when the chores were all done he went to the car and opened the trunk, and there was a tiny brown calf. He said it was for me to have for my very own. I raised that calf and she had calves. I traded her to Dad a few years later for another little Holstein calf, who I named Polly. Polly was my cow and when I got married and moved to our present home, my dad brought Polly and her calf and a saddle horse to us. We had her until she was sixteen years old.

I've always loved the cattle and horses and have worked with both all of my life. They are my way of life.

We have had hair-raising experiences with some range cows. They seem to leave their tales behind as they move on from here. Some of them have been a relief to see go down the road, but they aren't forgotten.

There was Bobtail, she was a real stinker when she calved. As soon as you topped a hill you could see the dirt clouds flying in the air as if to say, "That's as close as you dare come."

Then there is Roller. She likes to knock you down and then roll you away from her calf.

The Brown Bomber. It's like World War III when she calves. Best to check cows by walking on the other side of the fence when she's had a calf.

And then there is Sweetie Pie. Oh my, she's anything but sweet when she calves. As soon as the tassel of your stocking cap peeks over the hill, she's shaking her head and blowing snot at you.

Oh yes, we have nice cows to work with too, thank goodness. Or it wouldn't be much fun to do this job of ours. The mean old girls are just enough to spice up the job and keep everybody from falling asleep. We even miss them when they have to go, but it seems like there is always another to take their place and "make a name" for herself.

DONNA GRAY and URMA DeLONG TAYLOR
Frog Diapers

We went down eastward from Sheridan, got a eighty-acre place there thirteen miles out of Arvada. It would get so hot in the summertime — and of course we'd go barefoot — it'd feel like it was burning my feet on the floor in the house. Right after breakfast, my mother and my sister and I, we'd plan what we was goin' to have for lunch, and we'd hurry up and fix it and take it down in the root cellar. We spent the whole day down there. They crocheted, and I played with frogs! Yes! I diapered them and everything. I dressed my kids! They reminded me of little children because when I lay them down to put their diapers on, they just lay there and let me do it. When the little diapers got wet, I changed them. We always had chunks of outing flannel — the women bought it by the yard in them days. I had more fun with my little frogs!

MARY ALICE GUNDERSON   Black and White

For weeks my friend and I hoarded dimes and quarters, saving enough to rent a horse from the 3B Stables near my parents' cabin. But today — the Fourth of July — there would be no horse. Carolee was being punished for wearing her mother's diamond rings to Sunday School. This so embarrassed her mother that none of the family stayed for church.

At ten we were in between — not little, not yet teens — and were often ignored. We passed in and out of our families' attention like tourists. For convenience, we wore our hair braided: Carolee's blonde, mine brown. Once at recess we braided our hair together on one side, the dark and the blonde strands twisted, tied with a red bow. We paraded around the playground. Carolee was as skinny as I was fat. I drew animals, light and easily erasable, in the margins of my math book. Carolee was class clown, a wicked mimic with a mischievous side who sang with a clear, true soprano voice unusual, the grownups said, in one so young. I would have followed her anywhere. We'd been best friends since third grade, when I, as citizenship chairman, escorted her to the lunchroom. Best of all, we were both horse crazy.

We were young enough to be baffled by the news that something might soon happen to our bodies that meant we were "becoming young women." And while we were old enough to perform certain tasks like peeling potatoes for today's thirty-person potato salad, we knew if we worked clumsily enough someone would sigh and say, "Thanks, girls. Go on out and play."

My mother, Leah, and Carolee's mother, Irene, and three church ladies were frying chickens in cast-iron skillets on the woodstove, the men having gathered in the woods by the creek where my father kept a not-very-secret case of beer cold in the water, weighted down with a slab of flagstone.

Horseless this sunny holiday, we slipped through the pine and aspen woods. We crossed the dirt road, crawled through a sagging barbed wire fence toward an ivy-covered stone house we'd spied on days before. Lying belly-down in damp grass that day, we had watched four grownups play horseshoes. They were From Back East. The men wore light cloth caps and tan pants; the women, bright dresses, sandals, and jewelry that winked in the sunlight. The sandy-bottomed irrigation ditch we lay beside murmured below their laughter and the clang of ringers.

But today the yard was deserted. Stumps and boulders had been gouged out. A white string fence enclosed a patch of lawn, sprouting light green fuzz like baby hair. No one sat in the wicker chair or lounged on the patio swing. A lawn sprinkler, turned low, twirled slowly. The house seemed to float, suspended, waiting for something. Our eyes locked and we knew what that was.

Like Goldilocks, Carolee opened the front screen door. I followed. Over the red tile porch floor our tennis shoes were soundless. Someone had smoked here recently, and the smell of breakfast bacon hung in the air. I had never before walked on white carpet into such a large room. Carolee bounced on one of the matching blue velvet couches. I felt the cool, rounded stones of the fireplace. A fan of magazines spread over a low, polished table; on another lay a chess board and gold-headed pieces, some toppled as if the players had argued.

In the bedroom, a small blue bedside lamp glowed faintly, and a man's white shirt lay across the bed. Thick bottles of amber perfume reflected in the mirrored dressertop. Nervously, we touched the heavy stoppers to our wrists and earlobes, like women we'd seen in the movies. The scent was spicy, a little like oranges.

We heard them, then, before we saw them framed in the open back door, and we ran out, letting the screen slam behind us. Two horses — one black, one white — stood before us like a dream. Carolee squeezed my hand, sucking in her breath. "Black one's mine," she said. I had already chosen the white.

The horses nickered. Ears pricked forward, they waited at the manger. In the barn with its mixture of odors — sweet hay, saddle leather, and the thick, distinctive horse smell — we dredged up coffee cans of oats, pouring them through our hands into the trough. My horse munched noisily, jaws grinding sideways. I reached through the corral to touch his satin hide. When I scooped up oats to make a dish of my hands, his velvety, mumbling lips tickled and I laughed.

"Lookit. Look at me," Carolee said. She was astride the black. She had turned over the feed bucket to stand on. "See those white patches on their backs? Those are saddle burns. They're broke."

Edging carefully around my horse, hand steadied on his freckled chest, I moved the bucket for myself, stepped up and grasped the stiff mane.

When the black horse tried to steal oats from my horse, the white laid back his ears and we shifted sideways. Carolee pressed the black's neck, kicked him, and he circled the other way. Legs spread wide on my horse's slippery back, I felt myself carried along at a trot out of the corral, through the downed log gate and into the wide green meadow. Carolee grinned over her shoulder at me, and we felt like queens.

The horses stopped to graze at times, refusing to be moved. Then suddenly one would wheel and trot, the other following. We bounced and slid, not used to bareback riding, our hands twisted in their wiry manes. We named the horses as we rode along — Black Diamond and White Cloud.

We took off our shirts and stuffed them in the waistbands of our Levis. Then we were Crow warriors stealing horses from the Sioux. We watched the horizon, ready to gallop away if a Lakota band, feathered lances raised to the sky, should attack us from the bluffs above. We unbraided our hair to let the wind blow through it. How long we rode I cannot say, except that it seemed a long time and yet not long enough at all. Suddenly a dust cloud rose up at the end of the far road. A car! We might get caught.

We slid from the horses, ran forever through the meadow, past the house, rolled under the barbed wire. We panted and laughed with excitement, wiped sweat from our faces with our balled-up shirts. My wrists still smelled of cologne. Then Carolee took a penny from her pocket, wet it with spit, and slapped it onto the middle of her flat chest. "Hey, I've got three tits," she said laughing. Leaves fell from her sweaty back as she ran and I ran after her. We put our shirts on farther down the dirt road, and we made a pact. We promised to keep the secret of the unlocked house and the horses we owned for an afternoon.

When we looked back from a distance, the horses stood in the pasture, side by side, switching flies. Friends. Like us.

All that summer Carolee and I lived in two worlds: the everyday world of convention, and another richer, shimmering world we entered and left as easily as sliding from the back of a horse.

LINDA SLATER ⬅ *Porch-Sitting Passion*

Our porch in Montana, in the 1950s, was an intimate domain — a place to watch the world drift by, cars and clouds and dragonflies. Some days I sat there alone, reading a book I had stolen out of the back of my parents' bookcase, novels of searing passion like *Tobacco Road* and *Dark Came a Stranger*. The pages burned with love and adventure as I kept watch out of the corner of my eye for an intruding adult.

Other days, playing in my front yard, I yelled across the pasture to my grandfather sitting on his porch.

"Can I come over?" my voice carried over the pine trees.

"Ya! Come over and sit with me," was his answer.

I would run through the horses and wildflowers and mushrooms to sit beside him on his big front porch. He sat in a big, old, worn chair rescued from some past life, often reading dime novels he bought at the drug store in town — Zane Grey and Luke Short — he was strictly a Western fan. Every Friday night he took my brother and me into town to see a Western movie — Randolph Scott, John Wayne, Rory Calhoun — they pranced across the screen, free and full of bravado, while beautiful, quiet women waited for them back in town. After the show, we got huge chocolate ice creams at Bob's Soda Fountain for five cents and sat on the tall metal chairs at the marble counter.

On the porch, we did many things. We dreamed of next year's crop, watched new calves kick in the pasture, planned our trip to Yellowstone Park, and talked of my grandfather's youth. In the summer, I remember the smell of Grandma's old pink roses in the air, crickets singing and the sun setting.

We talked about the weather and the price of cows and whether the hay was ready to cut. Sometimes we ate popcorn and apples, peeled by my grandfather's worn jackknife. We rehashed the day together, going over the jobs completed, what needed to be done tomorrow. On auction day, once a week, Grandpa told me about the sale of a horse or how terribly low the prices were for cows. We exchanged farm gossip — who was about to lose his shirt and who was doing well. Grandma would often come out and sit and shell peas or snap beans while we talked. Sometimes we cleaned buckets of huckleberries or strawberries, which would be transformed the next day into jam and laid to rest in the cool dark cellar of the house. (My grandmother knew secret huckleberry-picking spots she shared with no one.)

If Grandma had been to town that day, she filled us in on who was doing poorly, who died, the price of cream and eggs, and who had won big lately at the bingo hall.

Sometimes we read the local newspaper by the darkening light, all the important stuff, like who had company, who had twin calves, which neighbor had gone to the gray stone hospital twelve miles away. We had no television but we had *Life* magazine and the *Saturday Evening Post*. Outside news was read, but did not have much effect upon the events in our little valley. Our lives were propelled along by the crops and the seasons. It seemed to be a very peaceful, secure time — Ike was in control, a solid, fatherly man who smiled a lot. This was the way I thought life would always be.

My dad and I sat on the porch a few rare evenings when he had no more chores to do. He built houses during the day and farmed at night and he ran from chore to chore. One summer he built a big white Adirondack chair from plans he found in *Popular Mechanics* and we sat there, he in the chair and me on the big arm, the smoke from his Chesterfields drifting past my nose. He always smelled like sawdust, and today that scent still takes me back to him. He would tell me about the spring lambs or the new house he was building in town or a memory from his boyhood during the Depression.

The space between all of us was short on those porches. We were a small clan, living in a small valley in a certain period of time. I could hear Grandfather's slow breathing, Grandmother's nervous energy. There was something spiritual about those moments on the porch — the pauses and the listening to the rhythm of words. We were not in a hurry and we had nowhere to go.

I grew up in a mystical place — quiet and peaceful in a piece of the past. I never went to an amusement park and I never had a store-bought dress until I left for college. When my mind gets overloaded today, I slide back in time to the porch for serenity and nurturance. I have made a pledge to sit on my porch with my children as often as I can. I listen to the words and hear the crickets sing.

JOANNE WILKE ~~ Geese

I cried when our geese died
   they were tall as me at six
      but mother taught us
     to hiss back at them
so we wouldn't get bitten

I cried when our geese died
   lions came from the mountains
     and killed them in the night
  We could see their tracks in the snow
and huge wing beats
   clearing the frozen ground

I never thought I'd miss
   those big mean birds

MAEANN B. JASA ~~ Tractor Travels

In the early 1950s our dad bought a used twenty-one-horse Ford tractor that was already as old as I was. My sister Jani and I looked it over contemplating its fit into our lives. We had always wanted a pony; here were twenty-one and four wheels to boot. We couldn't fall off, get thrown, or kicked. Just what could we do with it?

"Nothing!" Dad said. "You won't go anywhere with it until you can start it, work the clutch and brakes, back up, and parallel park beside the granary."

That day childhood curiosity and parental encouragement commingled, planting in us the seeds to explore through travel.

Tractor Driving #101 taught me to put my left foot on the clutch, right on the brake, and press the start button in the center with my thumb. Give it gas with the hand choke. A lot to coordinate. Shift. Lurch. Kill. Try again.

Then we attached a two-wheeled trailer and packed a lunch. Our world travels began west through our farmstead, past the hogs, chickens, and cattle, out into the pasture.

We crept across the pasture as immigrants and Indians; this was our Oregon Trail, our tractor the ox for the covered two-wheeled wagon and the pinto ponies.

We fought imaginary prairie fires, thirst, and death; we were the only survivors but we had to get to California.

As Indians we listened to the earth, looked at the world through their eyes; we walked proud and vowed never to work at indoor jobs when we grew up.

In the far northwest corner of the pasture stood a lone tree; driving twice around it, we had arrived in California. We'd unpack our cart, spread a blanket, lunch and dream. There were the good old days overseas in the old country to reminisce about, before we homesteaded in Nebraska, or rather our great-grandparents did. There was the future to contemplate, what to be when we grew up. We often asked, "Would we ever really travel around the world?"

I wanted to be a doctor and Jani an architect and Tide packer. She had seen a commercial of a woman working on an assembly line lifting the lid on a washing machine and inserting a box of Tide. This impressed her as a vocation worthy of pursuit.

Adventures continued back to the farmyard. As soon as we got home, we'd write horror stories of our trip for Mom to find. We enjoyed several years of tractor travels before moving into town. The tractor was sold.

We didn't grow up to be the doctor or the Tide-packing architect. Maybe we didn't have a strong enough belief in ourselves. Or we just followed an established pattern in our family of people settling for less. Aunt Nora gave up a life of her own to stay home and care for her ailing parents. Uncle Axel read everything he could get a hold of yet wouldn't share what he learned. Grandpa Williamson wanted to work on the railroad. Family pressure kept him farming. There was the fear he'd lose an eye to a cinder; he lost the eye to a wayward staple while making fence. Bobbe had polio at the age of six and spent the rest of her life on crutches and in a wheelchair. So many lost dreams, broken hearts.

Our lives grew apart until Jani's first son, Sean, was born in 1971. She asked me to come and stay with them in Kentucky. We reestablished our friendship and have grown closer ever since. We are best friends.

In 1980 Jani decided to do something other than bookkeeping — travel agent school. We had no idea where this would take us but one thing was for sure, we needed longer telephone cords. The mere mention of the possibility of packing a suitcase was a better laxative for both of us than a whole quart of prune juice. If Mom had only known.

Over the past thirteen years we have traveled to Egypt, Mexico, and Australia together, and many places within the USA — except California. We'll get there eventually.

Our dream of traveling around the world has come true in pieces these forty years. There's just that small distance to cross between the High Dam at Aswan, Egypt, and Adelaide, Australia, to complete the circle — once.

Early in '92 we began to plan seriously for a long jaunt to distant places. I UPS'd Jani twenty-six pounds of travel information. In July we spent a week sorting and planning. With travel documents in order, tickets in hand, we'll spend several months overseas — a trip for all those whose

dreams were unfulfilled, who lacked the courage or the strength to perse-
vere, whose time was occupied with survival. It's for you Bobbe, Grandpa,
Uncle Axel, Aunt Nora, and all the other broken dreams before you. Some-
where we'll probably find a lone tree we can drive around twice, lunch and
dream of California.

JONITA SOMMERS ⤙ The Ups and Downs of Driving

I learned to drive when I was two years old. If I stood on the seat, I could see
between the dash and the top of the steering wheel. The throttle was pulled
out, so *all* I had to do was hold on to the steering wheel and keep the truck
on the feedground while Bob threw the hay off to the calves.

It was hard at times to hang on to the steering wheel and keep my
balance because the truck hit the frozen cow pies and ditches. When the
truck hit one of these, it jerked and spun the steering wheel, throwing me
into the air. Sometimes I came down on the seat, and other times I ended up
on the floorboard. Every once in a while the steering wheel spun like a top,
and it would spin me 360 degrees before I came to rest on my feet again.

The next job was putting hay in the mangers for the expectant heifers in
the heifer lot. I had to drive real close to the manger so Bob could throw the
hay into it. One day I guided the truck a little too close and broke the mirror
off. I was afraid I would get in trouble. All Bob said was, "Well, I guess you
know how close to get now."

TONI VANCE ⤙ The Dangers of Meeting
Horse Trailers on Gravel

"Pull over.
Just pull over —
though he'll probably
get you anyway,"
Mother says
from the passenger seat
where she is busy sucking the life
out of a 7-Up can and twisting
the maroon seat belt that grabs at her chest.

My foot inches down onto the brake;
I can see the road swell to dust as the Chevy advances.

"Are you slowing down?
He's driving like a maniac, it's
probably that Baker kid; it doesn't seem like we're slowing
down very much."

My foot goes further through
the brake.
The dust snake advances,
its long tail sashaying back and forth
throwing gravel into both ditches.

With one finger lifted from
the wheel we are passed and left
to continue in a rain of rocks.
She points to a chip and asks me
if it was there before.
I say "I think so."
She returns to the half-squirming 7-Up
saying "We should have taken the highway."

LINDA KNOUSE STOTTS ~~~ The Essence of the Ranch

On a sunny midwinter day, the snow cover had melted, we were working on the old wooden corral fence and loading chute. I stood, holding a board, eyes moving across the south meadow for my youngest daughter, somewhere among the grazing red cattle.

I spotted her lying on her back in the sun, cattle grazing around in the golden grass. Mother's eighteen-year-old Red Angus twins, This and That, were nuzzling her; she looked small and vulnerable beneath them.

My mind began slipping back; I remembered Mother fondly, my mother-in-law for fourteen years but also my mother and mentor. As I watched my little girl, I wished she could continue to know Marie; then watching her manner, I realized she does.

Mother had died with Dad in a plane crash the month before; and yet she was still teaching, still living within us and through us, so her memory would not be lost to those who did not know her.

This ranch, this land, this family, and these cattle were her existence. At seventy, her face and hands were weathered by her desire to be in the midst of this life. She died in the sandhills twenty miles from her childhood home, coming home to her ranch, her family, and her cattle.

The first time I met Mother she was sitting quietly in a courtroom fighting for her land and her principles, defending what had belonged to her father as other family members contested her father's will, trying to divide his land. She lost that fight but her head was never lowered; her spirit never sagged.

She talked often of growing up in a pioneering family on a ranch south of Valentine, Nebraska, near the heart of the sandhills. She eloped with a young man shortly before World War II erupted. When Jack was drafted, she lived with his family and bore him a daughter, learning from example how to be a good mother-in-law. Their daughter was a few months old when Jack's plane was shot down in the South Pacific theater. She seldom missed a Memorial Day in fifty years to decorate his grave marker.

Later she married Dad, a man of few words but great generosity. They raised two sons and her daughter and were married for one day short of forty-five years.

In 1974, she and Dad moved to the ranch and began a life she loved, a part of every breath she took. Her desire was Dad's motivation.

Work was their way of life. She laughed when she told of sharing with him a Christmas dinner of cold hot dogs and crackers on the pickup seat; they were repairing a windmill in the chill of that December day.

They began mixing the Hereford herd with a Red Angus bloodline; in 1975, identical Red Angus twins were born during a spring blizzard on her birthday. Only Mother could tell those twins apart so they became This 'n' That. She said one had topknot hair that stood up and the other did not, but we could never remember if this was This or that was That or that was This or this was That.

This and That gave birth to "keepers" almost every year. Mother and her granddaughters, Jennifer and Anndrea, made a ritual of naming those calves. Each calf or cow wore an eartag with his or her name boldly printed on it, mostly to keep strangers from being confused. Many are still in the herd we will be forced to disperse when the loading chute is repaired.

As the herd grew, Mother knew each cow's face on sight. She could tell you the genealogy of each animal and instinctively knew which bull had sired most of the calves. Mother was the night calver, and the director when it came to tagging or sorting those calves; she pushed the calves up the chute for branding, writing vital statistics on each one.

Today Anndrea is a testament to Mother's patience and ability as a teacher. She spent hours talking to that little girl, sharing her secrets about the cattle, how they lived, what they ate, the best way to work around them, about calving and the process of deciding which ones to keep and sell.

Mother taught Anndrea about the land, the importance of the plants, the rain and the wind, about erosion and conservation. One day when the pickup stalled in the pasture while we were checking windmills and we could not reach Dad on the ranch radios, we walked back to the ranch. That walk was a lesson in nature with all the wildflowers in bloom, the birds flitting in and out of the sandhills' tall grasses that swayed in the breeze.

Mother taught Anndrea about the cycles of the seasons, and about accepting death.

Mother and Dad both knew the weather signs and planned their workday accordingly, finishing each evening in their recliners. Father read about computers and the stock market while snoozing to the sound of CNN; Mother read updates on health and veterinary medicine and wrote correspondence or recorded in her daily journal every event of their day.

She was the essence of the ranch, long lasting, forever there, caring, and beautiful. I loved her very much.

DEB CARPENTER ➤ They're Easy to Kill

"I bet I can jump from rock to rock and branch to branch, clear up to the next corner without even touching the ground," eight-year-old Frankie said.

"So what. Anyone can do that," replied tomboy Julie.

I couldn't. I was not a tomboy, and was scared of jumping from rocks or anything more than an inch above the ground.

"I bet I can run faster than you and beat you to that tree," Frankie yelled as he tore off running in that direction.

Julie, who was twelve years old, raced ahead and beat him.

I ran, but quit halfway because they were already there.

"That's no fair," I argued. "No one said, 'go.'"

We walked deeper into the canyon. Three explorers, equipped with the necessary walking sticks, plastic bread bag filled with lunch, and appropriate adventure attitudes.

"I'm hungry," I chirped, because I'd made lunch and wanted to eat it.

"Wait until we get to a side canyon."

Today's exploration centered around discovering side canyons, our term for washed-out gullies that wound from the hills behind our house to an immense canyon south of where we lived. We had named this immensity Spring Canyon for the spring that ran through it.

"There's a side canyon," I declared. "Let's eat."

"No, let's wait until after we explore it, then we'll eat our lunch where it comes to an end," Julie-the-leader commanded. Side canyons ended where they met the hills, some in abrupt cliffs, some sloping. Paradise Canyon, one of our favorites, mounted the hills in rock steps surrounded by beautiful red leaves we later discovered to be poison ivy.

We had stumbled into Paradise Canyon once — just once — and had never been able to find the mystical, moss-walled wonder again. Of course, we had found it from its ending, in the hills, and ended at its beginning, where it intersected Spring Canyon. To find it again, we should approach it in the same way — backwards.

This new side canyon was definitely not Paradise. Its walls towered twenty feet above us, seven or eight feet apart. As the walls tapered, we could see fifteen feet of sky.

We named all side canyons, as well as hills, rocks, and animals on our ranch. Cimmaron Hill was christened for a favorite television show; Pirate's Hill for a Hardy Boys book; Castle Hill because it looked like it should have a castle; and Dinosaur Rock because it looked like the head of a dinosaur. These were our playgrounds, and name-giving was an essential part of our life, an adventure, a ceremony.

"What shall we call it?" I asked.

"Let's call it Moss Canyon," suggested Frankie. "There's lots of moss on the walls."

"No," Julie said, scowling. "That's stupid. There's moss on all the canyon walls." She paused. "I like the name 'Rock Canyon.'"

"Let's go in farther," I replied. "Maybe we'll get some better ideas."

So on we went, the three sibling explorers, with Julie in the lead since she was the oldest and the least scared.

Noonday darkness closed in below overhead trees, the cold, damp walls encased us with eerie trepidation. The canyon narrowed, the walls got steeper.

"What if we see a snake?" I asked.

"We'll kill it," said Frankie.

"No sir," retorted Julie. "It might bite us, then we'd die."

"We'll run," I said.

"What if we see a porcupine?" Frankie asked.

"We'll kill it," Julie said.

I thought of a conversation with our father earlier that week. We'd heard over the news of a man lost in the mountains who survived because he was able to kill and eat a porcupine.

"Why a porcupine?" we had asked, thinking his choice was foolish. After all, there were deer and elk and fish in the mountains, weren't there?

"They're easy to kill," Daddy explained. "A porcupine is easier to kill than any other wild animal. They are slow. You just have to knock them in the head."

"We'll kill it," Frankie repeated. His eyes sparkled, an adventurer thinking of the hunt, the glory of killing a beast, the power of man over animal, the wit of the hunter over the instinct and strength of the hunted.

The essence of all our explorations was to discover nature, to discover the power we had over nature's friends. Of course, we hunted only in our minds. But anticipation made us smile.

"Look!" screamed Julie. "We've found one!"

I gazed past her finger and saw it. The pudgy, horrible beast, the enemy of our pilgrimage, the easily killed porcupine.

We approached slowly, not knowing what to expect.

"Don't get too close," cautioned our leader. "This is a dangerous animal."

"They can throw their quills," I whined, recalling a tale.

"Get your weapons," cried Julie. "We have to knock him over the head."

"They're easy to kill," said Frankie. "One thump and they're dead."

"Let's get out of here," I timidly trembled. "We'll get hurt."

"Not if we get him first," yelled Julie, throwing down the bread bag. She paused as the porcupine humped up to expose his quills and lifted his tail for defense. We didn't know how powerful his "sword," the tail, could be. We only knew that he was outnumbered and an easy victim.

We three explorers shouted and whacked the vicious animal with our walking sticks.

"Kill him!" became the battle cry.

"Kill him!"

Thump.

"Come on. Kill him!"

Whack.

"He's not dying!" I cried as the porcupine waddled quickly away.

"He's getting our lunch!" screamed Frankie. The bread bag was in the beast's path.

"Get him before he ruins it!" shouted Julie. She jumped ahead to save our lunch, since none of us had an appetite for porcupine, demanding, "Come on, help me!"

"I'm scared," I confessed. "He's supposed to be dead by now."

"His quills will hurt us," Frankie chimed, wide-eyed.

"But he's bleeding!" Julie screamed. "We've wounded him." Dread settled over the three explorers. No self-respecting hunter let an animal suffer; we had to finish the job we started.

Frankie and I joined in the rhythmical beating again. Whack.

Thump. "Oh, he's not dying."

We stepped back and looked at the leader, eyes imploring.

"Flip him over. He's getting away!" she said in a quiet but unmistakably frantic voice. Frankie helped while I retreated and fought back tears. Julie didn't try to hide hers as she beat the face of the porcupine with her stick.

Bash. I was close enough to hear the dull thud of his flesh receiving the blows.

Thump. I saw blood spurt from his nose as she hit him in the face.

"Oh, he's not dying," she sobbed.

"Daddy said they're easy to kill."

"Maybe you have to be strong to do it," Frank intoned.

"I don't know, but he's not dying," Julie moaned.

But then it was over. The porcupine stopped making his small whimpering noises. We continued making ours.

Meekly, we stood around him and watched the blood ooze out of his nose and from between his broken teeth. The small eyes which had blinked with every blow now stood open, glazed and accusing. After a few moments of silent graveside reverence, we were compelled to move.

We explorers had discovered the feeling of wastefulness, of taking a life that was not ours to take. But nature took something from us. No longer were we innocent.

At the mouth of the canyon we paused, looking back. "Let's call it Porcupine Canyon," I suggested.

ELIZABETH CANFIELD ⬥ **For the Grandchildren,
Coming to the Ranch**

Soon summer, returning, will bring you here again,
And during these sweet days of early spring
Coming after winter's stringent pause,
I hurry to make ready for you,
To gather gifts that will bring my own renewal
As I watch your days of childhood move along.

You'll kneel to see each flower,
Hear the songs of birds and frogs and crickets,
Find excitement in the rivulets
That follow thunderstorms,
Not pick up baby kittens until
Their eyes come open, and transfer
Tiny tadpoles from the dwindling puddles
Into the larger pond, so they may live.
You'll care about the little horse
Who carries you so cheerfully,
And leave horsehair from the currycomb
Where birds can find it to build nests.

You'll learn that wild things must be free,
Yet know your lot is to be tamed
By such small things as making beds
And brushing teeth and cleaning bathrooms
And finding hampers for the dirty clothes.

With sorrow you will see
There's no happy ending for the hawk
Who hit the highline,
Or the little lamb who couldn't nurse —

That the race is not always to the swift
Nor the battle to the strong.
I hope you learn that only under truth
Do we find solid ground.

I'll strive to guard you from
The permanent self-pitying adolescence
Where so many grown-ups stay,
And help you keep a measure of innocence —
Not enough to make you gullible, but sufficient
To guarantee you hope,
And a sense of wonder
As you step out to find your way.

Pay a Holy Kind of Attention

ANITA TANNER Ancestry of Cows

Lady is Sally's calf
and Skyline, Sally's mother.
From there, Anything, then Spot --
genealogy of cows
repeated to describe a temperament
as if decades on a place
means identity.

When Lucy kicks the hired hand
across the barn
a farmer can only say,
no wonder, considering her mother
and her grandmother —
Lucy's short for Lucifer —
it's in the blood.

Most people see nothing
from the ground up,
but old farmers can repeat
a milk cow's pedigree
like words to a favorite jingle,
what's lacking nowadays, they say,
is that kind of continuity.

MORGAN SONGI Stormy Weather

This is the story I want to tell you. I think now that the land helped save me.
The fine dust like hot powder between my knobby banjo-shaped toes. The
chocolate-brown earth smelling of decaying roots and honeycombed with
spiraling tunnels of wormholes. Daytime mud puddles alive with squirm-

ing, wriggling black tadpoles. The nighttime thrumming of toad concerts.

The lone nightingale that spent a summer singing in the night from our lilac arbor; the wake-up chirp of the meadowlark; the wild chant of the red-winged blackbird; the forlorn-sounding call of the mourning dove.

Crystal mornings after an ice storm, and the crystal-pink glowing midnight hour of an ice storm shot through with the color of aurora borealis. All that, and the storms over the west Nebraska high plains.

The ragged smoke-gray clouds that drifted in haphazardly on hot currents of wind to parade around the horizon like manic circus elephants, trunk to tail, before everything went yellow as far as you could see. The dust hovering in the air, waiting, and the air holding its breath while the leaves of the cottonwood, crab apple, locust, and chokecherry turned upright on their stems and vibrated in the singing silence. The upside-down gargantuan bowl of ocean wild, raging cloud ridges and hollows that appeared in the sky above us, just before the tornado took out a shed and an abandoned house a mile-and-a-half to the southeast.

The snowy white blossoming cathedral thunderheads that towered miles overhead. The lightning that crackled in zigzag arrows, that hissed in fluid sheets and turned darkness to light from west to east, north to south in a fraction of a second, that bounced along the ground in spheres of blazing energy and sometimes exploded inside houses.

Winter storms, the knife-edged, howling blizzards, didn't have the style and sheer elegance of summer storms, but they were unarguably awesome, in the old and religious sense of the word. You had to pay a holy kind of attention to them. If you didn't, you paid for it. A kind of sacrifice.

I could appreciate the violence of the weather. I understood it. It was magnificent. It had dignity, and was catholically impersonal in its choices.

My father was a lapsed Catholic. His raging violence was bereft of dignity or magnificence. It was nothing if not personally arbitrary.

We were a mile from the nearest neighbor, eight miles from the nearest town, and without a phone or electricity. I grew up wanting people-sounds and people-movement near me, and lights. I still feel the urge to jump and run for the train when I hear it whistle in the night and remember its rectangles of yellow framing flickering images of people as it passed.

Under the immense dome of empty sky that covers the plains, under its clear, hot summer skies, I felt as insignificant as a gnat. Under the clear, cold winter sky, I felt as vulnerable as a specimen under glass. As if at any moment I could be swept away, snuffed out. As if gravity would lose its hold on me and I'd go reeling off into the broad expanse of air and echoing light.

I know now that the storms anchored me. The lightning nailed me to the ground while the thunder growled and roared around me and through me, and let me know exactly where I was, and what I was. The cold bit into me. It pinched my cheeks and brought me to attention.

The night sky held me in its arms. I would go out into the pastures or tuck myself into a haystack and I'd lie on my back and look at the stars. On the plains of the forties and fifties, before the general blessing of electric light and the accompanying curse of light pollution, the night sky was as purple-black as the belly of a black panther. The stars were billions of crystal bits that flashed and sparkled and winked at children tucked into haystacks. I learned all I know about eternity from those night skies. It was a gift.

I've had to work for what I know of acceptance, for what I know about forgiveness. I'm still working.

I am a person who loves and requires solitude. Who continues to love storms and the night sky with a heart-lurching passion. Who feels my living connection to unseen roots reaching deep into the rich and living earth.

I am a person who loves where I live, in the heart of a city where I can hear people and all the people-sounds, because there's a wound in me that still twinges in a country night.

My father died last year. I had recently learned more about the "why" of him. I was able to tell him I loved him while he could still hear me.

This is the story I want to tell you. The land helped save me. The fine dust like hot powder between my toes. The earth smelling of decaying roots and honeycombed with tunnels of wormholes. Daytime mud puddles alive with black tadpoles; the nighttime thrumming of toad concerts. The lone nightingale. The meadowlarks, red-winged blackbirds, and mourning doves. Ice storms, and the crystal-pink glowing midnight hour of an aurora borealis. All this, and the storms over the high plains.

SUE CHAULK ⟑ The Ranch

This place is inherited through women's blood.
This place thrives on debt, drought and drink.
Nevertheless, we always ship fat cattle.

This place is inherited through women's blood.
No son to atone, a daughter will suffice.
A sweet sacrifice to the golden calf.

KAREN OBRIGEWITCH   *Growing Up Free*

There were three of us; three girls of the fifties, three country bred and horse-crazy teenagers. We were granddaughters of western North Dakota homesteaders. Our parents were friends and neighbors. Carolyn was tall, blonde, brainy, quiet. Yvonne was a self-assured brunette with a bubbly personality. I was a tomboy, tough-talking and daring. We shared our youth, love of horses and cowboys, dreams, music, and anything Western. We were joined by location and tradition and love.

Every summer during our high school years, we embarked on a short horseback trip to the past. We picked a date, gathered at my badlands ranch home, checked our saddles and gear and decided which horses to ride, and headed in a mutually agreed upon direction. It didn't matter where we were going, it was the going that mattered. We followed no itinerary, no planned route. We each carried a bedroll tied behind our saddles, and depended on springs or dams or the Little Missouri River for water for both our horses and ourselves. We rode with the assurance of the young that we would stop at somebody's ranch and they would feed us.

We would ride for two or three days in the one direction, then turn back and return home on a different route. We camped in branding corrals so we could turn our horses loose. We slept using our saddles for pillows. We would uncoil our ropes and loop them around our beds because we were told the rattlesnakes would not cross the ropes. Lying on the sod and trying to identify the stars, we knew where heaven was.

We shared our plans and hopes for the future. We knew we'd go to college, but marriage wasn't a top priority. (We liked boys, chased boys, went out with boys, but couldn't yet imagine ourselves in love with a boy!) We knew we were going to lose these days of girlhood soon, and it was as if we needed to store all the memories we could create.

We mooched cigarettes from an obliging neighbor, hid Beechnut chewing tobacco and a bottle of whiskey stolen from my dad in our bedrolls. Our hats were misshapen and old, our jackets dusty. We rode into Medora to show off for the tourists, and made sure the strings from the Bull Durham sacks were hanging from our shirt pockets. We rode through a herd of buffalo, not knowing we would be no match to outrun an angry bull. We were chased by a territorial half-wild stud horse who was guarding his small band of mares. We took the deer, antelope, bobcats, coyotes, prairie dogs, and badgers for granted; they were part of our badlands landscape.

We'd ride without our shirts to get a tan like the town girls had. During the midday heat we'd stop at a waterhole, hobble and unsaddle our horses, skinny-dip, and wash out our clothes. In the early dampness of the mornings, one of our horses would invariably buck, dumping the rider and her supplies. We would regroup, gather the scattered belongings, and keep going. Hey, we were cowgirls! We rode in the dark on a plateau looking for a trail we knew would lead us to a river and maybe a friendly barn. Once we were lucky and caught a ride with a rancher's son to a dance in a neighboring town. In an isolated cabin we met two college boys with summer jobs for the Fish and Wildlife Service. We made a point of riding that way again. Life was fun and we were so sure it would always be that way.

Now it is more than thirty years later. We got educated and liberated and married. Carolyn received her doctorate in botany and has stayed close to her country roots. Yvonne acquired her master's degree in social work and recently moved to New York after many years in Florida. And me? I dropped out of college, married my cowboy, raised four children, and remained the tomboy and rancher. The three of us have completely different lifestyles and locations, but we still have the same memories. We meet at least once every five years and the talk is constant and the connection complete. We still stand under the stars and talk about faith and loss and dreams, and we are still the teenage Western girls who grew up free.

SHELLY RITTHALER **High Plains Bride**

At the altar,
halo of lace,
pink roses in hand
and on her cheeks,
she promised to
honor, cherish
and love no other.

But he,
this child of the plains,
man of the sage,
promised
to love only her,
with fingers crossed behind his back,
taking this bride
when his heart
belonged
to another.

This child of the plains,
man of the sage. Before

he could walk
talk, ride horses, or laugh
his mother observed
the rites of passage
from birth to childhood.
Circumcision,
baptism for salvation at death
but for life,
for life,
she placed his infant feet
upon the gumbo soil
whispering
"Dig in your toes, Hang on
hang on
for all you're worth
for all your life
hang on."

He grew
then brought this bride
all pink and white
to the gumbo soil.

This bride
who would come to know
loneliness
as the land demanded his time,
energy, life.

At night when he fell asleep
beside her,
she pondered his reasons for
not meeting her needs
excusing himself saying,
"We have to make it pay
or we can't hang on
hang on
hang on."

With wind-blown dust,
she grit the litany
between her teeth until
one day,
weary, she quit watching the horizon
waiting for him to come home.

She looked instead to the land
between the house and sky
and learned.

Learned to celebrate spring
when the buttercups bloom
beside the last snow crystals
beneath the big sage. Learned
the first day of summer
comes not when the calendar says
but when the sego lilies throw
white blossoms toward the sun.

She learned practical, useful things:
to pull windmills, drive
egg-beater pickup trucks in
four-wheel drive. To keep two sets
of books, one for the bank, one to see
how they really stood. To bring
chilled baby calves and frozen lambs
back to life. To keep two dresses in
the closet, one for weddings,
one for funerals
both for church
when she could get there.

She learned to drive tractor, plant seeds,
feed hay. To sit a horse.
To cook for crews.
And listen to hired men's
women woes
without sharing her own.
But most of all,
most important,
she learned
from the gumbo lily
whose fragile blossoms
cry thick tears
and perish
the moment
they're plucked from their roots
set in the gumbo soil.

From this flower
she learned
to understand

the man she loved
who promised
to love only her
with fingers crossed
behind his back.

She looked to the horizon,
the land, her heart
and found

strength
to work at work
that never ends,

courage
to live being loved
second best,

faith
to love a land
she would never own.
For she found
you can never own the land.
It owns you.

At the barbed wire gate,
looking up the dusty road,
her cheeks
her hands
holding the tracks of wind
the kiss of sun
the scent of yarrow,
this bride of the plains stands.

When her babes come,
she'll carry them,
boys and girls,
in blankets,
to the silver sage,
and place their feet
on the gumbo soil,
whispering,
"Dig in your toes, hang on,
hang on for all you're worth
for all your life
Hang on.
Hang on."

CLARA L. SMITH 🖝 Spring's Promise

I wrote Spring's Promise in the late 1930s. I also lived it.

My husband, Ervin Smith, and I started farming in the mid-twenties, just in time to have our meager savings lost when South Dakota's Rural Credit Banks failed.

We sold our last good wheat crop in 1932 for twenty-five cents per bushel. Then came drought, depression, dust storms, hail, grasshoppers, army worms. We hung on, helped by FDR's farm relief programs. And finally Spring's Promise came true — a beautiful modern house, lawn, trees. I wanted somehow to hold the years of peace and prosperity — surely they were too good to last.

They lasted until May 26, 1958, when my husband lost his life in a farm accident. In a few days, on June 2, we would have celebrated our thirty-fifth wedding anniversary.

Our farm was located eighteen miles southeast of Lemmon, South Dakota. I sold it in 1964.

Spring's Promise

All day a soft spring rain had fallen,
but now the western sky had cleared.
Sunset rays struck across sodden fields
and touched with gold
the tender blades of grass
springing on sheltered slopes.

A farm wife drove the milk cows up the lane.
Her step was middle-aged and slow
but her heart thrilled
to this awakening of spring
and to the carol of a meadowlark
singing from yonder post.
Yet through her joy she felt a sadness
that it could not last.

The farmer met her at the pasture gate.
He too had felt the magic of the spring.
His voice was strong with hope renewed:
"This looks like a good year."

Then, stanchioning the cows
within the barn,
together they began the evening chore
of milking.

And in the tranquil quiet, as they milked
the farmer planned his acreage of wheat,
multiplied this into bushels
and transformed these into things
for which they long had wished.

She yearned to share his dreams,
but too often she had seen
this same rich promise of the spring
crushed in the thunderous path of hail —
withered in parching drought —
devoured by hordes of hungry insects,
come to curse this prairie land.
Her spirit, less resilient and buoyant
than his, could not forget!

Then, laden with foaming pails of milk,
wearily they left the darkened shed,
came out under the evening stars
and felt again the fragrant breath
of spring, cool and refreshing.

The farmer's wife forgot her fears,
the disappointment of the barren years.
They planned together —
"We'll start some trees again —"
"This year we'll plant a lawn —"
so in the magic of the fair spring night
they walked, and built again
their house of dreams.

AUDREY A. KEITH ⟍ Going Home

Lately I have been yearning to go home. Not to the little house in town, with its compact country-blue kitchen and the huge bedroom with plush dusty-rose carpeting and a closet my daughter-in-law said she'd kill for. That's just where we live. It's not home.

Home is an old farmhouse that has been added to at least three times. It has lots of room, most of it in the wrong places. The windows leak dirt and rain in the summer, cold air in the winter. The kitchen has been gutted of most of the cupboards and appliances. All of the floor and wall coverings are getting shabby.

I lived there from age six until I married, and a few years later moved back with my husband and two small children. It's full of memories, but there is room for books, records, photos. It's where Mother battled bedbugs left by the previous tenants. The walls were a dingy tan, bordered with a freehand design of teapots and cups, painted in a blue even I thought was ugly. At home we dressed, shivering, by a kerosene heater upstairs, but we also lived, played, learned, and brought friends.

Home is not just the house, in splendid isolation, but the big yard, native grass that looks good when it rains and survives when it doesn't, and the section of land surrounding it. The yard smells like heaven when the trees are in bloom, and I wouldn't trade my riding mower for the fanciest convertible ever made. Most of the apples and wild plums have died during five years of drought, but the flowering almonds, Juneberries, and lilacs are still there.

I used to know every inch of the land. While my sister helped Mother and learned to be a good housekeeper, I preferred being outside. Even then I sensed that "women's" work was less interesting and didn't count for much next to "real" work. I had also learned that you can't have much fun in a dress.

Being a tomboy I couldn't think of anything less desirable than being a wife and mother. I was certainly never going to get married! So in many ways my mother is a shadowy figure. I saw her life as dull drudgery. She was an avid Juneberry picker, couldn't bear to throw away anything remotely usable. She used to boost my sister and me up on our horses, and one day she boosted our much smaller brother up. He slithered down the other side and, once she was assured he wasn't injured, she joined our laughter.

How much more will I never know? How many hopes and dreams dried up and blew away in the thirties? She loved to read, but I never saw her sit and read anything except our bedtime stories, and then she usually fell asleep from exhaustion. We thought it was funny, God help us.

She was always working. She had a garden, she hatched and raised chickens, geese, and ducks. When Dad sent me out with the F12 and a drag, Mother worried. When I was in the seventh grade I spent all fall, after school, plowing sixty acres west of the house with an H tractor and a two-bottom plow. Plowing fifty-six inches per round at a top speed of one and a half miles per hour gave me a glimpse of eternity, but it was still better than doing housework.

I helped put the crop in again this spring. Like a long-ago love the land was hauntingly familiar, but the contours had changed. The fences were gone, and the sloughs had changed shape. Still I felt right, sitting on the tractor.

Why is it home? We belong to the land. It holds us with killdeer luring us away from their nests with drooping wings and pitiful cries. Nothing smells as good as the earth after a rain, although sweet clover comes mighty close. Sunflowers mature with a pungent aroma. We scoop up a handful of rich black earth and squeeze it, not just to judge it, but for the pleasure of feeling it.

We get pleasure from seeing any good crop, our own or someone else's. Watching a thick stream of grain pour out of the combine into a truck gives a feeling of richness that has nothing to do with money. I think it must be akin to the "fatness" spoken of in the Bible. Beyond sufficiency, it is repletion, and complete — at least at the moment — contentment. The land may not always belong to us, but our hearts will always belong to it.

GAIL RIXEN ➤ Contentment

Two sheep racing past the gate
kicking up their heels
shouted back to me,
"One pair for the ground;
one for the air."

A brown hawk holding fast
to the high cottonwood
in yellow morning sun
aimed her vivid eye and declared,
"I have flown my vigil in the fields
and found you."

One wren, like one last leaf,
flipping from walnut twig to bare bough,
couldn't settle long,
but whistled,
"So much luxury in the day."

The old tom cat,
his ears frozen down to stubs,
his face askew with scars,
slid along my leg,
saying in his throaty brogue,
"You're beautiful, you know,
Just lovely."

As I watched from the barn loft,
the blue-lidded moon
patiently placed little lights
across the face of the prairie

and all of them whispered together
across the still night,
"We are here
and you are among us."

DONNA GRAY and ETHEL GOUDY BRIGGS
～ I Don't Mind Milking

Ethel Goudy Briggs was born in 1910, four years after her father had proved up on his homestead claim on Mill Creek Flat in Park County, Montana. In 1931 she married Leo Briggs, whose family's land adjoined the Goudy place. Leo and Ethel lived on Mill Creek Flat, on a small ranch that Leo bought from his uncle.

Until recently, Ethel had a large vegetable garden, strawberry patches, and flower beds. She froze and canned fruit and vegetables, putting up countless pints of jam and jelly. Ethel is one of the hardest working women I've ever known, doing household chores and ranch work with equal ease.

My conversation with Ethel, a small, bright-eyed, lively woman who looks considerably younger than her age, was recorded on March 21, 1985.

I started to milk when I's about six years old. My sister and I would go down to the barn. When I was eight or nine — it couldn't have been any later than ten — I started milking by myself.

I don't mind milking, 'course I never like to have to do it all by myself. Now Leo sets on the bench watching me, and he's there to pack it to the house. We used to have to tie these cows hand and foot, and we had one down there that she'd come in the barn, that tail just *shhwit, shhwit,* swatting right and left. I's thinking just this morning, my gosh, she don't do that anymore, and I don't have to tie 'em up.

I know the last time Leo started beatin' the cow down there, I says, "Stop yelling."

"Well, she kicked it over."

I says, "If you'd have had your foot against the bucket, her foot wouldn't have bumped it. She wasn't a-kickin' the bucket, she was just moving her foot ahead."

Well, he was still yelling. "Quit yelling," I says. "You're stirring the whole mess up."

"Well, you're yelling."

"That's different."

If a cow needs bawling out, I can say one word to her, "Cut it out," or something like that. She'll shake her head; she knows she's being bawled out, but she don't get nervous about it. It don't worry her.

They declare that cattle don't see in color, but you know that's crazy. Heavens to Betsy, you go out there with a different colored coat and they'll all look atcha.

At night we milk at five o'clock, and then in the morning, it's whenever. Really odd times. Usually we're down there by seven, but then, they can wait. Leo always thinks we have to be there smack-dab at five, but they'll wait on us if we don't get there at that time.

These days, three cows is all I'm milking, because my tendonitis kinda gets to flaring up if I milk any more. We've got two real easy cows; the other one isn't so easy, so she's going to have to go down the road this fall. After I milk her, my wrists are startin' to feel uncomfortable. I have a yearling coming on from these easy milkers' side, but it's odd — this one that milks hard is a full sister to the one old cow that's so easy to milk. I don't understand that. It has to come through the bull, I guess, to make that difference. We got one calf from Don Clark's bull, and that heifer is the hardest cow I ever tried to milk! She had such teeny tiny little holes in her teats that we finally put a calf on her. All of that cow's other calves have been easy to milk.

If I didn't milk the cows, there's lots of times when I would, say like, go out to Washington and visit my sister and things like that. You can't do that, 'cause there isn't anyone around anymore that can milk cows or would milk cows. I intend to as long as I'm able, because in the wintertime I'm afraid I'd get so lazy, I'd be in a wheelchair if I didn't have that! It gets — when it's awfully cold — my, but it is miserable to go out and milk a cow, 'specially when it's so cold you have to put your hand up between the bag and their flank to kinda get the frost off the top of your hand. I did that several times this winter. But all in all, I don't mind milking.

BARBARA JESSING *Given Away*

In 1874, near Hastings, Nebraska, my great-grandmother Rosa Kleather was given away in marriage. Not walked down an aisle in a festive church, but given away; handed off in the dark of night from one man to another.

Her father, Sam Kleather, had made friends with a neighboring homesteader and fellow countryman. They helped each other plant and harvest crops, build barns and houses, and put up fence. Perhaps Sam Kleather was more in debt to the neighbor than the neighbor was to him, and giving his daughter away evened the score.

During a long night of drinking and gambling in celebration of a good harvest, he woke her from sleep. Then he woke a preacher, and the preacher's wife for witness, and gave his seventeen-year-old daughter to a man more than twenty years older; her new husband left another wife and three children behind in Germany when he fled to evade prosecution for what might have been a murder. Sam Kleather did not see, as the preacher's wife did, that the girl was shaking with fright. When the prospective groom asked if she wanted to get married right then, Sam said, "I am her father; she will do as I say."

In the morning, Sam lied to his wife, saying, "She ran away to marry Edward Rediess in the middle of the night." Rosa later recalled that her mother cried for a week, refused to speak her name, called her a stranger. As far as Rosa knew, her mother never learned the truth; it would have been disloyal to her father and her husband for Rosa to tell.

A year later, when Edward left the Nebraska homestead for Iowa, and then moved to Ohio, Rosa did as she was told, leaving her mother, sister, and infant brother behind. Forty years passed before she saw her sister again.

Edward grew debilitated by drink until he could no longer hold his job with a Dayton, Ohio, butcher; Rosa hired a nanny for the children and took over his job. When she located her sister, she moved with ten of her sons and daughters to an eastern Colorado homestead. Edward remained the nominal patriarch, but Rosa held the family together. She bore fourteen children with Edward, thirteen of whom lived long lives. It is said that her husband delivered many of the babies; the youngest is my grandfather. His daughter, Rosa's namesake, is my mother; Rosa died at eighty-four, ten years before I was born. But stories about her were woven through my childhood as my grandfather tended the garden, put up sauerkraut, made sausage, smoked fish and meats, and tinkered with inventions in a basement workshop. He even sunk a well in the tiny, urban backyard, hardly large enough to contain all the knowledge about survival he learned from Rosa.

I like to think of her long life as a triumph over those early misfortunes, and her loss of country, home after home, her mother and family, losses of choice — and of self. I like to think of the years of resistance just under the surface of her life, a force not to be stopped.

Ten years ago, when my grandfather began to write down the stories he had been telling and I helped edit and publish them, Rosa's story sank like a well into the reservoir of my own being. I date my formal knowledge of the facts from that time, but patterns in my life echoed Rosa's long before I truly knew her story.

As a young adult, I left California's crowded cities for the open plains of the midwest, crossing into Nebraska a hundred years, almost to the day, after Rosa entered it from the east. She arrived in a covered wagon at ten miles a day; I arrived in a sixties VW bug that could do sixty miles an hour on the downhill side of the continental divide.

A few years later, at my own wedding, I was neither given away nor gave up my birth name; I entered a marriage where my wholeness of self was safe. I slept for several cold Nebraska winters under a wool-filled comforter from Rosa's Colorado ranch; my grandfather remembered keeping warm in it even when the kettle froze on the stove. My dreams were more vivid, more primitive, under that comforter. I gave birth to two daughters, one named for Rosa; when I looked into those new faces I knew I did not own them, nor would anyone else.

I earn my living by psychotherapy; the stories I hear from women every day might be familiar to Rosa. She might recognize themes from her life: an instinct for integrity, a resistance to ownership, a struggle to maintain family connections, of saving and handing down stories along with quilts.

My connection to the land does not go far beyond geraniums on the windowsill and boxed garden beds on the southern slope of the yard, but I think of Rosa often when I care for those growing things. I have two pictures of her. One is a formal portrait with Edward and their thirteen children in Sunday finery, hair stuck in place.

The other shows Rosa in a farm dress and apron, windblown, feeding chickens, alone, tall as a tree on the rolling prairie where she made a lasting home. When I think of her, this is the image that comes to mind — just the other side of the geraniums.

PEGGY COOK GODFREY ⌒ Sing!

I used to cut and bale hay for my neighbors José and Vivianna. One wet summer when I'd cut it all and baled about two-thirds of it, daily rain showers began. After two and a half weeks, I stacked the baled hay and raked the windrows over again. By Sunday, they were dry, and after early services, I began baling. The stink of rotting alfalfa was dreary, and I began the first round unhappy at the waste of my time and machinery to tie up the blackened mess. Beginning the second windrow, I was close to tears for myself, and for José, whose share of the hay would be as sorry as mine.

Inside me, a small voice said, "Sing." I laughed; God has a wonderful sense of humor. With a heart of lead, tears rolling, I obeyed. I couldn't hear myself sing softly over the diesel tractor and chugging baler, so I bellowed "The Joy of the Lord Is My Strength," and every other praise song I knew.

By the time I started the third row, I saw my work in a new light. I thanked the field for faithful past crops, realizing that my labor would remove the heavy layer so the field could be productive next cut. My baling was a gift to the hayfield. The rotten bales would form the bottom layer of my stack, since those are the most likely to spoil anyway. They'd be excellent mulch for my garden and those of my friends.

When I was nearly finished, José and Vivianna drove up. Walking to the car, I noticed José was still pale and weak from his stay in the hospital. He told me he hadn't been out of the house until today, but he insisted on coming to say how much he appreciated my work. He knew how depressing it is to bale ruined hay. I told him how singing had changed my viewpoint; they were openly comforted for my sake.

Later that year, they decided to sell a young cow and her yearling heifer. She'd lost her newborn calf to scours while José was in the hospital. The cow gave too much milk and they weren't home to milk her out. I asked the price for both animals, thinking I probably couldn't afford them. To my amazement, they named a price I could afford.

During the next four years, the young cow, Red, bore and raised four sets of twin calves! José died after the first set, but I've always suspected he and God collaborated on this blessing. An insignificant act of obedience became a golden thread woven into the fabric of my life.

DONNA WALBERG ~ Our Onaka Ordeal

We were hired to mow six thousand acres of grassland, all contiguous, a total of ten and a half square miles. Only a cowpath road led through the middle of this land. There were no buildings, no people or farms, and only one lone tree. We used two tractors, each pulling two mowers hooked together, each mower cutting a swath nine feet wide.

We parked our camper in the nearest town, Onaka, South Dakota. My husband, Clay; our two children; my sister, Lory, who would baby-sit; and I lived out of it while we mowed. The town was so small that when we'd been in town half a day, everyone knew our names and what we were doing.

I sat high on the John Deere tractor and just drove. No one was going to get in my way. No traffic signs. When I saw a rock, I had to lift the mowers up and then put them right back down and keep on mowing. It was a nice feeling out there under a big beautiful blue sky with a warm gentle breeze coming across me. A very peaceful feeling, to be working the land.

I was impressed by how big the sky really was. Out there I could see the sky touch the horizon in all four directions — nothing hidden behind buildings or trees. A big blue bubble of sky.

These were peaceful days; the worries hadn't started yet. We got up early, packed our lunches, and kissed our sleeping kids as we passed Lory crawling into the camper to take care of them. We mowed all day, with only a short stop to eat our lunch. We quit around eight P.M. to service our machines: made repairs, greased sixty zerks, and filled fuel tanks. This took us about an hour. Then we drove back to town, ate the supper Lory had prepared, and kissed our children goodnight.

While I was mowing, the only noise was my 730 Diesel John Deere tractor — my Johnny Popper. I learned to appreciate its unique sound. With no radio, I got used to talking to myself; with no cab on the tractor, I had to bear the elements. It's funny how you can get attached to a piece of machinery; it took me to the opposite end of this land and brought me back safely. I depended on this machine.

I wasn't used to being outdoors all day, so I used lots of suntan lotion. But one day I was wearing shorts and a tank top and really started to get sunburned. Clay stopped and offered me his short-sleeved, lightweight coveralls. I took him up on the offer in a second. That left him wearing only a pair of underwear, but it didn't matter because nobody would see him anyway.

Sometimes this huge land started to scare me. Only grass and big sky and two people in ten and a half square miles. No electricity to light up the dark; there was no telephone to call for help, so I tried to keep an eye on where Clay was mowing at all times. Sometimes I loved the peacefulness; sometimes I did not like this feeling of total isolation.

One of my greatest joys came after we had been mowing for many days. I came over the hill and there was a *fence*. Yes, a simple fence. We had finally reached the outermost edge of this huge field.

Then we began to have troubles. We received a big rain. On the way to the field we got the pickup stuck and we couldn't just call for a wrecker to come pull us out. It was two miles to where the tractors were parked or two miles to the nearest neighbor. We walked to the tractors. Our feet sunk into the mud with every step we took. We had to stop many times to catch our breath. This land becomes a lot bigger when you walk over it one muddy step at a time. We got ourselves unstuck and decided it was too muddy to work that day.

Then it got hot. After a week of temperatures between 95 and 100 degrees, it hit 108. With no breeze, no clouds in the sky, hour after hour the sun beating down on us. We were at the mercy of this sky, which had once seemed so big and friendly. It was now like a test to see how much we could endure. It finally became more than we could take, and we went back to town.

We had repairs to do almost every day. In the pickup, we hit a rock so hard it ruined the engine and the transmission. The tractors required repairs — some minor like flats, others major like a new transmission.

One of the things that helped get us through was watching the animals. We saw badgers, hawks, and eagles. We watched pheasants and ducks walking their babies to waterholes.

We named all of the fawns Bambi. As we cut the grass, the deer kept going deeper into the field. Then they would come out and run to another patch of tall grass for security. We brought everything to a stop if a fawn was in our path. A big antlered buck watched us for days. As we got to the end of our mowing, the deer were thick in the remaining tall grass. Sometimes I stopped just to watch these marvelous animals and to give them a chance to move on to another field.

I began not to feel so alone out there. We had companions in the animals.

On the last day of mowing we were so excited at the thought of being finished and going home, but we were also holding our breath. This land had put us to a test every day, so why would the last day be different?

On our last round, all at once white smoke came out of my Johnny Popper's engine. It got so hot the engine had burned up. I sat on the tractor while Clay finished the last round.

In forty-five days we mowed 6,345 acres of grass. I greased a total of 2,700 zerks on our mowing outfits, and we drove 3,579 miles. Our vehicle casualty list included the 1968 GMC pickup, which needed a new engine and transmission; my John Deere tractor, which needed a new engine and transmission; and Clay's tractor, which needed a transmission overhaul. That doesn't count all the repairs we made as we went.

This mighty land had shown us both how tough and how peaceful and kind it can be. It had shown us no mercy at times, but it also had shown us beauty and let us appreciate the animals.

We call it our Onaka Ordeal, and we'll never forget it.

TENA COOK GOULD ⁓ The Heartbreak of a 4-H Beef

My first steer was Baldy, a big teddy-bear type. He was a great show steer. After I showed Baldy in the Scottsbluff County Fair, the judge suggested I take him to Ak-Sar-Ben, the state competition. What a big adventure for a thirteen-year-old from Henry, Nebraska. The trip was my first airplane flight and Omaha was the first big city I'd ever seen.

I knew Baldy was entered in a terminal show, but when they branded his jaw with an A K, I realized the fate of my big pet and tear-time came.

The painful irony is that exceptional animals worth keeping past county fair for fall and winter shows were usually the ones I became especially attached to — making the final sale even more difficult.

The sale could be heartbreaking. It didn't hurt too much to sell the ones that had only earned red ribbons, or stepped on me, or kicked me and ran away during showmanship competitions. But a bond developed when we spent several hours a day together and he depended on me for every mouthful of food.

The empty feeling of losing my friend seemed worst on the last night of fair, after all the shows and sale when the crews were cleaning the grounds, the carnival was being torn down, and snowcone and popcorn papers were blowing around the empty fairgrounds. For a moment I would think of never eating meat again and of getting out of the business altogether.

But each year it got a little easier to carry on the four-generation family tradition of raising beef. Raising a market animal was a responsibility and an excellent learning process. When the check came in, it hurt a little less, and the money helped to pay for college. I realize now that the auction ring is a rite of passage into adulthood.

SUSANNE K. GEORGE ~~~ Exploring the Plains, Yesterday and Today

Everyone lives several lives, and I've had my share. I grew up in the fifties on a farm near Minden, a small community in south-central Nebraska. The home we lived in belonged to my grandfather, who moved there with his bride in 1900. After my mother's death in 1959, we moved and became "gentlemen farmers," as my father termed it, living on an acreage near Kearney where he worked for the college and tinkered with horses and tractors, calves and sheep, unable to "take the country out of the boy." After I graduated from college, I married a farmer and settled down a few miles away.

After raising two children, being a farm wife for eighteen years, and going through a divorce, I began another life, that of a college professor. Ironically, my area of specialization is Plains literature, and I now own my own acreage outside that same university town, where I, too, tinker with horses and tractors. That special sense of place that figured so importantly in our foremothers' lives has pulled me back to the land with a force I cannot explain.

When I think back about my childhood growing up on the Nebraska plains and compare it to lives of pioneer children and again to my own children's experiences, except for technological and medical advances, not so much has really changed.

The prairie was the playground for the pioneer children, and they were free to roam and explore nature's wonders. When I was about eight or nine, my younger sister and I would jump on our paint horses and ride all over the farm. We rode bareback because my father wanted us to learn balance and the rhythm of the horse and because my mother was terrified that we might catch a foot in the stirrup and be dragged to our deaths. We learned quickly to hold on to the horses' warm sides with our browned and bare legs because the walk home was sometimes far, and on the plains there are few hills, gullies, rocks, or trees for a short child to use to remount a tall horse. We played cowboys and Indians, always arguing over who got to be the beautiful Indian princess, and we learned grasses, birds, and seasons by heart.

Later, when I was about ten, my father surprised us with an old buggy, and he helped me teach my mare how to drive. Then the whole plains opened up for my sister and me. For an all-day trip, we would pack picnic lunches of peanut butter and jelly sandwiches, with an extra one for Blaze, mason jars with rattling ice cubes and water, and chocolate chip cookies. Mother insisted that we occasionally drive the buggy close to the road's shoulder, especially on the corners, in case she needed to track us to check on our welfare. After we arrived home after dark several times because of our inability to calculate time and distance, she bought an old church bell at an auction and had our father mount it on a tall pole. One hour before sunset, we would hear the bell across the wheat fields, summoning us home.

The lure of the open spaces was irresistible to us, and we would often drive for miles across the farmlands to find a large old cottonwood tree under which we'd eat our lunch. Leaning back against its channeled trunk, we would look up through translucent leaves and pretend we were on the Oregon Trail bound for California, all of our earthly belongings in our wagon. We sang with the meadowlarks and sucked on the stems of the tall red grasses growing in the ditches. We preferred the dirt roads where hooves and wagons left powdery imprints, and we knew which of the neighbors would offer us cookies and lemonade if we drove into their farmyards.

Twenty years later, myself a farm wife and mother, I packed peanut butter and jelly sandwiches and watched as my own children headed off across the plains for a day of exploring. My daughter, her red hair shining in the sun, ponytail bouncing to the rhythm of her horse's trot, gripped the bare sides of her paint horse with suntanned legs, while my son, Pioneer seed corn hat set backwards on his head, rode beside her on his mud-splattered three-wheeler. I told them to remember to make tracks on the roads, especially the corners, so I could find them if I wanted to check up on them. I kept my mother's binoculars on top of the refrigerator to follow their progress as they explored the open plains of Nebraska.

LINDA HOUGHTALING OYAMA Mountain Made

My way of life I owe to the mountains and to my father, who was into mountain living. It was 1949, springtime in the Rockies, when our family moved into an old three-room log cabin on South Cottonwood Creek. The cabin had no running water.

There was one window in each room and mother sewed curtains from flour sacks on her treadle sewing machine. We papered the kitchen walls using flour paste and the inside layers of brown paper from the sugar sacks, then cut pretty flowers out of seed catalogs to paste all around for trim. We thought it looked pretty. It was a very hard life for my mother but I didn't see that until I became an adult. I had just turned six that spring and my adventurous life was ready to begin.

Late fall, after the temperature cooled down, Dad would shoot a deer, hang it up in the old log horse barn, leaving the skin on until freeze-up. Dad would skin down a ways and cut off a chunk of meat to boil or fry. We never had fancy meals, just meat and potatoes with home-canned vegetables from the garden.

My father was raised among the Cree people in Canada. He spoke Cree, French, and English. He passed much of this on to me, especially his love of Native people, the woods, and wildlife. Dad worked on different ranches wherever he could get work irrigating, haying, harvesting grain, or sometimes calving cows in the early spring. He also worked in a two-man sawmill owned by our neighbor across the creek. Then in the winter months he did some trapping.

We always had time to bundle up and go fishing in the winter. Dad built a big fire near a good fishing hole on the Gallatin River and all of us would fish along the ice, catching whitefish. We used the fire to warm our hands and to try to keep the ice melted off the fishing line. If fishing was good we would go home with gunnysacks full of whitefish. Then I remember Dad and I did a lot of gutting them out as I always enjoyed cleaning fish. He made a salt brine and got alder willows for smoking. The fish were washed free of brine after soaking overnight and placed in our old smokehouse. Oh, how wonderful that always smelled! The smoke curled out all over, but care had to be taken not to get too much heat. Everything had to be just right, and in about eight hours' time we had wonderful eating.

As a young girl I was fascinated with the furs and the traps. Whenever my father caught something, he skinned it in the kitchen as that was the only room with good light. I waited with great anticipation as frozen animals lay beside the wood range to thaw. I loved to watch or help as my dad skinned "those horrible creatures," as my mother called them. The little white ermine and the mink she disliked the most. I thought it was great.

The smell was no enemy of mine. Although I must admit that it reeked terribly if he accidentally cut into the scent gland.

By the time I was a teenager I was attempting to tan deerskins and make Indian clothing. I wanted to be an Indian. I tried to look like one, act like one, and even rode every horse I could get my hands on. We couldn't afford a horse but I made very good use of the neighbors'.

It was then that I came to the conclusion that I wanted to be a taxidermist, as I had been reading a lot of hunting stories and it seemed a lot of wealthy sportsmen had mounted big game heads hanging on their walls. I needed a way to make money. I didn't want to be a secretary and I disliked school in a big way. Then I married young, having my only son in this marriage.

We were ranchers, and even though ranch life was a real part of living off the land, I always longed to be in the mountains as they were a source of healing and comfort to me. I had begun a long slow term of losing my health and eventually this marriage ended.

I ran a trap line and did taxidermy work until I met my second husband. This marriage ended two years later when he passed away from Lou Gehrig's disease.

Shortly, I located an old cabin that had been empty for several years. I moved in and began trying to sort out my life. The old cabin needed a lot of repair; I threw myself into fixing it.

The mountains led me to develop my faith again and I loved my quiet life in my cabin, but as the years went by I realized I would live a lonely life as I was only in my late thirties. I was also beginning to suffer health problems, but doctors never found anything wrong.

My greatest adventure was when I caught a wolverine in a number three Victor trap on a toggle. I was working in a taxidermist shop at the time so I always checked my sets early. This day, however, as I snowshoed up to my set I could see a large round track in the snow. In the dark it looked like a large bobcat. It seemed strange that the cat would drag that heavy toggle log uphill.

I knew this was going to take some time, so I snowshoed back down and drove to the nearest phone, two miles away. I told my boss I won't be in today as I'm chasing after a big bobcat. It was daylight when I snowshoed back up to the set trailing my Walker hound, Montana Trouble. I could then see I had a wolverine in my set. Trouble and I went after the wolverine. The hair stood up on her back and neck as we trailed through some rugged country. But Trouble didn't really want to catch that keg of dynamite and eventually she got lucky as the wolverine somehow fought his way out of the trap. The toggle had been chewed to pieces, but the trap was okay so I picked it up. After trailing several miles through deep snow I headed straight down the mountain empty-handed. It would be another ten years before I would catch a wolverine.

As time went on I began to miss the companionship of someone to share my life with. No, it wasn't easy to find someone as I was so capable that most men thought I was too woodsy. Women weren't friendly either, as most of them wanted to compete or else felt very inferior. I was extremely independent and very confident, as the mountains had shaped me.

It was common knowledge that visitors weren't welcome at my cabin after dark unless I knew they were coming. I was quite capable with my .357 handgun. My rifle or handgun were constant companions as I loved shooting. One fall night, in the darkness I saw a vehicle coming but couldn't see who it was. So I loaded my .357 and waited. At the door appeared a Japanese fellow looking for a taxidermist. I could tell he wasn't a bit aware of my living alone, nor of the danger he was in if he made a wrong move. So began our friendship that eventually led to our marriage.

I continued to have problems with my health. It was during this time that I received two most wonderful gifts. I drew a permit for a Yellowstone buffalo. Because of my love of Native American people, that chance to shoot a buffalo was very special. Secondly, we were trapping pine marten but I had also made a cubby set with a 330 Conibear for a wolverine that was tearing up my marten sets. I hoped to catch him and to my surprise I did. What a thrill!

Although I've now been diagnosed with heart disease and Parkinson's, my husband and I have had some wonderful years of camping, fishing, hunting, and trapping. Since my recovery, life is exciting again and I feel those mountains calling.

For those of you who, as I, live to feel the intertwining of mortal spirit with the spirit of immortality, I found that special feeling in my mountains. The life that I was given beyond human expectation is a gift, simple and pure. For I have loved life with all my human heart, but the mountains and the creator are my balance beam, keeping me on course. I know mountain living has made me what I am.

PHYLLIS LUMAN METAL Abortion, 1925

I was seventeen and, when I got back to the ranch after graduating from boarding school and high school, I missed my period. When nausea followed I knew what it meant. In the ranch town where I grew up, when other girls were "in trouble" the older women would tighten their lips and give each other knowing glances.

I tried jumping off the barn roof and riding my horse as fast as I could up on the mesa — but the nausea continued day and night. I had to take a trip through Yellowstone with my family and pretended I was carsick all the way.

I could not imagine telling my Victorian mother the truth. So I wrote a letter to my mother's best friend's son in Salt Lake who'd always said "just call on me, your big brother." He immediately sent some pills which it took a while to get as we only went to town for the mail every two weeks. The pills did not work and I was frantic.

He then wrote me about Salt Lake's famous abortionist, Dr. Moormeister, who had practiced his art in Salt Lake under the nose of the Mormon Church for twenty years. He had never lost a case. He was called all over the U.S. to perform abortions for those who could afford it. I went to boarding school with his daughter Peggy and we all knew what her father did, but I never dreamed I would need him.

"We have to hurry," Big Brother wrote, "for he will not take you past three months. AND YOU MUST TELL YOUR PARENTS. I have told mine and it is fine for you to come here to Salt Lake and stay with us."

Sooo, "Mother," I said, "I have something to tell you," and I blurted it out. She was hoping it was the young man they had chosen for me to marry, but it was not.

So my mother and I went to Salt Lake with the hundred dollars Dr. Moormeister charged and stayed at our friends' lovely home. My "big brother" took me to Dr. Moormeister's office for the abortion. I went into a clean operating room with a nurse in attendance, had an anesthetic, and when it was over I waited for four hours for the cramps to stop. I went home free of nausea and in great spirits. The next day I returned to have the vaginal packing removed. That was that. It was over.

After a few days, my mother and I returned to the ranch. My "big brother" and I are still friends and that abortion is one of our many secrets. In the years that followed I referred several friends to Dr. Moormeister and they had good, clean abortions, no complications, and went on to marry and have families. What a blessing he was to young women "in trouble." We all knew the horror stories of back-alley abortions in that era.

Now I am seventy-four years old, so you can figure out when it was.

DIANA ALLEN KOURIS ━ Headlong into the Storm

I woke up to an October rain tapping lightly, persistently, in the early morning darkness. The sound normally brings me pleasure with its promise of life and honeyed air. Now it pinched at my spine.

The rain began to rap loudly on the Red Creek Ranch log house and splatter itself against the glass panes. I knew there was no way the cattle trucks could fight the gumbo mud, deep and slimy, to make it down the sheer dugway leading to the ranch. They had been trying for the last three days.

Bruised and worn out, my brother, sister, and I had been weeks gathering the cattle from their vast, southwestern Wyoming summer range. I thought about my husband and son at home. *Why do I do this every year, come down here and half kill myself?*

My brother, Bob, struck a match in the next room and a propane wall lamp yawned a soft glow. I heard Dad clear his throat and Bob's teenaged son, Rick, moan for more sleep.

Nonie, my older sister, strong and self-reliant like our mother had been, threw the covers back on her bed and said, "I guess we might as well get up. We're gonna have to do something; we're almost out of hay and the pastures are ate off."

When I entered the kitchen, the windows were still coated black. The only sound was the dinging of a spoon in a mug of coffee. Dad sat with his forehead resting on his crossed hands on the tabletop. He stood and walked to the window. Squinting to see into the dawn he said, "It's snowin' now." He shook his head.

Bob got to his feet. "I vote we head to the winter ranch with 'em. We're running out of feed and it's hard telling when this is gonna let up."

Nonie winced. "I don't know if we should do this, Bob. I mean I *really* don't know if we should do this."

"Yeah but, Nonie, if we don't get them out of here now, when are we going to? We've got to get the cows over there anyway, and with the highway close, we can ship the calves from there."

It was settled. We'd drive the cattle the eleven miles to Uncle Billy's deserted homestead, hold them there overnight, and get them to the winter ranch by noon the next day. Soon we were swinging into our saddles, the cold leather chilling us from our centers both ways. Wearing my boot overshoes and hooded yellow slicker, I reluctantly left behind my hat and spurs. The snow turned to rain, giving us hope.

The cattle refused to leave the field and walk headlong into the rain. We finally shoved them through the gate and they began the steep climb. Then snow started tumbling from the sky in pudgy flakes, coating the sagebrush and cedars with dollops of white.

Dad, Bob, and Rick went with the leaders and worked the sides of the herd. Nonie and I had the tail end. A dozen calves bunched up in the rear, confused and lost from their mothers. Convinced their mothers were somewhere behind us, the calves suddenly turned and streaked all directions. Nonie and I whirled our horses around; she went one way, I went another.

Wet sagebrush grabbed at my feet and chaps as my sorrel's hooves and knees cracked through it. I puckered as he cleared muddied crevices and badger holes. Panting, I sucked a couple of feathery flakes down my throat. When I made it to the lead calf, I waved my free arm wildly and screamed, "Go back! Get back, you dirty buggers. Turn."

Our calves came together on the road and we fell in behind them on a trot, both of us rubbing our horses on their necks. We were exhilarated and laughing.

Just then we saw a wad of cattle "falling" off the hill, spreading into the cedars. I stayed with the calves and Nonie hurried her quarter horse Sarley to get in front of the mess. When Sarley kept sinking and sliding I saw Nonie jump from his back and run a little ways. Each step got slower as the mud built around her boots. Packing feet the size of snowshoes, she went out of sight. I knew, though, no matter what it took, she wouldn't give up until the cows were turned.

When she caught up with me later, the cows were back on the trail and most of the mud had been scraped from her boots with a sagebrush rake. Her face was flushed and her hazel eyes glassy.

"Criminy," she giggled, "Sarley and I are both wore out and we still ain't even out of the dooryard."

The snow and rain took turns throughout the day. That same bunch of calves stayed in the rear and never passed up an opportunity to make a break for it. In most places the mud was ankle deep, tiring horses and cows with every step. We hollered and whooped until our throats were raw. We shivered, longing for the sun to pick a hole through the dripping sky.

Hour by hour the day wore on. I had long since stopped feeling like the spirited cowgirl. Nonie said I resembled a wilted yellow posy.

Then I heard the jangling of spur rowels behind me. I turned in the saddle and saw a vision. Three riders on fresh, high-strung horses and decked out in dusters, big hats, and inlaid silver, rode into view through the misting rain. As the Jolley girls and their Mexican hired hand loped easily through the brush, waving the skirts of their dusters and throwing loops with their lariats, the cattle hurried along the road like they hadn't done once all day. I was thankful for our neighbors' help but, feeling homelier by the moment, I wanted to wither out of sight in the presence of their magnificence. All I could do was pummel my horse along and wish for this day to be over.

Just before dark we climbed into the stretch-cab pickup and headed home. We bucked greasy mud the entire way.

Barely a heartbeat later it was dawn, and we were back in the pickup carving our way toward the cattle. None of us had our voices; the day before we'd left them scattered along the trail.

Bob shifted in his seat behind the wheel and hoarsely said, "I guarantee the worst is over. The storm's lifting and the cows'll have their bellies full and be ready to trail. They'll string out going down Rife's Rim and we'll hit the winter ranch by early afternoon."

We barely had our feet in the stirrups when it started to pour. The calves splintered in all directions and the cows balked at leaving the willows. With our ropes down, popping them on the hind ends, we fought them through the gate and up the hillside.

I saw Nonie and Bob leaning toward each other in their saddles, their eyeballs bugged out and their neck veins swelling. They were screaming at each other in frustrated squeaks. Nonie spun her horse around and trotted past me.

"I'd like to wring his neck," she croaked. "He thinks he's the only one who knows how to do anything. And I've lost my damn rope." Her raspy voice washed away with the rain as she trotted down the hill to pry cattle from the gully.

The cattle didn't string out. Cold rain and a brisk breeze washed our faces relentlessly. My knees throbbed, my toes went numb, and dampness seeped through my slicker and into my skin.

Nonie rode up. With her entire body shaking she chattered, "Are w-w-we having f-fun yet?"

As we inched the herd forward, minutes swelled into hours, gray skies darkened to dusk and then darkness. We were beyond exhaustion. My horse nearly fell. The blackness was so intense that at times I thought he was walking backwards.

Following the sound of our give-out voices, Nonie and Sarley swept the edges of the herd. Without warning the earth suddenly dropped from beneath them as a deep wash swallowed them whole. Miraculously, Sarley scrambled down the bank of the wash and scurried up the other side. Nonie squalled, "Whoa-ho taco!" and grabbed the top of her head, certain it was still in the air on the other side of the wash. Sarley dropped his nose to the ground and kept it there.

Dad found the fence when his horse bounced off it. At last the cattle trickled, then flooded, through the gate. We were giggly as we rode toward the corral. This job was done.

It was ten o'clock when we peeled off our saturated chaps and slickers in the warmth of the wood cook stove in the old ranch house. We gulped coffee made in a blackened pot before heading back to Red Creek.

Packed into the cab of the truck, we easily etched our way through the mud until we topped the hill above Uncle Billy's. Just as someone bragged on Bob's driving, the truck slid one way, then another, and dove into the deep barrow pit. Cradled in a sharp tilt against the bank, we all sat still, mesmerized.

Squashed against his door, Bob finally grunted, "Is — somebody — going — to — get — out?"

Dad's truck wasn't far. We walked down the hill to get it while Bob got a tow chain. A yank or two later and we were on our way again. Nonie and I rode with Dad. The trip down the dugway, mostly sideways, was terrifying and a fitting end to our day. Nonie gained a blood blister on her finger from her death grip on the window handle.

It was one in the morning when we shuffled into the kitchen. Dad looked down and said, "Well, lookee here. I've walked out of one overshoe somewhere." No one was surprised.

After a bowl of soup we got ready for bed. I slid between the covers and could hardly bear to think of our day. Closing my eyes, all I could see was cows.

Rain began to pat the roof and slide gently down the window. Warm now and cozy, it soothed me. I knew why I was here, and why I come every year. It's because here is where I'm most alive, riding through the brush on the back of a horse. It's what I love, and who I am.

GARNET PERMAN ⌒ Evolution of a Country Woman

I always considered myself a product of the prairie even though I grew up in town. After all, I could recognize a good stand of corn and I knew the difference between a heifer and a steer, which was more than I could say for some of my friends, and besides, a town of 1,300 is hardly a metropolis. So it was with a great deal of confidence that I said "I do" to my farmer/rancher husband and moved from the corn belt to the wheat lands, where I've spent the last twenty years discovering the real meaning of "rural."

I learned:

· about making a grocery list, stockpiling food in the pantry, and the art of substituting ingredients after too many forty-mile round trips to the grocery store for a gallon of milk and a can of mushroom soup;

· that sheep have an IQ three points below that of wormwood, and the truth of the adage that there is no such thing as a sick one;

· that the meanest tempered cow always calves at two A.M. in the middle of a snowstorm, and that consumers really don't appreciate what all contributes to the price of beef;

· that no matter where I am when we handle livestock, I am inevitably ten feet from where I should be;

· what a month of twenty-five-mile-per-hour winds and one-hundred-degree temperatures do to yearly income, and what several such summers do to a financial statement;

· that there were almost no people my age within a twenty-mile radius of our place;

· that some older rural people are intimidated by the vocabulary and interests of a recent arts and sciences grad; they'd rather talk about the weather, or the neighbor down the road.

I found my fun-loving college boyfriend turning into a workaholic who was too tired to care about fun as we'd known it and couldn't understand why his Phi Kappa Phi wife was so dumb about rural living.

By the end of the second summer, I was convinced that the drought we had been experiencing ever since our 1976 wedding day was the result of living too close to the outer reaches of hell.

By the end of the third hot, dry, isolated summer I was sick of being broke, lonely for people my age, and starved for a conversation of ideas. Standing on a hill at the end of our dead-end road, I faced the truth that living on the land is not an idyllic existence; that the mental and physical self-sufficiency necessary for existence on the plains is incredibly hard work with no guarantee of reward. I was less than enthused about the future.

Going home to my parents was briefly tempting, but I knew they'd send me back. I come from German-Russian Mennonite stock who have been adjusting to new places, customs, and people for four hundred years. Perseverance is part of the genetic code.

When my great-grandparents came to Dakota Territory, there were no trees, no fields, no roads; only hard work, and a chance that it would pay off. They survived by being committed to their faith, and to each other. How could I deny such a heritage? So I made a choice, a choice that I would love this land, that I would appreciate the people who made their living from it. I'd even learn to like those stupid cows. I also chose to be happy about the process, and my plains education continued. Seeing things through new eyes was the beginning of my really *living* on the plains.

Instead of missing the autumn color of my home country, all I had to do was focus on the ground in front of my feet to see the plains change with the seasons — from the lavenders of the early spring pasques and violets to the late summer sunflower gold and the burgundy of bluestem.

I learned to delight in the mud of March, because it means a hay crop is on its way.

I discovered majesty in a combine cutting a huge swath through a field of ripened wheat, and joy in the harvest camaraderie at the local grain elevator.

I found satisfaction in watching a crew of hungry men make short work of a homegrown meal.

I really listened, and I heard conversations about the neighbors indicating concern, not mean-spiritedness.

I've developed pride in being able to take whatever Mother Nature dishes out; she separates the hardy soul from the weak, and keeps away those crazies from the coasts.

I reordered my thoughts to believe that every day without rain is one day closer to the day it will rain. In the process, I discovered that God is never far away on the plains; He's as close as the next sunset, and as faithful as prairie winds.

Even if I never do get to the right spot when we move cattle, I've discovered the added dimension to a rural marriage that comes from working together. We've carved our own sliver of eternity, for this land will bear witness to what we have done here long after we go back into it.

I now appreciate that while city people spend much time and money to "get away from it all," I get to live there.

I've seen my children grow seasoned by the land and the love of it. The toughness of spirit I've observed in those who have survived years on the plains is budding in them; I measure my own growth accordingly. Those who have lived here are like the twisted, weather-beaten cedars on our hills; their toughness enables them to endure, providing shelter for young, growing plants and animals until they are established and can take their place in this gloriously harsh environment. It's an evolution worth journeying toward.

MARLAINE RUSTAD SLAAEN 〜 **Saturday Night**

Farmers gather to talk about the rain:
thirty-hundredths during the night
but Fortuna got
sixty.

Having learned to hide their feelings early,
here in this dusky room
they remain carefully free from expectations.

Down at the end of the bar
husband of some years, gray-eyed and good-looking
scrutinizes the wet ring left on the counter
from his beer can

and shelters me with the
power of
disregard.

PEGGY COOK GODFREY ✎ The Real Question

In the mid-1970s I developed a contract hay-baling business more as an extension of my own hay season than as a project. For the first few years my rural community expressed skepticism and disbelief — how many sunbonnets do you see trooping down the lanes from field to field?

The older generation contract balers were quitting the business, taking on fewer jobs, or weren't interested in being paid in shares. Dire times and blooming alfalfa make folks take risks: call the baler in the sunbonnet or stop her on the road.

One particular day I was towing my baler down a lonely dirt road. An older gentleman waved me over and asked, "Who do you work for?"

"Myself."

"Naw," he says, "what I mean is, whose tractor and baler is that?"

"Mine."

Clearly unsatisfied, he drew a slow breath and asked, "Lady, who greased that baler?"

I looked him straight in the eye and responded, "Mister, I don't think anybody but me knows where all those grease fittings are."

He grinned a toothless grin and said, "Can I get ya to do my hay?"

ELAINE M. OSTER ✎ Farmwife with an Attitude

Whenever I fill out a form that asks me to list my occupation, I put down "farmer," the same word I use when I'm asked my husband's occupation. The following is a true story:

The man reading the form says, "Your husband is a farmer?"

"Yes, my husband and I are farmers," I reply.

"You don't have a job?"

"Yes, I have a job. I'm a farmer."

"I mean you don't work outside the home."

"Actually, quite a lot of farming is done outside."

"I mean, you don't work for anyone else."

"No, I don't work for anyone else."

"So, you are just a housewife, or would you prefer farmwife?" (He is getting ready to change the word "farmer" on the form.)

I tell him, "Ted and I are farmers and I'm a wife and he's a husband. If you insist I am *just* a farm*wife* then he is *just* a farm*husband*. The fact that I'm the wife and he's the husband has nothing to do with our occupation. We are farmers, period."

PATRICIA MIDGE FARMER

Learning the Bum Lamb Business

I had two sons in the first three years of my marriage. The four of us lived in a two-room hired hand's house. My father-in-law paid my husband $125 a month and furnished the house and utilities — a better deal than he'd started with. For years, he and his family lived with his parents in their house on the ranch. I raised a garden, and we had venison and sometimes grass-fed beef to eat. I sewed clothes for the kids and the two grandmas bought them other necessities. I hadn't had many material possessions growing up, so I didn't think we were poor. But I didn't think a lot about anything. Wishing I could help financially, since I was experienced in office work, I talked of getting a job in town.

My husband spent a great deal of time (he had been a business major) figuring out to the last cent how much it would cost us for me to work in town. He included not just gas for the car, but every cent in oil, tire and part wear, baby-sitting, and my loss of support on the ranch. When he was done, a job in town would cost us money. That formula did not compute into his trips to the bars in town, often leaving me alone on the ranch with two babies and no vehicle. Somehow he always had money for gas and beer.

My father-in-law suggested I raise bum lambs. The ranch had carried sheep once, when they restocked after the war. He would help me, and bum lambs were free. As usual, I went dumbly into this venture without much information or planning.

The county agent gave me a name and told me he was going the next day to see a rancher with bums to give away; the ranch was forty miles south of Gillette by the Pumpkin Buttes. He'd watch for me. Since I was meeting new people, I wore stretchy black stirrup pants, a white blouse, long pull-on waterproof boots, and the new down coat I'd gotten for Christmas. Off I went in the two-wheel-drive ranch pickup to get bum lambs. I had directions, sort of.

Our ranch, situated twenty-five miles north of Gillette, was all hills and draws with pine and cedar trees and alfalfa meadows along a creek — almost like living in the mountains I'd left in Colorado. I could see the Big Horns from high hills on the ranch. I'd never been in the "south country" of Campbell County and didn't realize how different it was. As I drove, the land became flat and grassy, with trees only around ranches or abandoned homesteads. I was out in the big empty without a map, a little frightened; I saw few ranches.

At what I thought was the right place, I saw a turnoff from the highway; the dirt trail went through a cattle guard and over a low hill. This was March; we'd had a blizzard a week before. I had no experience driving

Wyoming trails, or driving a gutless two-wheel-drive pickup in mud. The men at home wouldn't have sent me on this errand alone unless they thought I could make it, would they? I trusted them.

Right over that hill, the road ran down to a low place that looked awfully muddy. I stopped and looked at it, and decided I'd better drive fast. I backed up, hit the gas, and buried the pickup in mud over the tires. I rocked the pickup back and forth. In absolute panic, I realized I was stuck. Not a building in sight and I was stuck.

I glanced in my rear-view mirror; the county agent sat behind me in his car. I was mortified that he'd witnessed my stupidity. As we drove down the highway to a neighbor with a Jeep, the agent told me he came over the hill yelling and honking just as I hit the mud, but I couldn't hear him. He laughed and said he never felt so helpless as he did watching me go right ahead.

The neighbors, five miles back on the highway and three miles off it to the ranch, were the friendliest people I'd ever met. We were there an hour, eating freshly baked cinnamon rolls and drinking coffee as everyone traded stories about getting stuck in mud. These good people were my introduction to my new homeland; their care and good humor are pretty much universal among country people. They didn't treat me like a dumb dude but accepted me as a soon-to-be rancher.

When we pulled the pickup out, the county agent drove it to the ranch. The rancher was only a couple of years older than me; two friends helping him lamb looked like members of a motorcycle gang. (I learned later that they were.) They all looked at me, traded some looks, and started pitching lambs out of a shed door into the back of the pickup.

I couldn't believe it. These were brand-new, half-dead babies; the thunk they made hitting the pickup box made me sick to my stomach. They threw in about thirty, said good-bye, and headed for the house. I tried to sort the lambs, and wrapped them in some old blankets and rags. I could tell by their glazed eyes some would never make it. All the way back to the highway, the county agent told me how to take care of lambs. By then, my brain was swimming with new experiences and shocks. I was exhausted when I got home; but I had thirty new babies, and supper to fix, and my own kids needed attention. That was just the start.

Five lambs died on the cold ride home. I'd gotten a sack of lamb milk replacer ahead of time. I mixed buckets of it, filled big glass Coke bottles, added long black calf nipples, and went to the barn for the first of the four-a-day feedings. More lambs died the first night. I got up in the night to feed them, and my husband put a lamp over their pen, but they still died. When I called the vet, he said they had overeating sickness, but it was too late. I sold five puny lambs that year; they didn't pay for the milk replacer.

The next spring, I felt like a pro; I went south again, to a different ranch on a graveled road close to the highway. The rancher wasn't there, but his

Mexican sheepherder gave me twenty-five bums. He stood, amazed, as I opened the back of the station wagon, full of boxes of soft towels and blankets, with warm bottles of milk replacer inside. I held and fed each lamb before covering it in the still-warm towels and blankets.

The man had a good story to tell about the crazy lady, but that year I saved all the lambs. We vaccinated them for overeating sickness, and they got sore mouth, but that wasn't deadly. I swabbed their gums with purple medication every time they ate; my hands were purple for weeks. I fed them every three hours, day and night, like babies. Made sense to me, but now everyone thought I was crazy.

Until I raised bums, I didn't know sheep were born with long tails. My father-in-law told me that he'd castrated lambs and docked their tails with his teeth because it was faster. I was disgusted; we used rubber bands on my babies. It was simple and clean; the parts just dried up and fell off. Sometimes wool would stick in the bands and I'd have to pull the tails off.

I loved my lambs and they thought I was their mama. I could raise my voice in the house and the lambs would thunder through, over, or under every fence between me and them to stand on the porch *baaaaa*ing for me. My father-in-law would cuss and mutter, grab pliers, hammer, wire cutters, and fence stretchers and rush out to sheep-proof the yard one more time. He never got the job done; my lambs always found me.

By late fall, when my husband said we had to sell the lambs, I knew we needed the money, but it was hard. When he came home, he said all he could get was $25 dollars a head. The buyer claimed they were too big for bum lambs; he just knew they were two-year-olds. That experience put an end to my bum lamb business.

By then, the family had seen that I could work with animals, put in long hours without complaint, and was a quick study. They put me to work as a rancher.

DELCIE D. LIGHT Janus Was a Two-Faced God

A sickly sparrow pecks at hulls
stuck in snow on an empty feeder.
This frail creature peeks at me
through my lace curtain this January Sunday.

And I am shaken by superstition:
birds touching windows augur death.
I feel chilled at this omen whose dark eyes
stare in through the pane.

Still, the bird sits bunched and shivering,
brown eyes dulled. I tremble
knowing I am witnessing a dying. Be gone!
Wings flutter and tap the frosted glass.

That was yesterday. Today the news
you died, my brown-eyed friend,
of your own hand, alone and away.
But I know you were killed long ago.

Your nest was icy, filled with shards
of father's lusting rage. He D and C'd your psyche
with his scalpel tongue, aborting your womanhood
just as Janus appropriated Juno's identity.

He had folks fooled, with his two faces.
White forehead and ruddy cheeks, he sat
in the front pew, on the school board,
the county commission. A fine citizen!

In the barn, between steaming, cud-chewing cows,
in straw he took you, his daughter, and
called you "whore." His heated breath and body
steaming, sated on your stolen soul.

You pecked at hulls frozen in ice and starved.
Women's seeds of friendship could not return your
faith in father, your self, nor sate your emptiness
so you ate the pills.

Your sparrow spirit fluttered across
the continent. Your brown eyes dulled to dust.
If I could have
I would have filled the feeder.

TERRY L. SCHIFFERNS ━ Is This Work?

What can I say about working women on the plains? I don't rope or feed
cattle or any other livestock. I did have chickens once. My chicken endeavor
was like a retirement home for old hens. I got a few eggs, but to be honest, I
was glad when my dog ate the chickens. It saved me that feed bill at the
co-op every month, or from having to eat stringy old hens. I know enough
to stew them, but I didn't look forward to eating them. Anyway, they
tormented the dog, eating his food while he was chained up. Little did they

realize, they were driving him to the end of his rope. I was not totally surprised to come home to heaps of feathered carcasses thrown pell-mell around the yard. I yelled at my dog, but deep down I gave a sigh of relief, knowing I'd no longer have to worry about keeping the damn chickens out of the garden or locked in their coop and the dog on a chain. I really don't think most people consider a dozen old hens that much work.

During the spring before we moved to the cabin, Doug decided to raise fryers, big fat white chickens that turned out pretty good. We lost a few in a spring downpour. Doug ran out and found them, beak first in a puddle with their downy feathers soaked and matted. He snatched them from the jaws of death, as he told the story, brought them in, thumped their once fluffy little chests, and gave them mouth-to-beak resuscitation. When they came to, he dried them with my blow dryer. Most ended their days in hot grease in my fry pan later that summer, but they were Doug's, and when he left, I gave up on chickens. I had too many other things to worry about, like getting enough wood to make it through the rest of the spring and then the next winter. I weatherized, finished that damn drywall, and fed the kids.

I'd just graduated with a teaching certificate, so I subbed. To get a real teaching job, I'd have had to move. I'm a Nebraskan not by birth, but by choice. Seventeen years ago I fell in love with a one-room cabin my friend Bobbie built, nestled against the south bank of the Platte. When Bobbie moved to Arizona three years ago, she left me the cabin. Now it sports a two-story addition, and the county maintains a one-mile stretch of dirt road leading in. I know the cabin's history; it included seventeen years of mine. I spent the day before my first son was born sitting in this kitchen, drinking tea. I'd always dreamed of living in a place like this, and after being here for only a year and a half I was not about to give it up. So I started my garden from seed that year, and I subbed when the schools called.

I worked on my bedroom first, where drywall had been hung, but not mudded. So I checked out an illustrated book from the library and learned the hard way not to be stingy buying or applying mud. If you're going to drywall more than a hall closet, buy the twenty-five-pound sack. Take my word for it. Add just enough water to make the mud the consistency of cake batter, but remember it thickens up after it sets for a while. Fill the cracks and nail holes, spreading the mud out and away. Feather it thin toward the outside but don't be stingy in the corners. Go ahead, dollop that mud like frosting on a cake, pressing the corner trowel in tight. The extra mud drools out the end like pasty white turds. And this is the good part.

After drying comes sanding, when drywall dust coats everything in the house. My snot was thick white stuff that made my nose wiggle and itch for days. How many days did I spend working in my bedroom? I finished three coats of drywall, then papered and painted. The healing power of drywall-ing helped me through spring. I needed to feel the ache in my arms and legs from stretching and reaching, to fall onto the couch exhausted. But most of all, I needed to know I could do something I had never done before. I trimmed the windows and doors with mahogany, but I might have done that later. I finished the living room later that summer. The first Christmas alone will definitely drive a woman to drywall, so I worked on the porch that winter.

But drywalling to keep sane probably isn't work most people associate with plainswomen. I should be out pulling the plow. Instead, for the first time in seventeen years of gardening, I planted flowers. I'd planted a marigold or two, justifying frivolity by saying they kept the bugs away. But flowers for the sake of flowers? I could never justify watering flowers when my tomatoes and peppers wilt by mid-July even with a heavy mulch.

So how does a rational plainswoman justify flats and flats of flowers? Well, I made five dollars at a friend's yard sale in town and went to a nursery I'd heard was having an open house. "The open house was last week," said the owner, "but these bachelor buttons and cosmos are getting leggy. I'll give you a flat of each free. And no one wanted to buy these nicotianas even though they are such a pretty pink. How about a quarter a six-pack?" When my five dollars was gone, the inside of my car was packed with tropical dreams. Since then, I have truly believed that I will get whatever I need. And that summer I needed flowers. I watered those flowers through a drought year and they bloomed and bloomed for me. The next year most came back from seed.

But growing flowers probably doesn't really count as work. I did weatherize the house that fall. I built window frames and hammered insulation where the wind poured through. Intimately involved with my miter box, I finally quit cutting my angles opposite to what I needed. I hung plastic. I caulked. I built door jambs until winter did not sneak in under the doors and around the windows. I asked myself why I had spent the winter before freezing and fuming because he had not done these things when I could have done them. I decided anything worth bitching about is worth doing myself.

I heat with wood and no back-up heat — that should count as work. I don't cut the wood myself now; I buy it at twenty-five dollars a truckload — cheaper than buying and licensing a truck and buying another chain saw. My teenaged sons carry in most of the wood, unless I'm home and feel the need to hold something in my arms — then I carry in armload after armload after armload. I love having it stacked high and tight. The boys always want to stop when they get five or six armloads heaped on the top. I know the security of having five days' worth of wood stacked inside while a January blizzard blows outside. I also know the art of filling the cook stove firebox to last until morning, choosing just the right pieces of wood to fit snugly against one another. I hold and examine each piece of wood to ensure it will curve tight to the next, fitting like a lover on a cold night. I'm partial to quarter-round pieces, leaving just enough space between them to allow breathing room for the fire. I twist the damper not quite shut. My cook stove is an 1881 Quick Meal that sucks air from cracks so a tightly shut damper allows a steady curl of smoke to escape, filling the cabin in no time. I fall asleep to the hiss of water simmering on the stove. If I'm careful, I'll wake to hot coals the next morning. Practicing and mastering this art, I always smell of wood smoke. My friend Shelley tells me I smell like a sausage. Knowing a compliment when I hear it, I grin and let her smell my sweater once more.

But is mastering the art of stove-stoking work? I did build a front porch last summer with my friend Mary Rose. And this summer I have to dig a new hole and move the outhouse. But I figure I'll invite some friends, buy some wine and beer, maybe barbecue some burgers and disguise it as a party. I have finally figured out how to clean the chimneys and that is work. I know because I had to pay someone else to do it after my son and I did it the first time. We didn't take the top section off and got that damn brush stuck in the chimney. I watched the chimney cleaner so now I know to take the top section off to get leverage to push the damn brush down and up again. Having once paid someone to do what I do qualifies it as work.

But a great deal of the time I do things like searching out the dead mice my cat catches and leaves to rot in the house. I feed the wild birds every day in the winter, but that's more like paying for my entertainment. I chase the cat late at night and she chases me, catching me by surprise when I come around a corner.

I don't cook as much as I used to. We eat a lot of sandwiches and popcorn. I spend the time I might otherwise use for cooking to do things like sitting in the snow next to the flooded slough, watching the beaver with my son, who agrees it's time well spent. I'm not sure what the beaver thinks. I guess he thinks we're crazy, my son and me, sitting in that snow bank when it's fifteen above zero during a February blizzard to watch him. He swam right up to us, turned, and swam back to his temporary shelter. I believe he intends to dam the slough behind my cabin, and if he does, well, then I will have some work to do.

What is the work that plainswomen do? I teach at the college part-time. Since they pay me, that might be work, even if I do enjoy it. I take classes at the college, and some days I'd swear that was work. And I write, but I love writing, though it is by far the hardest work I do. But writing, for me, is a lot like drywalling or growing flowers; it's just one of those things I have to do. I have tea parties with my daughter, and I read books to her, and we make snowmen, and we dig in the garden, and we swim. Mostly, I watch the seasons slip one into another over and over again and watch my children grow.

But work, I'm not sure any of this is work. For me this is just living.

TRUDY Z. WARDWELL   *Why I Didn't Write*

Forgive me for not writing sooner, but we were chosen as Ping-Pong balls in a World Olympics. A new law froze county salaries; our local honest and hard-working folks who never even took home office supplies for personal use were crushed, some trying to live on less than $1,000 a month. But the group took the bad news stoically, like rural people always do.

Then in January we got the Westcliffe Woozies, as usual. Worthless the horse went lame, and someone cut our fence; the donkeys walked down the road at night and were smashed by a speeding car driven by teen-agers. Baby Skipper had to be shot and Mama was expected to die. Since I reject all bad news, I spent hours that melted into days caring for her, hugging, singing, and praying for her to get well. And she did. Meanwhile I strung fence wire and repaired fence despite deep snow.

Next, the Green Berets arrived in Army trucks at two A.M., and Worthless tried to jump a fence but went through it instead. In February our pipes froze; after the sun came out, one shower worked but both stools stayed out of order for a month. We got flat tires every day from nails shucked into the driveway by a careless roofer years ago, pushed to the surface during frost heaves. The kitchen sink pipes plugged, blowing water over the floor. Mike got under the house to move the toilet and discovered we had ring-tailed cats living under there. They were no problem — they eat spiders and mice — until they climbed the mantelpiece and smashed Mike's antique gun and my cowboy statue.

Then Jerry Jeep wouldn't start; we were down to our '72 pickup that wanders down the road like a drunken goose and our '87 Land Cruiser with 125,000 hard country miles.

I got a sinus infection; heck, the whole town got a sinus infection and passed it around like a box of candy. In March, a hearing-aid man offered a free exam and since I'm deaf as a zucchini, Mike and I got tested, but we can't afford aids until I write a bestseller. So now when I say, "What do you want for supper?" Mike says, "No, I've been there and it's ugly." I say, "No, no, Mike, I said what do you want for dinner?" and he answers, "I haven't heard who won the Lotto." We laugh a lot! New glasses in March; aging sure costs money.

In March we went on a weekend vacation courtesy of the National Guard; I love being a military wife and would have joined myself if I'd been a boy. I love it that women pilot F-16s and choppers now.

I visited a neurologist for my migraines, and when she said I might have lupus, I went straight to the library and read how the body attacks its own organs, resulting in long hospitalizations, possible complications, or death. For the next weeks my migraines rarely left, my arm was numb, my right eye lost vision, I couldn't read and had to write with my eyes closed; my thinking was garbled and I hunted for words. Stress or lupus? I went for an MRI and blood tests, but the clinic *forgot* to send them to the doc; my fright grew daily, and I updated my will. Finally, I called and the receptionist told me the brain scan was normal, but the blood tests would take another week. I thought having a female doctor would result in good medical care; not this time. Again no one called me so I spent a nervous week until I called; no lupus.

Now I try to do what's most fun first, a change for me, the poster child for delayed gratification.

NANCY CURTIS ⌒ Cowmoms

Ranching is a job nearly perfectly suited to women. Most jobs that involve caretaking — raising children, teaching school, nursing, caring for the elderly — have traditionally been women's work. And ranching, at least the day-to-day tending of livestock, is based on the same skills as these traditional women's jobs. I can't imagine two more similar occupations than cowboy and mother. In fact, the similarities are so obvious that I wonder why cowboys weren't, from the very beginning, called "cowmoms."

The problem for women ranchers is that cattle can weigh nearly a ton each. While a good cowboy and a good mother do have many of the same abilities, the size of cattle makes it difficult for a woman to ranch alone. Fortunately, many ranch chores that young cowboys quickly complete with brute strength, other less physical people can accomplish with patience and an understanding of nonverbal communication.

That's the reason that many successful women ranchers have been tutored by a father or grandfather. Brothers, husbands, and young ranch hands all know how to get the job done, but when it comes to passing that knowledge on to a woman, they have two barriers. First, these men lift things. They shove things. They have nothing but impatience for people who are stopped by obstacles like wire gates that won't close, cattle that won't load, or bales that refuse to be tossed over a fence.

Second, these men have a complex image to maintain. They're faced with measuring up to both the hell-bent-for-leather image of John Wayne and the cutting-edge-of-science-and-technology image of the agricultural colleges. It's hard for them to admit tender feelings toward an old cow; hard because it isn't manly and hard because it isn't good business to give a cow a second chance.

Older men have had years to learn the intricacies of raising cattle and, as they've aged, they've learned to compensate for diminishing physical strength. I've known men in their seventies who would single-handedly go to a pasture, corral a herd of wild cattle, and sort out the drys. Nobody seems to give it a second thought. If a stranger questioned how this was accomplished — a job that might take three cowboys most of the day — you'd probably hear, "Ol' Bob is a hell of a hand with cattle." This "good hand" mystique prevents the acquired knowledge of experienced cattlemen from being passed down.

But aging fathers can tell their daughters the truth. Daughters won't snicker at the finer, more ethereal considerations. Sons are another matter. A father holds on to a bit of swagger with a son. But sons seldom ask anyway.

I began to ask my father questions. "Look at their eyes," he said. "You can tell when a cow's sick by her eyes. And the hang of her ears.

"Control them with eye contact, especially in a corral. Don't crowd 'em up or chase 'em around. You and the cattle got to be looking at each other. When a cow is thinking about making a break, you can see it in her eyes and her body.

"Give them signals they can understand. If you want a cow to stay back, let her know — look her in the eye, point at her, and tell her to get back. Say it so she knows you mean it, but be ready to swing the gate shut in her face if she tries you."

And I began to see that handling cattle is like handling kids. It's observation and communication. It's the subtleties of your voice, the calmness of your hands, the encouragement or discouragement in your eyes. It's having what people call "intuition" in a woman, but attribute to "savvy" if they're talking about a man working with cattle.

A person can get a cow to go through a gate by hitting her repeatedly with a cattle prod or by roping her from horseback and dragging her through, but a less physical person can probably get her through by making sure she sees the gate, giving her a reason to go, and being patient. Ray Hunt, the horse trainer, has built a reputation on the advice "Make it easy for the animal to do what is right and hard for it to do what is wrong." Cowboys pay good money for a two-day workshop to learn this theory. Good mothers have done it instinctively for generations.

The second quality that contributes to savvy or intuition is observation. Mothers notice changes in their children that are hard to define. They say their little Johnny looks "peaked" or ask him, "Is everything all right?" In the pasture I notice an old cow who licks her dead calf for a week trying to make it come back to life. I've seen a cow disoriented for a month after losing a calf, returning to the site of the birth, searching, calling. It tugs at me in a deep spot where the mothering instinct is never completely buried.

One winter an old redneck cow calved prematurely and lost her calf. I found the remains by following her tracks to a gully. Blood in the snow and a few fragments of soft bone were all that was left. The coyotes had found the calf first.

The cow disappeared for two days. I spent hours looking for her. When she reappeared, I corralled her and asked Fred to check her — he's a hell of a hand with cows. "Nothing the matter with her," Fred said.

She disappeared for days at a time. She didn't come for food or water, surviving by eating snow and grazing on dry patches of last summer's grass. Then I'd spot her — slow moving, skinny, losing hair, dull-eyed. I told myself if I saw her alive again, I'd take her to the vet.

We did tests. "Nothing wrong," the vet said.

"Maybe she's depressed," I ventured. I didn't have the guts to suggest that maybe she was traumatized. Maybe she'd watched the coyotes eat her calf — maybe it was already dead, maybe not. The vet didn't laugh at the idea of depression.

"What should I do with her?" I asked. "Is she going to be all right?"

He said, "Sometimes they never get over it. If she was mine, I'd send her to the canners."

Some changes with cows and kids are hard to define. But noticing the small things counts in any kind of caregiving.

It surprises me that ranchers haven't always been women, although I suspect the care of small herds of cattle falls to women more often than is commonly known. In Sweden, women take cattle to isolated meadows in the mountains each summer, sometimes beginning to herd alone at the age of eleven. The responsibility is considered a rite of passage. However, in the American West, where herds were often massive and few cattle were treated as individuals, the skills required were rugged ones. Then men who stayed in the saddle longer, rode faster horses, drank more whiskey, accumulated more cattle, slept with more women, and died younger were admired — not traits commonly shared by mothers.

Last fall I saw a help wanted ad requesting applicants for work on a ranch. In bold letters it said, NO COWBOYS WANTED. The term "cowboy," meaning a tough hombre who can manhandle livestock, is not necessarily complimentary these days. Profit margins are slim and cattle must be treated with respect. Detailed records on individual cattle give more assistance to a rancher making management decisions than a cowhand who can bulldog a steer in eight seconds. I think the rancher who placed that advertisement would appreciate a savvy cowmom. And after a while, he might even say "She's a hell of a hand with cattle."

LYN DALEBOUT Presence of Mind

Nature,
at last,
brings me no peace.
Everywhere I look
I see the rugged struggle:
ducks buffeted by wind,
elk running from me!
A prayerful person!

I see too much in things.
Read too much into life.
At the river
I find nothing I want to know.
Only the ceaseless, restless
cycling of things.

I come here today
and see nothing I could call
beauty.
Only wholeness, everywhere I look,
wholeness.

BARBARA M. SMITH It's Good to Have

I called my mother and told her I'd be coming up to Montana for a week to attend a workshop across the lake from their home on Flathead Lake. The kids and I would stay with them. "Good!" she said, delight in her voice. "I have twenty-five pounds of carrots coming on Saturday. See if you can come early. You can help can."

Oh, no. Canning season. But she knew I was coming and I was stuck. Twenty-five pounds of carrots translates to a whole bunch of cutting, scraping, washing, loading, canning, sweating. It wasn't what I had in mind. I was imagining a week of retreat from the daily life in my Wyoming town, a week of visiting the folks interspersed with great classes and conversations about the state of poetry these days, divided by leisurely drives around the lake. "Well," I said, "at least it's not corn." Corn is the hardest stuff to deal with.

"Oh, that's next week," Mom said. "Do you want to stay another week?"

I never complain about the price of vegetables in the store. As far as I'm concerned, whatever I pay, it's worth it not to have to put it up. My parents could buy canned or frozen vegetables, but they like to can. They were children of the Depression and they love to watch the pantry fill up with sparkling jars of veggies and fruit. There's something immensely satisfying about watching the trees change colors in the fall, knowing that the larder is stocked and there's enough wood cut, quartered, and stacked out in the yard for about ten years. They talk to other people of their age in a certain language, understood only by one another. "I put up twenty-seven pints of zucchini pickles yesterday. Tastes just like watermelon pickles. You wouldn't know it was zuc."

I can't understand this. No one ever wants zucchini to taste like zucchini, so why plant the stuff? My mother has zucchini casserole recipes that make it taste like corn, zucchini bread recipes that taste like banana bread, and now zucchini pickles that taste like watermelon pickles. I tease "Why not just toss this stuff when you're tired of it?" They look at me in disbelief. Throw food away?

My in-laws down in Arkansas are the same way. Their yard is gradually getting smaller and smaller as Granddad puts in more and more garden each year, experimenting with a certain kind of butter beans or figs. They had to add another freezer in the garage to hold it all. My mother-in-law is on a restricted diet and can't eat much of the produce, so they wait for us to come. Last year they put up forty-four pints of strawberries. While we were there for our one-week visit, we managed to eat three of them. But they've got it if they need it. Children of the Depression understand this.

Out in the kitchen, Mom is talking to herself. Actually, she's repeating the steps aloud so she remembers: "one-fourth teaspoon salt. There. I gotta, no never mind. That looks like enough. There." My dad always says that when Mom is talking to herself she is never really dangerous unless she's talking in Norwegian; then you don't ask. She hands me a knife and goes on repeating the instructions. The chopper whines, my daughter loads jars, I peel as fast as I can to keep up.

Finally a break, a cup of coffee and what I came for, what I always come back for: the stories, all about vegetables and family.

My mother says, "My mom and dad never would work on Sunday, except during harvest maybe. But they didn't consider it work to go down to the valley and pick fruit, so every Sunday my dad would haul all five of us kids down along the river there and we'd have to pick plums or whatever we could find all afternoon. We sure enough thought it was work, hauling those big gallon buckets full. Ma would make jelly and sauce and that's what we lived on. She always said, 'It's good to have.'

"I guess we would have gotten rickets or something like that if we hadn't gone berry picking all summer, but we kids didn't realize then how tough it was for my folks all those years. It took my dad years to pay off the grocery bill from the Depression, and that was just for flour and sugar; we grew or gathered everything else ourselves." I could hear my grandmother in my mother's voice. *It's good to have.* My mother wipes her eyes, remembering. My daughter, listening, hugs her.

Back to my job, I find a funny-shaped carrot with an interesting tripod of roots dangling and I hold it up. My mother laughs. I know this story.

"When we got married, there was no such thing as a honeymoon and we were living with Dad's parents. But Hazel had fixed up our bedroom and put bells on the bedsprings, stuff like that, and there on the dresser, on my nice new dresser scarf, was this big carrot, like this one. It looked like a naked man. Oh, that Hazel was a dickens! I was so shy in those days, I about died when I walked in there with your dad. Hazel and all the others were shivareeing us outside the window." My father listens to this story from the other room and they are both smiling. My children are gathered around as children do when they think they aren't supposed to be listening to something, and we are all smiling at the innocence, the fun, the romance.

Later, when I'm at the workshop, the teacher talks about discovery, discovering the true subject of the material. I wonder what the true subject is in canning carrots. It's more than the sum of its parts. It's more than just remembering the Depression, honoring the sweat and worry of all those grandmothers who got us here. My mother thinks she escaped the farm those many years ago, but the rituals are part of her and have been with her throughout her life. She has given them to me as well, and my daughter watches both of us, hears our stories. It's primal and mysterious, satisfying, this gathering of the harvest, like living between God and the ground. Something in us returns to it.

When my husband calls I tell him I've put up forty-four quarts of carrots. Corn is next. Don't worry, I say, we're OK. It's always good to have.

SHARON GUSTAFSON ⌒ **waiting**

back bend bent
eyes see fuzzy

while the mind
watches the body be busy

milking the cow
feeding the turkey

carry buckets of water
for clean clothes and body

act your age they cry
they are afraid i'll die

so i try to sit still
while the world goes by

tired of sitting
legs swollen like grief

promise myself to act
not the age they see

to act soon,
to set my age free.

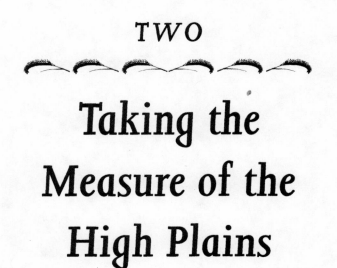

TWO

Taking the Measure of the High Plains

Grass Echoes Grass

FREYA MANFRED *Grass*

I lie in bed
with death on my mind,
with abused children, gangs clashing,
guns roaring, forests dying, lakes choking,
and I can feel it:
grass:
shooting up inside the souls of my feet,
tunneling through my knees,
tall and long and lemony,
tangled blades of green
feathering my thighs, soft as lips,
filling my belly,
hissing, rustling, into my heart.
I sit at my desk,
my best self unseen, unspoken
words of pain and love and praise,
words I owe, dying on the floor,
but the grass grows, the teeming grass grows.
The longer it grows the thicker it gets,
the thicker it gets the wetter it gets,
the wetter it gets the greener it gets,
the greener it gets the more my heart shines.
The grass flowers into my arms, my fingers,
up through my neck at a speed faster than the sound of it
thrashing and whispering in my throat.
It sprouts from my eyes, my nose, my ears.
With a green groan it replaces my greying hair,
my brain swelling with seeds of grass,
my mind supple, my throat singing.
Even in my despair with aching joints and withered breasts,

my feet twitch all night like roots,
my womb fills with the juice of the grass,
my heart fills with green light laden with green shadow,
    as grass echoes grass.
I expected to lie down and grow old and lose my grip.
I expected to weep and scream and apologize.
I expected to watch my loved ones get sick, go mad, or die.
I expected to fold into the death around me.
But one night when I wasn't thinking,
one night as I floated above sleep,
the grass started to grow in my feet,
and it's been growing ever since.
The grass sings, the grass cradles me,
the grass carries me out of myself into the world I hate
and first fell in love with
as a green child.

MARVELLE HANSEN   Memories of a Cow Wrangler

After my husband died, I knew I couldn't keep all the cattle. I had 135 head and sold some in the fall before the weather turned bad. Neighbors hauled some hay, and I had grain in the barn to carry to the feedyard cattle — some twenty-four buckets of grain each day. In January I started selling yearlings. But the cows were not finished with me. I got a couple of new calves in January, more in February. They knew I would never be able to sell those baby calves. Spring came again. The hay lasted until pasture time. I raised fourteen pretty Hereford calves that last year, selling out in 1989, and ending forty-two years in the cattle business. The hardest job of my life was selling my herd of cattle.

In all the years of checking on the herd, of looking for strays, and the endless fixing of fence, I was privileged to see many things that others only dream about. Once I saw a mink crossing the creek on a bridge made by a fallen tree. He spat at me and disappeared. I've seen an opossum on the back porch inspecting the cat dish. A pesky fox used to come out of his den in the old quarry and bark at me like a rat terrier dog.

The coyotes answered the six o'clock whistle from town. They peered out from the cedar trees and watched me feed cattle by the feedyard. Old Pinny, the boss cow of the herd, kept them in line. She was a big cow with a set of horns like fork tines; she could throw a coyote fifteen or twenty feet if she got a running start.

That was my lifestyle. I was envied by some and ridiculed by others. With grudging admiration, some neighbors called me the best cow wrangler they ever knew. Some looked at me with disdain. My father used to tell people I was married to this old farm. He may have been right. God willing, I will die still owning this land.

JANICE VIERK ➤ Noon Prayer

Homemade bread steams on the counter
fresh from the cook stove
where cobs turn white with heat.
Steak that was a crippled Hereford
only a week ago
sizzles and pops in the cast iron skillet.
Ears of corn, yellow and succulent
bob in the cauldron of boiling water.
Butter removed from the crockery churn
and molded with the rose pattern
graces the red-checked tablecloth.
Pies, cherry and apple, cool
on the wide windowsill,
recently relinquished by the calico cat.
The triangle sounds
bringing the men from the threshing
to the pump.
Cold water soothes red, leathery necks,
sweaty, dust-caked arms,
and throats parched with chaff.
Wooden chairs scrape worn linoleum
as the harvesters gather round the laden table.
To this gathering, Lord, we give thee thanks.
Amen.

LOUISE STENECK ➤ Sleeping with the Pigs

Words don't come easily now. I work with hands callused and scarred, dotted with brown spots from too many hours under a harsh sun. The nails are short and often ragged. My hands are strong and do good work; they have earned their ugliness.

But these hands have a hard time at the typewriter. In my other life, my fingers raced across the keys as I sat at my desk in the basement of the newspaper office in Nyack, New York, with a phone glued to my ear. Teletypes clattered to shouts of "Copy!" as the clock's hands moved down to deadline. Words flowed out of me effortlessly; my work, my life, my joy.

Not today. Here I sit, smoking cigarettes; perhaps I can smoke the words out, like that family of skunks I drove out from their home under the shed with a few burning rags.

I don't like change; I want to know what's going to happen today and next week and next year. I long for a road map for all the remaining years of my life. But I married a man who constantly stirs the pot. He loves change, looks for change, and blooms when under its influence.

Growing up in the suburbs of New York City, he lifted his nose to the wind and followed it. Armed with the conviction that anything is possible, and steeled with the knowledge that hard work solves everything, he set out to follow his dreams.

I, too, had dreams, but I hesitated to follow. Perhaps his fearlessness drew me to him. We met, we fell in love, we fought; we fell in love again and married. He would be my sail and I would be his anchor. Together we would navigate through life's rough waters.

One of his dreams was to own a hog farm. Don't ask him why. His only answer is that he likes pigs — a better reason than most people offer for their life choices.

Moving here was like coming to a foreign land, like falling asleep in one time and awakening in another, like walking down the street and realizing you don't know your own name.

We drove across two thousand miles of baking brown plains in August heat to a farm I hadn't seen. Cicadas whirred in every lonely tree on the endless plains, ashimmer with grasshoppers.

And there it was. A sagging trailer with windows missing; a few metal grain bins and a concrete-block barn; dilapidated hog sheds and broken fences; waist-high weeds, sand burs, snakes, a few dozen sorry-looking old sows, and some scrawny piglets. A wild cat hissed under the front stoop.

My husband hopped from the car, turned in a wide circle with his face alight, and shouted, "Isn't it great!" Tears gathered at the back of my throat, but the time for crying was done. Crying was for leaving; this was the future.

So I put my tears in a small place just below my heart. Sometimes at night, while my husband and son slept, I lay my hand upon my breast and imagined I could feel them there, hard as stone.

Each morning I woke with steely resolve and worked to clean ten years of cooking grease from the stove and cupboards. I put plastic on broken windows until we could afford replacements. We hauled truckloads of rusty barbed wire, tin cans, broken glass, and collapsed rabbit hutches to the dump. We chopped weeds and planted grass that the grasshoppers chewed as fast as it sprouted. Violent late-summer storms whipped the earth into huge clouds of dust. Four drops of rain fell. I stuffed rags under the poorly fitting doors and vacuumed grimly.

I feared the pigs. That first day, my husband took me to the pens and proudly displayed his animals. Sows with piglets barked warning and as they ran to the fence line to greet us I jumped back. "Do they bite?" I asked. The boars had huge tusks and wild, pink-rimmed eyes. They were so big. I felt so small.

I drove into town for groceries and supplies. In the heat, the streets were deserted and dust devils whirled between the buildings. A few women listlessly wheeled carts to the checkout counter where the clerk visited with a friend who leaned against a fly-specked Pepsi display. The clerk interrupted her chat to say, "Forty-four twelve." I paid in cash. I might have been invisible.

As I drove back, a farmer setting irrigation tubes lifted his head and one finger in greeting. No neighbors came to welcome us.

And so we set to work again. The days passed. At night we studied books about hog diseases, hog feed, hog buildings, hog finances. We put on our best clothes and drove into town to wheedle a small line of credit from the local bank. The banker frowned at us over the top of his little glasses while he shuffled through our papers. His frown spoke volumes about our strangeness, our inexperience. We vowed to be successful, just to prove him wrong.

And the weeks passed. We learned how to castrate pigs. The first one took us an hour and we only got him half done; today we can finish the job in twenty seconds. For extra cash, my husband took a job driving a truck for corn harvest. We put our son on the bus for the first day of school, his shoulders squared and his face frozen in fear. A little tornado came through and dropped a shed roof on our new truck. The milkmaid on the next farm was murdered; to this day, the killer hasn't been caught. And we worked and worked and I kept the tears frozen under my heart.

Sometimes at night I rose to wander the trailer and watch thunderstorms race across the dark. I longed for home, for trees that blocked the sky and breezes that smelled of ocean salt. I longed for a friend to call while I was making supper, to stand over the stove stirring a good soup while she rattled on about her children's colds and the new dress she bought but hadn't shown her husband. I longed for ethnic restaurants and art galleries and Broadway shows. I longed for black faces and strange languages on the street and people in clothes as brilliant and fine as peacock feathers. And I held my tears like a stone under my heart.

And so we worked and the months passed. On a late October day my husband left early to drive the truck. I cleaned house and watered the few sprigs of lawn for the last time and ate my lunch on the back step. The afternoon stretched before me; I had finally worked myself out of work. The tips of my fingers tingled as I played the record of anxiety and loneliness over and over in my mind.

I wandered the farm. The air was cool and still, the sun a whisper of warmth at my neck. Elm leaves hung listlessly green, tired and ready to fall with the first cold snap and gust of wind. Along the ditch, the cottonwoods blazed golden. In the far distance a lone combine inched across the horizon, gobbling the landscape, spewing yellow kernels into the mouths of waiting trucks.

Down at the pens I climbed over a fence and stood among young pigs who gathered about, sniffing my pants legs, wagging their curly pink tails like so many fat puppies. I sat down on a bale of sweet fresh straw. The pigs scattered, then inched back. They chewed on my boot laces, nibbled my fingers, turned long-lashed brown eyes to gaze into my face.

Oh, Lord, I felt so tired of work and uncertainty, of every day facing something new. So, so tired.

In that moment something in me gave way; I stretched out in sweet fresh straw, turned my face toward the weak warmth of the lowering sun and cried. I wailed and sobbed and shook, alone among the pigs, until the stone under my heart melted and I slept.

When I woke, dozens of piglets were curled about me, nestled against my hips, tucked under my outspread arms, piled like a halo about my head. I lay still in the whisper of sleeping pigs and let new life flow into the place beneath my heart that those tears had left behind.

It has been almost nine years since that October afternoon. This is home now, with good friends and good work. Nothing ever stays the same. Winds of change can blow out of nowhere, as startling as a tornado from the trailing edge of a cloud. If storms carry us away I will miss this life as much as all the others. There are more dreams to follow. I will be his anchor and he will be my sail.

SUSAN AUSTIN Land and Bones

The snow drifts onto the roof on the north side of the cabin. The fire crackles hot. I plug the notebook computer into the two deep cycle batteries with an automobile adapter then sit in the big chair and put my feet up on the bed, so the winter air that rises between the floorboards doesn't chill my toes.

Two brothers, Karl and Miles, built this fourteen by twenty-eight foot cabin in 1906. The logs they hewed by hand. No family here to tell their stories. The last old-timer who knew the brothers talks about courting in the heart of winter on a horse-drawn sleigh. She sings, "Sleigh bells ring, are you list'nin'?" She says lips were too cold to form a kiss. Hard winters are what all the old-timers talk about.

Greg's mother knows of winter not so far from here. She comes from Dakota pioneers. In the winter of 1922, in Bathgate, North Dakota, her mother, Mary Jane McAulay, went next door to a ladies' party. A flurry of snow drifting like soft down feathers became a blizzard. Francis McAulay went out in the storm to help his Mary Jane home, leaving their three small children behind. He didn't know that Mary Jane was already on her way, guided by the picket fence that separated the two houses. Francis floundered for hours as snow lifted from old drifts and made new ones in his path.

Lost to the fence, to the house, and to Mary Jane, he vowed that if he got home and found his family safe, they would never spend another winter in North Dakota. The following year, before the days turned cold and the light dimmed early, Francis McAulay moved his family to Kelso, Washington.

I wonder sometimes what the brothers who built this cabin might have thought of my computer. Greg's mother said, "I'm almost sure they wouldn't have been envious." I don't think so either. The brothers carved a field and hewed a cabin and didn't ask for much more. They farmed with a horse-drawn plow long after motorized tractors tilled the neighbor's land. In 1954, when the horses were too old to work, and the brothers too old to train a new team, they bought a used '53 Ford tractor. They shortened the tongues and replaced the hitches on the drill. The new Ford pulled the old farm equipment through the soil. Sentinels now, the drills, their rust polished smooth by weather, stand at the edge of the fields alongside piles of hand-picked stone.

What am I envious of? I don't need flush toilets, electric lights, or a plowed road in winter. All things that do not exist at the old boys' cabin.

I'm envious of the brothers, of this land as they knew it. People ask, "What's the hardest part of living out here?" Acre by acre, season by season, realtor by realtor: "Watching it go," I answer.

Come, winter, when Greg and I are dwarfed by the mountains and a quarter section of deep snow fields, edged into the forest, I like to believe that only the weather can change the homestead, wear it to dust by wind and rain and snow. First the brittle chinking will fall out in places and the wind will bore wider holes. Then snow piles inside in drifts; rain seeps and blows through. The wood will rot and the cabin will become a marmot house, with straw and fuzz from our winter hats matted in mouse nests. The foundation may settle too much in a fast spring melt and the cabin will lean to the north, then topple by wind. Bare bones bleached and scattered, like the cow moose who lay down in the aspen grove, leaving last year's young to fend off winter-starved coyotes just two weeks before the snow eased. The calf was smart to leave the rot of its mother. Coyotes and ravens and one bald eagle finished her off, scattered the bones.

One winter I went to the outer banks of North Carolina to remind myself how the ocean eats up roads, clears and dumps sand where it pleases, untamed. When I was a child, I walked to the beach on toughened feet with tar babies smeared in patches on my soles. I usually brought something, towel or surfboard, dropped or dragged, catching on sea grass and dried fence slats. When I was this child, I knew the tide and the surf just by the sound of the waves. By their lazy roll or thunder as they broke at the wet sand and the ground shuddered under my tarred feet.

I have taken this new land into my bones. How did it happen? I walked a lot at first across the open fields, down along the gullies, the creek bottoms, into the woods. I watched, listened. Then a new sense seeped in. And one winter night I found my way home by the feel of the land.

I had driven to the end of the plowed road and parked next to the dovetailed pine granary. I was tired, and warm for a moment. I thought I would stay there, curled on the truck seat, and sleep. But the cold quickly chilled my blood. I lifted the pack to my back and gathered the energy I needed to ski the two and a half miles home.

Under a new moon, dense fog meeting snow, I skied into the colder air that settles in the creek bottom. I felt my way along the road, cut drifts that soften into low hills on either side. The sharp corner of the dugway reminded me of the etched curve of Greg's hip. Instead of hurrying to his warm covers, I lingered. The scent of moose lingered, too, on the still air. Coyotes sang. When the coyotes quieted, I heard the faint hoot of a great horned owl.

Across the flat upper field I wandered off track, circled the chicken coop and the dog's shed. Then I reached out into the fog and touched the sawdust and splinter chink and hand-hewn logs of the cabin. Out of absolute darkness I finally felt what the old boys must have known — the dips and contours and flat reaches, with no other guidance than the familiar sway of the land through their bones.

MARGARET M. BARNHART Ghosts

Memory is a wondrous salve. It softens the rough edges of life, highlights the pleasantries, and makes what was cramped and confining seem cozy. In my memory I see a place in eastern Montana that I used to call home.

Although it had once been an active town, by the time my husband and I came to Enid, all that remained were the post office and the elevator — and the ghosts of an earlier time.

I remember the good things — the patch of prairie roses that grew behind our trailer where flocks of grouse took shelter during winter storms. I remember the breathtaking, unobstructed sunsets; the startling, brilliant night skies; the sounds of coyotes and pheasant roosters. I remember the stock pond where we used to fish.

It is this romantic picture of life in Enid that my memory paints for me. This is the picture Pat and I share with our children. It is this picture I had in mind when I eagerly agreed to revisit Enid last summer. I wanted to encounter some of the ghosts of the early years of our marriage.

Though some things had changed a little, time seemed to rewind as we approached Enid's familiar landscape. We drove into the townsite and climbed out of the car. At once a feeling of dread came over me. A knot tightened in my stomach. I did indeed encounter a ghost — a most unhappy ghost of myself.

I remembered why, when we left Enid fourteen years ago, I never looked back. I remembered the oppressive, unshaded summer days that smelled of dust and hot sage. I remembered the pale sandy soil that seemed hostile to trees and flowers, the water in short supply, the unrelenting prairie wind that rumbled the tin roof of our too-tiny trailer season after season. I remembered long gray winters of isolation. I remembered the dust that crept under sills and the mice that cavorted fearlessly between walls and in cupboards. Most of all I remembered the lonely person I had been, my lack of self-fulfillment, my sense of futility.

I am not the same person I was when I lived in Enid, but I can never stay there again, even for a day. My unhappy ghost lives there, suffocating, and waiting to smother me.

BERTIE ROBBINS COX ⟵ Dirty Dishes

I used to be a dishwasher, amongst other things. Never ahead, never a rest, in the sink a dirty dish to wash.

Now I'm working in a coal mine. The money is a lot better, but the work is the same: never a rest, always a load to haul, a bump in the road to blade; turn around, it's there again, just like a dirty dish. Always a pile of dirt to doze over the berm. Turn around and start all over again.

It must be because the world is round and always rotating, just as life goes round and round always back to where you began.

JUNE BRANDER GILMAN ~ Horses I Claimed

I live alone on the small ranch my husband and I built in 1951, and have done so since his death in 1973. I love the solitude of the winter months; it gives me time to just sit and reminisce.

Although cattle are the focal point of my life today, and I take pride in my small herd of Black Angus cows, this has not always been the case. Horses played an important part in my early life, as a means of transportation, pleasure, and a way of earning a living. My thoughts now turn to those horses who were my very own — those I could claim, care for, love, and not let anyone else ride.

When I was eight or nine, I got my first horse of my very own. My older sisters captured her out of a band of wild horses that roamed the nearby hills and gave her to me. She was a little buckskin filly with a brown stripe down her back and a white dot on her forehead. I thought she was the prettiest thing on earth. I named her Foxie. I always rode bareback, as saddles were a luxury and definitely not for us kids.

In 1954 I obtained my favorite horse, favored perhaps because I was older, or because he was with me longer. From an Indian rancher I acquired a well-broke four-year-old of Arabian descent, a sorrel roan named Nicotine; the name proved appropriate as he added stimulation to my life.

He was a free spirit and did not like to be corralled; a trait I could relate to as neither do I like to feel fenced in. Nor could he be enticed by a bucket of grain; to catch him was to outwit him. However, once he was caught, we became as one entity.

He was my companion for over twenty years, and when the end came I did not replace him. If I had the power to turn back time to recapture happy moments, he would be one of the main reasons for doing so. I loved that horse.

The day is now beginning to wane, and the magical, mystical wrappings of winter still linger; tomorrow promises to be another day of unforgettable beauty. It is time to go check on the cows; calving is to commence soon, and I keep a close watch on them. Life is good!

AGNES WICH ~ Voices in the Wind

Not infrequently today, farmers and ranchers are considered "rapers" of the land. I think incredulously, *this* land?

This land — my husband's father's father, and still *his* father before him, settled on this land over one hundred years ago. He planted the trees, helped bring water from the mountains, building canals and ditches with horse-drawn equipment. He dug the well, built the buildings, the barns, and corrals with the sweat of his brow and the strength of his back, tilled the fields with teams of horses, and raised his family, eleven boys and a girl.

An interstate highway and a frontage road pass by the front yard now. The original gate site remains, but the old house is gone. "Why would anyone ever plant trees so close to the highway, so near the power lines?" new neighbors have haughtily asked. "They look so ugly the way the utility company has had to cut them back."

"Because," I reply wearily, but attempting patience, "when those trees were planted, there were no highways here — only a dirt road. There were no power lines then."

But before my explanation is complete, the subject has moved on to more current issues, the history lost to the wind.

TRUDY Z. WARDWELL ~ **Come Next Branding, I'm Leaving Town**

It was time to gather the cows that Mike cares for; time to separate and work the calves. Since the owner, a city fellah new to cows, bought them at sale barns last year, the calves had been coming all year and most were darn big. Now they needed to be ear tagged, castrated, and given shots.

Mike was in Denver all week but he called to say the owner had called some buddies to help brand — dudes. The men would come up Friday night to camp out and the owner would bring all the food. But just in case, I grilled three pounds of Italian sausages, put spaghetti sauce on to simmer, and cleaned the *casita*. Since we still haven't saved enough money to buy a stove, I cook with a microwave, crock pot, or electric fry pan, and just like in *Green Acres*, the fuses blow. It takes forever and nothing stays warm, but I figured the owner would probably take everyone out for steaks anyhow.

When Friday night came, Mike returned and the owner arrived, but no one else showed up. We finally ate. Then about 10:30 a truck drove in and three men walked into the *casita* to sleep. Next morning the owner brought in his groceries: eggs, sausage, a coffee cake, apples, one small package of turkey slices, same of bologna, bread, a carton of pop and one of beer. "Ohmygosh!" I thought and threw together anything I had on hand (not much). I sliced my sausages for sandwiches, and made salad, dough-nuts, coffee, but it was a poor excuse for a branding dinner, even for a small crew.

But when I drove to the corrals, trucks, horse trailers, vans, and cars were parked everywhere with entire families, even babies, watching the branding. Some drove four hours from Lamar or Sterling. Dudes outnumbered cowboys twenty to one and watchers outnumbered everybody. Mike and the one other cowboy stayed horseback — roping, heelin', and draggin' to the fire — or they'd have gotten branded and tagged, too. Two cowgirls tagged and gave shots. The owner asked me to take pictures but I couldn't see the calves for all the guys sprawled on top of them.

Finished by noon, the hungry, bruised, and bloodied bunch crowded around the tailgate, for a fat-free turkey slice, thirty calories, on bread. Lordy, but this was embarrassing! And when I packed up and left and glanced in my rear-view mirror, everyone was following me home! When we arrived one fellah asked, "What time's supper?"

Meanwhile, the owner had to go home to his baby-sitter. He didn't know about branding protocol, being brand new at the business. The protocol says: When a man's come to help you brand all day for no wages, the food and drink better make up for it. In fact, each outfit competes to set the finest table. So Mike and I hurried to Jennings to buy food. Then the two cowgirls, who had rounded up a grill, went to work frying up Rocky Mountain Oysters (real fresh) and hamburgers with beans. A crowd of kids and dogs sprawled on the kitchen floor, but we stepped over them and kept working. After supper we had fifteen people left to sleep over and feed breakfast in the morning — and us with no stove, a one-bedroom house, and no idea we were hosting a branding that weekend! Oh, it turned out fine, we got 'em all fed and they were swell folks, but next time I hear there's going to be a brandin', I'm leaving town.

NORMA DUPPLER ⬛ Adjustments

As a child, I grew up carrying a gun strapped to my leg when I rode horseback out to the far pastures to check cattle. Our family has dealt with rabies, blackleg, blizzards, drought, floods, and tornadoes. Our ranching/farming operation has been in the family well over a hundred years.

Our house is just across the river from an old Indian village, burial mounds are located on all corners of the farm, and a prehistoric rock calendar lies on a hill to the west. The Sheyenne River snakes through our property, and prehistoric people appreciated the area for the same reasons we do — water, trees, shelter, game, and rich soil.

I just moved back to the area after twenty-four years in other parts of the state as a student, teacher, and later as a reporter for the *Bismarck Tribune*. Now I am the emergency manager for Barnes County, which is a nontraditional role for a woman. I still give penicillin shots, chase cattle, and stick my arm up to the armpit into a cow to pull a calf, but I don't make my living from the land. I would love to be a farmer, but there is not enough economic opportunity.

Symptomatic of these tough economic times, my husband lives in Fargo, where his job is, while I live on the ranch with my kids, my elderly uncles, and my father to be close to my job. We get together on weekends. These arrangements, or commutes rivaling the two-hour one-way trips to work in California, are becoming more and more common so people who adore this state can continue to live here.

My son is falling in love with the land, but all except five hundred acres will go to my cousins, so our ties will be broken in another ten years or so. He wouldn't be able to make a living on such a small acreage. It's sad, but we'll have to adjust.

ROBERTA Z. CROUSE   If I Had This Ranch I'd . . .

An unknowing guest once said: "If I had this ranch, I would do nothing but sit under these big cottonwood trees from morning to night and drink in the view." I tightened my jaw and said sweetly: "Yes, that's the nice thing about ranching. One is one's own boss. You just get some good cows and let them have those cute little calves. Then sell the calves in the fall and make a lot of money!" To myself I muttered, "Lady, if I can find five minutes to sit under these trees, with nothing to do, I wonder when it is!"

Or she might say: "If I had this ranch I'd do nothing but ride horseback all day." I'd said, "Oh, yes, that's what I do. It's so much fun!" To myself I grumbled, "There's nothing fun about riding all day. Especially if it means pushing those bawling cows over Centennial Mountain with mosquitoes playing hide and seek all over my arms and neck. The calves try to return to the ranch, or they hide in the aspen." It takes a good rider to push them ever onward and upward to the Medicine Bow Forest where we once had summer pasture. My husband didn't mind it so much, as he had become an expert rider as a child, but I . . . I'll admit that I wasn't a top horsewoman. I had never learned to ride as a child because my father had a "thing" about his kids and horses. He had witnessed the death of a child dragged by a horse and he would not have a saddle horse on our farm. We had two stalwart work horses, big, gentle creatures, but not suitable for riding. I was a social rider, only, when I could go at my own pace and at my own time. Just let George say, "Roberta, kick that nag into gear and get around those cows. Hurry now, or you won't get them." I would try, but I wasn't very helpful.

Being a ranch wife seems to have changed my viewpoint in many ways. It has left its mark on me and I sometimes feel that I am not at all the same person who started in this rough and risky game some forty-eight years ago.

I sit down by a lively, chattering brook with nothing in my mind but to enjoy the murmuring of nature and instantly I begin to assess the c.f.s.(cubic feet per second) flow of an innocent little stream. How many acre feet of water would it supply to thirsty soil? And who has the prior rights upon it? Is the land through which it passes the land that it moistens? Or does someone far down the line claim its precious gift? Impatiently I jerk myself into control and try to view it with the eye of an artist. My eyes follow the velvet green of grasses and plants that border the creek. Beautiful, so lush and verdant. Sure would be fine feed for our cattle. I can't even look at grass unless it is in terms of feed for cattle or horses.

I can't even drive by a meadow in summer and just admire the cattle I see grazing so peacefully. No, I must study each cow and calf and wonder how heavy the calf, how productive the mother, and just what margin of profit the rancher will realize from this pair in the year's tally. Novices to the ranching game see something quite different. They see an easy cycle of nature where cows have calves and ranchers take the money to the bank. I see, instead, days of hard labor feeding this cow in severe winter weather, hours of watchfulness so that her calf arrives alive, and months of protective care to ensure a husky, salable calf in the fall. I know that there really was nothing easy about it.

I study the turf of the meadow. Is the rancher overgrazing? Are his ditches placed to advantage for irrigation? Is that tawny quarter horse near the fence well broken? Will he come at a whistle, or will he dash madly to the far end of the pasture when his owner tries to catch him? Is he easy to ride or a backbreaker? Ah, but he is gorgeous. That should be enough, but it isn't!

Perhaps it would be nice, just once in a while, to again see things as they seem to be, rather than as I see them now, as they are.

One vow I have made: I will never, ever, say to myself or others, "*If I had a ranch, I'd . . .*" because, actually, that wouldn't be what I'd do at all.

PATRICIA ARCHIE   To Leave This Place

Cassidy, nearly eight, stands, hands on hips, looking up at me in disbelief. "Grandma, are you and Granddad going to live here for the rest of your *lives?*"

"Well, I certainly hope so, honey!" I answer. Satisfied for now, she runs off to play, leaving my thoughts swirling.

Leave this place? God willing, not for a long time yet. But I remember a time when we would have left it in a heartbeat.

We moved to our ranch in 1957, a good place, with two creeks running through it and plenty of meadows and shelter. We slowly built a small herd of cattle. Then came 1965. Half of our calf crop died. Then the rains came.

Horseshoe, the beautiful creek that flows across the base of the slope just one hundred yards in front of our house, was already full, as was North Horseshoe, the tributary upstream from our buildings. The ground was saturated with snow melt, and snow still lay deep in the mountains.

During heavy spring rains, Horseshoe oozed slowly out of its banks. We moved the dairy calves and the horses from the barn to higher ground. When the waters receded, we returned the stock to the barn. We weren't too concerned — the slowly rising waters never seemed a real threat.

By Monday, June 14, we had gotten twelve inches of rain in a month. Storm clouds roared in that afternoon, dropping hailstones the size of tennis balls and three more inches of rain.

We were preparing supper when I heard a roar outside and ran to the window. Water was already up to the front of the barn, about sixty yards from the house. I screamed for Lewis. "Omigod!" he breathed, and ran for the barn. Heart galloping, I picked up the phone to warn neighbors downstream. It was dead. Needing desperately to do something, I brought the children's bikes onto the front porch from the yard.

I ran to the yard gate and clutched the pickets, watching a wall of water and debris ten feet high, pushing like a live thing at the pole gate by the corner of the barn.

I screamed at Lewis, but he couldn't hear me. He drove two horses out on the slope toward the house, but Sleepy trembled at the barn door. Lewis, inside the barn, couldn't see that the water was up to the horse's knees. He doubled up a strap, and Sleepy snorted and lunged over the water.

When Lewis came out, I screamed, "Stay back!" but the wall of water broke through the gate and swept him down around the corner of the barn.

I was terrified he wasn't going to make it. I sobbed to the children standing wide-eyed at the doorstep, "Pray for Daddy!" I said. They started to cry before we saw Lewis waving from the hayloft door. I ran out as far as I dared, and heard him yell, "Get the camera and take some pictures!"

I laughed, giddy with relief. While I snapped pictures from the front yard, the children gathered hailstones for the freezer.

A cold fog descended, smelling of fish and muddy water. Down the creek, live trees floated, heavy root ends bumping and twirling, leafy canopies graceful.

We shouted back and forth from the house to the hayloft while the water streamed between us. Lewis indicated he had grabbed for the corral gate, the only strip of fence left, when the water washed him around the barn. Somehow he had crawled through a tiny side window to take refuge with the calves he'd carried to the hayloft earlier.

In about an hour, the water had receded enough for Lewis to come down. He carefully waded to the yard, where we all hugged and cried.

During the next few days, we counted our losses. We were on the wrong side of the creek from town and most neighbors, our electricity and telephone gone. We placed rocks and built a campfire outside for all our meals. The children loved the constant "picnic."

But we had lost our bridge, all our corrals, most fences, dams and ditches, a tractor, and cattle. The cows had run for the shelter of the trees along the creek to get out of the hail, and when the water came, they were trapped. We found many still standing, pushed against trees with logs jammed against them. We lost half of the calves we had left, and two of our three bulls. The whole creek bottom reeked of rotting animals for weeks.

Then one day, after the creek had gone down enough so neighbors could come to help, the men pulled a dead heifer from the trees downstream of the barn. I saw that she had been carried in the surge of water between the barn and the house, and realized that that could have been Lewis's fate. Remembering how lucky we really were, we began to count our blessings.

We grafted the dairy calves saved in the barn onto the poor numb creatures who had lost their calves. They offered no resistance to their new babies. They didn't even chew their cuds. They looked as if they had been chopped with an ax.

Lewis walked out to the big meadow to the west of the house, and found the hay ground was so covered with silt and flood trash, he felt it could never be cleaned up. He said, "If someone offered me fifty cents an acre for this place right now, I'd take it!" Fortunately, no one did. The rains of the next few days washed the silt down, and the hay grew as never before. We all pitched in to clean up the debris, and eventually we put up hay there again.

As for me, I was afraid to let my family out of my sight. We had lost many *things*. We must not lose each other. For a long time afterward, I would awaken to the sound of wind in the trees and think for a minute it was the roar of floodwaters. I still occasionally dream of water washing up on our front porch, which it never actually did. But in my dream it sloshes around and takes children's toys away, changing things forever. It wasn't water that did that — it was time.

The years flashed by as the children grew from toddlers to proud beginning drivers, trying unsuccessfully to hold back grins, to horseback teenagers. My memories are made of those days, and the unexpected poetry in the soul of my cowboy husband as he described the way frozen raindrops on a snowy doorstep looked "like a dappled horse," or the way red and black cows winding down a mountain trail looked "like beads on a string."

We didn't like floods or blizzards, but the struggle and the challenge of building something together, overcoming hardships — that's what makes life worthwhile. Now our grandchildren are coming back, and everything is exciting and new — for us and for them. No other place will hold those memories for us.

So when Cassidy asks if we are going to live here the rest of our lives, I can only say, "I certainly hope so." To leave this place would be to leave thirty-six years of ourselves behind. This place, yes, even the flooding creek, has been our life, and what a good one it has been. And what a good one it still is.

SUE CHAULK ✎ *Grave Gear*

Pad
Pencil
Copy of Bridgeport *Newsblade*
so I won't get bored.
Gallon of milk replacer
in case I meet some orphan calves.
A syringe
for the sick.

Kleenex
Chapstick
Headphone and batteries
I may not get to heaven I
might take a left turn and
end up in the hayfield
oops I mean hell.

Hooded sweatshirt
Two pair of socks
A night-light
for warmth and protection.
A bucket and rags to keep things neat.

My temper
My scarred heart
Pebbles from the Platte River
Cup of sand
Sprig of sage
so they will recognize me
and let me in.

SUE A. MORRELL   *Of Seed Catalogs and Spirituality*

In the early, almost hopeless times, when winter seems to have a firm grip on the prairie, the seed catalogs arrive, announcing spring, a pronouncement that the world will go on. I pull my chair close to the warmth of the fire grate, and those catalogs become an elaborate fiction, a dream of warm sun and spring seedlings.

The repetitious phrases within the pages read like a prayer. Those litanies appeal to my sense of who I am among the other women in my family. Words like "hardy," "northern-grown," and "heavy bearing" could be used as aptly to describe my mother, my grandmothers, and myself as they are used to describe trees and plants. Paging through the seed catalogs is a ritual that touches my past and its strong roots and expresses my hopes for my daughter's life.

Leafing through the pages of seed catalogs is also a spiritual ritual, the preliminary preparation to turning the earth, to opening and coaxing forth the deep inside. To open a catalog and dream, to turn the earth to seed, is a prayer of humility, reminding me of my duty to make something good of this space in which I live.

Seed catalogs also represent to me a tool of one of my many arts — rich artistic adventure. Like a painter who envisions a work on canvas, I see the garden, its perimeters, its shape, its substance. I sketch the rows and beds, erase and toss aside several plans before I settle on one.

The vision of that space in my head, for all its scientific accuracy, *never* becomes the real garden. Even when my plans are most specific and artistic, I realize I will turn this plan over to a Higher Power.

I am prepared for the best; I am prepared likewise for the worst. Nothing is so convincing of the frailty of human effort as putting seed into the ground.

Aside from the spiritual, an undeniable part of my need to garden is physical. I am proud that my sweat is irretrievably mixed with the tough prairie clay I mold into a garden.

By August, the seed catalogs are long abandoned to the mulch pile or the trash burner. The artistic vision is clouded by the very detail and depth that once promised so much. Now, labor is all. My muscles are weary. The careful plans of spring are sprawled with pumpkin and squash vines and tomato plants gone awry. My fingers are stained and my knuckles are nicked and red-raw. When the frost finally does come, I say, "Good."

But I don't say it too loudly. That would not be good sense.

The gardening experience becomes elusively seductive again in deep winter, when my memory is clouded. If God in Her infinite wisdom has any generosity, I will be lucky. The asparagus beds, hedge roses, and fruit trees I tend today may be here for generations to come.

From paging through seed catalogs to that first rich turn of the earth; from awed delight at the first green seedlings to impatient fatigue with the last ear of popcorn, my garden and I come full circle each year. It is all hard, rewarding work. As it should be.

CHERYL ARENDS **The Harvest Is Subject to the Weather**

I scratch the back of the earth
through thick inches of dust,
nesting each plant upon its bosom
as you once did me, hoping to somehow
make it all right, to pacify you,
Mother, for my not being perfect,
for me not turning out all right.

Year after year my hoe ruffles through
the loose garden dirt, against each weed
that tugs to live despite my onslaught for order.
I leave its roots to wither in sunlight
the way I fear you will leave me.

I mound the earth around tender stems
of cabbage, heap the mulch,
cover every inch of the corn patch
with hoe, fertilizer, water from my brow
to guarantee growth, failure only in hailstones
always a hailstone failure possible,
the sudden fierce uncontrollable storm
of revelations rolling in on green clouds
of guilt and fear, truth spilling in the downpour.

Even then I know not to disturb the plants,
that maybe some will recover,
will come back if I
resist trying to heal them, resist saying
too much, the results out of my hands
at last.

I sift through the soil for myself,
look beneath the fragile crust
to darker damp soil, let in air, drought,
look for growth, acceptance of myself

by me, by you, Mother,
each row straight, weed free, clean
as I'd like my conscience to be.

RUTH SCHUBARTH ✒ *Born Backwards*

I was born looking backwards. To my mother's chagrin, I believe my heart was born in the South Dakota prairies, though she birthed me in Denver. While the rest of the country was looking to the new decade of the sixties, I grew up wanting to save old bottles, collect rocks, learn quilting, and contemplate covering my hair. My mother, moving to California, can only see what is in front of her. She is a modern woman. I am a modern pioneer.

When I was a child, we lived in White River, South Dakota, a town of five hundred in the center of the Rosebud (Lakota) Reservation. We stayed there until I was seven.

Now I am grown and I have come back to the country. After high school in New Jersey, college in Chicago, a volunteer stint in a Thailand refugee camp, and perfunctory post-college waitressing jobs, I married Larry because of the poetry of his vision, and also because I was pregnant. I have brought my family back to the prairie. I look for the yuccas and the wide sky to give me back the confidence and trusting of youth; I look into the eyes of my children to see my confidence, transferred, growing there. At times my heart is full, while my hands grasp empty air. Other times all I find are cow pies. Most of the time I am honestly too busy (read: hard at work) for any of it to matter.

Here in Colorado's high plains I see nothing but cattle, sandstone bluffs, and four or five other homes and barns as far north-east-south as the eye can see. Antelope visit, coyotes howl, quail covey close by, jackrabbits, snakes, meadowlarks, and lark buntings — the state bird — are all abundant.

My husband is a beekeeper. We keep fifty or so beehives on five local farms. We are close enough to town to market our honey, but we also keep a sign on the highway in season: HONEY FOR SALE, 2 MI. SOUTH. Larry also works at a large hog operation just down the road. Sixty-hour weeks keep him away from home, but he's in charge of the nursery and farrowing, so his days are almost as exciting as mine, keeping up with our brood here at home.

We have five kids: Ruedi, seven; Willo, five; Evan, four; Abe, two; and Phoebe, one. We are starting to home-school.

Our first summer here, I fell in love with a couple of dairy goats at the county fair. I gathered funds till the following spring and put up a pole-barn — actually more of a pole-hut — then we bartered beehives for our first two goats.

We're a pretty efficient little homestead. Larry and his bees produce one to three tons of honey per year; the family uses about two hundred fifty pounds. His job at the hog barn provides all the pork we can eat. I milk the goats and put wethers (the castrated bucklings) in the freezer with ducks, chickens, rabbits, and lambs. I gather eggs and make vinegar cheese and whey cheese with summertime-surplus milk. I churn our butter with a blender and make our ice cream; I bake seven loaves of bread weekly. We use cloth diapers. We don't use the television or read a newspaper and often do without radio. Larry hunts in the fall, sometimes using a black powder muzzle-loader he crafted himself. On any night one of the boys might ask, "Which kind of meat is this?" and the answer might be one of ten or so: goat, lamb, rabbit, chicken, duck, cow, pig, elk, antelope, deer.

On the cover of one of my quilt books is a design in shades of brown with some accents in surprising blues. This quilt is my life. Five years ago, if I'd planned out a quilt for myself, I would have purchased fifty dollars' worth of wonderfully incredible deeply coordinating colors in shiny new fabric, as well as a new quilting frame and daycare for my children for a month so I could make an absolutely perfect quilt. But *this* quilt breaks all those rules. It's a *wonderful* quilt, but it wasn't planned; it happened. Nothing matches, no one block is repeated, everything about it is unexpected, and do you know what? I can't take my eyes off it. Quiet, but vibrant. It is the colors of my home. I love to look at this quilt, and every time I do, I see something I never saw before.

And so it is with my life. I feel most like a pioneer farm woman in jeans and comfortable shoes, sleeves rolled up and hair in a braid, walking easily from milking to baking, from mucking to hugging; walking easily, walking slowly, walking wisely, walking well. (It's a prairie walk, you know?) It's not found in the Bible to dress like that, but my heart doesn't feel like it's lying when I do.

TWYLA HANSEN   Instinct

Because it's spring and because
the sap rises steadily, so rises
today the farmer in me. The
outdoor beckons, renewal burns
in my veins this first warm
weekend. So strong is the
calling, I become the straw-hat

madwoman, mowing, chopping,
whacking the acreage with a
coarse-tooth rake. Out of my
way, the dog whimpers under a
tree, birds retreat to the
distant grove, squirrels blink.
Because it's spring and because
it's time, I till, gather, glean,
prepare to nest again
yet another season.

ELEANORE GARREAU   A Place Called Home

When my sister in Eagle Butte was having a baby and I was sent to help her,
I met my husband. A friend and I went to the drugstore for a magazine and
I saw a handsome Indian man sitting staring at me. I could tell that he liked
me. He asked me to go to a movie and I went and, of course, I knew that
I liked him. We weren't your ordinary couple, I was a full-blooded Irish
woman and he was a nearly full-blooded Sioux (Lakota) Indian. Some
people did try to talk me out of pursuing this relationship. I guess they
thought that the cultural differences would be too great and we wouldn't
last. Well, I didn't pay any attention to their words of warning and Sylvester
Garreau and I were married on July 24, 1937. We remained married until his
death on March 18, 1982. We had a full life living on the prairie. I guess we
showed people who thought it would never last! That's not to say there
weren't differences, but that's another story.

My husband and I eventually bought the place where I was born and
started our own cattle operation on the prairie. Since my husband's death I
have been continuing on with my cattle. Selling out and moving to town
wasn't for me. After my husband's death I was scared. I kept wondering if I
could do this and make a success of it. The choice was taken away from me
because I had debts to pay and I couldn't quit just because I was scared. I
think the prairie teaches one to be courageous. You learn courage over time
because sometimes the prairie can be an unrelenting and demanding place
to live. Before my husband passed away he kept telling me I could do it. He
was supportive of me and must have known that I knew a thing or two
about ranching. Well, he had more faith in me than I had in myself. Eleven
years after his death I'm still ranching. I managed to pay out on my debts
and I'm proud of that. I didn't do it alone. I have a deep faith in God and I
know that He helped me. I also have wonderful friends, family, and neigh-
bors who helped me.

As I write this I am in the midst of calving season. I am tired! If any of you have calved out heifers and your older cows, you know what I'm talking about. I could live without checking heifers every two hours during the night and day, but especially during the night. I know that to save every calf possible means success, but I'm glad when it's over. Raising animals on the prairie isn't always easy.

Being a ranch woman gives me a real sense of pride. I can look out over my small herd and I am so proud of my cows. Then, when other people notice and comment on how good my cows look, it makes me feel so good. It makes me feel like all of my hard work was worth it.

Living on the prairie, there's no other life like it. This is the only place for me to live. The prairie has taught me a lot and offered me a bountiful living. I am very honored to call this place home.

LUCY C. MEYRING ⚞ Ranching — In My Blood

I knew little about mountain terrain when I moved to Colorado and married Danny. One spring, during calving, I went into town for groceries and lime for the calving shed. As we live up on top of a hill (in the same house Danny was raised), I pulled up to the gate to unload groceries, leaving the pickup sitting on the hillside. I went on out to the calving shed and, realizing I needed some vaccine, went back to the house. Just as I got close to the house, I saw the pickup going off down the hill. I thought to myself, "I wonder where someone is going in the pickup?" Then I saw there wasn't anyone in the pickup and I ran, trying to catch it, but it caught up to the bunkhouse first, taking out the walls! Suddenly the door flew open and a man stood there in his long johns, eyes the size of saucers. I merely looked at him on my way to the pickup and shrugged my shoulders. The guy thought an earthquake had struck; the collision jolted the entire building, knocking things off the walls. That's how I learned that if the emergency brake doesn't work, always, *always* leave the vehicle in low gear, not in third!

We still feed with horses. Every morning through the winter we hitch ten to twelve head of big Percheron draft horses. Danny uses a six-horse hitch when the snow cover makes it a hardship to get around. One winter, I graduated from driving a four-up to his six-horse hitch. Quite an experience to have all that power, and learning to handle the lines and pull slack! These power machines are gentle giants. Their feet are about the size of dinner plates and you certainly don't want one of them to step on your foot! The teams all have names, Pat and Duke, Hank and Frank, Pride and Joy, Claude and Maude, and so on. They all know their names and are trained with voice commands.

We believe in hard work. I think of an older woman I befriended in

Dakota. One day, we were sitting at her small kitchen table visiting, and I said something about how dreadful my hands looked and immediately laid them in my lap under the table. She reached over and pulled them back up on the table and, running her small, frail fingers over my rough and callused hands, said, "Lucy, never be ashamed of these hands — they show you know how to work — be proud of that."

I've heard it said that this country is hell on horses and women, and it is no land for a lady. I look around me at other women in the area and at times, to be truthful, I envy them. There are very few women who are out day to day, all day, doing the things I do: breaking horses, feeding cows, calving, haying. Not having had a family, I missed out on the "luxury" of being a housewife, of being able to take care of a house and family full-time, of being able to pursue my own little projects and hobbies. Consequently, when I am old and unable to continue leading my active lifestyle, I will have to learn to do the things most women my age already know how to do, such as needlework and crafts. I just ask that God grants me good eyesight and the use of my hands!

I do have a few things over so many women, however. One is being a working partner with my husband. I have actually had people ask me, "How can you two be with each other twenty-four hours a day, seven days a week, and still like each other?" The answer is, we depend on each other. We are each other's greatest strength. Together we run this ranch, and run it efficiently and well. We discuss every major decision and decide together what and how we should do something. Ours is truly a working partnership.

Yes, ranching is a hard life. Sometimes I come in so bone tired and weary, I could literally sit down and cry. We give a lot of ranch tours to people from all over the country and the world. One beautiful summer day while giving a tour to a group of Europeans, one made the comment, "How romantic, all you have to do is ride around on a horse in this beautiful country all day." One of our hired men was standing there and he said, "Yes, and you should follow her around when it's fifteen degrees below zero with a cold wind blowing during calving." I was grateful he could see and realize what all is involved in what I do. I'm in charge of around two hundred fifty head of first- and second-calf heifers and cows.

Riding and starting colts has always been a great joy to me. Calving is a wonderful time to get a colt going. Colts learn patience with me constantly getting on and off, having to track cows. Weaving in and out of pairs makes colts light and responsive. We had one roan mare here at the ranch named Pinky who always had colts that were a handful to break. I have gotten broken up more off that line of horses than any I've ever ridden. Believe me, it's true that the older you get the harder the ground gets, and injuries don't heal as fast. One spring, one of Pinky's colts, a big, good-looking, easy-moving red roan, "boogered" and reared, coming over backwards. I knew he was coming on over so I jumped clear, but not before he hit me in the head with his head, breaking my glasses and cutting a gash under my left eye. I got up, never realizing my glasses were gone, got back on him and proceeded to take the heifer in. It was past lunchtime and when I got in the house, Danny took one look at me and shook his head — my face was all swollen, dried blood streaked it and my eye was turning black. A few days later, while I was riding the same colt, checking for new pairs, the wind in some willow bushes scared him and he used it as an excuse to whirl and stampede. Off he went in high gear till he fell in a badger hole, throwing me into a willow stump. I came out with a gash on the right side of my face and another black eye.

The joy of my life is having a good horse between my legs and a dog at my heels, feeling the warmth of the sun on my back, and smelling the earth after a spring rain. I look back at pictures in my family photo album and I realize that I'm merely part of another generation to live this life. One day, someone will take my place.

Things have changed so much in the last fifty years. My hope is that ranching, as a way of life, will continue. Just in the years I have lived here in North Park, I have seen a great change. I've seen several family operations sell to outside "money people." These outfits are managed and run so differently than those of us who have to make our living off what we produce manage our own. We become efficient because we can't fall back on outside money to subsidize us when we fall short.

TAMMY HANSEN GILBERT ~~~ You Live Where?

Oh, that poor woman at the JCPenney catalog ordering complex. Such a traumatic experience. And her first day, too. Her first lesson in "Do I go by the book, or do I retain my sanity?"

I suppose I shouldn't be so tough on the sheltered city person who took my order. I suppose if I had never lived in the country, maybe I would have trouble comprehending rural addresses and directions, too, but I like to think that the lack of street names and house numbers wouldn't send me into locational hysterics and directional chaos. This poor woman was convinced that no one would be able to find me — ever. And that if I had any misguided hopes that an item of clothing could actually be delivered to me, then I must be a bit soft in the skull.

My attempts to convince her that I'd actually seen the UPS man in my dusty rural driveway only weeks prior simply convinced her that I was delusional. *Then* she told me that in order for UPS to deliver to me, she is required to supply directions. No company had ever required this before but I tried one more time to tell her that the local UPS driver was familiar with this territory; he makes deliveries to my neighbors and myself frequently.

She actually chuckled. She firmly requested the directions again. So I told her.

I heard noises in the background that sounded a lot like a Tylenol bottle opening and then someone swallowing. Then she sighed, attempted to collect herself, and said, "I only have twenty-two spaces on my screen to use for directions." You could hear a scream building in her voice.

The way she reacted you would think I said something along the lines of: "Go north until you see a lake on the east side of the road that's wider than the second lake you came across after leaving town, and then go east until you have bounced across eighty-seven gopher holes, then turn left at the large cottonwood and proceed south to the skyline." Just when she was on the verge of offering me her one and only day's pay for gas money to drive to the nearest catalog outlet so she wouldn't have to type in any directions, we reached an agreement. I agreed to supply her with twenty-two-space directions, if she would agree not to take any more calls from rural areas.

Several different sets of brief directions using twenty-two spaces or less flashed through my mind: "middle of the country"; "8 trees east of WY"; "9,786 cows N of N.P."; or "ask somebody nearby."

I knew without asking that she wouldn't accept "right here, nitwit" or "UPS already knows."

When the package came, there in the corner of the label were the directions (really): 30M N H60 MM188 E 16M. It's a good thing UPS already knew where to find me.

LAURA OSADCHY ～ Call Me Doc

It was springtime in our hilly ranch country, and that meant calving was in full swing; also, grain seeding was underway. Some cows pick a secluded spot in a far corner of the pasture to give birth. This time, a black Holstein cross who had lost her calf refused to get up. Seems she had a partial paralysis in the hind leg — a pinched nerve, or something. It became my job to tend to her needs daily. This meant carrying a pail of oats three-fourths of a mile, then dipping water from a nearby slough. The cow lay near the alfalfa fence line as she maneuvered herself around on her tummy trying to get up. A couple of trips a day and a couple of days later, with no apparent improvement in her condition, I'd about had it. Disgusted with her, I gave her a push on the hip with my foot. She swung around as if to attack me. No doubt I hit on her sore spot.

The weather was getting quite warm and I was tiring of the daily trek, so I told my husband, "Shoot her and put her out of her misery. She won't get any better." One last time I trudged out with my pail of oats — but no cow! Now, how far could she go, and under the fence, too, in her condition? About one-fourth of a mile over a slope, as I approached a grove of trees, there she stood in the shade, grazing contentedly.

Come roundup day, seemingly cured, she galloped home along with the rest of the herd. My chiropractic foot action must have been all she needed to recuperate. Just call me "Doc."

MARY ANN HAUGEN ~ **Unconditional Guarantee**

Late afternoon sun warms my shoulders and relaxes some pent-up tension.

Swing hoe, up-down; slay weeds, up-down. Muscles grunt in surprise; weeks have passed since their last such workout. Dig out creeping Jenny. Roots break off in my hand, jeering a prediction of new growth to come. Chop, pull, toss. What the heck do they call this stuff? The way it grows, it could easily feed starving multitudes. Chop, yank. Uh-oh, too close to the pea roots.

There's just enough breeze to discourage horse flies and mosquitoes, to dry sweat from my neck and back. The moist soil gives up intruders easily; nourishment will be conserved for carefully planted stalks and roots. I find myself continually amazed by the miracle of growth, especially in this month of adequate rainfall. How did dried-up seeds create these huge zucchini leaves, or tiny, fragile cabbage sprouts explode into heavy spheres? All the intricate mechanisms of life cycles that fit together so well boggle my mind on a midsummer day.

The Care Center called earlier. My mother's only sister, an elderly lady, is deteriorating in body as she already has in mind. I'll take her to the doctor tomorrow for tests, hoping that she can be stabilized one more time, while not wanting to subject her to useless discomfort and indignity.

Her health was so precarious as a child that she wasn't expected to reach adulthood, yet she's lived on this earth eighty-three years, longer than her husband, sister, brothers, or their spouses. She's lived with good humor and calm acceptance of the frailty of life. Now she hardly knows me but often calls for my dead mother, and prays aloud that things will be better.

Weed strawberries. Not a good crop; think about a new bed for next year. I straighten up, jutting knees forward to accommodate a protesting back. Rest a moment. My gaze sweeps across the yard beyond the garden and focuses on an ash tree planted early this spring to replace the majestic cottonwood felled last winter. About twelve feet tall, the ash had a root system that would fit into a coffee can. Associate-in-wedlock frowned as he packed dirt into the hole around it and declared its chance of survival slim to none.

"Well," I comforted, "it's fully guaranteed. If it dies, they give total replacement."

We watered it heavily. As the other trees in the grove leafed out, including a linden we had purchased at the same time, the scrawny ash remained naked. More water. When the lilacs blossomed and bees hummed among thick caragana foliage, it still showed no signs of life. I quit watering and pronounced, "It's stone dead. Not a bud anywhere," and thereafter ignored it.

Then, on one of the few hot days we've had so far, I was walking up the drive and stopped in amazement. Tiny green leaves were appearing on the ash tree. Life was surging up the narrow trunk and breaking out of wispy limbs. Son of a gun. It was alive! Today I watch the leafy branches bow in the wind as if accepting applause from neighboring apple and plum trees and I smile, pleased as always when an underdog comes through.

It occurs to me, standing in the soft garden dirt, that maybe my aunt will be like that. Maybe she'll make another comeback and fool us all. Perhaps I'll still see the light of recognition in her eyes and share stories of our past as she sits comfortably in the recliner by her window. But maybe not. Her body may simply be too tired of fighting. And that would be all right, too, because she's been ready for a new adventure for quite a while.

After all, she has an unconditional guarantee. Of total replacement.

BOBBIE SAUNDERS ⟍ February Evening

The silent
sky
is
devoured
by thin-lipped
trees,
branches
intertwined
like tinderbox
hair,
bodies
of bark
grey
and misunderstood,
awaiting

confirmation
of yet
another
early
spring.

FLORENCE M. NEWSOM ⬤ They Cleaned Us Out

The bankers knew what was coming so by 1928 they began to call in loans. Our cows, horses, and machinery were mortgaged with the bank in town. Pa had tried to get ahead too fast and had borrowed money, often helping out his brother as well. At first Dad borrowed from his folks to get the stallion, Garni, and the Rumley tractor. He began to lose things in 1917, the year my oldest sister was born. They were short of food and burned only wood for heat. Grandpa Kennedy stayed with them and he lost the homestead to a loan company in Iowa. Ma said it was the worst year she had. The other bank held us kids' Liberty bonds; they went when the bank closed.

One day a man came with a truck. He loaded the milk herd up and took them to the stockyard. It was heartbreaking to see those cows go. Now we were down to twelve milk cows, a few heifers, and some calves, increase from the cows. They also had to sell the old work team, another team, the saddle horse and Dad's pony and her colt, and a race horse, leaving us the team of white mares. We began over. Dad was over forty with a wife and four kids, no job, no money, nothing but his two hands and the know-how of carpentry, machine repairing, concrete work — he was a good jack-of-all-trades. He traded the kicker cow for a roan cow that we kids could milk, her two-year-old heifer, and a baby calf.

Step by step we rebuilt, Dad doing any job he could get. I herded cows, raised chickens, and had a big garden. After I got on the National Youth Administration program, I bought a pressure canner and my bird book. Now I had a reference book for my writing on nature subjects and made enough for my own living. I sold a story and got a nice blanket I still have. Another story brought sixty dollars. I had good use of it and that story is still quoted today — "A Summer Evening" in *Dakota Farmer* in the 1950s. A yellowed copy was found in Mother's clippings. Just one of hundreds that I wrote. I realized that I needed to type, so a minister gave me an old battered Underwood and I taught myself to use it. I was a poor typist, mostly three fingers. A white piece of paper is a challenge; it has to have words on it.

After more than sixty years, we have made a comeback; I bought a heifer calf, an offspring of one of the first cows the folks had so long ago, Old Roanie. Now, ten cattle generations later, a heifer will calve this spring, a direct descendant of Old Roanie.

KATHLEENE WEST ⟍ Martin Luther's Children

Let it begin with the land, land patterned with field and pasture and a gravel road curving from farm to farm. A half-mile out of town, the road breaks from the blacktop and heads west. Winter winds drift it shut with snow, the spring melt transforms it into a narrow slough any hog would sigh to wallow in, and in July county trucks dump down its center a six-inch layer of gravel that pulls and sucks with the treachery of quicksand. Curve with the road over the Beaver River, the Skeedee Creek to a farm where the cornfields press the outbuildings on three sides. How are the crops this year? Is the corn bleached and dry or choked with sludge from the rain that pushed the creek over its bank? Who works this land where weather creases faces with lines deeper than time? Sun, wind, flood, and drought deliver their legacy of dust and mud to the people of the plains. Let it begin with them, born of the earth, marked by the earth.

Did they choose this place or did the land choose them? The Mormons gone to greener pastures, the Skidi and the rest of the Pawnee pushed away, the trading post and the old grist mill closed down, but the Union Pacific inspires a town and people to farm the land. These plains people are descendants of Scandinavian fisherfolk and peasants who followed no glamorous dream to America but hoped for something to live on, something to own. The surveyed acres hold them in the cycles of plants, growth, and harvest. This is the land of farmers and their children.

Let it begin with a woman born a hundred miles from the center of the country, so close to the heart she will always feel its beat within her skin. Her first memories are of fear and disappointment, and the love that prompts both. "Watch out," Mother says. Awakened from sleep on Grandfather's couch, she takes care not to step on the newspaper spread on the floor where Grandpa spits his snoose. Is it a nickel Grandpa hands down to her or a penny? "You're too young to go. Stay home with Nick." After the funeral, they find her on her hands and knees, trying to lure a black and white kitty out from under the barn. Mother lures her away from the cat with a cherry mash from the farmers' store. When she is older they will tell her the fluffy animal she relinquished was a skunk.

There is so much to learn. Who am I — and why am I here? Grandpa sailed to America on a one-way passage to collect a debt, and the country collected him. Back from California, with a piece of fool's gold and enough money to buy a farm — why not three hundred miles farther east in the rich Iowa loam, her brother would ask — a farm that in the Nebraska flatlands earned the nickname "the Alps," he settled and married Grandma. Their granddaughter is a child of farmers, sweltering her summers in the itch of hayfields, dreading the cold that wheezes and cracks the house with winter ghosts.

She shivers her Sundays in the Augustana Lutheran Church basement. Where are the stories of Lutheran childhood, of the child who twisted her Sunday school penny in a handkerchief and suffered the agony of knots during the disbelief of "Jesus Loves Me"? She drops the handkerchief into the wicker collection basket, afraid to ask for help, afraid to confess her inadequacy and tell Mother, "I lost it. I don't know how."

She doesn't know her history, could not understand, even though she shares the torture of a priest who gave his name to the guilty religion of the plains. Let it begin with Martin Luther. Anna Anderson squirms on the organ seat to reach the pedals and a flush creeps over her face, red as the hymnals. We sing. A mighty four dress is our God. All is mystery. The grownups herd the nursery class into a quavering group before the congregation and they repeat the Bible verse for the day. The just shall live by faith. The *just* shall *live* by *faith*. Wait for Sundays, watch for tornadoes, blizzards, and hail. Endure.

Let it begin with a Nebraskan, child of the plains.

She wrestles with Nick on a black horsehide, such a good work horse Sally was, and Dad felt so bad when she got old and blind and he had to shoot her, he spent twenty dollars to have the hide blanketed on the yellow and green felt. This all happened before. Everyone remembers more. They remember Grandma and kerosene lamps and wishing for water by the windmill. They remember when Katy was born, ten years after everyone else. Three days late for Christmas, tagalong, baby of the family, what can she remember? The last horse, Prince, they loaded into a truck and a man drove him away. *Don't cry. It can't be helped.* They didn't need him; he stood in the cowlot kicking furiously at the barn door, and the man said he'd take him back east to pull a milk wagon. In country school she squirted LePage's glue into brown circles on her desk and with her forefinger picked up each glob and licked it. "Don't you know what that's made of!" Teacher said. Prince is gone and it can't be helped. Don't cry, whatever's destroyed — weak-eyed kittens, crops, or dreams of growing up beautiful.

Winter ruins everything. Always winter. Snow and sleet and ice, those soft words, wrap her in a tight cocoon of winter, cancel the Christmas program, and if the ice doesn't weigh down the power lines, the telephone crackles, "We can't make it for Christmas Eve." Or if the phone goes out early in the day, she stands on a chair, looking out the window above the kitchen sink, hoping for a headlight to flash on the hill, until the electricity goes out and there's nothing to do but go to bed and wait out the cold and dark. It can't be helped, but she cries, under the weight of blankets, topped by Sally's hide, heavy as the night. The early years are always winter, snowbound, housebound in a frozen Whittier poem.

In the center she stands, a little onion, in layers of flannel and denim, a spongy brown snowsuit over all. She is a small brown circle on the snow, the dot to her father's exclamation, trailing him in a fox and goose path to the barn. Overshoes squeak on packed snow, oats rustle from bucket to feed box, and the cows munch, sigh, and shift their leg chains. Balanced on the T of a milk stool, slab of wood nailed to a chunk of wood, she watches. Not that she's too little to milk. Too slow. By the time Dad's finished with Old Roan, "How'd you do, kid?" she has but a thin white skim from Irene on the bottom of the pail. Her job is separator girl. Just before Dad strips the last drops from Fiddlesticks, she runs past the calf pens to the separating room, plugs in the motor, and turns the crank. She wants it perfect, the separator just warmed up and ready to go when Dad lifts up the bucket of milk foaming like Ivory Snow. Seven days in a row she sat in a tub to make her skin white as snow, snow-skin, paper-skin, ghost-skin, seven days of three-inch tepid water in the unheated bathroom and it didn't work. No go power from Cheerios, and even after building her body twelve ways with Wonder Bread, when Nick picked her up to swing her like a monkey, she cried from the pain.

Cream separates from the milk, yellow, thick, and clotting the spout, and the milk, freed from its butterfat, rushes out in a translucent milkfall of bluish white. "How's it work?" the Omaha cousins asked. City kids. Separators, corn pickers, and combines. "It's magic," she said. Everything divides. Wheat from straw, corn from cob, eggs-to-sell from eggs-to-eat, feeder calves from cows, kids from grownups. Cows beller and the combine plugs up. Blue milk in the winter, green in the summer.

Unless disguised by Rice Krispies and sugar, she hates farm milk, as she hates eggs, boiling meat, gravy, mushy applesauce, and sauerkraut. She loves town food, the milk bleached and clean in tall waxy cartons, cold meat pressed under cellophane with the grand names of thüringer sausage, minced ham; food with cartoon animals cavorting across the package, like Bunny Bread and Sugar Crisp bear food, boxes of cereal with surprises inside! She refuses all chicken but the wishbone, eats her cherry pie backwards, crust to point, to wish on the last bite. She yanks up clover and splits the third leaf with her thumbnail, stands at the window each night and waits, star light, star bright, I wish I may, wish I might, and falls into horrifying contortions trying to kiss her elbow. Mikey Wanek says she'll sneeze if she looks at the sun. For a wish, she needs six sneezes.

She learns to pray. Bless and ask. Please God bless me, bless Mother, bless Dad, bless Nick, bless Adeline, Barbara, Darlene. Please God, let me, please God, make me, please God. What are these wishes? These prayers? Born with a yearning for something more, something other, she spends her wishes as she can. They are her only currency, her medium of exchange. Let her begin with her wish, this prayer that she will die not before she wakes, keep her soul intact for the passing into the next season.

TWYLA HANSEN ⌐ **Wind**

Early spring, southern gusts
suck what little moisture
the ground has hoarded
over this dry winter,
similar, Father observes,
to the Dirty Thirties,
those drouth years when
corn plants seared in the fields,
so many gave it all up.

He survived, somehow, just as
we'll survive this odd spring
with no rain; the wind,
he says, is always with us.
I recall the farm —
the way the breeze whined
through the pine grove,
rattling leaves in the maples,
carrying the fine grit and
effluvium of clover, alfalfa,
Brown Swiss, sweet cud.

Father spends his days now
in a recliner, the past floating
out of and into his reality,
repeating the stories I know
backwards — his immigrant parents,
how they longed for their wooded
homeland, starting new in this
flat country. There were
slough grasses in those days,
through the bottomlands,
waving high over their heads,

and I picture myself lying
in a hollow on a tall grass bed,
seedheads nodding as my
lover's body sweats in unison
with mine, the sun warming
our skins, the whole universe
tilting toward harmony, but
when I look up, that, too,
seems passing, like the wind.

Not a Half-Assed Country

CAROLE WORKMAN-ALLEN ~ Passion's Climate

This is not a half-assed country. One
day soon, water will go raging down
the quiet creek, torrents of rain
and hail will challenge my existence.

Gentle breezes only visit here.
They quickly drift away to other
lands, replaced with wind that whips
the trees and send my skirts a-flying.

Soon, a blazing western sun
will march across the broad expanse
of heaven and disclose a sky so blue,
it's sure to break your heart.

There are no compromises here, no
clement, tender hearts to wile
the hours away. I've known no
easy loves in Colorado.

LORI HALE ~ Nancy, Heaven-Sent

In June of 1983, I lived with my then-boyfriend in Bismarck, North Dakota, with my two children from a previous marriage; Billie Jo was seven; Travis, five. Raised a city kid, I spent summers on my grandparents' farm and wanted my children to share similar rural memories. When an offer to housesit an old farmhouse for the summer came up, we jumped at the chance.

The house had been vacant for five years, since the death of the previous owner, Nancy Christenson Hendrickson. The acreage had been bought by a

South Dakota contractor who wanted to farm and ranch it. We'd keep an eye on the machinery and livestock in exchange for free rent. The house was rundown, but the surrounding scenery of the open plains was beautiful; I thought it was heaven.

Ready to be pioneers, we traded for a 4x4 Suburban and moved with a dog, goat, and two city cats.

After the electric company turned the power back on, a new pump supplied the running water — to the kitchen. Five years of cold winters had burst all the pipes in the bathroom!

"What are you going to do?" a coworker asked.

"Use the outhouse," I told her.

"What about a bath?" she asked.

"Use the river," I answered.

Having grown up on a farm, she loved the city.

Soon after we moved in, two men rode up on horseback, a tall elderly man astride a short and fat horse, and his son. They introduced themselves as our neighbors and my history lesson began.

All I knew was that the previous owner had died in her nineties. And I knew she wrote down everything on anything! I found scraps of paper tacked and stashed all over the house. I learned that her eyesight failed because her writing became progressively larger. Our new neighbors told admiring stories about a hard-working woman.

Nancy, born in the four-room house, lived her whole life on the homestead. Now the house had five rooms, plus two open rooms upstairs.

Nancy received only eleven months of schooling and was nine before she left the homestead. Shortly after her first trip into town, Nancy was given a horse she named Two-Bits, her transportation and companion for the next twenty-two years, until she replaced him with a motorcycle.

Besides doing homesteading — gardening, butchering, sewing bridal gowns, nursing — she kept collections and diaries.

In 1902 Nancy bought her first camera for thirty-five cents. In 1922 she added a darkroom, developing film for the area until WWII made chemicals scarce. Her photos of animals dressed in costumes she made and posed in human situations, were published in magazines, including *Life*. Most of her pictures earned her about three dollars each. Once she won a contest and received fifty dollars, the most she made from any one project.

Her father was already gone when Nancy's mother became bedridden. Though Nancy had claimed a homestead and built a house one mile from her birthplace, she moved back to care for mother. Her only contact with the outside world was by mail. Writing was her passion; if it could be recorded, she recorded it: rainfall, planting dates, crop yield, the river's height, what was in the root cellar. She kept her own nursery garden, raising a wide variety of fruits and vegetables. She made the best strawberry jam you ever ate, neighbors said.

After her mother's death in 1926, Nancy fell in love and married Herman Apenes in 1927, the same year she won the first Ford Model A to arrive in Mandan. Her friends told us how the old Ford caught fire one day in the barn, but they all helped save it. Herman died in 1934, leaving Nancy alone again. In 1935 she married her childhood sweetheart, Carl Hendrickson; they spent the next thirty-five years together, but had no children.

Nancy moved her homestead shack behind the original house, for a library. One day I looked up to see a pair of pants with a note attached, hanging from the rafters. I went up the ladder to the loft and read: "Apenes pants — he took the other pair with him." In the 1930s, I realized, men's suits came with two pairs of pants and Apenes had been buried in the other pair. Even in times of despair, the lady kept her sense of humor. Sitting on a box of old jars, holding the dusty pants in my lap and the note in my hand, I felt a deep loss for a woman I'd never known.

A strange-looking wooden ski with a large central post and odd hardware puzzled me until an elderly nephew of Nancy's explained it was the ski to her motorcycle, replacing the front wheel. In winter, when the river froze over, Nancy motor-skied to a relative's house for a ride into town for supplies.

The linoleum in the parlor was so worn I decided to rip it up. Tearing a large piece, I found a note, written to "Whoever finds this," dated in the mid-forties. She and her friend Mavis had made bread the day she wrote, hoping to go to town to hear about "the lawmakers and the lawbreakers."

I never got down to the bare wood. Under that letter, newspapers were shellacked by time to the floor. The whole house had paper stuffed in the walls and around the windows for insulation. I started in one corner of a room and read about the beginning of WWI, reading all the way around the room to WWII. It was easy to tell when the rooms had been added; last was the newfangled bathroom that didn't work.

The longer I lived in her house, the more I searched for Nancy. Once, ripping a board off a window between her darkroom and the upstairs, I found the original patch for the broken window — an old glass negative. In the picture was Nancy, a proud and beautiful woman, in a buggy with a man I learned was Carl.

The summer I spent at Nancy's changed my life — I haven't been able to live in a city since. I've lived on a remote spot on a mountain in Colorado for five years, but I think of Nancy often. The kids, almost ready for college, remember going down to the river to bathe, our goat bleating as it followed.

I remember my last look down at Nancy's, from the top of the drive the day we moved. The new owner planned to bulldoze all the buildings so the cattle could graze safely. I cried for the lost history of one woman's life, though I saved all I could for the Historical Society in Bismarck. I cried for the fact that one hundred years after her birth in that spot, progress had reached Nancy's homestead. I cried for the ninety-two-year-old woman who fell and broke her hip at home one day and was taken to the hospital. Told she could never live alone, could never go back to the place that had always been home, Nancy died two weeks later. Those who knew her said for the first and only time in her life, Nancy Christenson Hendrickson gave up.

People have called me a pioneer, living where I do, commuting miles to work, only to face having to get back up mother mountain (as I like to call her), especially in the wintertime. I was the only single mother on the mountain until my marriage a year ago. I tell them no, I'm no pioneer. Not when you compare my life to a real pioneer, such as Nancy. A mountain mama, maybe.

JOAN HOFFMAN ~ **Home on the Range**

It is a matter of knowing beyond knowing that this is a hard way. This living so close to the land you cannot separate yourself from it, this looking out that south window upon the eternal sameness and praying night after long night to the only God there is, the deaf one, that something essential will happen, something will change, someone will kick up a little fuss, maybe, and maybe someone will die and leave us enough money to get this place paid for.

This is the way it's been. My expectations have forever outstripped reality and guilt has settled in like a stone cross.

I can't say I wasn't warned. Enough people told me I'd rue the hour I came here to live, but I was young and more than half in love, and "ranch" was another word for "romantic." I have been slave to harsh, gritty winds and given in to gentle honey-breezes. I have worked my head off and considered selling my soul for a brief respite. I have wept at the meanness of it all, and laughed as I ran barefoot in summer rain. I have fallen into dark depression when the truth was more than I could face, and fought to grab light out of darkness. Ranch life has made of me a certified schizophrenic, cowering in dreadful doubt and pain, and just as surely a valiant woman unafraid of dragons and demons and stacks of overdue bills.

And you have to understand that I love this place. It is my home. I am free and bound. If that sounds a dichotomy, you have not caught the proper balance; I could not be secure if I were not allowed freedom. I have to have room to think and to call upon the strength I take from solitude. I have to run to the hills and look into the sweep of prairie and the river and the distance and I have to leave here and I have to come back. And upon coming home I must be welcomed and even needed. In these I find and know security.

GWEN PETERSEN ⸏⸏⸏ **The Legacy**

My grandmother gave me a gift today
(Now I expected socks),
Instead, an apron, clean but worn
Was folded in the box.

I know that women used to wear
Aprons to the floor,
Shapeless garments of muslin cloth,
Who wears 'em anymore?

My grandmother doesn't know, I thought,
The modern way of things,
That wearing aprons and serving others
Is what enslavement means.

When Grandmother gently chided me,
Politely, I said I'd listen,
And as she spoke of the threadbare garment,
I began to see her vision.

"Rest your hand upon the apron,"
My grandmother said to me.
"Listen to women who came before,
Women from history."

My fingers touched the roughened cloth,
I felt my spirit hasten,
As if the souls of those long dead
Were speaking through the apron.

I caught a glimpse of times before,
And I walked in ghostly shoes;
I fancied I was a frontier woman,
And wondered, would life I lose?

I held a baby as I marched
Beside a covered wagon,
And I was tired for the way was endless,
My weary steps dragged on.

Then howling warriors swept upon me,
Shooting from every side,
I ran till I thought my heart would burst,
There was no place to hide.

I slung the child, apron-wrapped,
Not knowing where she fell;
The babe survived, and I am her kin,
Her name, like mine, was Nell.

Again I touched the worn old cloth
And became a prairie bride,
New-settled in a soddy hut,
At night, sometimes, I cried.

For fuel, I learned to follow bison
And picked up chips of dung,
I heaped them high in my muslin apron,
And fetched till my arms grew numb.

I carried thick dark bricks of sod
Enfolded in my apron,
And learned to value prairie beauty
As homeward I would hasten.

Once more I stroked the muslin threads
And became a farmer's wife;
A skidding axe sliced through his leg,
Blood poured away his life.

To tourniquet the flow I tore
A strip from my apron's hem,
Then harnessed the team and raced for town;
Death was foiled again.

Smoothing the cloth of my grandmother's apron,
I saw a farmhouse shelter;
A toddler wandered close to geese,
She chased them helter-skelter.

Those flapping, honking, pecking demons
Gave the child a fright,
But right and left I thrashed my apron
And drove the birds to flight.

Once more the vintage muslin apron
Made pictures in my mind;
I was my grandmother in her youth,
My life was the Spartan kind.

When heifers broke the fence one day,
My apron closed the gap

Till I could fix the fence with tools
And chase those critters back.

And I often sat by the back porch door
And watched the children at play,
While snapping beans or shelling peas
In my aproned lap each day.

Then my grandmother's apron showed me
Western women when,
At branding time or thrashing season,
They cooked for hungry men.

I saw them in their kitchens,
Roasting, baking, heating,
Then folding hands across their aprons,
They proudly watched men eating.

"Have some more, there's plenty here,
Now, fellas, don't be shy!
More coffee Joe? Have some cake,
Here's a piece of pie."

"This apron is my gift to you,"
My grandmother said to me,
"Woven with truth and women's power,
It is your legacy."

I reached across my grandmother's apron
And touched her gnarled hand,
And felt the souls of all the women
Whose courage forged this land.

I thanked her softly for my present,
In tears, and filled with pride,
I greeted the shadows of aproned women
Walking — by my side.

KAREN OBRIGEWITCH Place-Bound

We plainswomen are realistic and romantic, tender and strong. Our small hands are invaluable when a calf needs to be repositioned and pulled. We haul kids to rodeos and watch them climb onto twelve hundred pounds of horse to try to make that eight-second ride, loving their determination but dreading the danger. On our way out the door to a school board meeting, we kill a rattlesnake waiting for us on the porch steps. We deal with life and death, and we respect both.

We schedule weddings after branding but before haying, or after fencing but before weaning. We wait to buy furniture or appliances or pickups until after the calves are sold, if there is enough money left after visiting the bank.

Our kids graduate from a high school barely large enough to stay open, and go to colleges with more students than the entire population of five plains counties. We educate them so they can live in the cities with their hearts in the country. They leave, but they always want to come back.

We are place-bound because we are not whole anywhere else and because there are familiar graves here.

CAROL BOIES ⬥ Like Grandma

When I was a single woman I lived alone in a city. I saw to the maintenance of my own vehicle, took care of my own home repairs, and managed my own finances. I felt like a capable adult with few self-doubts.

Before that I lived on a farm. I saw the farm through the eyes of a child, as a safe and happy home, with my parents as the caretakers. But as I grew, I couldn't wait to get out into the world on my own, and as soon as I finished high school, I left.

Fifteen years later I moved back to my childhood community with my husband and our two children. As an adult, I see things from a different perspective; I recall with my mature eyes the images I formed of my mother as a child.

I see my mom milking the cows, doing the chores when Dad was out in the field until after dark. And she did more than her fair share of taking lunch to the field, taking gasoline to the field, taking Dad to the field. She helped Dad sort hogs and load hogs. She watched gates and moved livestock, drove the tractor and shocked cane bundles.

These were not things she did in place of housework and motherhood, but along with them. When I see all the things she did and compare them to what I do, I have to wonder how she did it all with three children and few modern conveniences. She once told me she wondered how *her* mother did it all with five children and no modern conveniences.

I know I don't compare to my mother or grandmother. Even though I come from farm stock, a family of doers, I will have to learn it all for myself. When I left here, I was a child still more afraid of the noise that a hailstorm made than of losing a year's worth of expense, work, and income if it wiped out the crops.

Before we moved to our own farm, my husband worked on other people's ranches. I had little to do with the work or the livestock or the decisions concerning them. Now I am slowly becoming reacquainted with cranky cows and abandoned calves. I don't know how long it will be before I'm one of those toughened farm women that takes the three A.M. calving check and knows what to do if a cow needs help. I don't know if I'll ever be able to go outside after dark and not remind myself that there are bats around here.

Will I ever be as determined as my grandma was? Once when Grandpa was gone, she was outside by the corral and noticed one of the calves bloating. My mother, who was a little girl at the time, said Grandma ran to the house and grabbed one of her kitchen knives. Kneeling beside the poor animal, she clenched the knife in both fists, turned her head away, and plunged the blade into the swollen paunch. Yes, the calf lived.

It seems that with each new generation, life has become a little bit easier than it was for the one before. I realize what I am capable of doing only because I've seen my mother and grandma and what they accomplished in their daily lives. I also realize that my challenges will not be the same as theirs because our modern world is more technical and fast-paced. That doesn't make my life any more predictable.

I don't think my grandma got up that morning knowing what would be required of her. But then, none of us does. My prayer is that God will give me the faith in Him to do what is best, and the wisdom to know what that is. Then maybe in twenty-five or thirty years I will be as confident in the role of a farm wife as my mom and my grandma.

LUCILLE CRESS BAKER ⬩ *A Night Ride*

We moved to this very barren soil, built a boxcar-type palace — oh, palace, did I say? Oh no, 'twas what most would call a shack, but you know a shack can be a palace if it's where you live, where there's love and a family.

'Twas the beginning of the thirties, March 1931, a young couple with two little girls and a third one to come in a few months. That beautiful virgin soil had to be cleared of the native sagebrush. We were thirty-seven miles from town, four and one-half miles from a mail route with delivery three times a week. Our closest real neighbor was five miles away over roads that were just trails, ungraded; telephone service was unheard of, but it was our own land, our home, to us a bit of heaven on earth.

Not having a well, we hauled our water in barrels from natural water holes put there so mercifully by the Lord to hold rain for man and beast to share. We were careful to pick ones with frogs in them as they were cleaner and safer to drink from.

It was hard; it was all so good.

From March to August the days went by so very quickly and August 2 our third baby girl came. She was born in town so papa and two little girls spent eleven days alone.

Two days after I arrived home a virtual cloudburst came upon us, and it turned out that palace called home had been built in the wrong place. All the hills around us channeled the runoff right down upon it, that little one-room home, 22 × 18, with only flat rocks for a foundation, with a full basement beneath it, was almost afloat in a very few minutes. The basement had furniture, rugs, pictures, home-canned foods — most everything we owned was there. We were dry but we were very wet. No help near — decisions had to be made. My husband's sharp knife soon cut through the tarpaper that covered the outside walls the width of two boards; with lusty blows from a hammer he soon made an opening. Daylight streamed in; yes, also flies and mosquitoes.

Dipping water by bucketfuls was much too slow, so my husband went to our neighbor's place — they had moved to town — took their hand pump from a dug well, nailed some boards together for a trough, and began pumping the water out on the ground. As soon as he had lowered the water level, he took off his shoes and began to bring out all he could through a trap door in the floor — the box of pictures, books, rugs, and everything he could get his hands on. The walls were just dirt, and he had to work fast lest they cave in. He cut his foot on something and bled profusely but kept on.

How beautiful was the sun that came out after the storm; the yard was full of things to dry.

But all wasn't over, for in a short time his leg began to swell and streaks of red came from the wound; blood poisoning was setting in. He hurried to a doctor and came home long after dark from the seventy-four-mile trip. Since I hadn't known when he would get home, I decided to get the milk cows. Fourteen days after our baby was born, I saddled the horse, led him up by a pole fence. Our two little girls, aged three and five, held the reins while I laboriously mounted and started looking for the cows on a section of hilly land. I told the girls to stay in the yard and not leave until someone came.

I was not able to ride fast and a dark, moonless night was upon me, only stars to break the loneliness. About three hours later I came in sight of the house and saw car lights appear on the horizon and cried. There was no light in the house as my husband drove up to the gate and called the little girls. I was a mile or so away but in the still night air I could hear him say, "Where's your mama?" and they answered "After the cows." I could hear them crying; I could not hear the baby crying in the house, but she was. Then again, I heard him, "Good night! How long ago?" and between sobs they said, "A long time ago." He turned the car motor off, took the girls by their hands, went in the house to light a lamp — you know the good old kerosene lamps of the thirties. "Now, you stay in the house, shake the baby's bed, and I'll go find mama," he said.

I heard the door slam behind him as he ran to the old V8 Ford and started the motor, and I thought that a most heavenly sound. The motor raced as he started out to find me. I couldn't have gotten off the horse in my condition, or if I could have, it wouldn't have been safe in such darkness, so much cactus and rattlesnakes. Fortunately, he took the right trail and before long the lights found me. He ran to me, gently pulled me from the saddle, hugged me, carried me to the car as I cried big wet tears of relief. I'll never forget the comfort of those strong arms. We drove home slowly and led the faithful horse behind. Two little girls with tear-streaked cheeks were hanging on the gate; the baby had gone back to sleep with the light. Daddy carried me to the house, unsaddled the horse. The cows spent the night out amongst the sage, but at four A.M. they were in the corral. Thus came the end of one day and the start of another for a family a long while ago in the open range of old Wyoming.

CANDY VYVEY MOULTON Threads of Change

Every summer the poppies brightened the northeast corner of my aunt's house. Their furry, prickly green leaves swayed in the wind and their bright red-orange petals ruffled in summer breezes. They splashed color against the old log house and I liked to pick their seed pods and scatter the tiny black beginnings of new poppies in the flower bed.

Wearing a big white hat tied under her chin with a green ribbon, and about a half gallon of cold cream on her face, my Aunt Phyllis weeded and watered the poppies on her lunch breaks from the hay field. I took for granted those bright splotches of color.

When I was six, my dad took me to the hayfield, boosted me up to the seat of the John Deere tractor, and showed me how to start it. He put the tractor in low gear and I put my forty pounds into engaging the hand clutch so the tractor would creep, turtle slow around the patch.

My job was to pull the twenty-one foot dump rake over all the hay ground and leave scattered pieces of hay in a new windrow. Then Mom or Aunt Phyllis would zoom down the wavy line, scoop the fresh hay onto the wooden teeth of their power sweeps, and push it to the stackyard.

Dad rode with me briefly that first day, then I was on my own. Uncle Bert, who ran the stacker, would help if I had trouble. How Uncle Bert kept his sanity and patience I'll never know.

I was in my first year of raking scatters at the upper end of the snake patch, a long, narrow, crooked field, when I had my first real trouble. The patch was only about a hundred feet wide at the head. I started at the bottom ditch, dropped the teeth to the rake so they would catch the loose hay, and pointed the tractor nose toward the top ditch. I barely flipped the hydraulic lever to dump the sweet-smelling hay from the rake before I needed to turn to keep the rake out of the ditch. I swung the wheel and the tractor switched on a dime, the left big tire grinding the hay and dirt as the right made a quick full circle to go back the way I came. Like a cloud's shadow, the rake followed, the outside tire bouncing through the ditch.

On the third run, figuring I had the hang of it, I gave the tractor just a bit more gas and drove right into the ditch. Of course, I had to go get Uncle Bert.

Not in my whole life do I remember him moving quickly. He didn't yell as he got my tractor and rake out of the ditch. He told me it would work better if I drove the tractor and rake lengthwise on the field in that narrow snake's neck.

Less than a week later, in my effort to do a good job and earn my pay — which was nothing — I drove my rake behind the stack to pick up hay scatters. It was a good idea, until I hooked the tall backstop placed to keep hay from falling behind the stack. I pulled it halfway around before I realized it would keep following me as long as the tractor could move and the rake didn't break. I crawled off my tractor and went for Uncle Bert.

That time he asked me if I had any idea how long that scatter rake was and what the devil I was doing behind the stack anyway. I never tried to rake behind a stack again.

At age eight I graduated to side delivery rake and for two years I worked in tandem with my sister. We had great drag races, swirling the hay into big, sweet-smelling windrows. I'd chase her around the field in high gear. We'd either be doing play-by-play about the race or singing at the top of our lungs. Of course nobody could hear anything over the drone of the tractors.

Across the fence to the west our cousins and best friends, Billy and Cris, ran their own tractors, cutting, raking, and sweeping hay. Driving the John Deere tractors — the old Johnny Pops — we'd slow clear down when in sight of our cousins. Then we'd push the throttle forward. That made the black smoke roll out of the stack and the tractor go *poppety-poppety-pop*. Across the fence we saw answering smoke signals.

Finally, when I was ten we got a new seven-wheel rake, which I ran by myself. Several patches separated me from the rest of my family as they cut and stacked the hay. I loved the isolation. I have an older sister and a younger brother so for the first time in my life I was alone for hours at a time.

Driving around and around and making figure eights and circles to put the hay in fat windrows, singing "The Battle Hymn of the Republic" or "You Are My Sunshine" at the top of my lungs, waving at Billy or Cris over the fence, I could think and daydream to my heart's content. At least I could until I dropped the front tricycle wheels of the 730 Johnny Pop into a badger hole and broke them off. Then I had to walk to get Uncle Bert.

I can imagine his relief when I turned fourteen and got a job jerking sodas in town. I mixed malts and Green Rivers, put a spin on the ice cream in the soda glass, and stocked shelves until I turned eighteen and started writing for the local newspaper.

Like the back side of a piece of embroidery, my childhood days seemed unpatterned, with threads running in every direction and no design in mind. But the experiences keep coming back to me. They are more focused now. It's like I can begin to see the front of the needlework with its various hues and shades and an intricate design.

I draw from my days in the hayfield, at the head of the irrigation ditch, or on the back of a horse, to explain and interpret the stories I now write. I report on lawsuits, water calls, and weed control and I think of blisters on the palms of my hands, the sharp bite of a deer fly, and a shovel slung over my shoulder in imitation of my dad.

In 1990 I spent two weeks traveling by horse and wagon on the Bridger Trail in northwest Wyoming. While I ate dust during the hot days and slept in a floorless, tepee-style tent amid the cactus and sagebrush of the Bighorn basin at night, my family sold the ranch.

"It is time to sell. We're getting older. We'd rather not work so hard," my parents said of their decision.

They deserved that, but didn't they know, couldn't they see that it was like selling a part of my soul? It hurt inside as badly as losing Uncle Bert did a few years earlier.

The land was a part of me. It had shaped me as much as my mother's careful nurturing and my father's belief that his girls could do anything his boy could do.

Mom and Dad and Aunt Phyllis moved to town. It wasn't my ranch, it never had been, and I'd not lived on the place for years, but my own home is only a couple of miles away. I'm the only one who grew up on that ground who still sees it every day.

I see the land when I go for a walk, or to get my mail. I see it from my bedroom window and when I'm standing at the clothesline carefully pinning clean jeans and shirts and socks to the drying forces of the wind. Like a tangle of embroidery floss, changing colors mark the passing of the seasons: mint green grasses in spring; bright kelly green shaded with the deep purple of blooming alfalfa during summer; golden grain in fall; and white, lots of white snow in winter.

Within two years the ranch changed irrevocably. The new owner built different corrals, cut eighty-year-old trees, didn't let the alfalfa reach its prime, and sold the cattle. The poppies died.

SHIRLEY BLUNT   The Women's Club

The basically cruel existence on a dryland homestead in the early days in Montana was leavened by social contact with neighbors. Friends were chosen not so much for their compatibility as for their location. Horse-drawn transportation necessarily limited an afternoon or evening outing to a radius of maybe six or eight miles, which can be a long way behind a team of horses at thirty below zero or a hundred above.

Driven by isolation and the memory of community contact with kindred souls back wherever they came from, the homesteader women organized a women's club that exists among their descendants to this day. It was the social pivot of the time; I well remember my mother whisking through dinner and getting herself dressed in her best summer dress, hair rolled over a curling iron heated over a kerosene lamp. The thermostats on those old irons was spit on a finger and a careful estimate of the resulting sizzle. An attendant odor reminiscent of branding time and a faint brown tint in her graying locks told her if the iron was left over the flame too long.

Her dresses were flowered voile or other semi-sheer summer material. She treasured silk stockings, keeping them for best; they suffered in the weeds and barbed wire gates. Everyday stockings were a more practical lisle cotton, but it was a sad day if she had to wear them for dress, too. She prized wide-brimmed summer straw hats with flowers or fruit attached for many seasons, anchoring them with long hat pins. The usual Montana breezes of thirty miles an hour or so presented a challenge when she traveled in an open buggy.

My mother scrubbed her face with soap and water and applied a layer of a hoarded concoction known as "vanishing cream" — a type of cold cream that was absorbed by the skin. A dusting of loose powder dulled the shine on her nose and cheeks and mellowed a summer suntan. She never used rouge or lipstick and I don't remember any of the other ladies doing so either. They were all born in the nineteenth century, when ladies were ladies; they and their husbands took a dim view of such floozy trappings.

A full slate of officers served the women's group; election was from membership, sometimes accompanied by bitter campaigning among otherwise good friends. There was no nonsense; the meeting was called to order, roll call taken, minutes read and approved, and parliamentary procedure observed. There was always a program, either a book report or a report on some topic of current interest. Baby-sitters were unknown, so the children too young to be left with their fathers for the afternoon, or girls who would be underfoot at home, went to the meetings; we learned early to find something to do outdoors and out of earshot of the mothers' group. We were supposed to turn up for the lunch following the meeting with our clothing and persons in decent repair. This limited my activities somewhat, as it wasn't worth the repercussions to jump off the haystack in my best dress or skin my knee racing downhill and bleed on my good socks.

After the business meeting, the gathering got down to the basic reason for its existence — visiting, talking with other adult females, a luxury not otherwise enjoyed.

The program was laid out at the beginning of each year, so each hostess had the best part of a year to get herself and her house as presentable as possible. Members with smaller houses took the summer meetings, and those with somewhat larger quarters got the winter meetings, when the women were joined by their husbands immediately after the business meeting for a whist party with scorecards and prizes. If the hostess could scrounge up some new curtains or a new dress, she expected to be admired by all, and you can bet everyone noticed. If things were tough that year, homemade soap and elbow grease substituted for store-bought finery.

Lunch was as rich and toothsome as time and talent would permit. Whipped cream, lemonade, or iced tea were out, as summer weather precluded getting anything that cold. Some people who lived near rivers put up ice packed in straw or sawdust that would keep all summer, but in our area there wasn't anyplace to get ice except on the water bucket in the kitchen on winter mornings. The coolest place in the summer was in the cellar; milk, butter, and leftovers were dutifully taken down there after every meal. Liquid butter was taken for granted, and milk turned sour in a short time, since it was never really chilled after it left the cow.

If the hostess had a garden — and nearly everyone did — the whole troop inspected and admired it before they went home. There was never a weed in sight; if the hostess had some blisters on her hands she didn't mention it. I remember a meeting at our house one summer when it had rained some and the garden looked pretty nice. Somewhere I had gotten a few packets of flower seeds, and they were in full bloom. The next day there was a trail of high-heel prints on both sides of this colorful stretch of blossoms. Culture and beauty weren't too plentiful, and these ladies absorbed every last drop available. The women's club was their link to the more civilized world they had known before circumstances and adventure brought them to a raw land that demanded they mortgage their souls to conquer it.

C. L. PRATER ⌐ Eccentricities & Earthly Remains

She bought eight lots in the new section,
two plots in a north-south row,
and it's just for the two of them.

The first two lots to the south aren't any good
they're right next to the lane.

The last two lots to the north, next to the fence,
can't be used either, everyone knows Kinsley's cows get out.
(remember the cud on the Kruger stone?)

That leaves only four good lots in the middle.

It's always a good idea to have extra.

LUCY REBENITSCH ⌐ College on Twenty Dollars

I finished high school in three years by dint of hard work and fear that I wouldn't be allowed to go to school anymore. After high school I pestered my mom to let me go to college. My dad had died when I was in the eighth grade, and it was the Depression. She finally gave me twenty dollars and my train ticket to Dickinson; that was all she could do. I was to come home when I got hungry.

She helped me pack a few cardboard boxes, tied them with twine. An old suitcase took care of the rest; I took cooking things and some food as I would do light housekeeping at the college dorm.

I landed in a strange town, just turned seventeen, and scared to death. I asked the station keeper where the college was and he pointed it out — over a mile away — so I started, carrying my suitcase for half a block and then going back to get my boxes. I was exhausted by the time I got to the dorm and found a room.

The next day, at registration, I found that tuition was $15.50, payable right away; room rent was five dollars a month. I explained I only had twenty dollars and needed a job in order to go to school. They agreed to wait for the five dollars, and I went to work next morning cleaning the bathrooms in the college proper before 7:30 A.M. every day for $8.40 a month. Later, I also took an evening job cleaning turkeys at ten cents a turkey and thus earned my next quarter's tuition. Eventually, I also borrowed money from the college. As a country girl I was used to hard work, and I was delighted just to be able to stay in school.

EVA POTTS BURTON   *A Daughter Becomes*
                    a Cattlewoman

I've always been an outdoor person. I'd still rather be out on a horse at daylight, seeing the sun rise, than making breakfast. I grew up being treated like a boy and I enjoyed it. I always hoped I'd live on a ranch with lots of riding to be done and cows to tend.

I was riding bareback even before I can remember. When I walked out in the morning to catch my horse, I slipped the bridle over his head and swung on. It didn't take long to learn to hold on to the reins whenever I hit the ground. It was a long walk home.

My mother was the one who taught me to get back on when I was scared. The first time I zigged when my horse zagged to avoid a cactus patch, I walked home a stickery, tearful mess. Mom plucked out all the cactus she could find, caught my horse, and said, "Get back on! And hush your sniffling. Next time, watch your horse's head closer so you'll know which way he's going."

I've been picking myself up and getting back on ever since. Life has thrown me some stickery turns, but I've always "climbed back on."

I was not quite twelve years old when Daddy showed me how much he regarded me as "son" and helper. In those days, sons worked alongside their fathers, while daughters helped their mothers.

We bought about fifty head of cattle that were supposed to start calving within three weeks. Being in new territory, the cows were all inclined to wander. If they could find — or make — even a small hole in a fence, they were gone. It was my job to ride and check every cow every day. Each day there were new babies; when I'd find a cow struggling to deliver her calf, I would hurry home to find Dad and lead him to the cow. I provided help for safe delivery of the new calf, our ranch's future.

This was probably the most enjoyable part of my life. I liked the regular horseback riding. I worked extremely hard, especially for a girl, but I was big and healthy and thrived on the work.

I stacked hay the old-fashioned way, by piling the loose hay with a pitchfork after it was brought to the stack by a buckrake or sweep, as we called it. The loose hay was lifted up onto the growing stack with a hay stacker pulled by one or two horses.

My job was to spread the hay into an oblong or loaf-shaped stack. The trick was to shape it big enough to hold all the hay from the field, yet have enough left over to top it off. I built the stack, gradually drawing the sides in as the supply of hay diminished, so that there was a gently sloping but pointed top on the stack. This allowed moisture to run off rather than sink in and spoil the hay. It took close discernment to know when to start topping off the stack.

While stacking hay, it wasn't unusual to have stray items such as tumbleweeds or rocks thrown at me along with the hay. I even accepted mice and a few other little "pets" that found their way onto my stack. One load of loose hay came complete with a fiercely buzzing rattlesnake! The snake must have been as scared as I was, as it kept up a steady *whir-r-r-r* while I carefully got it sorted out of the hay. I was thankful for my long-handled pitchfork!

"Mother!" I hollered down from the stack. She was driving the team pulling the stacker. "Look out below! Here comes your pet! Now, you just have it right back and do what you want with it!"

One month I got the job of removing a fence, which entailed pulling all the staples from the posts, then flipping the barbed wire away from the fence and rolling it neatly. I wore leather gloves, but barbs cut through them.

I had to roll a half-mile of three-strand barbed wire and thirty-inch woven wire. The barbed wire had to be skillfully turned across each strand of the roll so it would stay compact and not spring apart. Many separated coils of barbed wire are a wicked apparatus. I learned quickly to do it right.

I rolled the woven wire last. It had to be laid flat and rolled into a thirty-inch-long roll, which steadily grew bigger and heavier. The uphills required a lot of muscle to get the roll of wire moved, but downhill I had to be careful not to let the roll get away. It probably weighed two hundred pounds before I got all of one length of wire into it.

I spent two years at college, then I got married. Dad and Mother managed the ranch with very little help, but every summer I went home and helped them. I had no thought that I would not spend the rest of my life there on the cattle ranch.

But this was not to be. My dad concluded that my husband was "not rancher material" and also that he could make more money by selling the ranch than he had thought possible. So sell the ranch he did.

This was probably the biggest disappointment of my whole life. I was very bitter and angry with my parents. When I finally had to leave the ranch, I vowed I would never go back, and I didn't for thirty years. Within six months or so, I did forgive my parents. Life is too short to hold grudges. I "climbed back on" and take comfort in knowing that I was an influential figure in the conversion of a homestead into a cattle ranch.

JOANNE WILKE ⌇ Marking Territory

I do not own
  this land I walk
  trudge steep uphill
where trees grew
where deer sprang

In diesel's silence
  I creep cat-mauled hills
skirt piles of green-needled trash
howl at the moon
  and piss around the edges

DONNA NIEDERWERDER ⌇ Hollyhock Seeds

I ran across the hollyhock seeds today. They were tucked away in a corner of a cupboard waiting for spring. Finding them brought a new flood of tears for I know now that these seeds will not be planted. We are moving — again. This will be the ninth move in nearly fourteen years of marriage, and this gypsy lifestyle is taking its toll.

Some of the moves were easy — moving from a rented apartment to our first house; moving from a house that was too expensive into one that would not be a financial burden; and best, moving from the city to a farm, fulfilling a lifelong dream to farm and ranch. I remember planting perennials around the farmhouse with such optimism. We would live out our lives there and raise our sons in the country. Some of the moves have been much more difficult — leaving that farm and returning to the city after becoming disillusioned and exhausted by the rigors of dairying; and now, leaving *this* farm for who knows what? Another temporary location — another rented house?

I'm finding that as time goes by, I don't move well anymore. Moving used to be just a physical chore. Now I'm finding there are more and more emotional strings attached. Eric won't be able to play securely in the fenced-in yard. Moving isn't just transferring furniture anymore, and I am saddened again by this great sense of loss.

I want to sink my roots deep into the soil and stay put. I want my sons to have the opportunity to bring their children home to visit Grandma in the same house they grew up in. I want to make my house a home — homemade crafts and decorator touches. I want to plant those hollyhock seeds along the garage and watch the stalks grow tall — their colorful flowers arching over my children playing in the sun. Then I want to pick those seeds in the fall to start new plants the next year and the next and the next. Well, maybe someday. I'll take the seeds with me when we move, just in case.

JEANNE M. BARTAK 〜 My Choice

As an only child growing up on a wheat farm in central North Dakota, I always had a love for the land. The beautiful plains sunsets or the spring wheat waving as the wind gently blew were wonderful parts of my childhood. As life worked out for me, I ended up with the land but felt I could not take care of it properly or make a living for myself. So as an older student of twenty-four years, I packed my bags and moved off to Montana to get a degree in range management. My secretarial coworkers thought I was nuts and going into such a profession only meant I was trying to catch a husband. But on our senior trip there were ten gals and three guys. Times were changing.

I worked for Irene Graves, who has a Ph.D. in range management and was a wonderful teacher and friend. I gained practical experience with a few wild experiences as a bonus. A few days after I arrived in Nebraska, we were moving some cattle, including a big Angus bull. Standing in the wrong place at the wrong time, I was in his escape route. He knocked me down, but I was not hurt.

I began wondering about my future. Irene raised Morgan horses and I got to know them up close and personal. As a child I had always begged my parents for a horse, but my dad had to use horses for farming and did not see them as a pleasure to have. On Irene's ranch I found out how much work horses were. My dad knew me better than I knew myself.

At twenty-seven I asked myself, should I run my farm or work for the government? Then Irene introduced me to a friend of the family, Steve, who was thirty-two and never married. Twelve years, three sons, and a daughter later, I am a happy farmwife who may not be utilizing her college degree as she visualized, but who has no regrets. My life revolves around my family and the farm. We live in an area with many acres of beautiful canyons, a creek flowing through the property, and pine trees. There are many opportunities to show the children the things that take place around us that I learned about in college. We always take a treasure sack on hikes and fill it with God's creations, whether that means that special rock from the creek, a turkey feather, or a simple pine cone seed. We are creating special memories with one another and filling up my closet as a bonus.

KAY MOON   Return to Elk Mountain

My future is this holy place,
where the mountains of my past
scrape the sky of my present.

Here, in the silence
between the trees.

B. J. BUCKLEY   *Mad Alyce as St. Therese:*
Mending Fence Near Powder River

Last winter's sea of snow pulled all the fences down
in the sheep pasture, and now the woven panels sag
slack-bellied like those ranchers who got through
the cold on bacon, whiskey, biscuits, too much beer.
Subzero dark clenched bobwire so tightly
that when warm comes like this, all radiant too fast,
steel sings and sparks and snaps and curls,
a solid thunderbolt, pulls the staples out
of cedar posts and sends them flying — pray
that you're not near it when it goes. I want
to sing myself, it should be this way, walls
brought down by a joy palpable in the air, no
obstacle to halt the deer, the antelope, coyote,
nothing in their way, the path on the ground
as clear as the one their hearts know.
Even the cows would manage, already they walk through
any fence they want to simply by forgetting
that it's there — they see the greener-on-the-other-side
and go. Of such deliberate vision saints are made.
But sheep — the sheep would falter. They'd stand
on the two-lane asphalt watching nervously as
trucks bore down on them, but not be quite so
nervous as to move in time. They'd bed out
on the railroad tracks or rush to baptize themselves,
a white multitude thronging into the muddy river
two weeks before shearing time, and not know enough
to come out — saved, but far too waterlogged
to save themselves. How woven wire or barbed can penetrate

the clouds of ecstasy they're caught in,
I don't know, but come to it they'll turn
so easily in one direction or another, it's as if
a way made straight were not worth going in.
This afternoon I'll stretch the fences tight
and high again, make whole what's broken.
Deer will still fly over, closer to God in leaping
than I shall ever be. Coyote will go through
or under, praising the Creator for His cleverness
in making all coyotes clever. For myself,
I long to see this grass go on unbounded
to the sky's blue edge, I want an end
to difficulties, to having to climb over, to
tearing my skirt — I want the road easy.
But the sheep who know so little know
what fences are for, and it's for them I'm going —
Praise the pickup if it starts, praise stretcher,
cutter, staples, hammer, great unwieldy bales of wire,
smashed thumbs and cuts and sunburn, praise this work
by means of which the sheep and I shall make our crooked way.

ROBYN CARMICHAEL EDEN   **Living on the Edge**

When you are born on the edge of the plains, you spend your life clinging to it, praying that you won't fall off.

The human offspring of the prairie are different at birth. Others spend lifetimes desperately seeking what we are born knowing.

In the vast prairie hyperspace, there is no room for clutter. Those who call the prairie boring and empty are those who pass through quickly, moving from one densely inhabited place to another, senses so dulled they need the neon gratification of mountains or seas or deserts. Born into a world of sensory overload, they are blind to the low-light vision of the plains. Used to perpetual motion, they cannot stand still long enough to feel the pull of roots just below the surface of the undulating grasslands.

Visitors may be hypnotized by the monochromatic repetition of groundswells rolling toward the horizon. They do not know the natives' thrill at seeing winter wheat breaking through spring snowmelt, a victorious emerald splash on the leaking soil. They cannot cherish warm and gentle summer breezes as we do, for they have not faced cruel, bone-stinging, subzero blasts or black tornadic skies.

Seasons on the plains give our lives definition. Climate and land challenge those who claim residence here. Those who choose not to be challenged leave.

Those who stay know that this is the only place that will ever be home for us. We are born knowing the world doesn't owe us a living; that work is expected and a source of pride; that life itself is a gift from the Almighty and that failing to utilize this gift is the worst form of sin. Children, we know, are to be loved and educated; homes must be made and families nurtured. We know we belong more to the land than it belongs to us, and that we are only stewards; life is tenuous. But we are stubborn optimists, never thinking we won't survive. The land is our trial, our comfort, and ultimately, our identity.

KATHERINE WOOD ~~ **Plains Preponderance**

She stops her four-wheel-drive Jeep Cherokee
at the two-mile corner
and gazes at the spread of her farm ahead —
A yellow barn, a red one,
the new ranch house that replaced the trailer,
three steel-gray silos, livestock pens,
the green John Deere tractors.
Then the dry spring wind comes up
billowing dust across the farm-perfect view,
swirling dirt against the Jeep,
making her feel desolate,
almost crazy for no reason.
She pulls forward
through a rolling sea of thick brown air,
knowing that vacuuming must be the first chore.

A fine silt glitters on the baby blue carpet
as she plugs in her Central-Vac and attacks —
powdered sand rises,
a layered curtain of prairie gold,
moving, shifting, uncovering time.
Her now-callused hands holding bunches of broom corns,
tied together and sweeping desperately
across a smooth earthen floor,
soil rising inside the soddy as well as out.
Overwhelmed by the vastness,
she turns to pull blankets up over the bed tick,

the rustling cornhusks and straw
unheard over the keening of mother nature.
She decides on elderberry jam
for the noon cornbread.

Reversed wind currents carry her deeper.
Tossing several buffalo chips on the fire,
she becomes aware that a gust
has torn the tepee's door open,
and the dusty dogs are gathered,
waiting for a piece of dried deer.
She stirs cornmeal in the pottery bowl
and sighs at Great Mother's anger
as She in turn stirs dirt about the camp.

Dispirited, despondent, depression descends
as a metal door slams.
Her men are home
ready for their noon meal.

Experience Counts

LAURIE KUTCHINS *Weather*

I am at home where weather is a big deal.
I belong in the flurry of nerves, in the wire and talk
when the front veers away from the forecaster's stick on the map —
guaranteeing he'll be sheepish the next day —
and comes slithering toward us, unexpected snake
of sleet, snow, squall, hail, rain, lightning, wind, blizzard.
I am at home where weather is the active link.

I am at home with year-round chains and blizzard kits.
Where skilled fingers fiddle with dials,
and ears once frost-nipped perk, mark the forecast
out of the chatter, jukebox, and pool-table din
like a woman plucking an arrow tip out of a ridgetop of stones.

It's March and it's snowing, and this is not the end of it.
At the bar, the ranchers stand around, warming up, checking in.
They are lambing and calving, day and night,
weather is either an intimate friend, nurse, or albatross.
They warm their hands on steamy coffee,
their lips on dry cigarettes,
they smell of smoke and wet wool, of snow and wind and uterine blood.
Outside their trucks idle, windshields and windows whitening
like old men's shoulders, heeler dogs curled on seats
in snow-cocoons, waiting.

I am at home anywhere men and women are telling weather stories.
The time when a single gust tossed a dog in its doghouse
out of the yard.
The blizzard of '84 when things modern shut down for days,
the livestock stuck under snow,
the storm when a pregnant woman left her car in search of gas,
wasn't found until the clearing, days later,

frozen against a pumping oil pump.
The Thanksgiving storm of '79 when stranded travelers
took up every inch of church in the towns between
Cheyenne and Sheridan.
The time when Horse, laying fence, trapped his thumb between wire,
stood there under the January sun hoping someone would come,
and by dusk whacked his thumb off
to get home before the dark froze him
stiff as a fence post.
The time when on a roundup the cows were deliberately turned loose
in a torrent because lightning is drawn to things in huddles.
I am at home in these stories.

It's May and it's snowing wet horizontal snow, and this is not the end of it.
The ranchers are up all hours, feeding and counting their stock,
standing around, warming their lungs, waiting it out.
The school bus brings the children home early.
I belong where towns end, the highways leading out
have metal gates across them
and twelve-foot snow fences hug the roads.
I am at home where root cellars and windows are left unlocked
and a rope is strung between the house and barn.
I am at home where weather is a parental voice I still listen for.

MARY LYNN VOSEN ～ Winter Crouches, Waiting

For three years I lived alone with my daughter on a farm sixty miles from anywhere. There I learned that the land and its seasons are not friends of mine. I know them well — they are not mine. I recall the morning landscape sloping down and easterly from the farm site where the house rested. Sloping for twenty miles, the fields met the ancient badlands whose hills rose up like dinosaurs. They were pink in the new light and bronze in the afterlight of day. We came to know this land and its seasons.

Winter — sometimes it chilled me, sometimes it warmed me. Mostly I warmed myself. Warmed myself to sweating, splitting logs blow upon blow and carrying them from the shed, through waist-high snow to the wood box near the stove in the house. I warmed myself with the thought that I'd gathered the eggs before they could freeze, cleaned the stalls, and fed all of the animals. There was no need to brave the indiscriminate blast of winter crouching outside the door. I'd already done it.

My home was a refuge I entered eagerly. Warm and secure, I busied myself baking bread and sewing quilts. My daughter, Brooke Lynn, got into everything: the flour, the pins, the cupboard. She would climb into the cupboard after removing all of the canned goods. It was her favorite vantage point while I cooked. The days drifted as haphazardly as snow. The nights did, too. I didn't notice the absence of adult companionship until daylight waned and darkness came in its place. Brooke Lynn was asleep. I felt emptiness. I guessed that I was lonely. It didn't matter knowing that the man who was Brooke Lynn's father might come home before morning. His token presence was hardly missed. These were his drinking days. He owned them. He was in his own world. Staying on the farm so far from town, I was in my own world, too. There were times at night when the wind shook the house and woke me; he wasn't home. He might have passed out in the pickup truck or been caught in some drifts trying to drive home. He might have frozen to death. There was nothing I could do. Somehow it seemed acceptable that he might die by his own hand from his own carelessness and insanity in this severe place. It was a fair game. One should not tempt these godless lands.

Sometimes a power line fell under the weight of ice and frost. Our power was cut off. Brooke Lynn and I were isolated. I didn't mind. When night came, I rocked Brooke Lynn to sleep in the candlelight. When furious snow obscured visibility to only a foot or two, I thought of how we hadn't been provided with a car — a way out in case of an emergency. Our nearest neighbor lived a quarter-mile to the south. I often wondered what our chances would be if I blindly blundered through the storm on foot across the fields toward their farm. With Brooke Lynn bound to my chest and zipped inside of my parka, she would be as warm as I. I have a foreboding that we'd have drifted with the flurry downhill in an easterly direction, to be found later piled against the barbed wire fence with the snow.

Winter was a harsh season where I lived. There was no forgiveness for mistakes.

The sharp air stirred my senses, awakening something in me — the nesting instinct, like women and animals about to give birth. Restlessness, which drives me to make myself ready. To prepare for the oncoming winter. This land and its seasons are not friends of mine. I know them well — they are not mine. Winter of starkness, I know that you're coming. I feel it.

SUE CHAULK ⟁ **Returning the Favor**

People say we should give this land back to the Indians. Some days I would pull the covers back and leave a meal on the table for them. If we returned it, I would not have to pay taxes, cook, pull calves, or put up hay. I would change my gender and move in with them. I'd keep my roan cowhorse, chase a few buffalo, clean my gun, and whistle at the women. If they asked me who I was in my previous life, I would say, "Ah, some old ranch woman." They would nod and let me join the war party — experience counts.

JAN RIPPEL ~~~ Daddy and the Ditch Water

"Cup your hands under that, Janet, and take a drink. That's the best water you'll ever taste," Daddy said. I was about ten years old and living on a square-mile farm in central Kansas with my parents and older sister, Mary Ann. Daddy and I were standing at the foot of the windmill. He had just loosened the lever that let the windmill blades start turning and the windmill began pumping up water from the sandy Kansas soil. The water was running clear and cold out of the pipe into the stock tank. I cupped my hands under the pipe and took a big drink of the cold water, and on that hot summer day Daddy was right — it was the best water I'd ever tasted.

Our farm was an average Kansas farm. We raised beef cattle and grew wheat. One thing that made it different from most of the farms was its very sandy soil. It was located nine miles south of the great bend of the Arkansas River, and perhaps at one time all that sandy soil was at the bottom of the inland seas that once covered much of Kansas.

One day in early spring, 1954 or 1955, when I was at country school, the teacher let the class take a big glass jar and scoop up a jarful of muddy ditch water. We looked at the jar as the water cleared and saw fat brown tadpoles. When I got home that day, I ran out and looked in the ditches and mud puddles around our farm and they were all full of the same fat brown tadpoles. The tadpoles were the size of plump grapes. They had stubby tails and some had tiny back feet. As the days passed, I watched them change into frogs.

Time quickly passed and I went away to college. I always loved coming back to the farm, and I was always glad if there was enough summer rain to fill the ditches. One summer in the sixties I was driving along the county road beside our farm. This was the road with the large ditch where I used to play. I was approaching a county road truck. The truck driver was going about five miles per hour because he was spraying the ditch, the water, and the plants that grew by the ditch with weed killer.

I slowly passed the truck and then looked over at the ditch. The plants that had been bright, green, and erect before the spray hit them had suddenly turned black, drooping, and greasy looking. If there had been any tadpoles in the ditch water that year, they were certainly gone along with the green plants.

In the late sixties I married and moved away from the farm, but my new family and I returned to visit as often as we could. A lot of things were changing, but Daddy still loved farm life and was still bragging about the water. Only now when we would walk out by the windmill and stock tank I was the one who said to my daughters, "Cup your hands under the pipe and take a drink. Don't be afraid, that's good water."

The seasons on the farm flowed one into the other. As the years passed Daddy began using more chemicals to grow wheat, corn, and now soybeans. In the seventies a big change came to one quarter of the farm. A quarter that had been a pasture of native prairie grass, one of the last patches in that part of Kansas, was put under center-pivot irrigation. To pay for the irrigation system, the pasture was dug up and planted to soybeans.

In the early eighties Daddy fell ill with what he thought was indigestion, but turned out to be inoperable liver and pancreatic cancer. Daddy came home from the hospital and stayed in his farmhouse for the remaining three months of his life.

By this time I was living with my husband and three daughters in South Dakota. I knew I had to drive back to the farm and see Daddy. As I was driving back across the Great Plains I thought of my life on the farm; how I loved the prairie and the tadpoles and how sad I was that Daddy was dying young. He was about ten years younger than his father was when he died. I started remembering things Daddy had told me.

When I got to the farmhouse I greeted Mother and Mary Ann and went back to the bedroom to see Daddy. He was in bed and looked frail and weak. Not realizing how weak, I took his hand firmly, as he would expect me to do, and immediately felt bad as I watched him wince in pain. We talked for a while, and then I left him to rest.

I went to the living room to visit with Mother and Mary Ann, and we talked about Daddy and other family news. It came time to fix supper so I went to the kitchen to help fix Daddy's tray of food. When I started to get him a glass of water from the tap, Mother said, "Don't use the tap water. Your Daddy only drinks bottled water now. He's afraid of the tap water."

Shortly after that visit Daddy died. That was almost ten years ago. I rarely, if ever, see tadpoles now. When I think back on those rainy Kansas summers and Daddy and ditches I think if we had more tadpoles and more roadside plants and more prairie pastures, I could be visiting with Daddy today and getting from him still a firm handshake and a warm, loving hug.

B. J. BUCKLEY ⌒﹨ *Last Words in October*

The Jerry-cat's gone, he's
a hair shirt, the unfleshed bones
of the idea of cat,

afloat like smoke
above the drought-singed pasture, blue
as the green-blue sage, at last

as transparent as he always believed
himself to be, a shadow's shadow,
stone-patient, quick

as razored lightning.
The prairie dogs can't see him
now, nor the cottontails

quivering beneath the tack shed —
his breath's gone silent as air,
the world's struck deaf

to moss-soft footfall
in the cheatgrass — it's the wind
this season that sounds whiskery

and dangerously wise.
Incorporate he was velvet black
with delicate white toes

and white mustachios, and he wore
a bib of ivory on his chest.
He could leap my height

into the air, weightless, his tail
balanced against nothing,
and snatch birds flying low,

though he forbore the swallows
when they spent whole summer evenings
diving at his head. Once

he caught two rabbits in a single
bound, and dragged them home
half a mile by the ears,

tumbling and tripping over their warm,
dead weight like a clown,
and then he left them

for the barn cat and her kittens —
presented them, rather, laid them out
paws crossed on the grass, and then reclined

against a stump to watch the babies'
dumb show of stalk and pounce over
the furry corpses. Once he shivered

up between the walls to oust
a nest of packrats from an upstairs
northwest corner of the house.

The noise of it! The snarl
and hiss and scream and squeak!
Mad cries of battle! —

Until at last he hauled them one by one
limp across the ceiling, down
the wall, outside into the dark.

He left the feet of vanquished mice
in little rows arranged precisely
on the doorsill, and he shared

his dish of kibbles peaceably
with the skunk lovers who one February
made a den under the bunkhouse.

I gave him milk in a blue bowl
and he drank it clean as sky.
Out there, out there in the autumn

gold and rust, any place the grass
bends he might be, my puss,
my little snow-foot, sweet soft hunter —

He's gone to chase the silver silent deer,
sleek and fleet, oh, ghostly fast,
he's the antelope's invisible pursuer.

ELIZABETH CANFIELD ⟍ The Informer

She didn't know that I watched from the north window. For several days I saw her move like a little ghost, alert, testing the air with her sharp vixen's nose, slipping out of sight at the least sound or movement.

She had denned, unknown to us, up the hill, under the big boulder. She couldn't know that she was absolutely predictable from this point on. I knew that when the weather warmed and summer came there would be times, as the evening shadows lengthened, when I could see her playful pups against the hill. Little foxes, learning what they must know to perpetuate their race. As do we all. So has it ever been . . .

Now I had a duty: She couldn't stay. Did she know she had a fine, well-hidden route to the chicken yard? And another to the barn where the ewes were lambing? Probably. It was not even a question of weighing equally undesirable alternatives.

Where do foxes, graceful, elegant, cunning, fit into our Peaceable Kingdom? I tried to blame Eve. *Eve*, I thought, *you should have left well enough alone, back there in the Garden of Eden. Now just see what a position you have placed me in!*

The little fox and I have the same goal in life: to protect our young and perpetuate our race. But unlike me, she doesn't have a conscience and doesn't know guilt.

My children are fighting all the battles they can handle here on this Wyoming ranch — and we are not living in a Walt Disney wildlife movie. I know you, little fox.

My son stopped his pickup at my door and I went out to tell him about the fox.

MARY DUFFY ⟍ *A Farmer's Grandchild*

My grandparents had something besides their love to share with me; something once common among grandparents in rural America but now increasingly rare; something that fewer and fewer grandchildren will ever know.

My grandparents had a farm.

Being a farmer's grandchild meant combining the best of what a farm has to offer with the opportunity to avoid the less desirable aspects. I could go home whenever I wanted.

Unlike a parent's farm, a grandparent's farm is only wonder, adventure, and fun. It is a hay mow filled with bales to jump on and over and around, to rearrange into forts and castles and secret hiding places, to use as padding for midair somersaults.

A grandparent's farm is the gentle old mare that allows you to ride her bridleless around the corral and the high-spirited shetland pony that delights in dropping its bareback riders at will. It is orphaned lambs to bottle-feed from big, black rubber nipples attached to quart-size soda pop bottles.

A farm is a stock pond to swim in when the August sun burns up everything else, even your fear of the bloodsuckers that will inevitably appear between your toes. In the winter, that same pond transforms itself into your own private skating rink and sledding spot.

A grandparent's farm is counting newborn calves in the early morning mist and being paid a nickel per weed for each cocklebur plant uprooted from the roadside ditches. It's exploring the abandoned farmsteads from someone else's past while your own future lies ahead.

A grandparent's farm is, perhaps, the best rural America has to offer. It is children interacting with nature and animals and earth in a way that can only make them better adults.

I mourn the loss of my grandparents, their farm, and the thousands of other family farms lost to the ever-increasing efficiency of agribusiness. But most of all, I mourn the loss suffered by grandchildren, my own kids included, who will never know the gift of a grandparent's farm.

JEAN KEEZER-CLAYTON ～ **The Last Coyote Hunt**

I curled the barbed
wire in a loose spiral,
threading it down
the coyote burrow
until I hit pay dirt.

The barbs held
in the critter's fur
and I pulled, slow
and steady. Took
about ten minutes
to yank her out.
She whipped her
head from side
to side, fighting
hard against the
wire, all the while
digging it deeper
into her sides
until the blood

puddled thick,
red on the ground.
Been pulling coyotes
twenty years without
thinking about
the sorry critters.

This morning, though,
I thought about that she-
coyote — and bankers,
wires and mortgages.

Grabbed the wire-
cutters and vet salve.
Doctored that stupid
coyote an hour or more,
watched her crawl back
in her hole when
I let her go.

TAMMI LITTREL   *Closet Animal Rightist*

As I sat in the accountant's office he began to tell a story about one of his
clients that he found amusing.

Listening intently and waiting for the funny part, I tried not to look too
impatient as I calculated in my head what this story was costing me by the
minute at the accountant's hourly fee.

He was telling me that his clients, an old rancher and his wife, had come
into his office for help in financial planning and in cutting costs. As they
pored over the books, the accountant made note that the rancher spent in
excess of two hundred dollars each month for dog and cat food. The wife
explained that her husband had a large number of cats and dogs and
couldn't bear turning away a stray.

This is where the story ended. I waited, thinking there must be more.
Finally the accountant explained the paradox he found amusing. He found
it ironic that a man who was callous and heartless enough to raise cattle
for slaughter would spend money he didn't have on dogs and cats.

I couldn't say anything. "Callous and heartless" circled round in my
head. Is this what people think of us? This accountant was not in L.A. or
New York, he was in a community where agriculture is the number one
industry. He made his living off these farmers and ranchers.

I don't remember anything else he said that afternoon. All the next
day while I went about my chores caring for the cows, I couldn't shake

his words. I had grown up in a ranching community and this slant on who I was in other people's eyes was a new one for me.

I couldn't stop wondering, do all non-farm/ranch people see us that way — as barbarians who butcher and slaughter at a whim? Mostly I wondered how could this happen here, where ag is supposed to be king? Have people become too many generations removed from the family farm to know what farming and ranching are all about, or are they accepting as fact the so-called "politically correct" but inaccurate animal rightists' views that are promoted in the media?

Later that summer my mother-in-law and her new husband, Jan, a college professor, came for a visit. I was relating to them how we had had several twin and triplet deer babies born in the hay meadow, and I really had to watch when I was swathing hay so I wouldn't run into a hiding baby. One fawn I moved out of the way several times. I thought it was the same baby, but later I saw the mother with triplets! Sometimes the mother will stand nearby if I am cutting close to her baby's hiding place.

As I was telling my deer stories, Jan looked puzzled. Finally he asked me, "Why do you bother to move a baby deer out of the way when you raise beef for slaughter?" Here it was again, that paradox that outsiders can't understand about ranchers.

I told him that I do like animals and that raising beef fills an economic need — it provides food for lots of people — while me killing baby deer with the swather would be senseless and wasteful and do no one any good. That seemed to satisfy him, but it made me all the more aware of how ranchers are perceived not just by folks in big cities but also by closet animal rightists in smaller rural communities.

I read a letter from a woman from New Jersey who was writing in response to an article in *People* magazine about ranchers killing coyotes. Her solution to the problem was that ranchers should simply fence their property so the coyotes can't get in. These people really have no clue as to what life is like out here, but they propose to tell us that we are doing it all wrong. The paradox seems to me to lie in the city dweller who can step over a homeless person without giving her another thought or ignore social disparity when it stares him in the face and yet turn on an industry he does not know or understand and cry inhumanity. If he knew any ranchers personally, he would know that they love their animals and have a great respect for them. If they didn't, they wouldn't sacrifice so much for their care. It's not a 9 to 5, weekends off, it's a 24/7 and the animals get taken care of first every day, even Christmas, and there's no calling in sick.

Our only hope in righting the many wrongs that have been hurled our way is through education. Mr. Greenjeans is long gone, and so it seems is the country's respect for the people who feed them, but actions do speak louder than thousands and thousands of words; we just need people to learn about our actions.

BARBARA LOVE ⟶ A Place of My Own

I have always dreamed of a place of my own — a house and enough land for a partial living, room for livestock and wildlife, family and friends. My husband and two kids share this dream, but like most young families in agriculture, the reality of owning our own place remains just beyond our reach. So we continue to work for others. We're not unhappy; we chose our work and way of life, and are thankful to be doing it. But I still dream of my own place.

My husband and I are third-generation Wyoming natives; we live forty-five miles from where we both grew up, near our families. We have been on this place for eleven years. I have learned where the mallards swim, where the blue herons stand on cool, sunny mornings. The neighborhood fox hunts at dusk in the field by the house, and rockchucks whistle from boulders across the creek.

The ewes and heifers lamb or calve in the coldest, windiest spot on the lot. Our saddle horses must be wrangled from the top of the big hill on sultry days when the flies are biting.

Sometimes I climb to the ridgetop and sit on a boulder surrounded by limber pines and ancient junipers. Wildflowers grow in protected pockets; mountain bluebirds chortle in the branches, and red-tailed hawks windsurf the thermals.

The infamous Wyoming wind patterns for this place are different from anywhere else I've lived. Lying in bed at night, I can tell wind direction and magnitude from the way the gutters on the house hum and the sounds through the trees. On a cool June morning the breeze comes down the creek like liquid crystal — clear and ringing. Dusty summer or fall gales carry smoke from wildfires in California or as close as the next drainage. In winter, arctic blasts whip the blood into my face and fingers, and soft eddies whirl shrouds of flakes in and around everything. A warm, snow-melting wind often means foot-swallowing, pickup-stopping mud that freezes at night and melts into inaccessibility during the day.

The mule deer doe with the split ear has been coming to my yard since she was a fawn five years ago, and now brings each year's crop of youngsters to learn the fine art of removing protective netting and fencing from my flowers and vegetables. They especially like the jack-o'-lanterns on our porch in October and the rhubarb leaves under the bedroom window.

My organic garden is filled with birds, insects, and small critters of the reptile and rodent persuasion. I've developed raised beds and water-saving methods, built the soil from gravel and sand into rich, productive loam. Every year I put in more perennials; this year I added bush cherries and raspberries to shelter the mountain bluebird house I put up four years ago.

This is a good place; I love it and would like to stay. But it is not ours. My knowledge and relationship with these hills and rocks, with the plants and animals, means nothing. My tenure here depends on someone else's decisions. I plant knowing I might never see the blooms or fruit, that there might not be pumpkins for the deer next October. When I leave, a piece of me will remain.

Whoever lives here next might not know the fuzzy gray-green leaves by the porch in June will be three-foot-high brilliant blue delphiniums in July, or that the great horned owl hunts the calving lot at night from the middle telephone pole. They might not care where the first tiny yellow and purple violets bloom in spring, or that the brilliance of the stars or the silent, flashing dance of the northern lights on cold winter nights are better than anything a television network could produce. Standing outside, listening to the wind sing with coyote accompaniment, I know why I want my own place. It has absolutely nothing to do with prestige or business, everything to do with the smell of sagebrush and warm earth, the Indian paintbrush and antelope fawns, hollyhocks that bloom every year, and bluebirds that return to sit in my raspberry bushes.

A place to call home. Someplace familiar and dear; a haven for my heart and soul.

VIRGINIA BENNETT ⌒ The Dead Yearling

The low-growth bushes were starting to bud
    And the first blades of grass began to appear
As my mare picked her way through rocks and mud
    Wearing her first set of shoes for the year

The raucous crows winged their effortless way
    Up over the ridge and clean out of sight
And I rejoiced in the promise of a longer day
    Followed by window breezes on a shortened night

The vows that Spring made of renewal and hope
    As I rode along, I succumbed to their sound
And we topped the saddle in one last, lurching lope
    While I delighted in finally riding on bare ground

Yes, Spring beckoned softly of her new life, new birth
    When we scrambled down the other side, I saw
A dead yearling deer lying on the sun-warmed earth
    At the foot of a cliff on the other side of the draw

I reined my horse over to it; she found her way with care
    And I thought almost out loud about its death

Why did he wait to die until the green grass filled the air?
Why didn't winter claim his last breath?

He'd made it through that tough first year
Of bein' a weanling and livin' on his senses
He'd obviously survived and been able to clear
In flightless bounds those lethal wire fences

So, why did he choose to give up the ghost
On this needle-covered, pine-coned forest floor
At just the time when the Earth gives her most?
He could've made it if he'd held on a few days more

He lies there, a metaphor of mundane rules
The epitome of a worn-out cliché
Leave the romancing to old women and fools
Stand here and grasp what happened this day

"With the good comes the bad," that's what they say
It's a truth that outweighs all the lies
But it's fact that for every birth on some warm Spring day
Somewhere, all alone, something dies

SHANNON DYER ~~~~ The Auction

After one date, I told my future husband, Doug, I couldn't go out with him again. My mother had always told me never to date someone I wouldn't marry, and I knew I didn't want to marry a rancher and move to the middle of nowhere. But he charmed me, and in February 1982 I started my ranching life.

My new in-laws bought an extra two hundred acres in the Nebraska sandhills when land prices were high. Soon after our marriage the recession hit and we couldn't make the payments. For an agonizing year we bartered with the Federal Land Bank. In 1987 the bank took our ranch, where Doug's grandparents had come when there was only a sod shanty and a corral. This family tragedy still affects us, and "The Auction" is about leaving the place we all loved.

The Auction

"Do I hear one dollar for this box of junk?" He held up a box most people would see as worthless, including the piece of metal I always hung the gas tank nozzle on and the bar I used to pry the grain door open.

"Okay, how about fifty cents?" As the auctioneer droned on, I turned to visit with some neighbors. When the group moved to the next row I slipped away to the house. My mother-in-law was sitting in a folding lawn chair in the shade of an oak planted by her mother-in-law when she came to the ranch to live in a sod shanty.

I put my hand on her arm and said gently, "How are you doing?"

She smiled brightly, hiding pain. "I'm trying to stay out of the sun. It sure is hot for April."

"It's a nice day," I said, rubbing my protruding belly while the baby inside squirmed to a more comfortable position. "There's a big crowd."

"We've got some good friends, don't we?" When Mrs. Buchfinck hobbled over to visit about the old days I opened a lawn chair for her. She was Doug's godmother and best friend to his grandmother.

Wandering out of earshot, I started for the barn, stopping long enough to spot our daughter Joslyn's shiny red hair. At three years old, she happily played hostess to the people who came to her house that day.

The first room of the barn was empty and clean, strange without nuts and bolts, wire and tools stored in the places where they'd been since before Doug was born. I stopped in front of the closed door to the back of the barn. I'd been taught never to barge in there in case I startled a cow and foiled some delicate operation.

I remembered standing in this spot at four A.M. a few years before, wondering if it was safe to open the door. I'd awakened to realize that Doug had gone to check heavies two hours earlier. When I woke alone, I decided to see if he needed help. Donning my usual hurry-outside-in-the-middle-of-the-night clothes, I high-tailed it to the barn. I stood, ear to this door, in my four-sizes-too-big olive-green parka and my moon boots, my white nightgown billowing around my legs. Chilly, I pulled the hood up, leaving only my eyes showing. While I debated whether to go in, Doug opened the door and I screamed. Doug wasn't expecting to see a green monster and he nearly fainted. I giggled again at the memory and walked inside. I ran my hands over the head gate, remembering the first time I ever watched Doug and his dad, Dale, pull a calf, six years earlier as a new ranch wife. While I got used to being married, I learned about ranching and country life. Anxious to experience the miracle of birth and see what they meant by "pulling" a calf, I traipsed out to the barn.

"Something's not right here," said Doug, pulling his arm out of the rear end of the cow with a sound like footsteps in muck. "I can't feel the head or the feet."

Dale shoved his arm into a long plastic glove and reached inside the cow. Gurgling noises accompanied his grunts until he said, "I don't know. Why don't you call the vet?"

Unfortunately, the vet was on another call. Doug and Dale took turns working on the poor critter, pushing and pulling to sloshing, sucking sounds, trying to turn the calf so they could get the chains on something solid. Their arms were covered with blood, all the disgusting slime that seeps from the back end of a cow. Soon the smell of Lysol mingled with the odor of dung. Nothing worked and the cow was beginning to go down. Finally, Dale took out his pocketknife and dunked it in the bucket of Lysol. I watched, horrified, as he inserted it into the cow.

That was the last thing I saw; my knees buckled and I hit the barn floor. Doug looked up long enough to say, "You better go outside." That was my introduction to the glamour of ranch life.

Memories kept flipping before me like some mental Rolodex. I left the barn, closing the door behind me. Dale was walking across the yard with a piece of cherry pie.

"That won't do your diet any good," I said.

"Who said I was on a diet? Besides, it looks like maybe you're the one who needs to diet." We laughed at his joke and I patted my pregnant belly.

I wanted to tell him I was sorry for what he had to endure today. Born here, Dale had spent his life on this ranch and today he would leave here forever. I put my arm around him and kissed his cheek. He smiled, "I better go keep that auctioneer honest." He handed me his empty plate and hurried away.

I joined the crowd around the International M tractor.

"Do I hear five hundred?"

"Yeah!"

"Five twenty-five?"

"Yeah!"

Bid it up, I thought. That tractor was special to me — the only one I was allowed to drive after I sent the swather spinning down the hill. That suited me fine. I'd sit on that little tractor pulling my side-delivery rakes back and forth across each pivot, through three cuttings of alfalfa every summer. To relieve the boredom, I'd sing ditties and make up sordid romance novels. Sometimes I'd get so involved with my storytelling that I'd forget to check the neat windrows that were supposed to form in my wake. One day I made up a particularly engrossing tale. When I finally looked back, I discovered that the rakes had fallen off almost a whole round back. Turning the tractor, I hurried back, hoping to hook them up before Doug came out. But the tongue was sticking straight up in the air and I couldn't pull it down to hook on. I walked two miles back to the house. Doug was annoyed, but he was also amazed. "Didn't you notice anything different?" he stormed.

"Well, not really," I replied. "I guess maybe the tractor pulled a little faster than usual."

I don't think he ever got over that.

"Sold!" The last item. I found Doug in the crowd and slipped my hand in his. He laughed at something a friend said and casually moved away.

While everyone headed to the concession stand for another piece of pie, or to the pickups for something more fortifying, I found Joslyn playing in her favorite place under the lilac bushes. The dog had made a dugout she called her hideout, but I could see it from the kitchen and from the front porch. Hand on my stomach, I thought of things we'd planned here for Joslyn, things the new baby would never get to do. Doug wanted to build a tree house in that big elm at the edge of the meadow where Dale had built one for him. There would be no more climbing that hill behind the house to pick wildflowers, trying to remember where the bush cherries were so we could pick them ripe. No more early morning snowmobile rides across the frozen meadow when the trees sparkled against the sapphire sky. Our children won't get to grow up here. That life ended today.

I picked up sleepy Joslyn and took her to the pickup. She stuck her thumb in her mouth and drifted off to sleep.

I climbed the front porch steps and dropped into the swing. Hearing people laugh and joke as they finished up their business and left, I recalled countless peaceful mornings I'd brought one more cup of coffee out here while the sun broke over the hills. Whenever Joslyn was fussy, I'd bring her to the porch swing bundled in blankets.

I sighed and stood; it was time to say another good-bye. The house was cool and quiet, but the silence was awkward. When I walked across the hardwood floor, my footsteps ricocheted across the empty room and bounced off the bare walls. The house felt deserted. Dustballs played tag on the barren floors. But I could feel the lives of three generations within these walls, and I imagined putting everything back. The couch was there. The television along that wall. Joslyn's toy box was under that window.

I went to the window. Pickups formed a line on the road, following each other out. I would never pace from kitchen to living room again, stopping at each window to study the storm and wonder when Doug would come in. I'd look out front; is he bringing in a cow that's calving? At the south window, I'd watch snow pile up. Is he in the shop working on a tractor and should I start making gravy now? In the kitchen, I'd look out back. Maybe he's on his way in; I should probably set the table.

In the bedroom, I shut my eyes and imagined the even rhythm of the pivot as it sprayed water on the alfalfa in the meadow. I loved to lie there in the sweet summer night and listen while it kept time to the cricket chorus. Bandit, our German shepherd, would run from the front of the house to the back, barking until Doug hollered at her. She'd quiet down until the breeze ruffled the leaves again.

I found Doug on the front porch. We stood looking across the meadow in a quiet interrupted only by the call of a whippoorwill. A deer and her two fawns ventured out to taste the sweet alfalfa. At a soft noise, I turned to see Doug wiping his eyes. I held him tight. This was the time for tears.

VIVIAN HAMBURG Gambling

James politely refused to play cards with my family at our Sunday afternoon gatherings. Poker was usually the game of choice. We used poker chips, matchsticks, or toothpicks to determine the winner, but even though no money changed hands, James would not be involved. "It's gambling; it's wrong!" he said pleasantly and excused himself to go for a walk.

I thought about this as I waited for sleep on "irrigating" nights. I had seen James cry only twice. Once when his father died. The other time was when, for the seventh consecutive year, a hailstorm wiped out the entire crop — a year's work. We'd have to borrow money from the bank to buy feedlot cattle and to buy feed for them, hoping for a profit when they were sold. Then we'd borrow more money for seed and expenses, hoping that, in spite of the seven previous years, the eighth crop would be a good one.

James could rationalize it any way he wanted, but my conclusion was: farming is the biggest gamble of all!

REBECCA WAMPLER Old Ponies

Skeletons of shelter belts
Support homesteads with their bony arms,
In a broken chain across the faltering plains.

Middle-aged folks go gray on the fringes of stagnant towns.
The ponies they learned to ride on
Disappear when the grandchildren come.

A tiny, hatchet-faced mare hides in the windbreak,
a faerie in her glade,
Cockleburs brush-rollered in her forelock.

Behind the barn dozes an old hoofer,
Leaning his ratcheting joints against the sun-warmed boards.
You could hang your hat on his hip bone.

Frosty mornings she humps up by the shearing shed,
He hunkers down in the haystack.
Waiting for a can of cake, scoop of grain, alfalfa flake.

Old witch and warlock, bluffers of dogs.
Classy and Chubby, tough as their practical keepers.
The vet is called only for those with future productivity.
Nobody goes hungry.

CAROLYN JOHNSEN 〜 Not to Farm

My father asks, "Do any of you kids wish now you'd gone back to the farm?"

It's a snowy day at my parents' home in the city; we're playing Trivial Pursuit and I'm winning. My sister and brother answer quickly, "No, Dad," and laugh.

My father would like to hear regret, some second thoughts from us children, who turned it down, one by one, when he and Mom offered us the farm.

My brother, sister, and I live and work in the city and have satisfied any longing for the farm with urban strategies: we've lived on acreages near town and we've had pets, gardens, ranch-style homes, and country kitchens — although no farm woman I know ever put ruffles around mirrors.

I could have farmed — for spring peas grown in a garden big enough to be tilled by a plow and for the sound of the squeaking windmill and the silhouette of the barn against a summer sky. I could have farmed for the green, humid shade between rows of glossy corn in August and for the itch of my sticky skin against it; for squealing sows and baby pigs, calves that sucked my fingers, and for cherry juice running down my arm in summer.

When my parents left the farm, my mother gave me a color snapshot she had kept pinned to the wall by the telephone. My father took it from the top of the windmill in late afternoon.

The pasture lane runs at an angle from the top and off the bottom of the picture. Sheep in a long crooked line walk toward the camera, following a leader out of sight in the shadow at the bottom of the picture. They stir up pale dust that floats against the gold corn stubble. That speck at the back, my father says, is me bringing in the sheep.

I picture me the farmer not at the back of a passive string of market lambs. Instead, I'm a farmer with grease to my elbows, working with wrench and pliers and oil can on the Farmall tractor.

I wait with a sow on a cold winter night — she on her side, grunting, her flesh heaving with labor, her breath scattering straw before her snout.

I thaw frozen water in the cattle tanks and scoop snow.

I borrow money to buy seed and I pray for rain, but not too much.

I could have done all these things. Neither work nor risk kept me from the farm.

My mother — a city girl — learned to farm. She walked our soybean fields to keep them free of weeds, yanking pigweed and cocklebur out by their deepest roots. She planted snapdragons and taught me that flowers die more easily than weeds.

She comforted frantic chicks and reached beneath complaining hens to harvest their sticky eggs.

My mother clipped discount coupons from the newspaper, counted change, and bought day-old bread — or made her own, kneading it with her fists.

My grandmother said my mother had it easy — with a wringer washer instead of a washboard and with a gas stove instead of cobs.

I've watched my grandmother hold a chicken to a scarred stump and strike it with an ax, clean through the neck on the first blow, and not wince at the blood or at the body dancing madly in the dust while she pulled another from the gunnysack held closed beneath her left foot. She kept the sack on a nail in the barn and used it once, my mother told me, to drown some surplus kittens in.

My grandmother lectured me on the benefits of the barn swallow and said I was cruel to knock the swallows' nests from the barn ceiling with a broom handle. For days she was sad about the broken nests.

My grandmother and my mother would have known how to remove a dead horse from the barn. My mare, Boots, died one night. My father had her hauled off by the rendering company while I was at school, saving me the pain, he said, of knowing she had died and having to see her go.

I imagine knowing by heart the phone number of the rendering company and leading the driver to a dead horse, watching him hook the chain to her leg, just above the knee, perhaps, and winch the body out of the stall, stirring up dust and straw, the pigeons on the roof nervous at the smell of death.

I could have farmed, for the sake of life and in spite of death.

There is an illusion about farming that the farm has less to do with hard work, delayed gratification, and loss than it does with security, clean air, and wholesomeness. My father contributed to this illusion, but sometimes he failed in ways he didn't know.

For a few minutes after dinner every day, he napped at the top of the basement stairs, sitting on the top step and lying back on the floor, his blue jeans hiked up above his ankles. It was then, while he was sleeping, that I once saw the bruises on his shins from the last time the pigs cornered him in the pen.

I know now that farming takes cunning, courage, endurance, and intelligence. And yet as a child I heard adults speak with respect of people who left to work in the city — whether they sold insurance, real estate, or Avon products — the farther away they got from the farm, from Cedar County, and from Nebraska, the more successful they were perceived to be by those who remained. And I understand now that I was being educated to leave, but I don't understand why.

My brother, sister, and I have brought a generation of farming attitudes to the city. We temper our urban lives with a farmer's resourcefulness, endurance, sentiment, and perspective. We know harsh reality when we see it, but we know that harshness isn't all there is to see.

Each of us could have farmed, I think.

We've let it go. The farm was sold. My sister says, "You ought to drive on past the place and see what they've done to the barn." I can only imagine.

VIOLA HAYS BLAIR ⌇ Remembering the Depression Years

December of 1934 is the focus of all that I remember about the Depression. Mom and we kids were home alone while Dad had caught a ride to Montana, hoping things were better there; he was trying to sell encyclopedias in Billings and he would be home by Christmas Eve.

Our only source of income was my paper route. About twenty-five people who worked for the Homestake Mine would pay five cents a week for the *Grit*, and I felt pleased to be earning about twenty-five cents a week. I was eleven, the only girl "paperboy" in Terraville.

I remember waking up in the night and raising up when Dad got home. He'd been unable to sell encyclopedias, but got a temporary job cooking pancakes in a café and earned a couple of dollars. On a snowy night, he tried to hitchhike home, but got no ride until he stood in the road and waved frantically. Long after midnight, he walked from Lead through the old mine tunnel to Terraville. A few days later, he got a job at Homestake.

We stayed in Terraville another year, then moved to Whitewood. Life seemed full of promise on a spring day when my sister was two years old and I was almost fourteen. One day in early March, my twelve-year-old brother came home from school and found our mother lying dead on the floor.

Having money or not having money has never seemed important to me since that day.

RHAE FOSTER ⌇ Curley

Let me tell you about Curley. He was born with diphtheria, he was blind, and his mother deserted him at birth. He couldn't suck or swallow. He couldn't stand, couldn't even lift his head. And, oh yeah, he was a Black Angus calf.

The spring of 1974 had been especially wet and the barn was damp and chilled, not a good environment for a sick animal. The morning after Curley's birth I pitted my one hundred and ten pounds against his dead weight and grunted and groaned him into our rickety wheelbarrow. Sunshine consistently covered a corner of pasture between the barn and the house. I pushed Curley to that corner and laid him in the grass. He rested, motionless and frail under the radiant Wyoming sky, while the sun warmed his hide.

Sunshine, penicillin, and nourishment became my routine. As I prepared to administer his first injection, I recalled my own experience with the cold, thick stuff. I remembered it hurt like mad going in and seemed to take forever.

Still, giving Curley his shot was the easy part. Feeding him was more complex. Curley could not open his mouth so I had to open it for him, and this required both hands. After I had forced the nipple into his mouth, the trick was to squeeze it and simultaneously prop Curley's head up so the milk would run down his throat, not out of his mouth and onto the ground. I had to hold the bucket at a certain angle so the inch or two of milk inside would cover the nipple hole. While squeezing the nipple, I rubbed the underside of his neck. This helped him swallow, sometimes. It was difficult to accomplish this and not drop the bucket. It took a lot of practice before I was certain I had gotten more milk on the inside of Curley than I had on the outside. I also put up with our big yellow dog as he poked his nose into my business. He didn't help with the feeding but he was one heck of a cleaner-upper.

I did little more that spring in the verdant mountains, surrounded by grizzled pines, than sit on the fence and stare at Curly. White clouds passed through boundless sky and crisp mountain air slid around me. I was waiting for a sign.

"Is this going to work?" I asked myself over and over.

"It's got to," answered a voice inside my head.

When we hired on to manage this small ranch in the southeastern Wyoming mountains, Allen and I didn't know the owner intended to use the place as a tax write-off. We started out gung-ho, made improvements left and right, and were happy, busy, excited, and fulfilled by our progress. About the first of April, the boss came by. We proudly showed him our accomplishments. Then we got the news. Our job was to occupy the place, ward off vandals, and handle any threat to animals or property. Keep the status quo, that's all. We were crushed. What had been an exciting situation for us, full of promise, became an overwhelming disappointment.

Word was sent out that we were available and seeking employment again. A number of good leads came our way, but until we received a definite offer we were pretty much stuck at Despondency Gulch.

The ranch was stagnant. Our labors stopped and we lived in a fog of gloom. Doing nothing was torturous. I needed to work, to do something worthwhile, see a task through to completion. Anything. Then Curley was born.

The boss was going to let Curley die as part of the write-off. I threw a stomp-with-both-feet, jump-up-and-down fit. The place falling to ruin was depressing enough, but the idea of letting that calf die put me over the edge. It was more than I could cope with. I wouldn't have Mr. Boss Man using this animal's life for his gain. No! So he gave Curley to me and the calf's recovery became my goal.

Late one gorgeous afternoon in May, I returned from doing errands in town. It was the magnificent type of day that only happens in the Western mountains. The sun, brilliant and direct, gleamed just above the pines. The air was dry, light, and filled with the scent of pine and sage. I felt a spiritual sensation of things growing.

Before leaving that morning I had performed my ritual; wheelbarrow, Curley, sunshine, penicillin, milk. I was anxious to get back and see how my patient was doing. Twice in the last week he had lifted his head, and once I saw him try to lift his shoulders off the ground.

As I topped the rise above the ranch I caught a glimpse of something there, in the corner of the pasture. I brought the car to a quick stop and stared. Was it — yes, it was! Curley, standing on four legs. I couldn't move. More than a few seconds passed before I reckoned with what I was seeing. Curley's black coat glistened. His head bobbed up and down as if he was using it to keep his balance. This was the first successful, encouraging thing to have happened in weeks.

I let the car coast down the rise and stopped next to Curley's corner. In this moment of happiness, I was overcome by all the disappointments associated with this job. Tears mixed with dust on the pole fence as I climbed through to get a better look. I stroked the velvet curls above Curley's eyes with my fingertips and praised him long and loud for his success. He was still too weak to walk, and at sundown it was back in the wheelbarrow and into the barn.

In a matter of days Curley was walking around as well as any healthy calf on the place. Feeding time became a lot easier now that he was able to stand. Holding the bucket knee high was a major improvement over the old balance-and-switch act. Curley learned that dinner was knee high and ran to suck the knees of anyone who chanced to come near him.

Allen taught him a head-butt game. It went like this: Allen would lean over and push his shoulder forward and Curley would butt it with his head. It was their own little tough-man contest. How did Curley learn to do that, being blind?

We tried putting him out with the herd a couple of times, but it didn't work. He had never been around other cattle and probably didn't know he was one of them. He stayed off to himself as if he were the only animal in existence.

Finally we took another job — hooray! Our new boss let us bring Curley along and he survived and grew. Even when he was a full-grown steer, he wanted to play the head-butt game. Not a good idea for Allen; Curley had gotten very big.

The sky was overcast and the wind blew out of the northwest the morning Curley became the ultimate of what every beef-steer can be. Allen carried the rifle and we walked silently from the house to the barn. I gazed intently at Curley and reflected. He had become a splendid, healthy animal. I was proud of him, and proud that I had saved him and helped to provide for my family. We paused a moment to thank Curley for what he had been to us, and for what he was about to become.

Several weeks passed before Curley joined us for dinner.

"Ol' Curley is the sweetest tastin' beefsteak ever," Allen said.

He sure was.

BETH GIBBONS ⬩ *Alone*

I kept thinking, *I'm too young to be a widow*. But thinking it doesn't change anything. There is work to be done here and no one but me to do it.

Each morning it was more of the same, I rose early to prepare cooked oatmeal and eat an orange after pulling on my faded denim jeans and a long-sleeved shirt. I fed the chickens, filled the tank, chased cattle off the alfalfa and sudan fields, then checked the tractor and machinery again. I put on a cap and gloves and spent twelve hours on the tractor. Most days I took the water jug and an orange and kept working. Tears would flow freely in that tractor cab as I had lots of time to think and pray.

Many nights the dogs would tree a raccoon and bark all night. If the coon came down while Aric and Brown were watching, the coon was done for. I didn't go out alone with the flashlight because it could be a rattlesnake. More than once we shot rattlesnakes at night, but now I couldn't hold the light and gun at the same time.

Baby, the bottle-raised calf, went wherever he wanted. I had called him Baby so he wouldn't have a real name and we wouldn't get so attached. Baby had bonded to me since his mother died when he was born. He butted me when he was hungry, but now that he was huge, I was afraid of him. He started going through the gate onto the road. He couldn't be shooed. He knew I wouldn't hurt him with a stick. The only way I could move him was with a bucket of feed, if he was hungry.

Late one night a neighbor called about a critter on the road. It was Baby. I told the neighbor I was afraid of Baby and couldn't get him in alone. "I hadn't thought about that." Click.

The alfalfa was drying. A friend called and offered to help. After suffering numerous bruises trying to hitch up the mower, I called for help. I concluded that I didn't need broken bones and knew I never could mow corners properly. My friend mowed, but I raked and stacked. My Harold had said I couldn't use the farm hand because it was something a man should do. Well, it took a lot of struggling until I managed to make decent haystacks. The hydraulic had to be filled, teeth straightened, and it was hot dusty work. I kept at it until the hay was all stacked. In a way I was thankful there wasn't a lot of hay.

Weeks turn into months when you are busy. Each night I came in when it got dark, covered with dirt and tearstains to an empty house. Brown dog wagged all over and Aric crowded close in the pickup. He had transferred his devotion to me now. He shadowed me and I needed his company.

There was no lack of work or exercise. One advantage was that I was so tired I had to sleep some at nights. When I woke during the dark hours, I often wrote in my notebook.

Sundays are terribly lonesome. I attended Sunday school and church then wondered, *What next?* Sunday afternoons seemed endless; they still do.

I managed to drill the wheat and keep busy with chores through the fall months. In winter there is ice to chop and very little else to occupy my hours. The lonely hurt continues.

I have decided that people apparently shun widows because they: 1. don't want to see tears, 2. don't know what to say, 3. are busy with their own families, 4. don't think about them, 5. don't care, 6. feel uncomfortable around them, and 7. are afraid of gossip or competition for their men. Maybe it's all of the above. Widows are the most lonesome, misunderstood people I know. Only other widows are able to really relate to the flood of tears at the sight of a picture, a thought, or a tune. It takes so long to be able to feel whole again. Then a comment can make you fall to pieces all over again. I still miss the only lover I ever had. After thirty-three years of marriage it just got better. We had hoped to have a lot more years together.

The hardest part is being alone.

DIANNE ROOD KIESZ ~ *passage*

Donna Kay still
docks lambs with
her teeth;
folks pale
at her frank admission
of the old
practice.

barn cats are easy:
just bag 'em and snip,
no fuss, no muss
or pain, it seems.
They trot away
self-image intact.

Joe and I cut Mike:
slit, stretch
sever.
trusting Lab eyes
betrayed, love me
anyway.

Urologists are kinder:
counseling required
anesthesia
half-measure
sufficient.

A sensible option
to the abortion
furor.

LINDA CRANDALL ➤ The Homestead

When I was a child, going home was as certain as the arrival of June. Home was the family homesteads in Nebraska's Platte River Valley, where grandparents told stories of the Depression and poor folks who lost their farms. "You must always keep the land," my grandmother said, pushing her bread dough hard against the red countertop. "If you have land, you can live a good life."

So when my father returned from World War II, it was no surprise that he entered the veteran's lottery to acquire a Wyoming homestead. To prove up on his claim, we had to live on the land for two years.

The night we arrived in Wyoming that bitter winter of 1947, the wind whipped dust and sagebrush across the road out of Powell. A sleepy guard draped in a green army blanket crawled out of his wooden shed and swung open a wire gate. He waved a gloved hand and we rolled down the path to the compound where we would live until one of the tarpaper-covered barracks could be moved to our farm site. We wound up and down the rows of barracks, finally stopping in front of steep gray steps. Mom pushed the heavy Packard door against the north wind and held her scarf across her face. "Two years," she warned. Daddy grabbed my hand and shouted promises of irrigated fields of alfalfa and beets.

Inside, the empty room smelled of kerosene, and the bare wood floors shivered and creaked as we stepped in. While Daddy struggled to light the heater and Mom tucked blankets around the feather mattress, I explored the drawers of a small cabinet in a corner of the room. In one drawer was a tablecloth, delicately embroidered in each corner with colorful flowers. "What's this?" I asked.

"The people who lived here before must have left it," Mom replied. I tucked the little cloth back into the drawer and considered it mine to play dress-up and to cover my doll in her cradle.

Most of the men, like my dad, had jobs with the Bureau of Reclamation, constructing dams and ditches for irrigation. The women passed the days mopping the splintery floorboards and washing clothes on washboards in deep gray sinks. Sometimes they met to play pinochle. They always let me have some cards and participate in the conversation. Mom scoffed at one of the older ladies because she kept a cat in her house, but I loved her because she let me have coffee, liberally laced with sugar and canned milk. Another lady gave me lessons on a pretend piano painted on a long piece of white paper. She hummed the notes as she placed my fingers on the appropriate keys. Before long, I could make music, too.

I can't remember the move to the farmstead. The barracks appeared one day in the expanse of sand and sagebrush. Nothing was so cold and empty as that one-room barracks. My mother carried in buckets of coal to feed the hungry potbellied stove; still, the water from the kitchen pump froze in the dishpan. Someone would come in the dark of each morning to pick up my dad for work, but sometimes Mom and I wouldn't go anywhere for days because our '47 Packard was frozen up. We'd spend long days wrapped in a quilt, sitting on the bed by the stove, sewing doll dresses and embroidering little sunbonnet girls on dishtowels. When a piece was finished, Mom set up the ironing board, heated her sadiron on the kerosene cook stove, and pressed my little iron on hers. We ironed to stay warm. One morning we watched out the window as a neighbor's barracks burned to the ground. They said it was a candle. Kerosene lamps and candles were all we had.

In the spring, my grandpa came to build an outhouse to replace the enamel pot in a curtained closet. I was outside watching the digging when I met my first rattler. He was curled up next to a clump of sagebrush. Our cocker spaniel, Digger, let out a whoop and pounced on it. Mom always declared Digger saved my life.

Before we left the homestead we got electricity. We had real lights on our Christmas tree, listened to *The Great Gildersleeve* on the radio, and cooked coconut cream pudding on the doll-size electric stove I got for my fourth birthday. My dad, an engineer, was offered a job to work on a nuclear power plant in Idaho, so the homestead was rented out and eventually sold to buy eighty acres in Nebraska next to my grandparents' farm.

Recently I went back to that homestead for the first time. Even though I was only four when we left, and the barracks has been replaced by a real house, I knew it. I knew the farmstead; I knew the alfalfa field that led down to the river; I knew the compound. After forty years, the heart-shaped mountain looks the same. No gatekeeper checked us in; the wire gate was not there anymore, but the sound of the car crackling over the rocky path was just as I remembered. One barracks remains on the site. The wind has stripped off its green shingle siding, revealing black tarpaper like that which used to slap against the wall where I slept. The windowpanes that aren't broken out are coated with dust and spider webs. My mother used to polish her little windows with vinegar and water until they mirrored the clouds gliding over the compound. She often set pans of hot fudge to cool on the windowsill. I can still see her hand-sewn green and white polka dot curtains blowing through the open window.

Only the tall stone chimney stands near where I savored Mom's fudge and pounded paper piano keys. In place of the splintery steps is a bland marble memorial for the interned Japanese families who lived at Heart Mountain before I did. I wonder if the Japanese woman who embroidered that delicate little tablecloth is still alive. I wonder if she thinks about Heart Mountain, about the cold winters, the wind whipping through those tarpaper barracks. I wonder if she talks of poor folks losing their land. I wonder if she comes back to Heart Mountain in June.

ROSALEE M. MICKELSEN ⌁ Surviving the Farm Crisis

Life is hard for farm women, especially if you are not prosperous. The events I am going to tell occurred in the later 1970s and the 1980s. One year it was so hot, temperatures ranged in the 118-degree range for days. Our corn stood in irrigation water and burned up. We've even seen years we planted expensive alfalfa seed and listened to army worms chew it off at the ground level. Yes, there were so many, you could really hear them.

I tried to get out the word about the grave conditions happening to the farms during the late 1970s and the 1980s. I talked to the local ladies' groups at churches. All I got was a bored "ho-hum"! I went through the newspapers and for one week I clipped all the notices of farm sales and hung them on a bulletin board. People let me know that all those farmers were at retirement age and were merely selling out. Suicides among farmers skyrocketed. It got so there were three or four a month across the state. Probably more, but there were those who were clever at hiding the circumstances.

Stories surfaced about women with children trying to survive in garages or chicken coops. North and west of our place, one family lost their home, and because their children were all teenagers, they moved into a small Quonset hut, not much larger than a chicken coop. The story we were told was that the father went into trucking to pay off debts. Rumors were that most of the street kids in Lincoln and Omaha, Nebraska, were farm kids.

I had only one son, my other two children were daughters, and I remember how hard it was to keep my son in jeans. Boys are harder on clothes and shoes, and I recall he had two pairs of school jeans. Seems like my washing machine was always acting up and other kids had so many clothes, and he didn't dare wear the same jeans two days in a row. So every other day he'd wear one pair of jeans. We did have enough shirts, and at that time buying clothes at Goodwill was popular, so we picked up several shirts he liked for $2.00 apiece. We always went to church on Sunday, and he insisted on wearing jeans, so those jeans really knew a lot of wear.

The problem during those times was all the work we could find paid $3.35 an hour: minimum wage at that time. Utility bills were running over a hundred dollars a month for our farm, and if we couldn't work forty hours a week, we could barely scratch up the amount of the utility bill. Every two weeks I was able to buy $25.00 worth of groceries for a family of five. We ate a lot of day-old bread, and potatoes and gravy. If there was an abundance of apples or cherries on fruit trees, I put up as much as possible.

We always put in a big patch of sweet corn. We almost always got a crop, but raccoons leveled the patch; after they left, it looked like someone went in with a stalk cutter. We always heard if you let the children run barefoot up and down the sweet corn rows, it would keep coons away. The coons had a banquet every night. One time as my son and I were walking through the sweet corn in our bare feet, he told me, "Mom, I hate shucking this corn and here I am walking through the patch barefooted to save it!" My only comment was "Ouch! Utch! Ouch! Owie! Doggone it!" as my foot hit another Mexican sandbur or small rock.

As a farm family struggling every way possible, sending children to school was nothing short of a nightmare. All I had to get to work and school was a 1975 pickup, top speed was thirty-two miles an hour. My son and I were late so many times, and the school wouldn't accept car problems as a valid excuse for being tardy, so we had to lie a lot about why he was late for school. To the west of us for several miles were no houses; if we'd needed to get help, we could have frozen to death.

When times are hard, there aren't many things to enjoy except animals and pets. Our family seemed to receive all the stray dogs town people dumped. We milked cows and our animals always had ample "dump" milk to drink. We bought dog food by fifty-pound bags. Over the years we had blind dogs, deaf dogs, big dogs, small dogs, good dogs, and bad dogs wander into our farm.

In the house there were always scraps of bread and meat to throw out, so I got to stretching it by cooking up a big batch of what we dubbed "cat crappe." I made up big pans of gravy from leftover fat and added dibs and dabs of leftovers, bread crumbs, oatmeal, corn meal, and just whatever I could spare. The animals licked the pan clean, and stayed remarkably healthy on this concoction.

This farm family survived these hard years. Once, within two weeks we buried a small daughter and had the bank foreclose on us. We didn't always hold our heads high; many times we wondered where we'd find the strength to survive another crisis. This mother prayed a lot. When it was over, I breathed a grateful, "Thank you, Lord."

JOYCE M. MILLER ⌒ The Morning Window

January is a month I can do without. While most people are getting on with the new year, cleaning up after the holidays, paying bills, and breaking New Year's resolutions, I spend my time like a ghost, prowling around the house at night, reliving the past, looking for something I lost a long time ago. I get cold and hungry as a coyote in winter and tired as a cloudy sky after a storm. But I'm afraid to sleep. I don't want to feel my cold dreams drift over me as I lay helpless.

Josie's a beautiful dog, she looks to me as fresh and lively as a pup. Seeing her helps me remember the day that is never out of my mind this time of year. Like the pain in my foot reminding me when I broke my toe, the January sky reminds me of the day I broke my own heart. Although for the longest time I'd blamed Wyoming's wind.

Josie and I were in a trailer twelve feet wide and forty feet long, seven miles from town, with my sick baby. Michael, my first husband, was getting ready to wake up and go to his classes at the university.

I was on the couch, under the window where the sun came in; the Laramie Range was beginning to take shape on the horizon. One big yellow star hung low in the sky like a dirty streetlight. It was Wednesday, January 12, 1972 — the day the eastern slope was nearly blown clear over the mountains. Michael and I had been in Wyoming fifteen months — long enough to have a baby and spend all our savings. We were lucky to have a baby boy, a trailer, and a rented piece of earth, and Josie, a full-blooded Norwegian elkhound. Josie was a mother hen with the baby, scratching whenever he itched, crying when he hurt. That morning she looked like a starved wolf, staring at the sky; we should have listened to her.

Josh awakened when his father did. He'd been sick with a fever for a few days. Michael, with troubles of his own at the university, looked at us with lonely eyes. This was his long day, classes from 8:00 to 1:00 and then labs until late evening.

"You have enough milk for the baby?" he asked, knowing I would be without transportation all day after he left.

I had tons of dried milk powder in the cupboard; maybe we'd freeze to death when we couldn't pay for gas, but we sure as hell wouldn't die from a lack of powdered milk.

"I'll put Josie out," he told me as he got his coat and gloves on. We had to chain Josie in our dirt yard or she ran away; since free dogs were treated as predators, she'd be shot or poisoned by our landlord. She tugged on her chain until Michael's car was too far away to see then collapsed on the dirt. A haze of moisture from her hard panting hung over her head like a cloud.

Like a blast from an explosion, a gust of wind ripped through the cold air and struck; the trailer tilted a little, so fast that I thought I'd imagined it. Josh was playing with a stuffed toy, humming. But when I went out to lead Josie inside, the hundred-gallon heavy steel barrel we used for garbage was lying on its side. I tried to right it; too heavy.

While Josh was in his highchair eating chicken sticks, the second gust hit. This time, the highchair moved back across the kitchen floor and hit the wall. Caught with a chicken stick halfway to his mouth, Josh laughed and dropped his food; Josie caught it in midair.

Then the wind rolled into Laramie at fifty-five miles per hour with gusts up to seventy-five, according to the radio. Tiny gravel the size of nits seeped in through the cracks in the walls and piled up along the floorboards like anthills. I didn't think my morning window could withstand the barrage and covered it with one of Josh's blankets.

From a sheltered window in my kitchen, I held Josh and watched tires blow off the neighbor's roofs. Garbage barrels like ours rolled down the muddy track between the trailers like a procession of military tanks. Cans, paper, pieces of wooden fencing, and clothing flew through the air like confetti in a ticker tape parade.

Our six-party phone line went dead, and the electricity went out; the trailer turned stone cold in the blink of my dog's eye. The furniture started to move across twelve feet of floor space; Josh, sitting on the couch, dissolved in helpless laughter.

I pushed the furniture against the west wall, hoping its weight would keep the trailer from tipping over.

I put batteries in the radio and listened to newsmen compare each wind gust to former ones like plays in a football game. I could correlate wind speed with furniture movement. At fifty-five mph, only the table and chairs moved. At sixty, the couch slid. Anything higher propelled the refrigerator.

My little "roll up to the sink, any sink" washer was all over the bathroom; I closed the door to keep it out of the narrow hallway.

The radio batteries died about 2:00. The last thing I heard was that all trailer parks and outlying buildings were being evacuated by the sheriff. I thought of rescue between furniture-control missions. Meanwhile, Michael was in class; he never listened to the radio.

Josh grew crabby and began to cough. Then he got diarrhea. For several hours I was busy with diapers and bathing Josh in the sink and changing clothes for the both of us, hearing constipated, compact balls of ice strike the tin trailer like sharp steel nails hitting a metal coffin.

During a calm, I made strong tea with lemon and honey and a pinch of salt to stop Josh's dehydration. It made him feel so good that I drank some and gave a bowl to Josie.

Then the wind returned with a scream. I lit the burners on my gas stove. Josh fell asleep in the relative warmth; I looked outside and saw the neighbor's trailer rise from the ground like a butterfly from a flower and crash back down again.

I made my decision then; we would not spend the night in the trailer. When Michael came home we'd find a motel in town. We had only the grocery money, but we had to do it. A few more hours in that wind and I'd need a straitjacket.

I packed Josh's clean clothes and a few dirty diapers; he'd gone through two dozen that afternoon. I collected cereal, chicken sticks, tea bags, bottles, powdered milk, jars of squash and applesauce, toys, bottles, and baby crackers. I made bologna sandwiches until the bread was gone and stuffed cans of peaches, pears, and beans into brown paper bags along with forks and spoons and a can opener. I even thought of aspirin and instant coffee.

By nightfall, I was ready. As darkness came, the trailer rumbled while the wind howled like a wounded mastodon. My mind screamed louder and louder; Josie sat, her feet wide apart, staring at the wall like she was watching a ghost. Josh slept restlessly in my aching arms.

I cursed Michael for escaping to his own world while I stood alone for our child and our home; I'd never done that before and it hardened some part of my soul.

When headlights lit the blackness, I ran to the window and saw an official-looking truck parked in front of the trailer. I positioned Josh on the couch with pillows on each side and on the floor in case a gust struck, then I pushed the door open against the wind. I yelled until I was hoarse.

Maybe I should have run to the truck, but I didn't dare leave Josh and Josie alone; I didn't trust them to survive without me. Then the truck was gone; its taillights flashing at the neighbor's overturned trailer. I thought the door would push right through me before I got back inside. In the bathroom, I was sick beside my washer overflowing with diapers and clothing soaked with shit.

Michael came home two hours later. Pale and shaking, he fell back on the couch in a heap. He didn't want to leave our home, but resigned himself as I threw our suitcase at him and grabbed Josh.

On the trip into town we were in the barrow pit a few times before we made it to the Holiday Inn where Michael wanted us to stay. With Michael I walked into the lobby, carrying Josh, Josie trailing behind.

In our room I gave Josh a bath and fresh clothes, then washed dirty diapers and T-shirts in the tub.

We slept, and then ate our bologna sandwiches until checkout time the next morning. The trailer was still in place on our rented piece of hard-packed dirt when we returned. Then Michael went to his afternoon classes while I cleaned up the place. No matter how I tried, I couldn't get it to shine like it used to.

Michael bummed money from friends so we could eat for that month. Later, I went back to work. We shuffled Josh between a string of baby-sitters who couldn't stop him from crying. Michael quit his day school and worked on special projects late at night, after I came home from work. We lasted a few more years like that, but it was never the same. Josh grew up pretty good. Michael and his new wife gave Josh a brother. I gave Josh a stepfather, a roof over his head, and all the time I could spare between work and housecleaning. But I didn't give him Donna Reed and, God help me, I always wanted to.

You're wondering about Josie aren't you? She lived sixteen more years, free to run, and died unchained one bright September morning in her own grassy yard.

Still, we'll go for a ride today, Josie and I, to see the old wreck, all forty linear feet of it still standing. It's mostly boarded up, my morning window long shattered by vandals' rocks. But that's as it should be. It wouldn't ever show the view I saw. I did so much damned dreaming by that morning window that I couldn't see what was right in front of me.

I lost two things in that trailer the day of the windstorm — my youth and my faith in love. I blamed both losses on the wind and the empty, hard plains. But I got one of them back, didn't I, Josie? Where is that dog? Gone for a run, I suppose.

ELSIE PANKOWSKI 〜 **The Home Place**

On the section we called home,
round-top hills rolled to the end
of sight: acres of blue flax,
whiskered barley, ripening wheat
shading light and dark in wind,
cucumbers and apple trees, fenced-off
squares of virgin grass. My parents
sheltered daughters disciplined with looks
of disappointment. They raised
chickens, cows, a pig or two. Long after
he had bought his first John Deere,
my father kept his horses, mostly Percherons,
dapple-gray, black as foals and lightening
with age to freckled white. On still days
as he mowed, his communion with his horses
carried to the house.

One burning summer, a gelding,
born and broke on our home place,
tired at his work. Holding me secure
before her, my mother rode him
to retirement on an uncle's farm.
Drought scorched the fields around us.
Thick with hoppers, grass parched
in the ditches. The gelding's hooves
riled ghosts of dust along the road.

Years later, on an April morning
when doves haunted in the grove,
a neighbor drove into the yard,
brought news of an ancient horse
trapped in his pasture, pacing up and down
the fence line, searching for an opening,
headed to our farm. My father went out
to the horse, toothless now and thin.
It nickered, mouthed the tender grass
he offered it, let the green shoots dribble
to the ground. Out of kindness, the neighbor
took his rifle from his truck and waited
till my father drove away.

MARGARET E. SMITH ~~~~ *A Horse Named Concussion*

Concussion was a great little cowhorse. He could occasionally be ornery for his master or other good horseman, but he was always gentle and dependable for any inexperienced rider. He seemed to be able to judge the ability of any rider, no matter what age, and to give them a fun ride without mishap. He excelled as a patient and gentle riding teacher.

Animals that spend a great deal of time with people seem to develop the ability to understand human language, and Concussion was especially gifted in this way. Concussion went to the fair every year from the time he was a year old till his master grew too old for 4-H, and he always hated being shut up in a stall for four days. He got so he didn't like to load in the truck or trailer. The key to loading him was to say, "Either get in or you have to run along behind." While we could always catch Concussion when he was out in the pasture, if he was in the corral, he would sometimes run laps around the pen — the more mud, the more laps — before allowing himself to be caught. We eventually learned that he would stop immediately if we sternly said, "Concussion, there is a horse sale next Sunday."

When we were washing horses, getting ready for the fair and parade, we would put the soap in a dish-detergent bottle so that we could squirt some on without so much spillage. Concussion would run by, snatch the soap bottle in his teeth, and trot around the barn with laughter in every move, tail waving and soap squirting all the way.

When Russell moved away, married, and set up his horse-training business in another part of the state, Concussion stayed at home. We were all afraid that, at his age, he would be very homesick and unhappy if he was moved away from the horses he had always run with. Over his long lifetime, Concussion had managed to founder on everything from grass to green apples, so his feet weren't in very good shape and needed lots of extra care. He was more or less retired to giving rides to our grandchildren and whoever else came along and needed a trustworthy mount.

One morning when he was twenty-something, I went out to the barnyard to catch a horse and found him lying dead in the corral. He had summered better than usual, due in part to the fact that we'd had his teeth filed in the spring and had found a short cinch that didn't rub an ulcer on his side when someone rode him. He had been happily eating grass all week, so his death was completely unexpected. We still miss him, especially when we have guests who want to ride and have no idea how. We have no other horses that we can trust the way we could Concussion, though I still remember one protective mother who stated loudly and emphatically, "You are not riding any horse named Concussion!"

MARIAN D. PETERS Circa 1992, New Salem,
North Dakota

Rebecca Fleeger, farmer's widow,
yearned for friends, peace, and beauty.
To those ends, she hired men to raze old
buildings on the farm her husband left her.
For days the workers wielded sledges,
ropes, and pulleys, tore down structures
as she ordered. Then they dug a shallow pit,
pushed rotten beams and siding in,
threw lighted matches on the wood.
Flames grew high, higher, higher,
sparks flew out, grass fires started.
Alarmed, Rebecca and the workers stamped
and tramped, threw dirt and water;
they stopped the fires in the evening.
But late at night Rebecca worried
sparks might fly from smoldering embers;
she shone her headlights on the pit,
hosed down the edges. All the while
her nightgown glowed in the light.
In New Salem's Koffee Kup Kafé, next day,
Rebecca's neighbor said, half joking,
"Strange goings on at Widow Fleeger's;
dancers prance around twilight fires."
A young couple said they made out,
while parked quite late atop a hill,
twin lights, like eyes, a ghostly
figure on Old Lady Fleeger's farm.
Those who listened tsk'd and giggled,
stored what they heard for gossip fests
at school, church, and the VFW. With each
telling, the rumors grew (and tellers,
too); what started out as tittle-tattle
turned to scandal: Rebecca Fleeger
practiced witchcraft on her farm.
But Rebecca didn't know it; happily,
she worked her plan for friends,
peace, and beauty. She hired a crew
to build foundations, move a guesthouse,
room for six on the farm.

From a discount catalog, she ordered
beds and dressers, chairs and curtains.
The delivery driver did his duty,
kept sharp eyes for sorcery signs
on the Fleeger farm. When back in town
he told about a pit — not deep — dead coals.
"Ah, a place for sacrificial burnings,"
mongers hissed with glee. A little later
rumors flew of headless goats, no-tail cats
lying dead near Fleeger's place. When
the sheriff checked, he found no clues;
"Dogs ate the proof," informers claimed.
Meanwhile, Rebecca painted, papered, scrubbed,
and waxed, planted trees and flowers.
When all was set, she asked six she'd met
on trips to spend the summer on her land.
The rumor-makers added six, said thirteen
women covened on Rebecca Fleeger's farm.
Rebecca's guests read and rested, jogged
and walked at dawn and dusk, enjoyed
the beauty of the land. Some watched birds,
some went fishing, three went biking, two
went riding — plenty to do, each to her liking.
The guests, all from some distance, relished
books and talk of Indian people, planned
a project with Rebecca to bring peace
and healing to the land, using native customs:
they gathered stones then relaid them like
the Indians, in a medicine wheel design.
Rumorers found this disgusting, yet
another witchcraft sign. Two men
at the Pickup Tap said, "This is awful;
we're tired of this witch crap."
As the evening wore on, they made plans
to rid their area of witchy powers;
they felt it was their civic duty.
Well in their cups, they drove their trucks
to Fleeger's farm, intent on murder.
As they crawled to Rebecca's window,
armed with knives and a shotgun,
the sheriff stopped them — he'd been warned
by a barmaid of the men's bad intentions.
Rebecca slept throughout the action,
so the sheriff drove out in the morning

for a visit; he told Rebecca that her life
had been in danger. Shocked, she asked
about the murderers' motives. As kindly
as he could, the sheriff told her
of the witchcraft rumors: fires, signs,
ghostly figures, sorceries, dancers,
lights, and covens. Rebecca laughed,
then she cried, then she told how she had
worked to make herself a better life.
As she sobbed again, she said,
"I've lived here for forty years,
my neighbors know me well,
if they wondered what I was doing,
all they had to do was ask."
The sheriff patted her shoulder and said,
"I'm sorry, ma'am, that this has happened."
Wiping her tears, Rebecca answered,
"All is forgiven. It doesn't matter,
for I have friends, peace, and beauty."

LINDA M. RACE ～ Markers

I share pride in the fact that each farmer today produced enough food for 140 people, but what are *we* losing? Maybe those of us who are left in agriculture are so frantically trying to hold on to what we have that we are letting something else slip away.

When did the company and chatter of radio and TV replace the company who stopped by for dessert and coffee, and the chatter that lingered over the church potluck table?

Has the friendly clang of a dinner bell been replaced by an appeal made on the Motorola?

And when did the fence posts turn into highway mile markers?

MARY LYNN VOSEN ⬅ Rotten Squash in the Cellar

Last year's squash disintegrates in the dark
on a wood plank spanning two walls of the cellar

its flesh softens,
concave wounds
the skin puckers there
misty with mold

If I pick it up now, even by the stem
It may stretch heavily and break, weeping life fluid on me.
In a few more months —
when I return it will be a flat black form, its dry edges clinging
to the plank

In an old folk's home
Old Woman
sits unstirred, in the dim light of
rest, under wrinkled skin

If I go to see her now
she will want me to take her into the sunlight and tears will
leak onto our cheeks.
If I stay away longer, she will forget to depend on me
And when I return, there will be an old shape in a box.

JODY STRAND ⬅ **The Only Thing We Will**
Not Do Is Give Up

When I got up on Wednesday morning, it was just like any other day. The
sun shone as brightly, my world was secure, and the most important thing I
had to take care of that day was baking cookies for my son's Christmas
party at school.

I still had no suspicions when my husband came walking up to the
house at mid-morning. If he wasn't too busy he often came for a cup of
coffee after morning chores were done and before starting his other work.
As he sat down at the kitchen table, I poured him his coffee and was
chattering on, reminding him what night that week we were invited over to
our neighbors' for a Christmas get-together and what day I would like him
to take off and take us shopping, and asking him what he wanted for

Christmas this year. When he didn't answer me, I turned to him and that's when I saw the look on his face and knew something was wrong.

He looked at me and with no preamble said, "The boss came and talked to me this morning. Honey, he sold the ranch."

I said "What do you mean, sold the ranch? To who? Are we going to be working for them now?"

"No," he said, "you don't understand, they don't need any help. They'll be running the ranch themselves, we're out of a job."

To those of you who have no knowledge of ranch work, this might seem like nothing more than what happens to hundreds of people every day when some big corporation decides to cut back and they simply lay people off through no fault of their own. You just go out and look for a new job right? Well, it's not quite that simple for us. You see, when you work on a ranch, you are required to live there because so many things have to be done at odd hours. Consequently, when you're out of a job, you're out of a home. And home is definitely what this ranch had become to us. We had ridden every pasture, checked every fence line, sat up all night in the barn with calving heifers, prayed for rain when the pastures started to dry up, and had come to love this ranch and think of it as our own. Oh, we knew someone else owned it on paper, but what's a name scrawled on a dotted line compared to caring for and working on a place three hundred and sixty-five days a year? In our hearts, the land belonged to us and we to it, and now it was being taken away.

For the next couple of hours we discussed the pros and cons of what we thought we should do and how we should handle telling our son. By the time the bus came into the yard, we had finally decided. With my husband making phone calls looking for a job and me starting to pack things up, it would be virtually impossible for us to keep it from him, and if we didn't tell him, someone in school would. In a rural community, everyone seems to know everyone else's business. There is a grapevine that's faster than Western Union, so we were sure a lot of kids would be hearing their parents talking about how the ranch we lived on had been sold and wondering just what we were going to do now. After supper that evening we told him what had happened and not to worry because Daddy would just find another job. I stressed to him how much I needed his help in doing the packing and getting ready to go, and he actually took it better than either of us had. They had a going-away party for him on his last day of school and when I picked him up that night, I saw by the look on his face what it had done to him to have to stand there and say good-bye to all of his classmates. We had another difficult time a few nights later when our neighbors all came to a going-away party for us in the church basement. After that we all seemed to shut down and try to feel as little as possible. We were all kept very busy packing and I was glad I didn't have much time in which to do it — it saved me from staying in any one room too long and going over memories in my mind. After my husband and I had gotten married, this had been my first real home. My son had been conceived and born there.

My husband did find a job, not the kind of job he wanted but then, any job you can find in agriculture in January is a godsend. My husband went to work each morning; my son, with more than a little fear and anxiety, started back to school in a new town; and I put away our possessions and went back to the job of chief cook and bottle washer.

It didn't end there. We've moved since then and the way things are beginning to look here, I don't doubt but that we'll be forced to move yet again. Between the vegetarians claiming meat isn't good for you and the environmentalists wanting to turn all of the grazing land back to nature, they are driving more of us out of work every day. Where will we eventually end up? I don't know. All I know is, no matter how many times we have to move or start over, we will be able to do it. Ranching is not only what we do, it's who we are, who our ancestors were. It's a heritage and a legacy. No move will ever hurt the way the first one did because none of us will let it. We have learned we cannot let ourselves become attached to a place that doesn't belong to us, and we won't make that mistake again. If we have to keep starting over, we will. The only thing we will not do is give up. We will not quit ranching. Because that too is who we are.

AURIEL J. SANDSTEAD ⌒ Postwar

In our early days on the farm and before the installation of parking meters in Sterling, Saturday night was the big business night of the week. Rural towns were like beehives. Stores stayed open until 8:00, 9:00, 10:00 P.M., and some were open as long as anyone cared to shop.

Once, in town with my husband, I had an experience I'll never forget. It was a very warm summer night and we had been lucky to find a parking place on Main Street in front of Hecker Drugstore to "people watch" before we headed west on Highway 14. The "pole road" from Atwood to Willard was a terrible dirt road, so the Willard-Sterling travel was generally via Highway 14. It was harvest time, which meant extra of everything. Tired, bloated, sweaty, in advanced pregnancy, I was feeling particularly unlovely despite the new boxcar-size wraparound tent I was wearing. In my whole life I have only seen two people on whom I thought pregnancy becoming, and I certainly wasn't one of them.

Willard and I were sitting in the car watching friends, neighbors, townspeople scurrying around before closing time, when an extra-large woman, dirty, unkempt, dressed in men's overalls, hair disarrayed, came ambling down the street. I could scarcely believe that woman could be so uncaring about herself when friend husband piped up, "There goes Auriel," and that was the last straw. Auriel dissolved into tears. Nor would she be comforted. A first pregnancy was scary and disruptive enough in her life when she was so busy she could scarcely keep up with the demands of each day. How would she ever manage with a newborn to love and care for? The joy was gone from people watching on Main Street.

DIANNA TORSON **kirsty ann's mule**

you lay poignant and composed
in the pasture
under a fierce noon fire
drying your flesh to jerky
blowflies ravage your knees
scraped deep past skin
scavenge your broken hoofs
kiss your twisted jaw

banned from your herd
you returned

whiteman's rage
galloped you to this
knoll west of her barn
tied to the pickup
you ran the road with
elegant ears and expressionless
eyes till he shifted into high

then crashed into gravel
sharp as a grater

you cannot hate
but we can that man
who dragged you, ancient animal,
your kind face not made to
express this pain.

JACQELINE S. ELLIOTT **From Short Ears
to Long Ears**

Once I lived on a ranch in Colorado, raised registered quarter horses, and believed I'd found my niche in life; horses, I thought, were the most magnificent animals ever created. Then a neighbor's renegade burro crawled through the fence to breed my favorite mare. When the offspring was born, I stared at the little red mule's big brown eyes and enormous ears and said, "What will I ever do with a mule?"

A few years later, training my mule, Sarah, to ride, I took her to fall cattle roundup on the Clevenger Ranch outside Pueblo. Horse lovers sneered, but verbal confrontations were the least of my problems when a gust of wind scared my mount into the middle of three hundred steers. Running hard, she passed the steers *and* the cowboys on their good quarter horses. My boss was too polite to suggest I shoot her; he said, "You should take that mule to the races in Durango in the spring."

Attending the mule races in Durango turned me into a mule lover, as other enthusiasts shared their knowledge with me. I found a bonding quality that is not found in the horse world.

Sarah Sue Anne, my first mule, competed in gymkhana events with another mule, Suzette; the team won the American Mule Association medium-size chariot world championship two years in a row. Sarah also won halter shows, barrel races, pole bending, and flat saddle races. After that team, I co-owned two world champion large chariot teams and several other fine saddle mules. Then I bought Maude, a world champion racing mule who'd won thirteen straight races three years before. I paired her with Sweet Sue and won top driver of the year in the American Mule Association competition, outrunning the previous world champions by nearly ten lengths. Maude became my best friend; when she was fourteen, I rode her to two wins and a second place. We've both retired from racing now, but she's a grand old gal.

In 1986 I divorced and had to sell my first mule, Sarah, to pay my way through college and support my two children. I was brokenhearted, until I met and married another crazy mule enthusiast. In 1990 he bought Sarah back for me and made my life complete.

Through mule racing and showing I've met wonderful friends, and acquired five mules. But I am ever grateful for the little red mule who introduced me to a new way of life. She taught me exactly what I'd ever do with a mule. Thanks, Sarah Sue Anne.

ANITA TANNER ⌐ Butchered: A Cattle Song

We couldn't imagine
the dull thud muffled by animal hide.
Even the sound of the verb
brought shudders.
We didn't dare ask about

How our farm cattle were led
up a ramp
that rose above the world
to the black iron door,
we never questioned,

obediently herding them into corral
and up to loading
where the trailer hinges
grated shut
and our minds took over.

They were always victims, then,
shying at the sight of the black gate,
trying to whirl in the narrow corridors
that led to their ascensions,
every nerve and sinew cringing.

We had little inkling of their calm,
their cud-chewing composure,
climbing higher above us,
lifting their eyes to the hills,
carrying their ordinary cattle songs.

THREE

Savoring
the Prairies

Choose the Music

EVELYN HARD ⁓⟍ **Evelyn's Garden Bug Spray**

Put in a large pail:

> 1 cup freshly dug horseradish root or leaves, ground up
>   (if you don't have horseradish, use stinging nettle
>   or elderberry leaves)
> 1/4 cup Fels Naptha or Ivory Soap flakes
>   or 1/2 cup molasses
> 2 cups ground-up onions or 8 cloves ground garlic
> 3 tablespoons ground cayenne pepper
> 1/2 cup vodka

Add almost a gallon of warm water, stir, and let set overnight in a covered container. Put through a strainer, then strain through a cloth. Spray on plants, covering the underside of the leaves. Store any left over in a covered container in the fridge, or give to a Skid Row bum!

You can add two cups of water in which one cup of cheap tobacco has been steeped, but do not use tobacco on tomatoes or peppers, as there is the possibility the tobacco may contain the Mosaic virus, to which tomatoes and peppers are susceptible.

MARILYN HENDERSON ⟍ **The Year of the Grasshoppers**

Down through the years, I have heard my parents tell stories of the '30s. I have never doubted the severity of the conditions, but I never expected to live through anything like that.

My garden in the yard was not hit too badly by the hoppers. Across the road about one-third of a mile away, I had permanent plantings of raspberries, about three hundred feet of them. I also had all my potatoes, and fifty hills of squash, and about one and one-half acres of sweet corn.

My mother-in-law tells of having to put her apron over her face to protect it from the flying grasshoppers during the '30s. They were especially bad in the pasture when she went to gather the cows for milking. I never thought I'd see that, but I did. Walking across the width of the road, I'd get hit by flying grasshoppers. I had to cover my face to make any progress.

The potato vines were wiped out in a flash, and they ate the potatoes that were exposed on the ground. I dug what was left, but it took several hills for a meal.

I went out one morning to dig potatoes for dinner and found only twelve squash plants left. Two days earlier all fifty hills had been there. I counted the hoppers on one plant and quit at five hundred, when it dawned on me that all of these plants would be lost, too. I didn't have any pesticide, as I try to go organic, but I had to protect those plants. I started calling neighbors, looking for pesticide. After several calls, I finally located some about two miles away. I jumped in the pickup, got it, brought it home, and mixed it, then drove out to spray. When I got back to the garden, about a half an hour later there were no plants at all. Even mature squash were gone.

I just sat down and cried for a moment. Then I got up, dusted off my pants, and sprayed those guys.

A lot of hoppers survived and went on to the raspberry plants. Not only did they eat the berries, they ate the leaves, and they ate the stalks down to the ground. The Boyne made a comeback the next spring.

The sweet corn patch was a little ways away, so it took a while for them to move in there. The raccoon ate its share, but the grasshoppers started on the silk, then moved to the tip of the cob. Sometimes they'd eat the whole cob; other times what looked like a cob was just husks. Out of one and one-half acres, we had one meal of partial cobs I rescued. There were few stalks to disc, so one less job. There was no second-cutting alfalfa. My dad tells of hoppers eating fence posts down to nothing. If I ever had any doubts, I don't anymore.

CRYSTAL SHARPING ASHLEY ⌒ · Cows on the Loose

"We'll just turn these heifers and their calves out, then move that old ewe into the clean pen, and then you'll have all the time in the world to get the house cleaned and bake your cake."

Doesn't that sound like everything is going to go smoothly and without a single hitch? Guess again.

What he forgot to tell me was that first we have to drive some cows out of one small yard, sort the heifers off, eartag the calves, and set up a temporary fence before we can even think about turning the cattle out.

Actually even that is easy, until I realize we have to tromp through a foot of mud, run each calf into a corner in order to tag it, and search all over the place for panels and gates to use for our fence.

Finally the heifers are started down to the pasture. They deviate from the straight and narrow only once, when they find the only open gate on the place — one that would have taken hours of struggling to get the cows through if we had wanted them in that pasture.

While going down the section line, the cows try to double back to the barn. Of course my husband is driving the pickup, so it is up to me to take up the slack on the right side of the pickup, so the cows keep going down the road. Luckily, the pasture is only half a mile away, so it amounts to just a short walk for me.

It's a good thing I'm not too tired out after we get the heifers in, because Mrs. Bull Derrick went through the corner gate and needs to be shown the way back into her pasture.

We hop into the blue 1948 Studebaker pickup and the chase is on. Mrs. Bull Derrick has decided that the empty field is a nicer place to live than the pasture with all the grass in it. We have to chase her to the far end of the field before we can even get her turned. This is where I have to get out of the pickup in order to turn her back. And since my husband, in the pickup, has her headed in the right direction, he can't stop for me to get back into the pickup.

So there I am at the far end of a field, watching a crazed cowboy trying to work with a pickup instead of a horse and a rope, trying to get a cow named Mrs. Bull Derrick back through the gate she broke down. Mrs. Derrick's eyesight and memory fade in and out. She can see me and she can see an old blue Studebaker bearing down on her, but she can't see or remember the hole in the fence she came out of.

All this time Mrs. Derrick races back and forth next to the fence line. I am expected to keep even with her so she doesn't decide to travel straight across the cornfield. Trying to keep even with Mrs. Derrick becomes a real challenge since she is running on grass and I am tripping over old corn rows.

Finally Mrs. Derrick is cornered; she's fifty feet from the gate. The pickup rattles to a stop, spewing out grease guns, gas cans, and one very angry cowboy.

Now with the Studebaker used as a barrier and the two of us acting as a human fence, Mrs. Derrick calmly walks into her pasture, stops within five feet of the gate, turns to look at us, and with what I would swear is a smirk on her face, begins chewing her cud.

ROSE POTULNY 　　 Broomstick Therapy

One incident is vivid in my mind. Just after a two-day snowstorm, when the cattle had been in the Quonset for two days, my husband, Vic, let them out. Thirsty, they drank a lot. Then Vic fed them potato culls and alfalfa hay. The combination of the feed and liquid filled them with gas and they began to bloat.

He rushed to the house to call the vet, then said, "Come and help me." As I followed him out the door, I saw him grab the broom from the corner of the entryway. I wondered, but knew better than to ask questions.

In the barn, Vic pushed a large cow in distress into a corner, shoved the broom handle horizontally into her mouth, and said, "Stand here and hold the broom handle until the vet gets here."

I held the broomstick, pushed hard, and thought about the vet coming seventeen miles. I wasn't afraid of cows because I'd milked ever since I was a young girl, but this was different. The cow and I stared at each other. Her foul breath came right into my face as she belched. It seemed like hours before the vet arrived, but the cow didn't even try to move. We lost only about three head that time.

EDNA MILLER 　　 Designated Turkey Herder

In the 1920s, when grasshoppers were a real threat to ranchers' grass and feed supply, my mother, Fern Bomgardner, went into the turkey-raising business with hundreds of birds and little equipment. Every broody chicken and turkey hen was pressed into service. Turks were given to turkey hens, fifteen to twenty per hen to raise, at first in A-shaped coops arranged in groups of five or six in our south meadow. As soon as the turks were feathered or able to travel, they became grasshopper catchers. To really fulfill their purpose, the entire ranch had to be freed of the pests, which meant herding turkeys like sheep.

Much of the time, my mother was the designated herder. Each day was planned, decisions were made as to who would help with chores, do housework, help herd turkeys, cook for the crew, etc. There were several hired men who were employed in the fields, farming, irrigating, and haying. I was usually the one who prepared the noon meal, while my younger brothers helped herd turkeys. However, when Mom was taking the turkeys on a long run, I went with her.

One long run I recall was through the west pasture across Prairie Dog Town, down that valley, over the hills heading south and east, ending up north of the house along the river where the turkeys really enjoyed a drink and the shade. My mother usually walked, but we little folk had a choice of walking or riding a pony. For all pony rides, Dad had a warning, "Get off and lead your horse across Prairie Dog Town so he doesn't step in a hole and break a leg!"

I remember following those chirping turkeys as they fanned out, racing along catching hoppers. As we approached Prairie Dog Town, those little barking dogs added to the chorus until they sighted the approaching turkeys as they topped the hills. (The prairie dogs had chosen a low-lying area partially surrounded by hills — some higher than others.) What fun to watch those funny creatures as they would run for their holes and disappear but for only a moment, then you'd see those beady eyes checking, "Has the danger passed?"

PENNY S. DYE *Woman Vet*

I have practiced veterinary medicine for the last five years in Rapid City, South Dakota. I am a partner in a three-doctor animal practice, working on cattle, horses, dogs, cats, and exotic animals. Every once in a while we see a pig or a sheep. And, to answer a common question, no, I don't work on just small animals. I guess I get asked that a lot because of my size. I'm 5'2" and weigh . . . well, let's just say I weigh more than I look like I do because I have to stay in pretty good shape. In my spare time from the clinic I am a full-time ranch wife! My husband and I live on a ranch by Hermosa, South Dakota, where we run about two hundred fifty head of cows.

They say I've broken a lot of hard ground, being a woman in a typically male field. I guess I never really looked at it that way. I know that every new vet has to establish herself or himself as a competent practitioner, and whenever there was a question as to whether I could handle something or not, I tried not to take it personally and just dove in and proved that there was really no need to question my abilities. There are times I rely on my strong German background and the stubborn streak it gave me! I have found it interesting that more older women doubt my capabilities than men do, or perhaps it just irritates me more. This spring I was called on a Sunday afternoon to work on a uterine prolapse; a lady placed the call. When I got there and stepped out of my vet pickup with my coveralls on and started getting my things ready, the rancher asked me, "Are you doc's assistant today?" I answered, "I am doc!" We put her uterus back in, one of the easier ones I've done — thirty minutes from the time I got there to the time I left. Three men had worked at it for two to three hours before they called the vet!

A typical spring day went something like this: first thing, I had a sick dog to check; it had been vomiting and had had diarrhea for a few days. Diagnosis was dietary indiscretion, also known as garbage-can gut. The next patient was a geriatric dog to be vaccinated; I checked its heart murmur and prostate problems. I was preparing to castrate a yearling stud colt when the call came in from a ranch that Jay was on his way in with a C-section. The other two doctors were already in the country doing calls, so I stayed for surgery. The calf was too big to be born naturally, so we cut it out. As I was putting the final stitches in, the technician came back to ask if I could stay for another C-section if Mike could get the animal loaded and into the clinic. I asked her to reschedule my castration and grabbed a Coke and a candy bar for lunch. Then there was a vaginal prolapse, but luckily Dr. Allan showed up to do that so I could get started on Larry's dog, which had gotten kicked by a horse and now had a fractured kneecap. The surgery turned out to be a little more complicated than expected, as the kneecap was broken in two places rather than one as it had appeared on the x-ray. I got the kneecap reconstructed as well as could be expected, but the surgery took about two and a half hours. We took a post-op x-ray and it looked good. The technician took over the recovery.

I then went to work on a yellow-naped Amazon parrot called Poncho. His sinus passages were blocked, so we did a nasal flush and collected the fluid for culture, drew a blood sample for a complete blood count, and began antibiotic treatments.

My next appointment was a coughing horse owned by Joe, so I left for his place. The horse was sicker than most with very congested lungs. We began aggressive antibiotics and an expectorant. My last stop for the day was Dallas's house to check a horse that had developed a large number of very small bumps all over its skin. The diagnosis was an unusual viral skin disease that would go away with time. This ended a rather typical day, if you can call any of our days typical!

When my days aren't filled with veterinary medicine they become filled with ranch life. It seems that we are either out working, moving, checking, or calving the cows. I also try to keep the house and yard looking nice. It's nice to get laundry done every once in a while too! There are times that you have to let a few things slide, though.

Last winter we had one of the coldest Februarys in a long time, and our cows started calving at the beginning of the month. We calved out 260 head, with 100 of those first-calf heifers. Seventy-five percent of them calved in February. The morning of February 23 started at 5 A.M. with my husband, Jack, coming in the bedroom saying "I need help!" He had overslept his alarm, and with subzero temps you're going to have trouble. One heifer had calved and its calf was chilled; another heifer was in trouble, with its calf's tongue very swollen and practically frozen. Jack had brought the chilled calf in with him; we covered it in blankets in front of the woodstove that had gone out overnight and plugged in the heating pad, but forgot to turn it on. We grabbed the calving chains and ran out to pull the other calf. We got the chains on, hooked up the calf puller, but we were unable to work it because cleanings from the previous pull job had frozen the works solid. So we tried to start the space heater, which has problems in severe cold as it uses diesel fuel. As Jack cussed the space heater for not starting when you need it the most, I ran to my jeep to get my calf puller, dragging it through the snow on the way back. Consequently, it didn't want to go back together quite right. We started pulling the calf anyway. With the calf half-way out, the calf puller fell apart, so I wrapped the come-along chain around a post and kept pulling. The calf was alive, so we ran it over to the house to warm it. The temperature of the first calf didn't register, which means it was less than 94 degrees. So Jack got our old washtub (we don't have a bathtub) and filled it with the calf and five gallons of warm water. While I kept the water warm, and the calf from drowning, Jack went out to milk colostrum out of the two heifers that had just calved so we could get the lifesaving first milk into them. He came back with one and a half pints, combined total from both. We added warm water to reheat it and tubed the first calf, whose temp was now 96.4. We changed the water in the tub and Jack left for the neighbors to see if they had colostrum. (I had sold our two bags of powdered colostrum to a neighbor the night before.) The dairy didn't have any colostrum on hand, but could milk a cow out. By the time Jack got back, the first calf's temp was 100, and I had put it on an old oil tablecloth to keep from soaking the floor. We tubed the second calf with the fresh colostrum and gave it a shot of banamine to help take the swelling out of its tongue. Now it was time to feed the third calf in the house — our little premature calf, which despite all odds was doing pretty good. Its birth weight was a whopping 21 pounds. So we put milk in the nurser bottle and while we were trying to feed it, the first calf wanted a piece of the action! It's now about 8:30 and time for me to get ready for work. I don't need to be there until 10:00 since I work the late shift tonight and then take emergency calls. Of course I got to work to find that we were not the only ones with chilled calves! That evening we put the two calves back with their respective moms. Both sucked and were doing fine.

I am happy to live a life where very seldom are two days alike, and if they are, they tend to be spread apart.

CAROLYN JOHNSEN ⚊ Baling Wire

When my parents held their farm sale a couple of years ago, my brother and sister and I collected various useful or memorable items before they were offered at auction. I took some small pieces of furniture, a couple of gunnysacks, and an iron ring from the side of the barn where my grandfather used to tie his horses.

I wish I'd taken a hundred feet of baling wire.

The use of wire to hold together bales of prairie hay or alfalfa seemed incidental to its other uses. Baling wire held the droopy pasture gate shut. It formed a loop for the hook on the screen door and fastened the rickety wooden sideboards to the old green feed wagon. From the ceiling of the brooder house, the chick feeders dangled by baling wire. Baling wire and a nail held a rain gauge to the garden fence, and a little loop of it replaced a broken buckle on my brother's four-buckle overshoes.

My father started the windmill by dropping a wooden bar out of a baling wire loop. For my mother he made long twisted baling wire hooks and hung them from the great maple tree east of the house. When butchering chickens, Mom hung the plucked birds from these hooks by their ankles so the cats couldn't reach them as she worked.

My folks didn't bring any baling wire with them to the city. Now they, like me, have to settle for the unsatisfactory urban equivalent — new wire with none of the flexibility of a wire that's been wrapped around a bale of alfalfa. In a city hardware store, when I'm asked what gauge wire I need, I say, "You know, something like baling wire." Few clerks know what I mean.

Driving across the Great Plains, I've noticed the big round bales of hay wrapped in plastic, and I wonder what use farm families make of the plastic once it's off the bale.

Last summer my morning glories hung on a sagging trellis. I could have fixed it with a foot of baling wire, but the only piece I have is four feet long. I always use it to stabilize the Christmas tree.

VIRGINIA A. CASSELLS ⌒ Women's Work

All of the work on the ranch was done with the help of either our team of work horses or the cow horses. I used to drive the team for my brother when he used the fresno to scrape sand from around the tanks, and I also drove the team on the hayrack when we put up hay for the winter.

I would drive Teddy and Jake down the rows of shocks of grass as my father and brother threw up the large mounds of hay that would bury me if I wasn't careful to scramble up on top and tamp them down. I hated the needle-sharp grass that would stick through my overalls.

I knew my mother was overworked, but it never seemed fair that when we returned with the hay, I had to go to the garden, dig the potatoes, pick the peas and other vegetables, scrape, shell, and prepare them for cooking, while my father and brother lay down to rest.

Then I would set the table and help with the dinner and dishes, finishing just in time to go back for another load of hay. If I complained, Mother would say, "Well you don't have to go with them." But of course I loved working with my father outside, so I would endure anything.

MARIE ELLENBERGER ✦ Just Like a Woman

When my husband announced that he and the hired man were going on a three-day machinery shopping trip, he said I'd be in charge of mixing the ration and feeding the steers with the loader and feed truck. I nodded knowingly. Then with pencil and paper in hand, I found the hired man by himself and asked how to operate the two vital vehicles. As he talked and pointed, I took notes as I had not done since college.

The next day, I pinned the notes to the leg of my jeans, just above my left knee, so they were easily visible. Then I referred to them as I drove the loader, mixed the feed, and drove the truck.

Two more days remained on this work schedule. The notes remained pinned to the leg of my jeans, but my need for them lessened with each feeding. If he had stayed away three more days, I would have had it committed to memory.

OLIVE M. RABEN ✦ The Winter that Was

On January 1, 1949, weather forecasters predicted snow flurries but the day was bright. My husband fed the pregnant cows while I dressed and photographed our four sons in the matching outfits they'd gotten for Christmas. On the way to a New Year celebration with relatives in town, my husband, Elmer, mentioned that the cows were all acting restless and uneasy; we joked that perhaps they'd been celebrating the night before, too!

I will always be glad we had that day, because it was the last outing for quite some time. By morning we were in a full-blown blizzard, with the temperature dropping and inadequate shelter for the cattle and our team; the car, pickup, and tractor stood in an open shed. Elmer walked the floor all night on the second and third as the wind blew and more snow fell.

Our house was originally two schoolhouses put together in 1910, and added to, around, and on top of by everyone who lived there, not well insulated, nor snowproof. The older boys slept upstairs and they had snow sifting down on them. So we moved them downstairs and hung a blanket over the door leading upstairs.

After several attempts to start the tractor, Elmer gave up and found the team about a mile away. They had drifted down over the bank into White River. One landed upright and was standing in deep snow; the other was laying on his side in the ice. We found someone in Crawford with a big winch who got the animal free, but a lot of his hide and a hindquarter came loose in the ice, so he had to be destroyed. We had to keep all the cattle near the house and try to feed them as best we could.

We were better able to fend for ourselves than many. The fall before, Elmer had taken a pickup load of our wheat to Chadron and had it milled into flour for our use. I could bake bread, biscuits, corn bread with the best of them — luckily. We finally did run out of yeast, but we had lots of other things. Just a few days before Christmas we butchered a beef and hung it in an old shack near our windmill. Naturally, with the intense cold it was frozen stiff, so when I wanted some meat, Elmer went out and sawed or chiseled a piece off. I also had a large bunch of hens, though we lost a lot of them, and I had done a lot of canning.

With the electricity put in a couple of years before, we managed to rig a heater for the tractor.

We lived just 1/4 mile from the Crawford cemetery. The only time we could get to town was when enough people had died that they had to clear the road so they could be buried. Then Elmer took down a couple of pieces of fence, jumped the ditch, and went in a hurry, as with the constant winds the road didn't stay clear long. People who lived farther from town were sometimes luckier than we, as they could just go across the pastures where they were blown off, but we had two railroads and White River in our way, so we could not get out through the fields.

It was one of the best of times for family togetherness — when we weren't worrying. We taught the children many card games, played board games, did jigsaw puzzles, had much music around the piano, and read to each other. Also we popped corn, made chili, and just plain had a lot of family fun. When all else failed, we went outside with the sleds and slid down the snow banks in the highway! We lived where it is really flat, so the snow banks were fun.

Eventually all this ended and it began to warm up. Unless you experienced it, you have no idea of the runoff that occurred. We had ordered a new car at Christmas and when it came in, we drove into Crawford and picked up an aunt and uncle to take them to Chadron for supper. The rivers were all running very high, but we gave that no thought. When we started home, the river just this side of Chadron was way over its banks. We came home through Hot Springs, Ardmore, and then home. We didn't make it until 3 A.M. It was not a fun trip, with four adults and four kids in one car.

After the storms were over, I was sitting in the living room reading when I heard a terrible crash-bang kind of noise and the whole house shook. I thought there had been an explosion of some sort, but I didn't smell any smoke. After I got my shaking self together, I set out to see what had happened. Our house had a flat roof and so much snow had blown into the crevices in it that as the snow melted it caused the entire ceiling in one of the big bedrooms to collapse.

SHIRLEY LILLEY ⟋⟍ **Storm at Chimney Rock Ranch**

In the fall of '69, during the years that we worked for the Grazing Association, we pastured about 1,600 heifers, 1,500 steers and 500 pairs of cows and calves — about 25 different brands. We'd already shipped out some stock when a storm hit.

During the night, eighteen inches of snow fell. There was no chance of getting trucks in, so we fed the cattle hay and hashed over plans to trail the steers out the next day.

On October 13, we started out from our shipping pens at daylight with 950 head of cattle. It was ten degrees below zero. I've never been so cold before or since. I had so many clothes on and my bones were so stiff that I had to climb up the fence to get on my horse.

We trailed the cattle eighteen miles to the railroad at Red Buttes. Several of the farmers (owners of the cattle) were helping us. Our horses nearly played out, but a few miles from the stockyards, neighbors came out to help us. What a welcome sight that was!

The steers were corralled just before dark, but it was hours before the cattle cars came, and it was four A.M. when we left. We didn't get to bed until twenty-five hours after we'd started out from home.

After a few hours of sleep, and more snowfall, we were back outside, taking care of the cattle still left on the ranch.

TWYLA HANSEN ⟋⟍ **Snow Crazy**

They say it wasn't so much
the snow that made her crazy,
what with winter pressing hard
so early on the heels of autumn,
as the *thought* of snow,
listening as she did each storm-
impending night to forecasts,
off in the west storms loom-
ing large as the Rockies,
weighing on her as heavy;
her nightmares claustrophobic,
inside the cab, the motion
back-and-forth, back-and-forth
of the blade, the endless hours
in the night and the *thought*
they say, the responsibility

for moving all that snow;
in the cab alone with only AM
late-night radio, the swirling
flakes on the windshield, in
front of the auxiliary headlights,
swirling, swirling hard. Yet
she knew what the job entailed,
with all its seasons of duty,
and wanted it, they say, more
than most; they say she should
have known.

NORMA F. PLANT ~ *April Blizzard*

After both my sister Irene and I were married, we went home for a visit on April 6, 1935, with our children, Irene's three-month-old son, and my thirteen-month-old boy. Our younger siblings, Betty and John, were to appear in a school program, and we decided to go while Mother baby-sat her grandsons. We wore high heels, spring dresses, and hats; our older brother, Ralph, drove us to the school, six miles away. Before long, a blizzard began, and we started for home in Ralph's car. Within a block, the car stalled. While Ralph tried to fix it, we returned to the school; I had difficulty walking in the wind and snow, five months pregnant and wearing high heels. Fifty people spent the night in the school's basement, singing or trying to nap.

At dawn, the wind and snow continued; a bachelor named Lloyd offered to try to get us home in his truck. With Ralph, we squeezed into the cab and drove two miles on the highway. As soon as Lloyd turned into his side road, the truck stalled at a drift caused by a half-buried car. The two men found the driver slumped over the wheel, drowsy. They pulled him out and we all started to walk the half-mile to Lloyd's house, holding a blanket before us.

Exhausted and shivering, we reached the house and Lloyd lit his black stove with corn cobs and coal, then heated bricks to put in the bed; Irene and I crawled in, and so the first day ended.

Next morning, the blizzard still raged. The men hitched horses to a lumber wagon, heated bricks for our feet, and wrapped blankets around us. At a deep gully where we should have found a bridge, we found only a steep slope; the horses were unable to pull the wagon, even with all of us pushing. We unhitched the horses and walked a quarter-mile to the next farmhouse, the quarters of bachelors noted for their bootlegging and gambling. They were kind, preparing food and giving us a bed, into which we crawled wearing all our clothes since it was far from clean.

On the third morning, while the sun shone, the men dug the wagon out, and the bachelors loaned us two horses. Together with the other team, they pulled us home to our anxious parents. With no telephone, they had no way of knowing where we were; Mother had fed Irene's baby on oatmeal gruel. Seeing the bright warm sun glisten on the snow was the most beautiful sight nature could have given us.

KATHRYN E. KELLEY *Witching Saint Anthony's Well*

When our old well began to fail in the 1940s, Dad called a well company for recommendations. I watched as two of the men considered more "sensitive" wandered the farmyard dowsing for water, holding metal wands in each hand. Believers said short bobs, deep dips, and rotations in the rods meant water lay below. When the wands pulled together at the far tips and bent down, they pointed to water underground — somewhere. The men were methodical, covering the ground piece by piece, hoping to find water near existing buildings and feedlots. I left to meet the school bus before they finished.

My dad found it hard to put his faith — and money — into a project based on such an odd and old-fashioned technique. I'm sure the word "witchcraft" must have passed through his skeptical mind. So after school and chores, he collected metal rods in several forms — coat hangers, welding rods, lightweight fencing materials —- and we did our own test. Feeling silly, but thinking about serious questions, we stepped across the grass. We willed our minds to be free of distractions, afraid our need for water would convince us wrongly. Dad and Mom carried heavy rods; I carried coat hangers, holding to the hooks.

Time after time, Dad and Mother walked the same ground with no response. I moved slowly from the outer edge of the yard toward the center. To my intense surprise, the hangers dipped down. Uncertain, I backed up and tightened my grip, then stepped forward again. Slowly the ends bent toward the earth and swung inward to meet in front of me.

Startled, I looked at Dad, who confirmed that the well crew had discovered the area, but abandoned it. I moved toward the middle of the yard and felt the wires move as I approached a cottonwood tree. My fingers ached with tension, but I couldn't hold the wires still; slowly they bent down and inward.

Again, I turned to my parents, who confirmed that I'd found the spot chosen for the new well. I shivered; what did any of us know about finding water, especially a ten-year-old? The new site was so close to the old well, we feared we might be boring into the already failing source.

In a few days the crew returned. On their second day of drilling, the bit broke at two hundred feet. Sweating, dirty men replaced it, exchanging grim smiles. They usually found water at that depth, but saw no sign of it even at two hundred fifty feet. When they stopped for lunch, they talked of dry holes; the equipment couldn't go much deeper.

My aunt, who had driven out from town, was skeptical. She told us all she had prayed to St. Anthony, who found lost items. The men smiled politely. Prayers were women's work; men worked with things their hands could touch.

In the cool shade of the house the men talked until we became aware of Mother, calling from the yard. "Come quickly," she screamed. A heavy rumbling came from the new hole. The crew rushed to the rig, knowing they had to back-fill the hole at once.

Frantically my mother tried to make them understand, but the men were busy. She pulled my father by the hand over to the raw edge, went down on her knees, and motioned him to look in. In that dark place there was no mistaking the rush and curling sound of moving water, nor its sharp bright aroma.

Puffing, my plump little aunt arrived on the scene, confident her prayers to St. Anthony had been answered. Thereafter, we called it St. Anthony's well.

THOMASINA PARKER 〜 Corn Cob Cuisine

Bushel baskets piled high with corn cobs stood behind the kitchen range. I'd put baby Ronny on the bed to watch me from the window as I picked them up from the hog pen. The clean cobs from the corn sheller were used to start the fire, but they burned too fast and didn't make a steady hot fire like the muddy manurey ones from the hog lot.

This was the first part of the daily ritual. The next was carrying out the ashes. It wasn't bad if you remembered to do it every day. You just put a paper on the floor under the ash door, pulled out the ash pan, carried it outdoors, and dumped it by the chicken house. The hens like to scratch and dust themselves in the ashes. I believe it helped rid them of mites, too. But if you missed a day, the pan overflowed, the ashes spilled onto the floor, and dust settled on everything.

The third part of the routine was the constant washing of your hands. When you were ready to begin a meal, you filled the stove with cobs. Then you washed your hands. Next you got your roast ready for the oven, or cut up your chicken, or prepared a meatloaf. Then you put in more cobs, washed your hands, fixed a dessert, washed your hands, on and on.

Then sometimes you didn't accurately calculate the amount of cobs you'd need before you had time to get more — and you ran out. So you grabbed a basket, climbed over the hog pen fence. The gate was wired shut to keep the little pigs from wiggling through. Your dress always caught on the top wire, overalls weren't worn for everyday, just when you went to the field and sometimes to milk. You scooped up the cobs as fast as you could, listening for the babies' cry, and dashed back to the house. Then you filled the stove and washed your hands again! I kept a wash pan on the back of the stove; it was handy and the water was always warm.

We'd buy a little coal but it was saved to try to hold a fire overnight in the range. There was little money, hence little coal, and there were lots and lots of cobs!

Despite the inconveniences, the range was an ideal cook stove. You could adjust the cooking temperature just by moving your kettle forward or back. You always had a reservoir of hot water, and a warming oven to keep the food warm when the men were late for supper. The oven was always hot, ready to pop in a pan of biscuits or corn bread. And what was more relaxing than to prop your cold feet up on the open oven door? It was also the perfect place to dry wet mittens and boots, and served as an incubator for wet, chilled chicks and baby pigs, snuggled in an old flannel shirt in a box.

You regulated the temperature of the old range by the number of cobs you put in. Grandma Parker was a genius at this. When we were first married, a neighbor asked me to bake a "scratch" angel food cake. I'd never made one but agreed to try after Gram volunteered to "man" the stove. The cake turned out fine, thanks to the rapport between Gram and her old range.

We bought a microwave oven a year ago, how did I manage without it? I bake, then freeze our bread, rolls, and cookies. They come from the microwave tasting fresh baked.

But no matter how much we advance, some things never change. We'll always need:

> persons like my mom, who loved to cook
> kids to help Grandma (and Grandpa) bake cookies
> little boys to lick frosting bowls
> little girls to stir cake batters
> family and friends to share the love and warmth of a kitchen

Yes, some things change, some remain, "and the greatest of these is love." (1 Corinthians 13:13).

VIRGINIA BLACKFORD ⟿ Majestic Range

Mother and Dad had bought a new Majestic range before we left Minnesota to homestead in Colorado. This was Mother's joy but she had no coal to use for fuel and learned to use dried cow chips. One day she was baking bread and some town ladies came to call. Mother was so ashamed to keep her fire going using cow chips that she let it die down and lost a whole baking of bread. Come to find out all the ladies used cow chips and should have told Mother, but they too were ashamed. Years after, they used to laugh about it.

During World War I, the Colorado Extension service promoted the canning of vegetables and meat. I was on a 4-H canning club team that won first place at the Colorado State Fair in Pueblo. We were asked to demonstrate canning foods safely to clubs of women all over eastern Colorado. Our leader was Miss Amelia Alexander; her sister, Addie, also helped. Miss Alexander had her car fixed up with a box on back to hold our pressure cooker and canning equipment. We also took camping equipment as we sometimes went quite a distance and had to stay overnight.

Years later, I was sent to Lubbock, Texas, to learn how to organize and manage canning stations where we canned the beef that the government was buying up. Because of the drought there was no pasture for the cattle and they were all dying. I had canning stations in several towns, including Rocky Ford and Lamar. We had huge pressure cookers and canned in tin cans. This put a lot of men and women to work.

After the beef was canned people still needed work so the government sent me to learn how to make mattresses and we had a factory in Lamar.

ELLA SCHLATER REICHART ⟿ Making Do

Our farm was eighty acres located southeast of Springfield, Nebraska, on the Platte River. One summer, my sister Annette and I lay on cots in the yard, very sick with jaundice. The doctor didn't know what to do for us, but our neighbor brought us some elderberry wine and honey, and I guess it helped because we started getting better.

Our front yard was surrounded by huge elm and cottonwood trees, but there was no grass. Therefore, every week when our mother finished washing clothes, we got to sprinkle the ground with the rinse water, which was great fun and usually ended in a water fight.

The only bed in the house with a store-bought mattress was Mother and Dad's. The other mattresses were "ticks." Each spring after corn shelling, the ticks were emptied, the coverings washed and dried in the sun, then refilled with fresh corn shucks. In the fall we emptied and washed them again, and stuffed them with fresh prairie hay or wheat straw.

We always watched for the big brown and orange butterflies in the spring, because as soon as we spotted one we could take off our shoes and socks and go barefoot. We usually got two new pairs of shoes a year: a new pair of patent leather slippers in the summer to wear to Sunday school and to start school with in the fall; then, when it started to get cold, we got a pair of high-top shoes with laces for winter.

In winter, the kitchen got very cold at night after the fire went out, so anything that would freeze, like eggs, potatoes, apples, we carried into the living room before we went to bed. One strict rule my dad had — nobody sat down to the table to eat without washing hands and face. Many a morning we had to break the ice in the water bucket to wash.

Summertimes the washtubs sat under the eaves of the roof to catch rain water. It was always a treat to have soft water to wash your hair. Or if we caught enough water, we could wash the clothes in it. There was no detergent or soap powder. Once a year Mom made soap, but as a general rule she bought P & G bar soap to do the wash, and we used this to wash dishes. One strict rule: after washing, all dishes had to be rinsed in hot water from the tea kettle and then dried. Wednesday and Saturday mornings we filled the washtubs with water and left them sitting in the sun all day. This was our bath water, and we all took baths in it. You were really lucky if you were the first one in!

MARGARET CARR   **Tree Limb Checkers and Mustard Plasters**

While growing up, we often got by with what we had on hand. I recall this particularly in two areas especially important to children — toys and medicine.

Thread came on wooden spools, which we used for knobs on doors, drawers, and pot lids. Dad whittled wooden tops for us from the spools, sometimes hammering a shoe tack into the point to make them spin better. Ernest could make his top spin a long time; I improved at spinning tops as I got older.

Dad showed us how to make ratchets from spools by carving notches around the edges of a spool and wrapping string around it. When you held the ratchet against a window or door and pulled the string, it made a horrible sound; Mom hated the noise. Ernest could get away with it sometimes, but I waited until Mom went out to help Dad with chores; then we tried to see who could make the most noise.

Granddad Nelson's cigars came in wooden boxes just right for a wagon Ernest made. He put a twig through the spool holes and used shoe tacks to keep the spools on the twig. Then he nailed the twig to the bottom of the cigar box, attached a string, and had a wagon. I inherited it when he grew tired of it, and I pulled kittens or rocks around; rocks stayed put, but kittens were more fun.

One time Dad sawed a piece of board to a point on one end, drilled a hole in it and inserted a stick, and impaled a piece of Mom's writing paper on it for a sail; we used that sailboat for a long time. He also made us checkers from tree limbs. Half of them were blackened with stove polish. He marked off squares on a wide pine board, used stove polish for some, and left the rest as they were. He and Ernest often played checkers on winter evenings after chores were done, by kerosene lamp light. Dad also made willow whistles. When I learned to make my own, I found that green chokecherry worked as well as willow, but Mom wouldn't let us blow them inside the house. Ernest made a big one that nearly broke our eardrums.

My hoop was from a thirty-gallon wooden barrel; I used a stick to roll it and had a hard time keeping up. One time it got away from me on a hill, bouncing this way and that, gaining speed all the time. Finally it left the road, hit a rock, and leaped into the air. I thought I saw the grove of trees and bushes it bounced into, but Ernest and I looked and couldn't find it. That fall when the leaves fell, there was my hoop, way up in a tree.

On long winter evenings Mom read books from the library in Sundance to us by the light of a kerosene lamp. The more exciting or scary the story was, the closer Ernest and I edged up. Zane Grey's books were favorites; Jack London's *Call of the Wild* had me in tears, as did *Black Beauty*.

Ernest had read about stilts, so he made himself a pair and could really run on them. Dad made me a small pair but I fell off more times than I was on them.

Medicine usually looked terrible, smelled awful, and tasted bad, as if it would be more effective that way. Home remedies were all we had. Dad made Mom a medicine chest from a hand-planed flat pine box with a lid. It had a hasp and eye for a lock, but I don't remember it ever having a lock. It was kept under their bed, and we children never dared touch it.

For croup, Mom made us swallow a brew of one-half cup of molasses, a little hot water, and one teaspoon of soda. When it foamed up, you swallowed it quickly.

We had several remedies for chest colds. Mom made a mustard plaster of two parts flour to one part dry mustard, with enough hot water to make a paste. She spread this between two layers of cloth and slapped it on the chest hot, wrapping towels over it. I usually sweated, and sometimes got blisters. When we didn't have mustard, Mom made a chest plaster of sliced, lightly fried onions.

For a sore throat, Mom made us gargle warm saltwater or vinegar, salt, and pepper; for a head cold we snuffed saltwater up our noses; we rubbed salt in our scalps for dandruff; and put salt on a cloth to scrub our teeth. I was at least ten before I got my first toothbrush.

Every spring, Mom gave Ernest and me a tablespoon of kerosene with sugar as a tonic, to "clean the system." Wonder it didn't kill us. Another spring tonic was sulphur and molasses. She used coal oil (kerosene) on chilblains after our feet were frosted; it felt good on hot, swollen feet. We also used coal oil or turpentine and sugar on cuts or punctures in both animals and humans, and sometimes we put axle grease on animal wounds.

Dad liked to use runny pitch from pine trees for his cuts, and smeared it on calves' heads when they were dehorned; it was messy, but it kept dirt out and flies away, and cost nothing. When I was roaming around and found trees with runny pitch, I'd go back later with a cup with no handle and a spoon to gather it for Dad. Mom wouldn't use it, but Ernest and I did.

Mom always kept a jar full of scorched linen rags she had heated in the oven for dressings for wounds and burns. For infections and boils she boiled flax seed, mashed it, and plastered it on, or applied hot milk and browned bread, or sheep dip, diluted.

She tied slices of raw bacon around our necks for swollen glands; I hated the greasy mess, so sometimes Mom used castor oil, the remedy I hated even worse because it made me throw up. I remember Mom coaxing and wheedling me to take it, until Dad held me while Mom pried open my mouth and held my nose to pour a tablespoon down my throat. I always fought and cried. As soon as it hit bottom, my stomach began to roll and cramp until up it came with a vengeance. That always left me weak and shaky; don't know what good it did. Once, Mom said I bit her finger when she pried open my mouth, so she put a clothespin in my mouth instead. In my teens, I used castor oil to clean shoe leather.

Dad always got chaff in his eyes while thrashing. Mom would put a flax seed in his eye to work the chaff to the corner where it could be removed.

For an upset stomach, Grandma made bay leaf tea, but Mom probably didn't have bay leaves, so she made "charcoal tea" by pouring boiling water over burned toast and adding a little sugar. We kids thought it was good, so it probably helped us. Sassafras tea was supposed to be good for a fever, and it was just plain good to drink with a little sugar. Mom's relatives in Indiana often sent us some, made from the bark of the sassafras root. A little went a long way because it got stronger each time it was boiled.

For an earache, Mom blew smoke in our ears; I know firsthand this is effective. For colds, Dad made us a hot toddy of whiskey, sugar, nutmeg, and hot water. This made me sweat and sleep, and usually broke up my cold.

In spite of, or maybe because of, these remedies, Ernest and I grew to adulthood, and I'm still here at eighty-six.

GRACE E. KYHN ～ Building the Straw Shed

It was the dry years of the early thirties, and our farm was in need of shelter for the farm animals, with the coming of winter. The cost of lumber and posts was more than the upcoming corn crop would pay for. It was a family discussion to save funds that brought to mind the idea to build a straw shed.

I was ten and my brother was twelve years old and we looked forward to trips to the river to gather the cottonwoods and willows for the building project.

The largest cottonwood trees Father used for corner posts and center division for the two-roomed double-walled shelter. The four- to six-inch diameter logs were rafters, cross pieces, and gate material. The one- to three-inch diameter willows and long straight branches were hauled home after we children chopped off the small limbs with our hatchets. The fun of this soon became work and night found us with throbbing arms.

We children helped to line the walls with old woven wire. We held the willows upright against the woven wire and even tried to nail them. My luck was a smashed thumb because the green limbs bounced around so much.

In preparing for the filling of the walls Father had mowed all the tough coarse slough grass and weeds around the fields and hay meadow. Now he forked this dry stuff into the walls and all of us walked around packing it down. When he ran out of this junk, he finished with wheat straw. That sticky, itchy, scratchy straw made us miserable. We were glad to finish the job and have a bath.

Father finished the roof like the walls. He laid a generous amount of limbs on top to keep his thatched roof from blowing away in the Nebraska winds.

When I look back, I realize how much about life we experienced for as long as that shed stood, and the memories we cherish. On our trips to the river, we talked with Father about everything along the way. The meadow-larks on the fence posts, pasture owls that turned their heads and necks until we thought they would drop off. Snakes that left trails on the sandy road, gophers running zigzag everywhere. The wild bluebells forming seed pods, wild roses, grasses, the kind of trees and bushes. Watched the clouds make shapes and forms. We must have asked a thousand questions.

It was in the shed we caught the colts and calves to pet. When winter came, the warm air from the animals' bodies caused steam to escape through holes in the walls and freeze in honey-colored icicles along the outside walls.

When spring came, the walls were filled with sparrow and wren nests. On top of the roof the turkeys and chickens nested. The rooster would crow and all the birds felt safe from the nightly visits of our neighbor's dog. The snakes and toads sought shade from the sun and hot winds. They would frighten me as I went to gather eggs. Now and then an opossum would venture within and our dog would bark until we removed him.

Each fall we refilled the walls. The filling settled and Old Bess, the mother of our horse and mule colts, pawed and nibbled at the bark and the horrible brown decayed stems and knocked loose some of the upright limbs. We could not part with her, even though she had this bad habit. I think she missed the shed when Father pushed it into a pile and burnt it, for in its darkness she also found relief from summer flies. Now we children found it harder to study baby birds, as we could no longer climb the walls and see them cry for food.

There is not long life in a shed constructed by such a method, but it served a purpose and got us into more profitable years. It taught us that things are not forever but to enjoy them while we can; it taught us to learn from them and to put effort into life.

FRANCIE M. BERG Meadowlark

The meadowlark is poised there on a weathered fence post, singing joyously.

"It's time," he sings out in his melodious tones. "Time to plant your sweet potatoes."

Different versions take root in listening ears. "Can't sing, but I feel pretty good," is what one woman wrote me that her father kept hearing.

But to me he sings ever of sweet potatoes, however inappropriate that might be to this open northern plains country.

HELEN MOORE HENRY Milkweed Silk

In the fall of 1943 all rural schools were invited to participate in a milkweed pod contest. This was an effort to help during the war. The government had no use for the pods, but the silks inside were used as a substitute for kapok. Kapok was used inside life preservers on ships. There was a shortage of kapok, so the silks of the milkweed pods were used. My students and I decided to try to win the contest. It took about 10,000 milkweed pods to fill one gunnysack. We counted the ones in the first bag and estimated the rest. Every day that fall we took the noon hour to look for pods in neighboring fields. We soon discovered there was no shortage of milkweed pods. We not only collected during the noon hour but each child and I went through our own fields after school. After the bags were full we would hang them to dry on the fence line at school. When we finished we had fifty-six bags of milkweed pods and won the county contest. Many years later the land owners told me that we must have done a good job hunting milkweeds because their fields had no milkweeds for years.

FRANCES BURJES FITCH
I've Been There, and I'm Still There

As I sit in the comfortable cab of our four-wheel-drive tractor, pulling a thirty-two-foot chisel plow, air conditioning on, and the radio playing my favorite country and western tunes, there is time to reminisce on the changes I've experienced.

It seems but yesterday when my Dad placed the line of a four-horse hitch in my small hands and let me drive a short way. He was drilling wheat with an eight-foot horse drill, and I was his shadow, riding alongside him, standing on the platform at the rear of the drill. I was pleased that the rows I made were very straight, not knowing that the teams were trained to walk straight.

Yes, from the days of the four-horse hitch to the four-wheel-drive tractor, I've been there and I'm still there, tilling the soil.

I love the land. Land remains the same if you care for it. Many times I've seen my dad pick up a handful of soil and hold it. Now I do the same.

Born on my parents' homestead and raised in an all-girl family, I learned early in life what it takes to run a farm. Everything was "armstrong" power. We carried all the wood, coal, ashes, and water. We milked cows by hand and carried the milk to the house to be separated by a machine that was turned by hand. We carried the milk, minus the cream, out to the calves, pigs, and chickens.

Every morning we brought in the horses and milk cows with our horse Dinah. Dad's big Belgian work horses were too tall for me to harness; I could place the collars around their necks by standing on the manger, being careful to keep my feet away from theirs. Dad's love for history was reflected in the names he gave his favorite team, Cleveland and Tecumseh. During haying season, we had as many as four teams in the horse barn. It has been a few years now since I've driven a team, but there is nothing like feeling the tug of the lines as a team heads home to their oats.

It's been more than fifty years since a threshing machine pulled into our straw yard, lined up the belt to the engine, and waited for the bundle haulers to pull up alongside the feeder and start pitching in the bundles of grain. Once the grain was cut and bound, we stacked seven or eight bundles to a shock, so they would stand up and shed water. I used a pitchfork when shocking, as a weapon against mice and rattlesnakes.

Now I run our self-propelled combine, adjusting the reel height and speed with a little lever and using the variable speed as the grain gets heavier or thinner. Is this really progress? I'm munching on a protein bar and an apple for lunch. No time to stop and eat a meal. Gone are the days when neighbors helped each other at harvest.

I miss the whir of the mowing machine as the team pulled steady and their heads nodded slowly, keeping time with their feet. There isn't a wind-rower made that can cut a square corner like a good team of horses. After a day's work, when they were unhitched, the lines coiled and hung up, I climbed up on the gentlest horse, hanging on to the hames, to ride home-ward.

My husband contends that we couldn't run the farm without the four-wheel all-terrain vehicle. Maybe so, but sometimes I long for my first saddle pony, Dinah, who carried me to school every day and took me home through many a storm or blizzard. Our four-wheeler never meant as much to me.

A few years ago I became lonesome for a kitchen range and bought a gray and white enamel Home Comfort with sheaves of wheat and a small scythe pictured on the warming-oven doors. This beauty crowds my kitchen, but I love it. No longer do I dread a power outage. Every day in the wintertime I take out the ashes, build a fire, and have the tea kettle steaming. Many days the stew pot is on and my bread is rising in the warming oven. It serves as a humidifier and is a great conversation piece.

In 1989, the year of South Dakota's centennial, I decided to have an old-time Christmas so my grandchildren could learn something about the past; the best way is to recreate it. The REA was the greatest thing that ever happened to rural people; we'd do without it for one day.

Our son and his wife and family of seven children were coming so my husband Ed and I decided to dress old-fashioned. I never realized how awkward a long dress can be. I made a noon meal over the fireplace by baking a cake and apples in a Dutch oven with the recessed lid and making ham-and-bean soup in my big stew kettle. Cooking the evening meal on my little range was easier, with a large surface for my kettles of chicken and dumplings and all the trimmings.

When the grandchildren arrived, their first task was to clean the lamps and fill them. Grandpa and the children's father took the boys out to the wood pile to saw wood by hand and carry it to the house. Meanwhile the girls were churning cream to make butter, and sprinkling clothes to iron when the flatirons got hot. Their mother was practicing with the treadle sewing machine. Grandma, keeper of the fire, was very busy; it takes about two hours to get the coals in the fireplace just right to bake.

We spent the afternoon playing games and singing songs accompanied by the children's mother on the old piano. They learned to wind the Edison phonograph and play the cylinder records; Grandma taught them the waltz. The little ones posed for pictures in baby dresses made by their great-grandmother. Then there was water to fetch. We had no pump on the well so we had to dip it out and carry it up the hill in buckets. For the first time, the children knew where our water came from. Needless to say, after a trip or two up the hill they were more conservative with the water.

I have a floor loom so we did some weaving, and I explained how the spinning wheel would work. (Mine is so old I don't dare use it.) As the darkness set in, each child lit a lamp or lantern. We sat at the table with the Aladdin in the middle, joining hands for the blessing. The circle of light from the lamp was small, but our circle as a family was complete.

Naturally our old-fashioned Christmas was not one-hundred-percent authentic. Once we forgot and snapped on a light. And we had to use our indoor toilet; we have no outside one anymore. For one day we did shut off the TV and the stereo. I learned how tired Grandma could be when the day ended! But the children had been an important part of the celebration, and they learned something about their heritage.

We cheated a little; our son videotaped it all.

MARJORIE SAISER ~ Making Noodles

Choose the music before your hands get
into the flour. Choose Christopher Parkening
to be followed by Perlman and Heifetz.
Music enough for
seven batches of noodles.
Lay the disks into their circles
and push buttons. Play the music loud to
yourself and to your house on a Sunday morning.

Watch a finch at the feeder.
She looks at the sky, the ground.
The feeder sways with her.
The pen and ink of her wingbars.
Her head and shoulders moving
like lights turning on.
The chaff drifts away in the wind.
Break the egg. Beat in milk,
salt. The flour white like a luxury.
By the time you get to the Heifetz
you will have enough to feed a houseful.

One of your grandmothers must have done this.
Not any grandmother you've seen or
seen in pictures. Perhaps one with a cotton
scarf around her head, one whose hands
like yours took the flour
in white lines in the creases of the skin,
under and around the nails, inside the rings,
if she had rings
if her knuckles were the kind to swell,
to prevent taking off rings
even for making noodles.
Roll the dough without fuss.
A sureness in the hands.

Her hair, if it had not been for the
cotton scarf, surely hanging and swaying
around her face. Cut the noodles and sing
with Parkening. Lay the noodles
on the floured cloth. Each batch different
because you can do nothing the same way twice.

Praise the father. Praise the mother.
The spirit whose power uplifts.
The finch who faces into the wind,
who finds her seeds.

Cut and sing and lay the noodles on
the cloth. Your grandmother fingers,
your grandmother hands, your song going
out to your house, to the chairs and rugs,
to the walls, the pictures. Beyond the windows,
beyond the frost on the grass,
beyond.

The Good Dance

SUE CHAULK Matinee

You arrive
wearing tight jeans
soft as deerskin
worn thin
defining every muscle;
sunglasses
black hay hat
dust speckled gray;
your open chambray shirt
no match for tanned skin.

I am freshly bathed
damp hair
robe clinging to wet thighs.

I open the door.
Body heat envelops me.
Your shoulders fill
the room as you ride my loins.
Your slender butt
welcomes two hands
mine.

We drink iced tea
from the same beaded glass.
Your stark white skin
carries flecks of the red porch floor.
You rise
work calls.
I watch you drive away
hay dust in my hair.

JOAN L. POTTS ~~ Harvest Season Is a Tense Time

I've been watching the side profile of my farmer husband from across the dinner table for twenty years. And before that I watched my farmer father's profile.

When a farmer stares directly into his dinner plate, things are going well with the farm work and he's enjoying his food. When a farmer stares past and over the edge of his dinner plate, the weather hazards and financial matters are bothering him. When he stares at his plate with glazed eyes and doesn't notice what's on it, he's tired. When he glares at the dinner plate as if to burn holes in it with his eyes, he's upset about a machinery repair, a sick critter, or the creek going dry.

Farmers wear the weather on their faces. No words can change the bronzed, rough appearance of a farmer's face. There are no words that make their faces shine until the sun shines so they can get the harvest done.

The dust in the wrinkles of a farmer's brow is as indicative of his work as the creases and calluses on his hands. Farmer's faces tell stories of determination and persistence to survive.

The harvest will get done. Farmers will not be as tense. And farmwives will again quietly observe happier profiles.

PEGGY R. SYMONDS ~~ Dear Daughter

Dear Daughter:

I'm sitting here thinking about how our lives are alike, yours and mine. When you were telling me about your tractor troubles and trying to get the corn planted, it brought back a memory.

Your dad and I were trying to plant corn also. It was when you were too young to remember. We had some pretty old, sad machinery. Dad had a job off the farm. I farmed, hayed, whatever needed doing. When your dad came home at night, I had the day's machinery problems lined up in front of the garage waiting for him to get home. It's a good thing he was a good mechanic.

The combination of old machinery, too much work, and a mere twenty-four-hour day to get it all done didn't always make for sunny dispositions.

Back to my story. We were gonna plant corn. We had about sixty acres that all the neighbors said was Good Corn Ground. Being alfalfa people, we decided to take their well-intended advice. There was a bumper crop of creepin' Jenny and foxtail on this sixty acres, with a few sprigs of grass and a lot of gopher holes tangled up in this mess.

We laid a plan. I would plow and disk this ground and get it ready to plant. We had a 2010 John Deere tractor and a three-bottom rollover plow and that was working so good I plowed one way, then plowed the other way. I disked the same. This would really slow the weeds down.

Every morning I did the chores, put you kids on the school bus, and farmed. By the weekend, I was ready.

We had a John Deere A and a John Deere B — narrow front ends and older than me. The plan was for me to harrow ahead of the corn planter. There was a nice feature about the narrow front end tractors — they turned sharp. I had the harrow behind the A. Your dad had the planter behind the B, and away we went. I needed to get a couple of rounds ahead. After several rounds, Dad decided I was making a real mess and wasn't harrowing straight enough. Besides that I was really wrecking the corners. This wasn't our first farming experience by any means — just our first with corn. Dad decided he'd demonstrate and show me one more time how to do it right. He jumped on my tractor, told me to watch and learn, and away he went. Nice straight harrow marks right up to the corner. He whipped around to come back and when he turned, he turned so sharp he picked up the outside section of the harrow with a hind tire and brought the harrow right up in the seat with him.

It took about one hour to get the harrow off the tractor and ready to go. Not a great deal was said about my harrowing after that. Don't know if I learned a lot about how to do it, but I certainly learned what not to do.

This isn't the end of the story. This isn't being told to you to make your dad look bad. It was just the way of things.

Dad got back on his planter tractor and started his first round. I always thought he was keeping more than one eye on my straight rows or what happened next would never have happened.

He got to the end of the field, hit the lever to raise the marker-arms on the planter, and whipped her around to go back. Two things happened real fast with this sharp-turning John Deere. The arms never raised! Instead, the outside one hooked in the woven wire fence on its way by. Posts started snapping, staples flew, and about one hundred and fifty foot of woven wire, sheep-tight fence — to keep livestock out of our new cornfield — started following him up the field.

I was so busy watching where I was going that I never got to see the whole show, but I saw enough to make me whip a U-ey in the middle of the field and go back.

Don't ever let anybody tell you women aren't just as good at farming as men. Just be sure you marry a man that can laugh at himself, especially if you mess up and laugh first.

Also, he needs to be a good mechanic!

Love, Mom

JUNE WILLSON READ 〜 Running Water Ranch

Wyoming's isolation and distances have produced a special type of inhabitants — hardy, self-sufficient people who believe they can take care of things without much outside help. And if that doesn't work, too bad.

My legacy from growing up on the Running Water Ranch in Wyoming also included beliefs about the roles of men and women.

Sometimes I rebelled. My parents believed that girls should work inside and boys should work outside. I became proficient and bored with housekeeping, food preparation, dishes, and laundry for seven to fifteen people (when hired men were added). Besides, the outdoors looked more exciting.

I argued with Dad from time to time for a place in the outdoors. One loss occurred when a high school classmate wanted to sell his Model A for fifty dollars. I had the money from the sale of my 4-H cattle, but Dad said no. Too much work for him and the boys to keep it running. Funny, but it never occurred to either of us that he might have taught me how to take care of it myself.

I scored a win the summer of 1952, after my senior year in high school. It was branding time, and I pestered Dad to let me help. He finally let me inside the corral to record the cow's horn brand and calf's ear tattoo number. I was proud to be part of the team.

Hunting was a particular vexation. My middle sister gained the privilege of hunting when she turned fifteen, so I figured it would be my turn one day. Imagine my disappointment when my dad said no. I had put most of my .22 rifle shots into the bull's-eye at 4-H camp that summer, but he heard me comment that I flinched. Again, it never occurred to either of us that he might have taught me how to shoot without flinching.

Because the men drove most of the long distances and drove during the winter, I did not learn to drive on snow and ice. Actually, I never drove on snowy or icy roads or more than fifty miles at one time or changed my oil or pumped my own gas until I was an adult.

Although I felt denied access to independence, I did gain the feeling that I was valued as a person, and was protected and cared for.

LINDA VELDER 〜 Dear Tomboy

You passed by me on the street today. You may not have noticed me; I am the elderly woman who was standing in front of the post office. You walked down the sidewalk dressed in a man's shirt, jeans, boots, and feed company cap. As you passed, I felt a twinge of sadness.

I feel I must write you this letter now to help you in the future. Please read it thoroughly and carefully consider what I have to say. You may not choose to accept my advice now, but please tuck it away in your heart for it will revisit you as you mature.

My dear, after a certain age tomboys are no longer cute. Preschool or preadolescent girls are acceptable as tomboys and may draw a few compliments, but they will too soon fade away.

I can tell you from bitter experience that if you dress, act, smell, and talk like a boy, you will be treated just like one of the boys by both the boys and the girls. When you wish for the young men to look at you in a different light, they will be unable to take you seriously. Men don't really like to compete with girls in sports or work. They may feel that they have to "throw" the contest or change the rules; or they have to contain their strength and skill to keep from injuring you, or, when your hormones kick in, avoid your tears.

Boys want to hang around with other boys, and only boys. When they want to be around girls, they don't want a tomboy.

It is great to be knowledgeable about machinery and livestock, to an extent. The lyrics of an old song, "Everything you can do, I can do better. I can do anything better than you," sometimes means backing away from a task and allowing a man to do the work himself. In truth, in that way you still may be doing it better than him.

When a man marries he wants a wife, not a hired hand. If you continue to dress as you do and usurp his role, you will be treated like a hired hand. I have seen women doing all of the farm or ranch work while their husbands are at the auction barn, downtown café, drinking coffee and gossiping, or at the bar.

Men lose their nurturing instinct when exposed to the tomboy type. They are confused by a role that blurs what they have always known. If a boy spends his time playing rough with a girl, he may not know how to be gentle and sensitive. His basic natural male instinct to protect mother and young may never emerge.

Honey, you don't impress the men or the women by acting as you do. Men enjoy sitting around the machine shop or on the corral fence talking man-to-man stuff in their own language. It is hard for them to relate certain farm or ranch operations, express their private feelings, or tell their off-color stories with you listening. And the more you hang out with men, the more your language will become unbecoming of a lady; I know that for a fact.

Of course, as you get older, women will feel threatened by your presence with their menfolk, and at some time in your young life, you won't have either men or women who are close friends. Wives will be nagging their husbands about you. Even though you may be innocent of romantic tangles, everyone watching will believe you're guilty.

There are a lot of things in life we don't like to do, but we must. I know how difficult it is sometimes to be a girl; there are times when it is just no fun at all. Dressing like the men is a practical thing to do, and men are more interesting to listen to than women who sit and discuss sewing, recipes, fashion, and clubs.

I am not saying that women should not work on the ranch and dress in clothing that is safe for working around machinery. I am not against a woman's right to do as she wishes, but I feel a woman should walk beside her husband, not in front of him. If you lead the way doing the work, you will find you have the pleasure of doing all of the work by yourself.

My dear, you are an intelligent, sweet young lady under those jeans, boots, and man's shirt, with your hair tied up in a knot under that cap. Please try to sit with the women from time to time and develop a rapport with them. Someday you will need the advice of another woman, but you won't know how to relate to one. Read a few women's magazines to polish your rough edges. I am confident that someday, long after I have passed away, you will thank me.

I hope I can save you much unhappiness, isolation, and the pain of the mistakes I made so many years ago.

Love, An old tomboy who has been there

LAURIE WAGNER BUYER ~ Hanging in Balance

I was not born to the land. I came to the land by choice when I was twenty, when my dreams of college degrees and a teaching career turned pallid, when letters from a Vietnam vet turned mountain man sparked my latent love for the land and filled my heart with renewed purpose.

I came west from Chicago, with a backpack and twenty-five dollars in cash. I came with the idea I would stay one winter season and I ended up staying for life. From the outset, for me, it was never easy. I had nothing to lose but I also had everything to learn. I had to start over, begin again. The rudimentary skills of a homestead lifestyle were no part of my suburban childhood, so every lesson I learned, from splitting wood and carrying water to birthing and butchering, came hard for me, and the hardest lesson of all was death.

The eye of the hen was dark, unblinking and ringed with gold. Stretched out on the wood block, every tiny burnt-red feather on her head was perfectly sculpted. The concentric age rings in the old and weathered wood wove circles around and around her head like a haloed aura of light. Gripping her stiff legs, my left hand was festooned with homemade bandages, badges of honor earned while learning to split kindling. My right hand held the big double-bitted ax aloft and trembling. The hen had shared my attic room for several weeks, penned up with food and water and warmth to help her heal from the brutal pecking she'd received while cooped in with the flock. Now she was fat and well, destined for the dinner table. For over a month we'd been eating smoked bear ham and elk steaks sawn whole from a frozen haunch. Chicken would be a welcome change. "Don't swing too hard. The weight of the ax will chop through her neck," he coached me. I hesitated. "Just toss her into the snow." I let the ax fall. I felt weak and sick but remembered thinking later that the plucking and gutting was far tougher work than the killing.

Snowed in eighty some miles north of Kalispell, Montana, my first months on the land were often desolate and lonely. The mail came twice a week to a box on a forest service road when the four-wheel-drive postman's rig could get through. Pride helped me stay. I learned to cook on the wood-stove; I split wood and carried water. I washed clothes by hand and rinsed them in the ice-bound river and hung them to freeze in the bitter night air. I was impressed with the root cellar, all dank air and darkness, the timbered roof covered with thousands of hibernating daddy longlegs spiders. The root crops stored in bins of sand and the hundreds of jars of fruit, vegetables, and jam were reassuring. Once I learned how to milk the goats and fork out hay for the horses, I enjoyed the early morning and late evening routine of chores. I was always tired. Always sore. The silence and the soothing sound of the river sustained me.

By spring I was a hand of sorts. I was continually busy with chores or cooking and cleaning. When I had time, I learned to bead and I read or wrote letters to family and friends. The air was pungent with manure and earth smells when the snow left. The river ran high, mud-rich, teeming with frantic sawyers and nameless black debris. Cleaning the chicken house one day, I was using a scoop shovel to scrape up droppings and dirtied oat hay. Squabbling hens, a new batch of chicks, and the cranky, irascible rooster were shooed outside in the sunshine. It was dark and the air was heavy and lung-burning, tinged with ammonia. I was in a hurry and my shovel came down hard and fast on a fluff ball chick who had scurried back inside. Cheeping loudly, it dragged its broken toothpick leg; I picked it up and carried it to the cabin cupped in my hands. He was playing the piano, Rachmaninoff, something bold and brilliant. I dared not interrupt so I simply held the chick out, its leg dangling. Not pausing, he said bluntly, "You hurt it. You take care of it." I was afraid then and crying, "Why are you so cruel?"

"Cruelty counts," was what he told me.

I assumed that death came easy for him. He was a hunter, a trapper. He'd been a medic in the war. He was remote and mostly silent. He considered his life hard-won and his outlook was fiercely intent. He carried his aloneness like a shield and his callous disregard of others gave him a separate peace. I did admire and respect him, and, yes, in my own young, untaught way, I loved him. I yearned for his selfsame strength, his conviction, his courage. Ignorant and innocent, I suffered in his realm, but I learned of many things, things of darkness and despair, things of joy and light, things of the land and the wild ones who walked there. I learned of the seasons and the value of food and shelter. Cold and fear took their place alongside laughter and warmth. I learned the incredible power of a single kerosene lamp burning at the window on the nights he did not come home. I learned to be alone.

The second spring came early, the snow line retreated each day and left miniature, majestic lakes on the meadow. Wild swans glided in late in the evening; they came for last summer's seeds and their calls were dusk soft, eternal. The crazy cries of loons echoed back and forth across the land, drifting high, lonesome, and eerie in the night skies.

I'd learned to ride, bareback, by demand. We went one day, late in the afternoon, to see the country opening up. He rode the sorrel mare, Jubilee, and I, her three-year-old bay colt, Ahkee, named for the piercing scream of the sparrow hawk. We left the sheltered timber surrounding the cabin and barn and headed cross-country along the edge of the snow-free meadow, winding our way through willow-choked beaver sloughs, headed for higher ground. Suddenly I was cold and afraid. But he went on and I followed and the beaver channel of black water and ice and mud was wide and bottomless and the mare lunged in and splashed and sprang ahead, scrambling for footing on the steep, slippery bank. Ahkee was young and uncertain. He minced and backed up, shying; then he plunged in after his dam, lurched and drew up in an explosion of terror, leaped the bank, crashed through the dog-hair pine and was still; terrified and still. He would not move. I kicked and beat him with the reins. Releasing my death grip on his mane, I slid off on jellied legs to lead him forward but he would not move. Finally, desperately, I whooped a come-back call to him who had disappeared downriver.

We could find nothing wrong. No blood; no broken bones. Nothing but that the colt was wild-eyed and trembling, coated with icy sweat. He would not move no matter how we coaxed and cajoled. So we took off his hackamore and turned him loose, assuming he would follow or turn back for the barn. We rode off double on the mare, crossing the wide, roaring river channels, making our circle for home in the day's last silk-soft air.

He dropped me at the cabin door and raced away on the trail we'd first taken. I waited and worried, sitting on the wood block while the goats and cats gathered around and the sunlight faded into pink and orange shimmers on distant snowcapped peaks. The thunder of hooves scattered the goats and brought me to my feet as the mare slid to a stop, all foam and frantic dancing. "Get me the .30-.30." And I did. And he was gone.

I started a fire and lit the lamp. I half held my breath waiting, waiting until the sharp crack of the rifle told me Ahkee was dead and I did not know why. And I was frightened.

Stepping out into the moonlight I took the clammy, heavy rifle and I held the mare's head. His cheeks were silver streaked with tears, the first I'd ever seen, but his face was horrible to see so I looked away, ashamed, and hid my face on the mare's hot, sweat-stained neck. Then he was gone to the river, down under the dark bank where the water ran glacial and pure.

Later, we did not sleep. The moon was bright as day and the upstairs room filled with an unearthly dance of light and drifting shadows. For a long time he would not speak and I lay very still and scared until his tense voice, harsh and choked, said, "A beaver stob poked a hole in his gut and he trailed his intestines for a quarter-mile and tromped them in the mud. And he was down." And I could think of nothing to say; not one thing for comfort, nothing to take away the loss of a hand-raised colt, gentle broke and trusting. And I have never known, in all these years, if I was to blame.

Death became easier for me, though it was never easy. I began to see that everything we did had a reason and that every day of life was quite precarious and delicate, hanging in balance.

In my third year there a letter came from the absentee landowner saying we must leave. His twelve years of caretaker's residency in the cabin above the river was over. He was sullen and angry. What we had together became as tenuous and fragile as a spider's web. It grew strained by my insecurity and fear, by his unbridled hatred and silence. We wandered with the horses and the hound, living in a tepee camp wherever we could find a flat, grassy place to lay our beds. I left and came back again, and again. We moved and settled six times in five years and never found again what we once had. Worn weary and wanting so much more, I went to work on a ranch, skiing four miles each way to my one-day-a-week job of cooking and cleaning and caring. He was not pleased.

When calving time came, the boss was on crutches from a knee operation so I learned to help harness the team of Clydes and feed off bales of hay to snowbound Hereford cattle. It was a bad spring, wet and cold, and the calves scoured and died. We dragged them off for the coyotes and poked pills down the cold, raw throats of the ones left alive. I nursed a paralyzed calf for days, massaging its useless legs, coaxing it to stand, which it could not do. Its ma was gentle and wise and she stood over her calf so it could raise up on its front knees and suck. But it would never be well and the sight of it lying wet and dirty in its own excrement sickened me. So, one morning while the boss held the lines with one hand and his crutches in the other, I slid off the sled and went into the barn alone. It was dimly lit by early sun and awesome, the silence like a cathedral. I sorted off the cow, used a sledgehammer to stun the crippled calf and cut its throat. When I stepped outside to wipe my knife in the pristine snow, I looked up and said, "I'll drag it off later," and saw the boss's home-from-college son staring at me. His eyes called me cruel. I wanted to tell him that the line between cruelty and kindness was fine, so very, very fine.

When branding time came, the corrals were dry and a thick haze hung in the air full of hot iron smoke and dust from four hundred frantic hooves tromping the ground. The boss's knee gave out and he couldn't kneel to castrate the bull calves, so I quit wrestling, took his knife and emasculator, and went to work. As she turned her head away from the knife, the boss's daughter grimaced and laughed and began to call me Miss Blood and Guts and I found that I did not mind but rather smiled, knowing that, at last, I'd grown tough enough to do the job.

I doubt he ever understood what I found on that ranch. I'd come into my own and finally knew what kind of life I wanted and needed to sustain me. I did try to talk to him. He stood stoic and silent, his arms crossed, his face blank, his eyes flint-hard, sharp and fathomless. I did not have much to pack. I simply took all that I had learned from him and left the rest behind. In the end, he was kind. He let me go.

RHAE FOSTER  **The Hometown**

I hated it.

I hated the wind that blew all the time.
I hated the countryside, dry and brown.
I hated the barrenness,
Isolation, people separated by distance.

I hated a settlement too large to be a town,
Too small to be a city.
I hated that everyone knew my family.
No matter who I became or what I accomplished,
I would always be known as someone's granddaughter
Or daughter
Or cousin
Or niece.

I hated that everyone knew each mistake I made.
I hated the boredom.

I hated it.
I hated it.
I hated it.

When I went back I asked myself, "Why?"
I was happy to leave again.

BETTY STARKS CASE ⌒ Tractor Tales

I heard a nostalgic spring sound one April morning and looked out to see my beaming mate aboard the humming old Ford tractor. Apparently, I thought, the little blue machine has agreed to serve one more season.

Watching the two of them chug down the lane together, I wondered if tractors might grow to be more than mechanical things, perhaps in years of companionship with man becoming some kind of storehouse of philosophy or wisdom. Some pretty heavy stuff is laid on them out there. Who else besides God and the birds could one talk to those endless days?

No doubt tractors catch more profanity than is their due, but I suspect they also share a man's dreams, frustrations, and prayers. There's a lot to absorb.

My father's old John Deere must have been saturated with philosophy. Clearly, it imparted wisdom to him from time to time. He had only to consult its "innards" to find the answer to a problem. One case in particular impressed me.

When I was sixteen, we moved to Wyoming from South Dakota, where I fell in love with a schoolmate a year older that I. He gave me a beautiful gold-filled locket ordered from Montgomery Ward. A week later he mailed me a letter.

"I'm not coming to see you again," he wrote. "In plain words, you sort of get in my blood. Anyway, I have no faith in marriage."

I was devastated. "Plain words! What does it mean, I get in his blood?" I wailed.

Though my father preferred to shy away from emotional encounters, his automatic response to challenge, including my teenage love affairs, continually led him into them.

"Means — he thinks — maybe — he loves you," he blurted.

"But he said he wasn't coming back!" I cried.

I clutched the locket to my breast and wept for days.

Finally, one morning Daddy called, "Come help me repair the tractor. I need you to hand me the wrenches."

Beside the old John Deere out by the shed, Daddy tinkered away for what seemed an hour. Nothing much appeared to be happening except for a running stream of pleasant, pointless conversation on his part. I stood by the big toolbox, waiting. He didn't seem to be needing the wrenches. I wondered when he would.

At last Daddy cleared his throat. From the bowels of the old tractor, where his voice sounded like he was consulting the carburetor, I heard, "About that letter from your boyfriend. When he's old enough, if he really loves you, nothing in this world could convince him you couldn't have a happy marriage. Remember that. Now put on a smile and go out with the other boys who ask you."

The tractor repair apparently completed, I was dismissed to go help Mother prepare supper.

A few years later, the young man whose blood I'd invaded asked me to share his life, absolutely certain the future was invented just for us.

Many years have passed and the locket still gleams, intact and treasured, along with the marriage.

And old tractors? I'll bet they could tell more about human nature than mechanical power. They probably should be revered in museums. Some are there, of course, but as worn-out relics of a mechanized world. If we'd listen with our hearts, they might reveal poignant tales of real lives. Like the stories we hear from old saddles and guns.

JULENE BAIR ~ A Guy Could

When I was a girl I longed to drive the tractors my brothers had wearied of by the time they were twelve. But my chores were kept within the limits of the chicken coop, garden, and house. Kids have built-in radar that locks onto parental injustice, so my parents got the opposite of what they'd intended. My brothers found jobs elsewhere, and I came back to farm.

Like many farmers in our area, my parents once measured their success by the quantity of bricks they used to build their ranch-style house in town. As a consequence, Dad has to commute to the farm. He pulls into the yard every morning at about eight, two hours past the time he would have been in the field when I was a girl.

We "hired hands" cluster around his pickup window. We are a choice group. Two are my uncles, one who came to work on the farm after his real estate business bottomed out and the IRS was after him because he'd neglected to pay his income taxes, and another who spends his winters in a Veterans Administration domicile because of a mental disability. There is also Long John, a big, six-foot lug with a toothless grin, a visceral mechanical ability, and a tendency to add y's to his words. For instance, the other day he told me he was going to go "up northy and change the sockies" on the irrigated corn.

Most women would feel out of place on a farm crew, but I never have. I came home at thirty-five, pregnant and destitute after a failed marriage. I qualify for this bunch not just because I've failed and am odd, but because I like the work. The men didn't accept me as easily as I did them, however, especially since the first task I undertook once on Dad's payroll was to clean the shop, just the kind of menacing activity expected of a woman.

Sympathetic to Dad's hoarding instinct, I retrieved nuts and washers one by one from the half-inch layers of dust-caked grease on the work benches, then removed the remaining crud with one of the many broken hoes I'd found. I sorted cans of rusted bolts and fencing staples, and occasionally turned up long-lost costly items — a complete set of new belts for every grain auger on the place, missing socket sets, and a power take-off adapter that Dad had suspected a former hand of swiping. I dislodged wasps' nests from the cubbyhole shelves and stirred up enough dust and mouse manure to replace all the topsoil lost on the farm to wind erosion in the last ten years.

Despite my willing immersion in grime most women wouldn't come near, the men considered any kind of cleaning a feminine chore. But when planting season came and Dad magnanimously consented to let me drive the planter a few rounds, he was dumbfounded to find I drove straighter than he. Suddenly I was valuable. Forget that I had remodeled the house that winter, proving I could handle tools, lay Formica countertops, hang and finish drywall. This ability to drive a tractor in a straight line was what separated the men from the boys.

Uncle Raymond, who was our number one tractor man, was still unimpressed. Being exceptionally humble, he figured anyone should be able to do what he could. My chance to win him over came one June morning after a wind storm when I was the one elected to climb the Quonset and re-nail the ridge roll. Dad's arthritis prevented him from climbing, and Uncle John was out changing irrigation sets. Long John and Raymond were afraid of heights.

Different methods of climbing the structure were discussed. "A guy could put a ladder in the tractor scoopy," suggested Long John. But the extension ladder was too short to reach the building's peak even with the scoop hoisted as high as it would go.

Finally, Dad came up with the winning idea. "A guy could get a long rope, throw it over, and tie it to that big old tractor tire on the other side."

I climbed up the building along the rope while Long John made wisecracks about my weight lifting the four-hundred-pound tire off the ground and began hammering, happy to be doing something the men lacked the agility and even the courage to do. Dad and Long John went to the field, leaving Raymond to "Keep an eye out." He came out of the Quonset every so often and shouted, "How ya doin'?"

"Just fine," I would reply, and he would shuffle back inside the Quonset to the dusty old couch he liked to sneak off to whenever there was a lull in a day's activities.

At lunchtime Raymond announced, his voice full of wonder, "Julene's the bravest one out here. She climbed up on that old Quonset."

I felt a little guilty that one hour of hammering had made me a hero in

Raymond's eyes. I worked only mornings and spent those summer afternoons immersed in the enchantment of new motherhood, taking dips with my baby, Jake, in his play pool, watching Raymond disk long, slow loops in the section of summer fallow north of the house. By then I was tired of the tractor work I'd envied so when I was a girl.

"A guy could work harder," I said, hugging Jake, who was chuckling at his own exuberant splashings. "But most guys aren't your lucky mom."

GLORIA VAN DYKE ~~ My Man Isn't

You've heard the phrase "self-sufficient" —
Well, if you ask me, my man isn't.
Like when it's time to milk the cows
He comes and says, "Can you help now?"
The times he couldn't fix a bite to eat
Or wipe his dirty, muddy feet.

In the wintertime and he's shoveling snow,
He says, "Can you finish? I froze my toe."
He can't put a paper back in the rack,
Clean the drill or put grain in a sack.
And chase a pig if it's loose in the yard —
Heavens no, you'd think him lame or standing guard.

If the house or barn needs a hammer or nail,
You suddenly see him become weak and frail.
When it comes to looking for socks or clothes,
He couldn't find them if they hung on his nose.
You've heard the phrase "self-sufficient" —
Well, if you ask me, my man isn't.

DIXIE DeTUERK ~~ The Great Bull Roundup

"Hey, wife," yells the rancher from atop his sixteen-hands-high horse in the yard. Once mounted he never dismounts unless absolutely necessary. His wife does have a name, although he seldom uses it. He simply calls her "wife" or sometimes "hon" if they happen to be in public. "Hey, wife, you ain't doin' nuthin' right now are ya?"

The wife, a small woman who is in the process of removing the built-up no-wax linoleum wax from her kitchen floor and fixing supper at the same time, grits her teeth. She hates being called "wife" and she hates how he never asks, "Are you busy?" but always declares, "You ain't doin' nuthin' now, are ya?" She would like to scream. "Of course not! Why would I be busy? Who do you think cleans the house, cooks the meals, mows the lawn, weeds the garden, dresses the chickens, washes your clothes, and always drives to town for parts when something breaks down?" Of course, she doesn't say it, but she knows that now he has some job for her to do that will throw a wrench into removing the wax from her kitchen linoleum, let alone completing supper.

Looping an electric cattle prod over the saddle horn, the rancher spies the kid dressed in a T-shirt, sneakers, and shorts sauntering across the road, headed for the creek with his fishing pole and can of worms. "Hey, kid," he hollers, "come here a minute." The eight-year-old boy also has a name, which the rancher never uses. When he wishes to be more personal, he calls the boy "Bub."

The kid rolls his eyes, kicking himself for not being sneakier about his getaway. He, too, knows he's being finagled into a task that will wreak havoc with his fishing plans. He wants to protest, "But, Dad, I already fed the chickens and the calves. Can't I go fishin' for just a little while?" But of course he doesn't; he walks over and stands by the horse, waiting for his mother to appear. Like his mother, he discovered years before that whatever he might have to say makes no difference to the six-foot rancher.

When the wife comes down the back steps wearing cut-offs and sandals, the rancher says, "We got to move them five bulls to the little pen. It won't take but five minutes. All you got to do is head 'em off from going in the corn and the hay." And he heads down the road on the horse with wife and kid trotting along behind.

The bulls have been in a small pasture about a half-mile from the small pen where the rancher wishes to place them now. Both the wife and the boy know there is no good reason they need to be moved at all. But the rancher has decided, and since that is tantamount to a declaration by the Almighty, they obey.

The four-foot-seven-inch boy is stationed in a nine-foot opening in the fence around the cornfield. His job is to keep the five 1,600-pound bulls from entering the field. He is on foot and defenseless except for the fishing rod and can of worms he still carries. The 102-pound wife is stationed in the middle of the lane surrounded by wide ditches; her job is to head the bulls into a small pen to the right and to prevent them from entering the unfenced hayfield directly ahead. Swinging his lariat and yelling "Hiya," the 248-pound rancher rides his big sorrel gelding down to the bull pasture and begins to herd the five giants up the lane.

The kid manages to prevent the first four bulls from turning into the field, but the fifth one shoulders him aside and heads for the corn.

"Get him outta there!" yells the rancher, waving his lariat at the boy.

The boy would like to yell, "You get in here and get him. You're the one on the horse with the rope!" But he doesn't; he's too busy running to head off the bull.

The rancher is not about to ride after one bull, leaving the other four unguarded to the rear, a direction they have no intention of heading.

The boy literally flings his seventy-five pounds in front of the bull and comes face to face with 1,600 pounds of determination to taste corn. Out of sheer desperation and the instinct of self-preservation, he flings his can of worms at the bull. It hits the bull on the soft tip of the nose, cutting it a little. The boy snatches that moment of hesitation and pops the bull between the eyes with the fishing pole. It works; the bull shakes his head and ambles back into the lane.

Meanwhile the five-foot-three-inch wife is doing a frantic one-hundred-yard dash back and forth across the lane trying to turn the other four bulls into the pen and away from the hayfield they can see and smell directly ahead. Her only weapon is an old sunflower stalk she has snatched from the side of the lane. She wants to scream, "Get up here with that darn horse and turn these brutes!" But she doesn't; she is too busy trying to jump high enough to hit them between the eyes with her sunflower stalk.

The rancher is not about to ride ahead of the bulls, leaving them unguarded to the rear, a direction they have no intention of heading.

The wife finally manages to turn the bulls into the pen just as her left sandal falls apart and the kid rushes up behind the fifth bull, who has cooperated nicely after being stung on the nose by the can of worms. The wife and the boy strain to pull two steel panels, which weigh more than both of them combined, shut on the bulls.

The pen is actually only panels on three sides. The side nearest the hayfield is a rickety remnant of a wooden corral. As the wife and child search for a piece of wire to fasten the gate panels, one bull pushes his head between the boards and crashes through the dilapidated wooden fence. The wife dives between the bars of the panel, gallops across the pen, and flings her 102-pound body across the gaping hole to prevent the remaining bulls from escaping. On the way, she steps in a fresh cow pie and loses the other sandal. All four bulls are breathing moistly in her face.

"Oh, hell," exclaims the rancher from atop his horse. "What are we going to do now? That bull's gonna git away."

The wife wants to scream, "Ride after him, you idiot. You're on the horse with the rope. And give me that cattle prod before I get trampled here." But she doesn't say it; she's too busy trying to keep her bare toes out of the way of eight hooved front feet.

"Git after him, Bub," hollers the rancher, waving his lariat first at the kid and then at the bull who is fast disappearing into the distance of the

286 · LEANING INTO THE WIND

hayfield. The boy races after the bull, the fishing pole whipping in his hand.

"I suppose I got to git down off this horse and haul one of them panels over here to plug that hole," growls the rancher.

The wife wants to say, "No, I'll drag one of those panels that weighs twice as much as I do so these bulls can have time to get through this hole in the fence." But she doesn't; she can't even get enough air to whisper it. The bulls are crushing her against the fence with their massive heads, slobbering all over the front of her shirt.

Flying after the escaping bull, the boy steps in a badger hole and slams to the ground. The line on the fishing pole wraps around his head twice and the hook embeds itself in his left ear. He can't help it; he yelps in pain.

"By God!" roars the rancher, slamming the panel over the hole in the fence and rescuing the wife at last. "Can't that kid do anything right? Now I gotta go after that bull." He swings his six-foot frame over the saddle of his sixteen-hands-high horse and lopes off past the crying boy, swinging his lariat and yelling, "Hiya!" with whistles in between.

The boy limps over to his mother, carrying the remains of his broken fishing pole and holding his hand over the fish hook hanging from his ear. Fortunately the barb has not penetrated to the shank; she removes it easily and wipes his wet face with the tail of her shirt which has been ripped in two places in the fracas with the bulls and the rickety fence.

The escaped bull returns to the pen, bellowing in disappointment at getting only a few mouthfuls of hay, with the rancher right behind him on the gelding. The wife and the kid drag the panels open and herd him into the pen, at the same time trying to keep the other four bulls from escaping.

It is now one hour and fifty-three minutes since the start of the great bull roundup, which was to take not more than five minutes. The kid no longer possesses either worms or fishing pole. The no-wax linoleum wax remover has congealed to a glob of indestructible plastic on the kitchen floor, and supper has been burned beyond recognition. The wife is now barefoot; neither sandal is salvageable, nor is her shirt. Everyone, including the bulls, is hot, sweaty, and filthy, except the rancher perched on his horse in his Levis, Western-style shirt, cowboy boots, and hat. He looks through his sunglasses and the bedraggled pair before him.

"You know," he declares, "these things wouldn't take near so long if you two could ever do what I tell you." Then he gallops off toward the barn, leaving them in the dust.

The wife and the kid look at each other. Only their combined primordial screams release enough hostility to prevent them from committing murder.

Note: My first husband was a cowboy, the product of a farming-ranching family. The women in the family have always thought this story was hilarious. The men have never seen the humor in it.

TAMMY HANSEN GILBERT ━━ **Ranch Communications**

This is the age of communication. In addition to the commonplace house phone, there are cordless phones and car phones. There are even phones that you can carry in your pocket wherever you go. If you can't be there to answer your phone there are answering machines and services to answer it for you. No matter who you're trying to get hold of or what you want to say, the odds are certainly in your favor. Unless, of course, you're trying to reach a rancher. He could be off driving cows, sorting cows, doctoring cows, feeding cows, buying cows, selling cows, checking wells, fixing fence, putting up hay, or helping new baby calves into the world. And that's on a slow day.

The basic ranch communications system has not changed a great deal over the ages. While CB radios in pickups and telephones in barns and shops have certainly helped a great deal, the rural communications system's main receiver is unquestionably the same as a century ago. It's called the WIFE. As a multitude of women know, that basically stands for: "What If Finding him takes forEver?"

The scenario is always the same. You have your day mapped out perfectly. Down to the last detail. You have just the right amount of time to do everything you need to get done. You might even be humming to yourself, things are going so marvelously. Then it happens. Huey from the parts dealership calls and wants to know if a one-fourth-inch seal will work just as well.

"Just as well as what?" you ask.

That's when Huey realizes he's got a real mechanical genius on the line. "Just as well as the other shiny round circle deally your husband called and wanted to order, Ma'am."

"What if it doesn't?" you say, knowing full well who will be blamed if one shiny round circle deally doesn't work just as nicely as the other.

"Well, I've never actually been present when somebody tried it, Ma'am, but they say there's a lot of swearing and small explosions."

"Hmmmm. I suppose we really ought to try and avoid that. Can I have him call when he comes in?"

Huey sighs, and decides right then and there that if he ever gets to talk to who he intends to talk to when he dials the phone, he'll eat his parts manual. "Ordinarily that would be fine, Ma'am. But we only get shipments from the warehouse that makes these reinforced ultra-steel seals every two years, and if I don't have the correct order within the next two hours, we'll just have to wait."

"I don't suppose that whatever he needs the shiny round circle deally for could run without it?"

Huey bites his pencil in half. "No, Ma'am. The owner's manual strongly advises against it. Something about smoke and gears locking up."

So there you have it. Now you have no choice. You have to pack up and go hunting. Normally you get to make a decision about whether you go looking or not. Normally you get to decide if you're going to drive through every pasture to find him only to have him say, "That really could have waited, you know." Or you can wait for him to drive through the yard and then have him say, "Why didn't you come find me for pete's sake?" But, this time, the decision has been made. Huey will go into cardiac arrest and some unidentified piece of machinery will be rendered useless unless you save the day. Pack up the kids, turn off the stove, take enough food and toys to last the trip, and off you go. Over hill, over dale, we will hit the endless trail. You rack your brain to remember what he said he'd be doing and where. You remember. You go there. He's not there. Surprise, surprise. Now you've got enough grass in your grill guard to feed a pony, and you still haven't found anyone. You try to think of how you will possibly convince Huey that you tried — really tried — to find him.

What's that? Could it be? Many thanks to the patron saint of lost causes — it is! A pickup on yonder ridge. And there's actually still time to make a call to Huey before the deadline. You hop out and quickly, but efficiently, explain the entire situation. You figure you'll just plain make Huey's day when you call back. He might even quit early and go celebrate.

"Huey? From Wegottum Parts? Oh. He didn't have what I needed so I called Bart over at Parts R Us. He's mailing it to me. By the way, did the feed man call?"

PATTI DeJONGE ⟶ For the Farmer's Wife

Advice for having a successful marriage breeds faster than a farm cat, especially when a farmer's daughter marries a farmer.

Believe you me, even if a girl has been raised on a farm all of her life, there are some things she just doesn't ever take the time to really notice.

For example, I really doubt that my daughter, who just married a farmer, understands what the phrase, "Honey, would you like to go for a drive?" means.

"If he asks you, don't ever think you are really going for a romantic Sunday-type drive," I told her. "More than likely you will be alone in the pickup following either an orange triangle sign to another farm or else the rear end of your least favorite cow."

If by chance the two of you are alone in the pickup, make sure you sit in the middle of the seat, real close to him. That way, when he just "happens" to check the cows in the pasture, you won't have to open the gate.

Farmers also have different driving habits.

"Be prepared to stop at every implement display while traveling," I told her.

"Don't be surprised if the same man who doesn't have time for you to buy any necessities while you are in town, like food, will probably always have time for a quick look at new equipment while you sit in the pickup.

"These are all words of experience," I told her lovingly.

"Never ever be the 'puller' in any situation where a piece of equipment is stuck, always make sure you are the 'pullee.'

"By being the pullee you will be the one inside the stuck vehicle and all you have to do is make sure you follow the puller and never rear-end him.

"Pullers always get into big trouble whenever the chain breaks or the vehicle doesn't get unstuck at the right moment," I told her.

SUSANNE K. GEORGE ~ Poster Girl

In her tight blue jeans, nipples perked
beneath a baby-blue "Let's Rodeo" T-shirt,
the urban cowgirl
taps the toe of her high-heeled boots to
"Mama Don't Let Your Babies Grow Up
to Be Cowboys,"
and looks out from under a tangle of curls
and a new straw hat
at the cowboys lining the bar.
She knows she's lookin' good.

And the cowboys are lookin' good, too,
at what she's advertising.
More just like her,
artfully packaged in denim and leather,
cluster like billboards along a highway.

Finally
one cowboy,
lean-legged and pearl-buttoned,
spits into a beer can,
shifts into low and
pops the clutch.

ready to buy
what she wants to sell
and it's a buyer's market.

NANCY HEYL RUSKOWSKY
The Seventh Direction of Night

According to some Native Americans, the seven directions include the four compass points, the heavens above, the earth below, and the seventh, the most important: inward, into the territory of the heart and spirit.

When one chooses the rural life, many of those reflective opportunities come with the night watch, matching patience with that of Mother Nature.

When I imagine life on the plains, I can't think of tales from big ranches. I only know the small of country living; I spent my early years on a 160-acre farm in eastern South Dakota where corn ground was plowed each spring by our horses, Tommy and Dewey.

That was where I first learned the truth of the night when, as a ten-year-old, I took my turn studying the final stages of sleeping sickness and the palest palomino filly gave me some of my early lessons in courage. From her I learned the first brutal facts of life and what can lie just outside the sunshine.

After birthing four children in four major cities in four far-flung states, I came home to new country — Wyoming — and a little homestead, fitted neatly like a thin chapbook amid thousand-page ranches. Here I would learn my own lessons of ranching and hopefully share those "lifeway of the night" hours with my daughters.

Night, like a film's negative, places all we see in starkest black and white. Unlike that development process that reverses life as we view it, darkness does cause us to discourage our senses from speaking the truth too clearly or suddenly. Our instinct talks to us of what it knows to be true while common sense whispers doubts. My younger daughters discovered the power in that gift while fighting those questions as they presented themselves in a field within shouting distance of help.

They needed to milk extra early one cold spring morning. Of course the two Jerseys were out in the field, a small strip of pasture that reached out toward our neighbor's driveway.

As I put together a hot breakfast, they were suddenly back in the house, whispering frantically in the entrance. A too-early-in-the-morning argument ensued. When I stuck my head around the corner, Patti spit out a whole list of reasons why she'd not return to the dark of that field. Each reason ended with, "There's something out there."

Believing in Patti's intuition, I grabbed a coat and joined them for a trip back to the pasture. While we moved ever farther from the circled guidance of a distant yard light, I reached out to touch the message Patti felt so strongly. It was there surrounding us. Unarguably we were being watched by fearless observers.

As the unity of our joined hands and spirits seemed to sharpen perceptions, the pre-dawn sky lifted the veil of blackness, altering it to an inky shade of gray which left body after body silhouetted against the shadows. The three of us had intruded upon a band of sleeping deer, all bedded down, unwilling to leave this alfalfa nest for any human invader. Only a few seemed to acknowledge our passing as we glided step-by-step through the herd.

When we located the cows, they seemed mindful of the comfort of our guests and moved quietly toward the cattle yard. Of course Patti couldn't resist whispering to me as we separated at the barn, "I told you there was something out there!"

Seldom do those rural situations solve themselves so easily. Many require long periods of wait followed by short chunks of hurry.

It's not unusual for me to sit, long before dawn, at an old oak table weak with age. I appreciate the solitude while another thirty minutes measures itself against my concerns for the old milk cow laboring in the barn or, more recently, a ewe suffering from pregnancy toxemia from my overcare.

I write poetry to a grandfather who marked his pain on a rocker, a secret groove under the arm filed sharp with his thumbnail. They tell me he ate here even on the worst days of his illness. "Carry me to the table," he ordered each noon when they tried to take a tray to his bedside.

Birth is not the only obstacle to sleep. Death, too, often lies awake in those midnight shadows and, if the old tales are true, most often comes in threes. In 1990 we struggled for several weeks with a disease of toxic proportions that found me lacking in the skills to stave it off. We had lost two of our best ewes. The next to go was a wether, and finally my best black ewe, a Rambouillet cross with a light white patch over her forehead. She was large, well-constructed, minded her own business, and took care of a big, bold, black ewe lamb. When she died, I took the shears and claimed her fleece. At the beginning it was not a good experience. I learned what grave robbing must be like. She was no longer able to protect herself; my act seemed like rape, a violation of her will. I didn't steal from her in life, waiting to take what I was not generous enough to bury her with. The struggle went on. I snipped with my hand shears, placing clutch after clutch into the bag. I avoided the touch of her body; the warmth reminded me, like an electric shock, how alive she'd been just minutes before.

As the early morning light leaned into the shadows where I hovered over the body, it happened; gradually. I became immersed in the wool, entranced with the color growing stronger with that light that sometimes comes and goes before dawn. Faded brown, the surface grayed into deep silver with the power of my thumbs holding it back, the cutting sound like that of cloth being ripped against the grain. Yet in places the wool held its blackness. There were long straight sections and others deep like the best of mink and multihued with a crimp that would hug itself easily into a strand of yarn at the wheel.

My fingers wanted to spin as I worked, to show this life that had lived three years that it was worth it, that her fleece would be spun into a long-lasting piece. Years from now someone would wear her; would it matter that she had been a big black ewe with a white face? Productive, somehow she should have earned her place in history. Few can hope for immortality. But now — I don't want to lose any more. With the help of a local vet, the siege ended.

Each night arrives with a new story to share, most of them experienced in dreamland. The lessons I've learned from inner travels come not just through that step into a blackened sky; not all dark spirit travel occurs beneath the stars. Some can be internal.

Although I wanted my children to experience every aspect of this existence that seems to be getting squeezed to the edges of life, I seemed to find those dark times especially informative myself. Long after the girls were grown, done with the ritual of "taking your turn" under the yard light, I continued to renew and connect with them through those late hours, always seeming to sense their own after-midnight struggles. The call came at ten to tell me that Julie, my oldest daughter, was in the early stages of labor, thirty miles away. She was expected to rest quietly during the night, and receive a labor-increasing shot about six A.M. We could come see our first grandchild sometime tomorrow so, "Sleep tight, Grandma-to-be," were the last words she said.

When had I ever slept all night while a child was in pain? At what point does a mother turn over the care of her youngster to someone else? My left brain knew that I did not intend to be there, this event was for parents only. My right brain wondered if anyone could care for my daughter without my experiences of battling chicken pox, broken bones, or emotional trauma.

I crawled deep into my bed and deeper into the recesses of memory. I hadn't felt this separation at her wedding. There was no loss, only the celebration of taking our first son into the family. Tomorrow we would expand that gift with the birth of the first of our next generation. But I felt a loss, increasing all night. Whether she slept or tossed on the waves of contraction, I could only imagine.

Could I will my energy to reach across the farmlands to her hospital bed? Would she know my caress across her forehead, my arms around her like so many times? My mantra became, "Julie, I am with you." She was no longer my child, she was the wife of a man who had become my son, at the pinnacle of a family I would not make decisions for, could only love separate from my own now. That unseen cord, so strong that she continued to renew herself for life's battles, now stretched itself beyond existence.

Finally I dozed to dream of Julie's birth in a hospital in Omaha where I was sedated but aware of that tiny life being presented to me. I did not know the real value I received, nor even the best way to nurture it, but I tried over the years to prepare her as an adult to enjoy every day and every minute of growth.

The phone rang shortly after six. I noticed the pre-spring sky preparing for the day as I picked up the receiver. It was Julie. "Mom, we've had a baby girl. You should have been here."

"Honey, you're not going to believe this, but I was — every minute."

As all mothers have discovered after the birth of a child, few remember the pain for the celebration. In spite of my ache-filled night of discovery, the new day brought a commemoration of my own gift twenty-five years before. Now I could accept the truth of the separation. But in the cathedral-like glow of early light that throws reflection against the trunks while leaving the grove in darkness, and with the seriousness of another watch concluded, I could appreciate the rightness of that revelation.

Just as I survived my big city opportunities through the gifts from that South Dakota farm, I see the girls turning childlike experiences into adult solutions by remembering to follow the seventh direction. As our Native Americans know so well, the truth, though often elusive, is frequently nearby; the night knows the answer best of all.

MAE HOFFER ~~~ *Never a Gold Digger*

I set here at the kitchen table wondering how am I goin to start this, so I figured the first time I saw North Dakota. I remember the first time I saw North Dakota with its rollen plains and elevators. I was on the way to meet my husban for the first time. We had been written each other for quite a while. So we decided we would get married, as we had so much in common and liked each other. We both enjoyed worken with cattle.

My brother brought me to Columbus from Jackson, Ohio, to catch the Greyhound Bus to Jamestown, North Dakota, then another small bus to Harvey where he picked me up. He could not come to where I was at because he had his cattle.

Back in Ohio, they would say, "It won't work out." I didn't know some was also sayen in North Dakota, "All she wants is his money as she is a Gold Digger." But we have proven them Wrong as we cared for each other when we met, and have grown to love one another.

I know the first time I saw North Dakota, I fell in love with it. The sun comes up with a Bang, and the clouds after a rain float so close to the ground you feel as if you could reach up and touch them, and the Northern Lights are something to behold, and the sun dogs, I call them little rainbows.

So different than what I had been use to as I come from the southern part of Ohio. There was big hills and lots and lots of trees, copperheads and rattlesnakes.

And things was different out here. Even their speech, as most of them are German and they talk a lot in German, and I can't understand much of it, just a few words. And my Southern accent didn't help much, as they couldn't understand a lot of things I said either.

Everyone is so friendly and wants to feed you. When I came here ten years ago I was thin — but not any more. Everything was delicious and very hard to resist.

When walken across the open prairie looken for the cows, you see a few things that looks like Indian dancers when the wind blows. Then you come closer then you see it was only a slender tree with a few leaves at the top.

The winters some times are a little tough, but so butiful and lots of wide open spaces for snow mobilen. Would I go back to the Hills? For a visit but North Dakota is my home now.

We raise cattle, also farm, but my love is for the livestock, as to me there is nothin like seeing a baby calf been born and takin those first hops and jumps.

The year we got married there was only a few there, as it was November 14, 1986, and we had a big snowstorm, dumped a lot of snow on us. He had to get a snow remover to get the snow out of the road before we could get out. The snow was almost over the chicken house. We had a hard time feeden them.

That evening it started snowen again; we thought we might miss our own wedden. But it was a lovely wedden and everything went along just fine. The only honeymoon we had was cleanen the barn, shovelen snow, fighten a few blizzards, and feeden the cattle. We get along pretty good, don't quarrel, and work the land together, and is very happy. So you see our marriage worked out good.

BETH HATHAWAY COLE ⌒⟍ Side By Side

I was twenty-five when I married Randy and began life in a whole new environment. I was raised in a small town in Wyoming but had no connections to a life in the country until I was fifteen years old. Then my parents purchased a dryland wheat farm and moved. I remained in town most of the time, however, to finish high school, and spent very little time on the land my family purchased. I was connected with the farm and farming activities enough to get a taste of how things operated, and how impatient and demanding the land is to a farmer.

For six years after I graduated from high school I was away from the farm, attending college and spending three years working out of the state. It was those three years that gave me insight into the world I had left behind — something I may never have learned any other way than by living in a different area with a very different style of life — in a city.

When I returned to Wyoming I wasn't prepared to stay, but I met Randy and my life changed course drastically. I still thank the Lord for that moment of revelation! I wasn't looking for romance.

I met Randy in a ripe wheat field in August; he hid behind the combine after he glimpsed me. We only dated three months and were engaged to marry. I was, and still am, taken with his honest, simple, yet profound outlook on life and the people and events in it. I learn prodigious philosophical lessons from him every day, and usually when I am least expecting it. Growing up where hard work and learning to accept it came like breath is the main reason that makes him so special. Working at back-breaking tasks to achieve his goals has given him a different outlook on life. He is vastly patient and forgiving. The rest is a mystery and must be divinely granted.

I have never been as happy doing anything else. I am not always this happy; here is an entry from my diary:

> I found a baby lamb today. He was laying still in the grass on the flat out there; but I didn't get there soon enough. His mother stood by as if protecting him from all the world's harm — and she had done a good job — before Heaven took over. I stood closer as if to say good-bye, a bird flew over and sang *tutt tutt*, as if to say, *what a shame*. If only I had come sooner, if only the night were warmer, if only I had more control. But that is such nonsense, because I have no control at all. I looked up, thinking this wasn't fair, all that live must die but life so short is not fair. I must be wrong. Being wrong might ease the ache in my throat that reaches clear to my heart, but it changes nothing.

Some days are miserable and sad but never as miserable as a day spent away from the country nor so sad that the surrounding beauty won't bring solace.

The most bitter pill to swallow is the death of animals, especially the young. The lambing season one year brought us severe financial strain as well as heartache. The rain was relentless that May and our losses were very high, nearly fifty percent. Breeding and raising livestock was completely new to me and to see so much death that first season was devastating to my soul. We were not prepared to shed-lamb but attempted it due to the weather. We ran out of hay that was high enough in nutrients to satisfy the needs of the pregnant ewes and lost many lambs to spontaneous abortion. It was sickening to see the nearly formed babies in amniotic sacks, red and purple and distorted. It breaks the spirit to see nature betray itself. But only the human spirit.

Humans can only intervene so much and there it ends. This was the heavy-hearted realization that caused me to make the decision to shoot a newly born lamb. His legs were deformed, curved backward, he had no equilibrium so he could not stand. He seemed dazed and to have a deficiency of the brain. I knew immediately that it was futile to try to feed him; he would never survive on his own or be salable with such problems, but I tried to convince myself otherwise for several hours. Finally something had to be done. He was dying anyway from starvation and other causes. I could not bear to see him suffer. It's one thing to find a dead animal or see it after it dies, but to watch an animal that agonized in life — surely death must be better, some sort of relief from this world. So after holding the lamb on my lap in the sunshine and shedding many tears I asked Randy to please shoot him. I don't know which was harder for Randy, seeing him die or killing it, but he granted my wish. I always plug my ears when the gun goes off, even when I'm in the house. I can't stand for their passing to be so harsh. I can only hope when we do this that it is the best thing.

I enjoy this life because it allows me to work side by side with my husband on a daily basis and work for the same goals at the same time. Life in the country is good for a marriage; I believe it has given us time together we never would have had doing anything else, and has strengthened our bonds as a couple. The down-to-earth hardships and happinesses are good for anyone's perception of life.

DEIRDRE STOELZLE ~~~ **The Curtsy: May Day in Casper, Wyoming**

When you park at the Beacon Club, you get out and walk through a sea of pickup trucks and big, 1970s-model gas guzzlers and through lots of broken glass and trash and sometimes ravines of rainwater and mud to the walkway and finally to the front doors.

You walk in and the man behind the counter looks you up and down and checks out who you're with. You either pay a cover charge of a few dollars or he tells you to spend your money at the bar.

Once past the gate it's tense for a minute, but then you know exactly who all's there and it's time to order. Which gives you a chance to look around for someone you know but make no acknowledgment. And that tells you something about Wyoming: we only talk to people when we have to or when it's convenient. Besides, the only people you want to talk to are complete strangers, strangely; but hell, it's a small state.

The fake cowboys are the ones wearing hats and Western shirts and are often overweight and have full beards. The real ones look oddly unobtrusive. Lots of them are fairly lanky, some are short, most of them don't wear boots but sneakers or leather shoes. They're the ones who'll dance with you and, depending on the guy, don't dance as well as you'd imagine.

We two-step around counterclockwise — one, one-two, one, one-two, one, one-two, and so on. Maybe a couple twirls here and there.

We were talking when we could've been dancing together, he said. So we put our cups of water down and walked through the swarm onto the floor and we danced the next song deep within the crowd, close to his friends who looked us up and down, which confused me, but Dale explained it was because I was a good-looking woman.

"You are so much better looking than I am," I said. "If I were a man, I'd love to look like you."

When I first saw Dale he was standing with perhaps five other people, and he was drinking water. He told me they'd come from Kaycee looking for "wammen." He had full, pale pink lips that exposed perfect top teeth, as if his mouth was fixed in a permanent smile. His skin was a brown milky color. He was twenty-three.

"Are you the designated driver?" I asked.

He said no and asked me to dance again. And when we danced he touched my back and my side and I felt his hand in mine, rough and callused and mine, sweaty, and I wished my perspiration would soften and soothe him.

Dale wore glasses before deep brown eyes that shone and looked right at you. For me that instantly created competition between his eyes and his perfect mouth and in my gaze I vacillated.

He was German and Irish and a little Indian or Mexican, perhaps, he said. His hair peeked out, light brown, from under his baseball cap.

I introduced him to my companions, a veterinarian and a biology professor. I told him I was a reporter for the *Casper Star-Tribune*. He'd studied business in school. He told me that the sheep market is in bad shape and the cattle market is doing well. I told him that I'd just worked at Dow Jones and his eyes widened.

I told him Kaycee was my favorite place in the world. He said, "That's what we like to hear."

I didn't notice whether he wore boots.

The first time I ever went into the Hole in the Wall bar in Kaycee I was on my way to Sheridan to see Pettit. I went in to get a beer for the road and everyone in there — and there weren't many people — looked me up and down and didn't smile, just gawked, and they scared the shit out of me.

When I asked Dale about this, he told me they'd never seen a woman before, probably.

I got some rocks in Kaycee. My favorite is the pinkstone, rife with soft quartz.

I heard cowboy poetry last Father's Day while trying to get through a chef's salad at the Feedrack.

The last time I was in the Hole in the Wall it was fall and I was on my way back from covering a Corrections Department meeting. I wrapped Molly's dog chain around a post out front. I sat and drank a beer on the porch of the bar, set up a bit from the street on planks of wood, just like you'd imagine it.

I sat across from a desolate museum and the Kaycee post office and I wanted to leave, but I also wanted some sort of connection. I got none, except if you count some people walking in who petted the dog.

I like to cast spells when I dance, when I remember to think in pentagrams and light, and I remind myself of the power and the dignity that comes from strife and experience and teeth-grinding faith.

A good dance means feeling every muscle and moving everything that moves and to express and to release. To whom just ain't important, I am only flesh. And blood. And air, water, and fire. Concentrate and breathe.

My companions found me and told me it was time to go and look for Pete, Alan's best friend. Dale asked me for my phone number and I told him he could reach me at the newspaper.

I said we will never see each other again. He calmly asked again for my phone number. I shook his hand and then I kissed his cheek and left him.

We drove around for a while but couldn't find Pete.

I was nervous when we returned to the Beacon Club, embarrassed to have come back. Mary and I went to the bathroom and I had a bit of a smoke and then we walked back out and I saw him and my heart went to my throat. I had no choice but to walk right up to him, though he was standing next to a fat farmgirl who'd moved in on him in my absence. I asked him to dance and we danced.

He told me he was flattered to have been missed. He told me he knew I'd come all the way back to see him and he said he appreciated it. I was vulnerable.

He asked me if I was married.

He held my hand and kept an arm around my waist and I liked that even if it was fairly awkward. But he was soft and he was smart and sweet and he worked hard and you could tell.

My favorite piece of stall writing is this: "This is goat roper country, love is a great eight minutes."

Ride 'em.

I go into the women's room at the Beacon Club to smoke cigarettes and waste time and determine how drunk or sober I am. I have written political graffiti on the walls of many of the stalls, graffiti endorsing Jerry Brown, and some graffiti that is a line or two of my own poetry.

When a slow song comes on every woman in there wonders what to do — go back out there to whomever? Hide out? Not give a shit one way or another?

There's a sign behind the bar at the Beacon: "Nobody's Ugly After 2 A.M."

Plaintive.

That's closing time and the lights come on, exposing tired and drunken faces. That's when everyone is asked to leave. With the lights on now it's a warning to the drunk and the foolish that they should each take a good long look at the woman or man beside them.

The drunk are taken to breakfast with the squeeze of the evening, presumably to sober up enough to make a decision: Are you really going home with this person?

The last time I saw Dale Graves I asked him to spell his last name and he did, in a singsong kind of voice that entranced me. I reminded him he knew how to reach me and I took his hand and shook it and curtsied.

He bowed.

In Wyoming the natives call people from New Jersey and the rest of the East "carpetbaggers." The East is anyplace east of Wyoming, which includes Houston, in most cases.

I am a carpetbagger who loves the natives so entirely and zealously that I feel honored to be asked to work with them, to brand and to dock sheep and to ride, ride, ride. They've lent me fine Australian saddles to which sheepskin cushions have been attached, and they've shown me how to rope and to tie ewes and to say things like, "That cat'll tear you a new asshole."

I spent most of my first year here with a New Zealand stockman who couldn't see the forest. But now, amid my darling natives, I am almost thinking straight.

I can personally smell a man and know him well in a matter of moments. And I inhaled Dale so deeply I am still intoxicated, still beside myself.

But he is staring at the canyons wreaked by the Red Fork and I am battling killers and rough wind and waiting, impatiently.

For the five days after I met him I cast spells and read tarot cards and otherwise obsessed, because I'd fallen in love. I read books about the Red Fork in Johnson County and his family and wished for solace from my longing and received none. And I knew that in a week or two the longing would be over and besides, I already had a boyfriend.

And so it went that Sunday I did my radio show and Monday I went south, to Douglas, to cover a murder, and Tuesday I rested and started a story lawyers exclusively were going to read and Wednesday I was awakened by Lieutenant Washut at 5 A.M. and staked out a hostage scene all day, and by Thursday I knew the tarot cards had lied and I'd never see him again.

Thursday night the moon was completely full and there was a clear blue sky with wind that blew like you wouldn't believe and my boyfriend came over and I choked back my longing for Dale Graves and took a walk.

For I am a meek and humble carpetbagger with a large sliver of endowment that I take only a small portion of, i.e., the shirt on my back and that's it, and give the rest away, although I wanted him near me and missed him fiercely.

My first full year in Wyoming I spent doing ranch work and a lot of riding and I was partially depressed, lonely, and in the dark of winter, exhausted.

I came out here because it is the middle of nowhere and I like the vastness.

One morning I awakened after drinking myself to nonexistence with some Mexican agriculture dignitaries. I drove to the end of the ranch road to where it meets Hat Six Road, and I stared out at nothing at all and laughed and puked my guts out and cried and laughed and got back into my car and went to work smelling like a distillery and so hung over I should've been hospitalized.

After the first year I anticipated the next year. I'd made it through a hard and ugly winter with a dog I couldn't handle and two foster cats I enjoyed and fed and kept indoors. I'd made friends and surrogate parents and got better and better at work and at law and at being a good-looking woman and building strength.

I knew who Caroline Lockhart was. She liked buckskin horses and wore boots and spurs into the *Cody Enterprise* and had lovers and friends like Buffalo Bill who admired her and let her do anything she wanted to do. She was as novel as a talking frog.

With the full moon I thought about how this always happens. I fall in love and can't surrender it and I am longing for the days before I knew the person was alive and wishing I could hold his soul. It's always a risk and I always take it. I hold my breath and cast it all, with everything at stake.

It is at every point that I procrastinate, because I know very well how it ends, and I don't want to write it.

Friday night I went down to the Beacon Club and danced with Dallas Laird, the attorney. There wasn't a Dale, and after a few dances, I left.

I'd walked into the newsroom Friday afternoon and looked at my messages. I hoped, bargained, you know, that Dale had called.

Some men try to help me out. They wonder aloud why I'm not knocked up or why I'm alone. I tell them that men can't deal with me and they always say, "Because you're attractive and intelligent." Plainly, they must know. They, the perpetrators.

But here's a little secret: I don't always wait around and when I don't, I am proud.

I wait.

It is often very difficult for me here. Of course I have certain rewards and am thoroughly entranced by my surroundings. But culturally I aim and shoot low, or much too high, and when I realize the height or the climb itself, I am swayed.

One of my surrogate mothers told me what her mother told her — find someone as much like you as possible, because men and women are different enough as it is. And here I, for twenty-five years, have tried to connect with those most unlike me, for growth, exchange, for education, so to speak.

Chalk it up to an end of an era. Equality no more. No, now it is something entirely different that we must call individualism. The appreciation or enthusiasm for what Is.

I must make it work somehow.

If I didn't have Casper, I'd have eaten my gun by now.

He was out there on the Red Fork west of Kaycee trying to count the new calves and studying brands. He got off his horse when he came upon a dead calf lying there, a newborn, maybe; he didn't know for sure how long it'd been there. Not too long. He flipped the calf over to see how old it was when his horse spooked, reared up, kicked him in the head, and ran off, and it wasn't until the next morning that they found his body, the teeth bashed in.

BETTY L. LYE ✏ Saying Goodbye

I walked in the pasture today,
  Trying to say goodbye
To the fields that quietly lay
    Fall plowed.

With a sigh I closed my eyes —
  And remembered when
My children were little,
  I had no time then.

To walk the fields,
Or enjoy solitude
Or the creek that runs
   Through our farm.

Too busy, driving tractors
   Preparing fields for planting grain
Raising my family — What did I gain?

   A farm to sell
   Children all grown
   Tears in my eyes
      At the happiness known.

Lying in the soft grass,
   Soaking up the sun,
Hating time passing by,
   Knowing my work here is done.

The River of Stories

MARY KATHRYN STILLWELL ～ **January 4, 1991**

The moon, what's left of it,
brittle with cold,
casts a blue glance over the snow.
The shadows are so deep
that if I fall into one,
I might not return.

PATTY LITZEL ～ **Gifts from the Sky**

I would love to be on the land, up to my elbows in crap and blood, trying to pull a lamb. Tick-ridden at shearing time, and sunburnt from riding. Leathery and wrinkled and worn like the land and a horse's hooves. I'd like what I do to be important and make a difference and make me happy even though the next guy may not understand why.

But, like my dad, I wasn't born into ranching, have nothing to inherit. I would be laughed out of any bank for trying to get a loan to buy a place and some cattle. Being female and having little experience makes it almost impossible to find work as a ranch hand. But that's the only way I can think that I could do what I love. Other than marrying into ranching. How do you live in an area remote enough to meet single ranchers when you have to live in the city to support yourself?

The rewards of ranching on the plains are the greatest things I know. But why is such a simple, honest lifestyle so hard to find in today's world?

December 15, 1992: Today I remember blessings from the land and sky. I was searching when I turned to the land, but not for what I found. The land and sky gave me gifts, and along the way I found what I was looking for.

When I was eight years old, we visited my mom's old home and she told me a story. She was my age when a tornado came through the area. After it had passed, she went to the well on the same path she'd always used. On the ground she found a perfectly knapped spear point. A gift from another culture, another time, another place. She has it to this day. I know; I cut my fingers on it when I was little.

By then, my grandparents had moved to town and only the barn and chicken coop were standing. The only sign of a house was a crumbling foundation and deserted belongings in a hole that had once been a home. I heard the story and saw what was left and blamed the tornado for what time had done to my mom's youth. I was scared of tornadoes for a long time after that. Then I watched one myself.

It was a ways off, not heading toward us, so I felt safe standing in the doorway. Everything I could see shimmered with the vibration. The air sucked the breath out of my lungs, made them feel like bass drums do at a street dance.

I followed the tornado's path toward Sweet Pea Hill. I jumped down off the barbed wire fence and there — where yesterday was only a strand of tangled, rusty wire — was my gift, a baculite, a fossilized creature that lived when these plains were sea floors. I belong to it. It fits in my hand like it was born with me, and I feel warm shivers and deep peace when I hold it. My mom's spear point has never cut her fingers, and my fossil doesn't fit her hands.

Horses: Once we were going riding like we'd done countless times before. My cousins had their own saddles and horses and they rigged up my brother so he'd ride alone, but me and my little sister, Teresa, had to ride double on Pepper.

My sister has a stubborn streak and wanted the saddle to herself. I knew a little about reining, but I ended up on the horse's rump.

My cousins and brother rode away from the barn, but we had a hard time getting Pepper to move. We kicked and kicked until one of my cousins came back and led her away from the barn. She followed the other horses until they outdistanced us, then she spun around and raced back toward the barn. Teresa screamed, threw up the reins, and grabbed the saddle horn with both hands. Then she went over backwards, knocking me off the horse.

My folks and aunt and uncle, who were watching, say we just fell off. They didn't see the death grip we'd had on the saddle. I felt numb, like I was seeing from someone else's eyes as I got up and followed the horse toward the barn. My left arm hung funny so I held it with my right hand. I didn't say anything or cry.

We got to the house at the same time as the grownups. My dad wrapped magazines around our arms and tied them with string to keep them from bending for the trip to the closest hospital. They laid us down in the car. I don't remember how long the trip took, only that Teresa had her feet in my face and that I was really tired. I remember being in the emergency room getting ready for surgery. Teresa had broken her right wrist and arm. I broke my left. She got a cast and got to go home. With a pin inserted through my elbow, I lay in traction with my arm above me for a month.

Summer, 1992: This afternoon I was sitting in the Oasis, the only café in town. Some tourists had stopped for lunch. Since they were in the booth behind me, I listened to their conversation about how deprived we are.

They'd driven the seventy miles between Belle Fourche and Buffalo seeing only one farm. We call it "Redig, population three." Driving the same route, I watch clouds playing tag with the wind; they always lose. I see mountains and mud buttes raging up out of rolling hills, stone johnnies stark against the tallest. I see ghosts of the past and some terrors of the future. I see roads leading to neighbors and cars full of people I know waving to everyone in the fields.

I have never seen the wasteland the visitors described. They said their trip took forever, they almost hit a deer, and there are no radio stations in this godforsaken country. I know they drove seventy miles an hour and the trip took less than one hour, it was probably an antelope, and they don't know how to hum. I also know that they have never driven in Montana. For that, I am grateful. Grateful that our Western neighbors don't have to bear curses for a land they didn't create. Grateful for the land. Maybe I'll never be crowded by people the land doesn't welcome.

I love the land so much I feel joined to it. As you walk over the prairies and hills, walk softly, for you tread on my soul. I've shed blood here and fought some here, both people and the elements. I've lost loved ones here. Placed their bones in the care of the land. This is my history and future, the wind blows so fierce it might blow through my veins. Everything here comes as a package deal.

ROSALIE VIGIL ⟩ *Arnold Pig*

One day, visiting on the phone with my sister who lives in the city, I told her about Arnold, our pig, who had pneumonia. I gave him penicillin shots and kept him under the heat lamp, but still couldn't keep him warm enough, so I put my old turtleneck on him. My sister laughed and said that it sounded like *Green Acres.* I knew Arnold appreciated the thought because he grunted at me and got comfortable. We had a proper burial for him and every other animal that has ever died in my care. My city kin think it's ridiculous.

KELLY REBECCA DEREEMER 〜 Wild Cows

Not all cows are tame, and the bad ones usually have bloodshot eyes or maybe horns. Dad says that's a bunch of foolish ideas but I know from past experience — having to hit the cows in the head with a stick while Dad tags the calves — that the "snorty" ones all had bloodshot eyes.

EDNA MAE LINK HEHNER 〜 Feeding Cows

In 1934 it was a problem to keep enough feed for our cows. A half a mile of road along the east side of our farm, lush with grass, was used very little. Each day I took the cows to that road and let them graze. I sat in the car at one end of the road and appliquéed quilt blocks. When the cows reached the car, I herded them in the other direction.

PHYLLIS M. LETELLIER 〜 Tested Rules for Ranching

There must be a special place in heaven for the horse that teaches a kid to ride and the cow that lets him learn to milk. Both have to be long-suffering creatures of infinite patience, and both are worth their weight in gold.

The dog loves you best just after he's rolled in fresh cow manure.

One thing for sure, that ridiculous phrase "gentle as a lamb" wasn't invented by anyone who ever had anything to do with one or more bum lambs.

The only thing harder to fence in than a determined bum lamb is a bunch of baby pigs.

There's nothing safer than kittens in a woodpile — you'll find out when you try to catch them.

There's nothing like having the milk cow die to make you realize that you have too many cats.

The main reason for keeping the old dog going: You know he'll be replaced by a puppy and few things are harder to endure than living with a puppy until he turns into a sedate dog.

If the tractor you are driving is going to break down, it will do it at the far end of the field, away from your pickup. And the worse the surface underfoot is for walking, the farther that will be.

No matter what they tell you, ranchers really get married to have someone to open gates.

DONNA PARKS From a Meditation

Dear heavenly Father,
I've been thinking it over and I
    Just don't know.
Are there horses in heaven
    or hayfields to mow?
In this sweet black soil
    How the roots grow!

Maybe for me,
    less than eternity
if I could just stay.
Earth is enough.
My hands are restless
    and rough;
All wrong for the harp anyway.

TONI KIM FRENCH *They Still Make*
Country Schoolteachers

5:15 A.M. Alarm clock jolts me out of a deep sleep. That time already? My
husband, George, rolls over and says he'll get some coffee started. I think
how wonderful he is until he throws back the covers and lets in a massive
cold front.

5:30 A.M. Got to pack my lunch. No leftovers today. It'll have to be a sand-
wich again. I always pack extra food; some kid will forget her lunch at
home or won't bring enough.

5:45 A.M. George comes in and reports that we have six inches of new snow
and all the horses are fine. Besides me teaching school and George being the
anesthetist at the local hospitals, we have a horse-boarding business.

6:15 A.M. I look like I'm going to be gone for a month. An extra coat and
shoes. All my books, papers, and lunch. A couple of things I colored and cut
out for a new bulletin board. Six bottles of a new paint recipe for art class,
and the new soccer ball I picked up last night. A little snow doesn't bother
these kids!

6:30 A.M. Country schoolteachers usually beat the snow plows, so it's go-
ing to be a slow trip.

6:45 A.M. Made it! First thing I have to do is turn up the furnace and shovel
the walks.

7:00 A.M. This is my most productive time of the day! I am the only one here. I check over all lesson plans, review the new algebra equation, make sure all materials are at my fingertips.

7:25 A.M. Alex is here. He always comes early. He won't be far from my side the rest of the day. He just spotted the new soccer ball.

7:30 A.M. I take the new soccer ball and a jump rope away from Alex after they both land in the sink where I'm making a fluoride rinse for the kids. He asks me for the third time if we have to have math today.

7:45 A.M. One of my favorite times of the day. All my kids are here now so I sit down and listen to everything that has happened since yesterday afternoon. Some cows on Kelly's ranch fell through the ice on the river and they spent most of the night trying to save them. Diane gives me a full and complete description of the new 4-H project she started last night. Alex wants to know *why* we have to have math today.

8:00 A.M. We go outside to pledge the flag and all get snow in our shoes. Alex wants to know if we can have math outside today.

8:30 A.M. Everyone is busy working on math. Lee needs extra help so I pull up a chair. Soon Sarah announces she is going to flatten Alex if he pokes her with his pencil one more time. Sarah doesn't make idle threats. Alex sits on the other side of me and whispers that he really thinks my hair is pretty today.

9:00 A.M. In our school, where all different ages and grade levels are in one room, all of the kids get involved in lessons I teach out loud. As the eighth graders and I discuss World War II, the whole room comes alive! Jeff is amazed that anything like that could happen. Diane has tears in her eyes thinking about the victims. I take all the pens and pencils away from Alex. Lee and Scott debate the timing of the U.S. entry into the war. The whole room seems to vibrate; the kids are coming up with questions and answers on their own. I need to rescue Julia from Alex, who is about to demonstrate what he would do to Hitler if he met him on the street.

10:00 A.M. Recess! We decide to play Fox and Geese. The kids vote to make the course in only geometric shapes. I remind Alex not to throw snowballs or push the younger kids down in the snow.

10:05 A.M. Alex threw three snowballs and pushed Lee down in the snow, so he sits by me on the swings. I want to play Fox and Geese! Alex tells me he doesn't think he has ever seen a nicer pair of snow boots than mine.

11:00 A.M. I make Robin promise that when I am old and in the rest home, she will come read to me; I love to listen to the kids read out loud. Alex interrupts Sarah to ask if we have to have math tomorrow; Sarah glares. Some of the older kids pair up with kindergartners and first graders to read. A good chunk of my monthly paycheck goes toward making sure we always have new books for them to read together.

11:30 A.M. Time for our twice-weekly spelling test. Each grade level has separate spelling words, but with so many grades in one room, there isn't time to give separate tests. The kids say that we don't have spelling tests, but rather spelling dances. I get all the kids ready with paper and pencils. (Whoops! Forgot I took all of Alex's pencils and pens.) Then I do a sort of dance from one grade to another, pronouncing spelling words as I go. There is a certain rhythm to it; the kids sway in their seats. I can pronounce over two hundred spelling words *and* use them in a sentence in under ten minutes. In the end, every kid has the right words for his grade level on his paper.

11:45 A.M. Lunch. Anyone who has ever been to a bidding auction will have an idea of what our room is like at lunchtime. These kids are masters at the swap, trade, bid, and con-your-neighbor lunch hour. As soon as the lunch boxes are opened, a roar goes up. Homemade desserts are the most expensive items. Homemade chocolate cake can go for two pieces of fried chicken, eleven M&M's, three peanut-butter-stuffed celery sticks, and being the pitcher for the next softball game. This ordinary group of easygoing kids turns into ruthless cutthroat wheelers and dealers. I got a slab of banana bread covered with fresh butter for one bag of barbecue potato chips, two pieces of gum, and five butterscotch candies. Costly, but worth it. Alex has to sit by me again. He blew pop out of a straw at Kelly. Alex thinks the color of my sweater makes my eyes pretty.

12:05 P.M. As we get all bundled up to go outside, Julia proclaims that she is too old for these baby games. Julia is almost fourteen, trapped between adult and child. All kids go through this, especially girls. I show her the new soccer ball and she decides maybe she can suffer through one more recess. Kids in western Nebraska learn early how to play any game in the snow, even volleyball. I won't be able to play soccer this recess either. Alex has to stay inside and write apologies to Sarah and Kelly for poking and spitting. That means not only do I supervise playground games, but also stay close to a window so I can keep an eye on Alex. I'm glad I brought an extra coat. Our resident herd of deer comes around to see what the kids are up to.

12:30 P.M. Now it's my turn to read aloud to the kids. I'm reading *Where the Red Fern Grows*. This will be the only time today that I won't have to worry about Alex. He loves to listen to stories and won't move a muscle. Diane has misty eyes, and we haven't even gotten to the sad part yet.

1:00 P.M. I am having a group lesson in English today. We put up huge sheets of newsprint on the walls and are writing down as many homonyms as we can think of. I'll leave the sheets; I'm sure we'll be thinking of more for days to come. Alex has to sit in his chair; poking with pencils again. One of the little girls comes up with "so" and "sew," earning a round of applause. While one of the big boys helps her write them on the newsprint, Alex whispers to me that I am his favorite teacher forever and ever, and maybe I could just think about not having math tomorrow.

1:30 P.M. After science lessons, it's Robin and Alex's turn to rotate the eggs in the incubator. We are waiting for eight chickens and four ducks to hatch.

Alex drops a chicken egg on the floor. He feels so bad that he cries. We have an impromptu note-taking session comparing this chicken with a full-term chicken.

2:00 P.M. Julia talks everyone into playing soccer at recess again. The game doesn't last long; the ball hits the barbed-wire fence. We play kick ball the rest of the recess.

2:20 P.M. The kids love the new paint I made; it puffs up as it dries. I am going to have some real masterpieces! Alex is sitting outside the door to paint; he thought Lee could use puffy hair.

2:50 P.M. Just enough time for a quick spelling bee before dismissal. The words are flying fast and furious. Kelly wins on "impervious."

3:05 P.M. Time to go home. A big flurry of coats, lunch boxes, mittens, homework, and books. Alex gives me a big hug as he runs out the door. I try not to look at all the papers waiting for me to check. I clean up the bathrooms and run a broom over the floors. I make a note to myself to remember Sarah's piano recital in town tonight. I find a note from Alex stuck in my lunch box.

> Dear Mrs. French,
> Most of the time you are my best friend.
> Can I go home with you someday?
> Love, Alex

5:00 P.M. George has supper started and all the horses, dogs, and cats are fine. Music to my ears!

5:30 P.M. Alex just called to find out if I got his note. I promised I'll bring him home with me someday in the spring — close to the end of the school year.

5:35 P.M. Alex called back to see if I knew exactly when that day would be. We settled on May 7.

8:30 P.M. I smile to myself while reading the local paper. The town teachers are demanding another free period during the day. I wonder if they get bored. They don't have recess or lunch duty; they don't teach their own music, art, or P.E. And they have free periods. Maybe I should move to town. Nah, I'd probably miss Alex.

9:30 P.M. In bed, almost asleep. The phone rings. When I pick up a little voice says, "Mrs. French, do we have to have math tomorrow?"

GAIL RIXEN 🖌 Why I Build Things

I'm asked, more often than I like, how I ever got into carpentry. And why would I live out in the middle of nowhere, working a few acres by hand?

The short answer is: I know it and I like it. I was raised on a farm and have always done physical work. It's not that I have no other options; I have a B.A. and secondary teaching license. I like this life and don't find the work demeaning. I'm not sentenced to it.

Physical work is peaceful, setting the mind free while tiring the part that worries. Digging post holes clarifies one's place in the cosmos while giving one the chance to hack an irritating person or problem.

I believe we were made for physical work. Nothing seems more ridiculous to me than people tying themselves in nervous knots on office chairs all day, then driving to a club to race a stationary bicycle to nowhere inside a concrete building. It seems strange to work so hard to avoid physical labor just to waste our energy on play.

I don't subscribe to the whimsical notion of the laborer as noble savage. Any crippled old hard laborer reminds me of moderation. And, yes, in the middle of a one-and-a-half-acre field of oats half-scythed, I'd take a little moderation and a mild breeze. But now that the oats are in the granary and I'm housebound during storms this winter, I think fondly of the field and the rhythmic swing of my arms.

I do carpentry for my living because it's creative and satisfying; it's what I choose to do. It can be frustrating and debilitating, but it allows me the freedom of self-employment and outdoor work.

When I'm not working off the place, I'm building things in my head, or writing, or tending my animal menagerie, or coaxing something green to grow. In a world of options, I can't think of a better life.

EVELYN HARD ~ How Not to Sit in the Shade

Early Spring — 5 A.M.: Start fire in wood-burning cook stove, put coffee pot on, take fast walk to outhouse, take a "spit" bath and get dressed. Cook breakfast, let chickens out of hen house, feed and water them, milk the goats, wash and sterilize the milking utensils, do dishes, check brooding hens for red mites, make a couple of pies for dessert, sterilize another bushel of soil to sow vegetable seeds in, water seedlings already up and growing, prepare lunch, do dishes, put stomach tube down sick calf's throat, spray fruit trees, take ashes out of two stoves, bring in more wood, sweep the floor, dust furniture, check on the chickens, shovel some litter out of hen house, cook supper, gather eggs, do dishes, milk the goat, patch some jeans, close hen house door, take a bath in large laundry tub. Stumble to bed.

Late Spring: All of the above, plus feed and water baby chicks, baby guinea fowl, and mama fowl all in their individual coops, made by yours truly. Incubate some goose eggs, butcher some early frying chickens, remove mulch from under each fruit tree, work in the strawberry beds, set out the last of the broccoli plants (in a pouring rain), make six loaves of bread and/or cheese, dry some herbs and teas. Fall into bed.

Summer: Do more weeding, watering, and cultivating; can, freeze, and dry food. Butcher more fowl and pack for freezing, make salami, more pickles, mulch the potatoes and garden; take shower under outdoor solar-heated shower. Collapse into bed.

Early Fall: Can, freeze, and dry foods. Show Miss Smarty — one of the milk goats — that she can too get zapped if she doesn't cease and desist going through the electric fence! Make more fruit leather, butcher more fowl (and some of the pets?), fry up gallons of pork patties and pack in lard for unrefrigerated storage, make more pickles, fruit juices, fruit butters, applesauce. Hope to live 'til bedtime!

Late Fall: Can, freeze, and dry. Store apples, cabbage, onions, winter squash, and pumpkins in fruit cellar. Dig potatoes, make and dry goat jerky, make sauerkraut, more applesauce.

Early Winter: Mulch fruit trees, strawberries, and so on. Winterize the hen house, make and freeze egg noodles, make jellies out of previously canned fruit juices, butcher some hens, geese, and guinea fowl.

Late Winter: Start visiting friends again! Begin planning the coming spring's work, start some vegetable seeds in flats, read — and read some more — how-to books. Cook up a storm, i.e., experiment with recipes using home-grown foods.

I've necessarily left out numerous other chores one does in the course of living the good life, but this should give the reader some food for thought.

JANN POTTER 〜 A Ranch Woman's Week

Being a ranch woman means being an all-around woman. For example, here's most of what I did last week. Keep in mind that our son, Jabe, goes to school at 8:30 A.M. and gets out at 3:30 P.M.; that's at least forty miles a day on the road. We don't have a school bus. Our daughter, Carly, stays in Dillon (sixty miles away) during the week to attend high school.

Sunday, 5:30 A.M.: I helped Gene feed the cows and yearlings, then loaded up three horses and two kids and headed to Whitehall, 120 miles away, for a 4-H rodeo; Gene stayed home to calve. We got home at 9 P.M.

Monday: I helped feed cows and yearlings, then hosted our quilting club and the quilting club from Salmon, Idaho, for lunch and a day of quilting; there were twenty-two ladies here.

Tuesday: After feeding, I hauled four dry cows to the sale in Dillon. That afternoon Jabe and I practiced roping, running barrels and poles in our arena. After supper I helped Gene pull a calf.

Wednesday: After feeding, Gene and I sorted and vaccinated our yearling heifers and steers, then turned them out on grass. We'd been feeding them since November. At 6:30 we had a Little Guy Wrestling awards dinner in Wisdom — pot-luck; I took barbecued beef.

Thursday: We still have a few cows to calve that we have to feed. I did some brushing on one pasture and got caught up on some household chores.

Friday: We branded calves; Jabe stayed home from school to help. Also had help from some neighbors; we help them and they help us. After school our 4-H club picked up litter on eighteen miles of road between Jackson and Wisdom. We all then came here and had hot dogs and our monthly meeting.

Saturday: Loaded horses and kids and drove to Hamilton, ninety miles away, for high school rodeo. Carly participated; we stayed all night and rodeoed again on Sunday and were home by suppertime.

TERRY HENDERSON 〜 Ranch Widow

April 21, 1981

Dear Mom and Dad,

This has been a horrible week! I am so thankful you let Robin come stay with me this spring. I never thought I'd lean on my little sis. Larry's folks seem to expect that since I'm getting paid by the ranch and live so close, I'm at their beck and call from daylight to dusk, and sometimes beyond. I have my own household to run, and a husband and two kids to take care of, in addition to the ranch work. I'd go crazy puttering around the house after being a ranch hand here since college days, but it gets overwhelming.

When we got back to home ranch from cow camp Sunday, Larry had a terrible headache. I knew it was bad when he agreed to go to the doctor on a weekend in the middle of calving season. What really frightened me — Larry asked me to drive him to town.

At the emergency room an intern found Larry's blood pressure unbelievably high, but gave him some pain pills and asked him to see his regular doctor during office hours.

On Monday it wasn't hard to get Larry to go to our family-practice doctor. That quack said it was just a sinus headache.

April 26, 1981: Robin came in from camp looking scared. They had an old cow trying to have a backwards calf. By the time the calf was born, Larry was done in. When he got home, he didn't even take off his calving clothes, but staggered into the bedroom and collapsed on the bed.

His mom drove us to town. Larry lay on the back seat with his head in my lap, almost in tears with the pain. He kept saying, "Don't let them take the kids away from you if anything happens to me."

The hospital tests showed Larry had no peripheral vision, so it's either an aneurysm or a tumor. We'll know more tomorrow.

April 27, 1981: The doctors are operating on Larry's aneurysm as I write. Starla doesn't understand where we are. How do you explain to a four-year-old that something is terribly wrong with her daddy? The baby's ear infection is still making him miserable.

Grim news: the aneurysm has a weak, unformed neck. It was difficult to repair. The neurologist fears Larry may have extensive brain damage.

May 19, 1981: If one more person at the funeral had said, "You're young, you'll marry again," I'd have poked them in the nose. Larry wasn't even in the ground. Why do they think being twenty-six means I immediately want another husband? I still love Larry. What do I do about living and working on the ranch? If I don't work here, I have to find a place to live and another job to support the kids. I'm too numb to know anything.

I finally cried, Mom, after you left, yet the hurt hasn't gone away. I'm so full of empty, I can barely function.

June 1, 1981: This would have been our eighth anniversary, as well as that of Larry's folks. They came down for a little while, but none of us knew what to say.

Larry's dad asked Robin to move to summer cow camp this year since we're short-handed. I'm going to miss her.

I may buy into the ranch corporation if the family agrees. As long as I'm working here, I might as well be working for myself. Before Larry died, we were considering going off by ourselves, to have our own place. With him gone, that's not possible; another dream put on the shelf.

July 12, 1981: I spent the life insurance money on a partnership in the ranch, with a few shares for the kids. This way I know I'll have a house and food for my family even if all else goes haywire.

I'm having fits with live-in baby-sitters I can afford; just lost my third one in six weeks. Living in the country sounds lovely until they realize I only get one station on TV and I don't get a daily newspaper.

I doubt if I can hire a suitable nanny for my entire salary, with room and board thrown in. Larry's mom will watch the children in a pinch, but that's never been a lasting solution.

August 20, 1981: When Larry was alive, ranching was a shared lifestyle. Now it is just a job. When I check cattle, I get off my horse to open a gate and I remember the last time Larry opened it. Or I check the fence line and remember the spring day when the whole family bounced along in the old power wagon. I dug out the springs at the yearling pasture last week, getting soaked and covered in mud. Before, there was the camaraderie of Larry and I both coming home a mess from similar chores. All I come home with now is a backache.

I'm doing all the swathing this summer. It's hard to try to keep things normal around the kids. I blame my hay fever for my swollen eyes if anybody notices. The ranch bought one of those self-stacking wagons. There's no way I could have stacked over one hundred stacks of hay this summer without Larry.

September 25, 1981: I have to push Starla out the door and onto the school bus. The counselor says Starla is fearful I will leave her and not come back. I don't know how to help her with her grief. One morning, I heard her in the music room asking the angels to bring her daddy home. Several times I have found her sleeping at the foot of my bed in the morning. She keeps saying, "I want to go home," but we are home.

I was in one of those tight spots the other day with no nanny and Larry's mother in town. So both the kids went with me to trail dry cows off the mountain. Starla rode her Shetland and I stuffed a pillow in front of me for little Monti. It's awkward controlling a horse with one hand and holding a baby with the other, and ten miles is a long way. Robin helped on the lead and I mostly rode at the back. Monti dozed most of the way. Getting off and on the horse was a problem at the gates. Monti and I were both stiff when we got home.

January 14, 1982: We made it through the holidays. The kids didn't seem to notice much amiss, although I still catch Monti looking for someone or something. I have several years of memories of Larry but soon Monti won't have any.

Larry's folks had company during Christmas Eve dinner. One lady said, "Oh my dear, I just don't know how you manage all this work and raising a family too!" Like I had a choice! I want things to be the way they used to be. I didn't ask for this change. I'm only doing what I have to, providing for my kids.

I've got a new nanny, Gladys, a grandmother type. I'll see how long it takes before the isolation gets to her.

March 1, 1982: I finally got up the nerve to go dancing with a fellow. Larry's folks were up when we got back to my house at the outrageous hour of eleven P.M.! The next morning they quizzed me on who I'd gone out with, how long he stayed at my house, how old he is, and so on. It's not worth the hassle.

April 30, 1982: So much has changed in just a year. The hardest part about the calving season has been the night checks. Gladys quit. On my nights, Larry's junior high sisters take turns sleeping on my couch in case the children wake up. They don't like having to sleep at my house.

It's three miles down the creek to check the heifers. The only vehicle that can wallow through the muddy, frozen ruts is the tractor with no cab. By the time I've spent forty-five minutes outside I'm usually chilled to the bone, no matter how well I dress. It's hard to warm up enough to get back to sleep. Often my feet are so cold that I lay awake from the two A.M. check until five.

July 15, 1982: Gladys is back, but I think the high elevation at summer cow camp is hard on her. I tried to get her to cook on the cow camp stove one day, but she isn't comfortable with the wood part of the stove and the gas side doesn't work very well. She prefers to stay down at the home ranch with the kids. I know they're disappointed when they can't be on the mountain with me, so I drive ten long rocky miles up and back every day. The dew isn't off the grass until after ten A.M. and I'm generally home by six P.M. to milk the cow. Evenings, the kids can go with me while we unload the hay hauled off the mountain, which gives Gladys a break.

August 28, 1982: Gladys decided to go back to town for good. I'm surprised she stayed as long as she did. However, I have finally found a solution. Ernie, the bus driver, comes right to my door, since we're the end of the line. Monti rides the bus ten miles to the neighbor's ranch and gets off at Joyce's. She watches him along with her two little boys during the day. At night, when Ernie drops her older kids off, Monti comes home on the bus with Starla. On days I know I can't be at the house by bus time, I call Joyce, and Starla gets off the bus at their stop. All I have to do is drive to their ranch and get them when I'm done. This seems so easy after all the hassle of baby-sitters.

I hadn't realized what a strain it was having other people living with me. It's so peaceful to spend the evening with just the kids. Once they're in bed, I don't have to make small talk when all I really want to do is sleep.

October 23, 1982: A while back, somebody was walking around here at night. I heard footsteps on the swinging bridge outside my window and I peeked out. It made me realize how vulnerable I am with the children. I know you taught me to shoot, Dad, but a gun may not always be available if I need it. I've started taking tae kwon do lessons, the only reason I go to town outside of business, groceries, and Cow-Belle meetings. The kids go along and play around the edge of the gym. I hadn't realized what a hermit I'd become. Running to town for social activities just doesn't seem worth the effort.

Even though we keep distinctly separate households here, I never realized how much family politics influence the little things in my life. Larry's family is so different, so segregated. I worry about the effect on the kids.

November 20, 1982: Winter has come to the mountain. We trailed the cow herd off yesterday. The snow is so deep we had to take snow machines and the D-6 Cat, but the cows were ready to go. We just opened gates on the way up and trailed behind the slower ones coming off. I've never wrangled on a snow machine before. It was dark, after eight P.M. when we got down. The kids were tired of waiting for me. That's one of the longest, coldest days I've put in. Snow machines are even colder than riding horseback. I can't put my hands in my pocket and alternate warming them. I have to keep my hands forward for the throttle and steering.

December 28, 1982: Celebrating on Christmas Eve still feels like we're jumping the gun, but with feeding cattle, mornings are just too hectic. This way the kids can have time to enjoy opening their gifts under the tree. For

Christmas, I bought myself a new coat. We had Rudolph; I taped a red light bulb to the nose of the elk head hanging in the living room.

April 22, 1983: Old Spec tried to pull a run-away at winter camp today as I was bringing an old cow in that had been calving for a couple of hours but was making no progress. Near the barn, Old Spec shied and we were off and flying. I pulled his head around and we piled up on the ground — knocked the wind out of both of us. When I crawled back on, he was much better behaved. We put the cow in and she calved by herself an hour later. I was afraid it was going to be backwards and I wouldn't be strong enough to get it turned.

May 30, 1983: I was just installed as Cow-Belle president. As long as I'm in the beef business, I might as well be promoting it. We only meet once a month. The women are people to talk to who understand this way of life.

July 10, 1983: I'm plugged up with hay fever so bad I have to sit up at night to breathe. There has to be an easier way to make a living that gives me time with the kids, but this is so secure and I love the work. I'd never make a secretary. If I had to work inside, I'd be a basket case.

September 5, 1983: I can't believe I just turned twenty-nine. Sometimes I feel like an old lady. I wonder if I'll die of old age by thirty-five.

Do you remember Jim, the older neighbor you met? He was helping us trail yearlings off the mountain for shipping and heard me cussing the cattle because they kept wandering off into the trees. He laughed because I don't cuss like the guys do. I have my own vocabulary — just as emphatic, but not as vulgar. I guess that comes from my upbringing, Mom; even though I'm doing a man's job, I want to be as much a lady as you are. Larry's dad told one of the neighbors that I'm the best hand he'd ever had.

Therein lies the problem. When Larry's youngest brother finishes college and quits playing around, he is going to be boss here. Even though I'm a partner, I will always be just a hired hand. I am not really part of the family. Larry's little brother's going to come home and start giving orders without ever having to work his way up. I've been taking pride in something they don't consider mine.

October 29, 1983: Larry's dad has a hernia, can't lift, and plans to have surgery soon. I walked his D-4 Cat off the mountain and realized I have operated every piece of equipment and can ride every horse on this ranch. I don't know that it amounts to anything except my own satisfaction.

December 20, 1983: This winter is old already, though barely begun. I'm tired of breaking ice on the creek every morning, especially when the water freezes in two layers. The banks are getting too slick at the heifer hole, and the hired man and I had to chop ice steps in the frozen ground so the animals could get up out of the creek.

Winter camp isn't much better. The wind has been blowing so the windmill tanks are full of frozen slush. It's almost like rubber when I try to break through it with a shovel or an ax.

February 15, 1984: Monti was upset because I didn't let him go along to help feed. I've had him all week because Joyce's kids have the chicken pox. The snowdrifts are getting too deep for four-year-old legs. Larry's mom watched him.

March 30, 1984: Both kids ended up with severe cases of chicken pox. My only choice was to have Larry's mother watch them while I was feeding. I was able to spend the rest of the day with them. At least they got through it before calving season started. It seems when trying to juggle motherhood and a ranch job, I often drop the ball.

July 2, 1984: I am going to leave the ranch. I finished my year as Cow-Belle president and am going to school in Denver for a degree as a veterinary technician. I asked Larry's dad to pay me a director's fee on my ranch shares to give me some income while I'm in school. I've applied for grants and I've got a student loan.

The kids don't quite understand what moving involves, but they are reassured when I tell them we can visit. Denver will be quite a culture shock, but I promised that as soon as I'm done, we will move back to the country and they will have their horses and animals again. I can graduate in eighteen months. Surely I'll survive in town that long.

August 28, 1984: This is it. My last day at the ranch. A friend is helping me move with a four-horse trailer. I took the first load to Denver last weekend and found a place to live.

I will have a part-time job the first quarter of school. My classes are half a day since my other college credits transferred. I've found someone to watch the kids, and Starla will start school the first week of September, three blocks from our new home. She'll be able to walk with a couple of other kids.

Today is both sad and happy. I am leaving the last tangible bit of Larry behind. Without the hassles of family politics I can finally be my own person. I am losing my security for my future, but replacing it with unknown opportunities. Wish me luck. I know you do.

August 28, 1992: When I left the ranch, I intended to leave all the pain and frustration of family differences behind. The local paper recently ran a story on my cowboy poetry and the cow/calf operation I've built up since I finished vet tech school and remarried. The article explained that I had taken over my first husband's job on the family ranch following his death. This week, Larry's mom wrote a letter to the editor emphatically stating to the world that I held no management position on their ranch and was simply a hired hand at the time. I am going to request that they buy out my ranch shares.

August 20, 1994: I never dreamed Larry's death would strengthen me for future disasters. Monti will always have a mangled foot from the four-wheeler wreck. Larry's folks claim that although Monti was working for them, *he* was negligent. Since he is a shareholder and fourteen years old, they refused to pay any medical bills. In addition, I was shocked when they requested that I pay for the repair of the machinery. Optimistically, I believed he could somehow be part of that family. Time has proven, once again, he's simply another hired hand.

Their reply this time to buying my shares was to offer me forty cents on the dollar for what I paid thirteen years ago. The reason: I have minority shares, which devalues them. If I had only known then what I know now.

Love, Terry

PAMELA J. OCHSNER ⬎ frustration

frustration . . .

This morning, I will let the chickens all out; I will tear down the hog fence and scream and shout. I will fire a shotgun outside in the herd, and burn down the house without saying a word. I will break all the windows and break every dish, and I'll go out for lunch to wherever I wish. I will cut all the fences, and poison the pond, and I'll plow up the trees, or the corn, or beyond. I will go today and do whatever it is I have to do, but just for one day give me strength *not to argue*.

Amen.

REBECCA WAMPLER ⬎ Dark Billowing Flowers

October, 1951, rural Niobrara County, Wyoming.
The young wife's first pregnancy wracks her with nausea.
Her heart is sick, too.
One brother lost in Korea,
Another, her closest, shot in a hunting accident.
She cannot rejoice for the new life within her.
A radioactive cloud from above-ground nuclear tests in Nevada
Boils over Wyoming from Rawlins to Redbird.
Fallout thicker than Chernobyl's hot dust over Eastern Europe
Sifts down on the woman, her sisters, and the fetus.

April, 1952.
Southeastern Wyoming is blanketed by atomic clouds.
The woman is resolved to the birth, but still punky.
The flu, the old folks say.
She will never finish grieving for her brothers.

May, 1952.
A spring blizzard beats down through three waves
Of nuclear radiation.
Radioactive rain and snow pelt the prairie,
Like a winter's dirt shaken from a rug.
The woman's belly is fat as she chores in the sleet,
Gathers eggs, milks the cow.

June, 1952.
Another month with four days of invisibly falling poison.
And I am born.
Before I am ten, eighteen more filthy storms dump on Wyoming.

1992.
Small-town papers mark their deaths,
Women stopped in mid-stride.
Dropped by creeping rot.
Their liveliest cells gone rogue,
Black roses bud and bloom.
Mothers in their prime waste and fall,
A shocking plague that is statistically insignificant.

Bewildered mates and abandoned children suffer in silence,
Western stoics.
We're practical here.
Death is always part of a balanced equation.
We're isolated here.
Unaware that we were invaded,
We fly loyally the flag of our conqueror.

DONNA WILLIAMS DEREEMER

The Day the Uncles Bought the New Truck

Of the many adventures I have had while living on the family ranch, The Day the Uncles Bought the New Truck is one of many vivid pictures in my mind. It rates right up there with other adventures like The Day I Backed Over the Mini-Bike My Husband Had Just Traded In, or The Day I Nearly Killed the Horse When I Fed Him All the Cream that Wouldn't Turn to Butter, or The Day I Tried to Stop the Bulls from Fighting by Driving the Pickup In Between Them, or The Day I Stuck My Head in the Gate while Sorting Cows and Received Black and Blue Ear Muffs.

MARILYNN J. VAN WELL ⌒ My Dear Grandchildren

My Dear Grandchildren,

Granny was just remembering how very special you made our week when you came to visit us on the farm. What a joy we experienced when we watched you ride the pony, chase the dog, carry the kitty, and investigate the old barn. It was the same pony your daddies rode and the same old barn your daddies explored. It seems like only yesterday.

Granny's memories were mixed with a bit of anger, too, because somehow we thought our family tree would center around the family farm. Inflation has taken its toll and making a living for more than one family on our farm is no longer possible. You hear a lot about corporate farming now and they say the family farms, like buggy whips, are no longer needed.

Well, my little ones, today's system would do away with a lot more besides families working together to produce food. We would lose other priceless ventures, such as trips to the summer pasture to check the cattle herds right at sunset. We'd lose Monopoly games and jigsaw puzzles on a cold winter's evening while snowbound on the farm. And what about all those homemade rafts built to float on stock dams whose builder pretended they'd take him to faraway places?

Granny is all for progress, but when progress rips from us the core of our nation's roots, the family farms, then progress becomes, like everything else without a core, rotten from the inside out.

Oh, dear children, I remember so well all the small towns that served their own local farming communities. They each had their own hospitals, schools, theaters, banks, drugstores, clothing stores, and many more businesses. On Wednesday and Saturday evenings, the small towns were alive with the hustle and bustle of the farming community. Children ran and played together, the women visited as they shopped for the weekly supplies, and the men stopped to chitchat on the way for feed and repairs. The teenagers went to the movies, and dogs and cats ran about town, joining in on the excitement.

When the farmers succeeded, so did everyone else. Everybody worked hand in hand to keep their community alive. Now, when Granny drives to the small towns, she sees hospitals either closed or struggling to stay alive. Schools have been closed or consolidated. The clothing stores are gone, as well as the theaters. Main Street just doesn't have the activity it once did, and that saddens me.

We needn't wonder why. Many farm families could no longer survive on low prices for their commodities and high prices for the products they needed. Mother Nature often helped to close down the farms with droughts and hailstorms. When the farm family finally gave up and moved away, a lot of the community died, too. Each person was vital to the heartbeat of the land. Our Main Street businesses soon felt the loss and closed their doors, and once again we died a little more.

As I write my thoughts to you, my little ones, I wonder what will be left for you in the way of family farms. Your grandpa and I are so happy you've had the chance to experience what it is to feel the land breathe through the grain fields, producing precious food without the help of chemical fertilizers. We're happy you were able to see life born anew in a baby calf as it came into the world cradled in the arms of Mother Earth. And especially for you, our little grandson, that you walked beside Grandpa all day, still smiling and full of energy at the day's end, filled with wonder in all you saw and did.

Granny wants to hold it together for you and future generations. I will continue to write my senators and congressman, asking their help to preserve this way of life. My letters alone won't do it, but many letters from many farmers will make the message heard. I always try to remember the saying, "It is better to light one little candle than to curse the darkness."

Well, it is time for Granny to close this letter to you. The evening air is filled with the sweet smell of Russian Olive trees and I hear a coyote calling in the distance. The birds are quiet now, for it is their bedtime. I guess it is Granny's bedtime, too. So until next time, we'll have to be content remembering all the fun we shared on your visit to the farm.

Love, Granny

JANE ELKINGTON WOHL
At Fort Phil Kearney, December 1991
Site of the Fetterman Fight, December 21, 1866

It is as if I must blacken my face
with the charcoal I would find here
beneath the snow, sagebrush, grass roots,
topsoil new this century,
and thus blackened
wait for the December night to fall
clear and still on this hilltop.
Then I would see Orion in the southern sky,
shoulders, three stars for his belt, three for knife
and, if I had a telescope,
the horsehead nebula whirling, dense and distant.

And I wonder if a woman, officer's wife or laundress maybe,
in the dim light from small papered windows,

smoke rising in the cold air,
stood here in the center of the fort
looking at the stars.

At the museum now they tell us
those in charge put all the women and children
in the powder magazine, underground.
In case hostiles attacked, they could be blown up
and saved from capture.

I watch my children follow coyote tracks
across the snow where palisades once stood,
and guardhouses.
Small signs mark officers' quarters,
blacksmith, infirmary, commissary,
magazine and barracks.

In the distance, bare trees line Piney Creek
where Sioux and Cheyenne camped that winter.
With cooking fires burning low, they too
could watch the December stars.

With black grit across my cheeks,
I could lie hidden in the shadow of the creek bank,
quiet, unseen, safe.

I see that woman standing here
watching the night sky tilt above her,
pulling her wool shawl closer,
memorizing Orion's knife
before she joins her children underground.

SHARON FRANK ~~ **Dearest Little One**

April 14, 1993

Dearest Little One,

Your Daddy and I are looking forward to you joining our family. The doctor says we can expect you the first week of September. Your older brother, Joshua, figures he'll have enough time to practice at being a good example for you by then.

Your Daddy is a hired man for a very kind farmer who has a cow/calf operation. I mention that the boss is kind because we haven't always been so fortunate.

Working for a fair man makes it so much easier to enjoy life. You don't have to be afraid of making a tiny mistake, or saying something not quite right, or just having an off day. You see, when the boss decides he wants you gone — you go immediately. We lost our home and our livelihood for a man's bad mood. We always knew that he considered us "less." His daughter came down once to tell us that we were lowlifes because we didn't own our own land and had to work for someone else.

It nearly broke my heart when I had to sell the horse I'd waited twenty-eight years to have. I had to do it so we could keep up with our obligations and move on.

Don't be scared about this boss. He knows we are people and he treats us very well.

You'll be coming to live in a little white farmhouse. It's old but cozy and we live near many ponds. The Canada geese will often wake you with their honking. They always have a lot to say to each other when they get ready to leave.

Cows and calves will be nearby. You'll have your own bunny when you get older and you can help me gather eggs. You'll have a dog to run with and a kitty to curl up in your lap.

I want to tell you about me, too. I'm my Grandpa's boy. You see, it was my Grandpa who gave me my appreciation and love of animals. He loved cattle and wanted to own a ranch. He wanted a son of like mind to follow in his footsteps.

Grandpa never got his ranch. He became a very successful salesman of health products for livestock. He never got his like-minded son. He got a granddaughter who wished she were a boy and followed after him anyway.

I work in the livestock auction yard on sale days. I get to work outdoors and be near cattle. I am with people who have a close relationship with the land and their animals. It's wonderful to be near people who know where they come from — the land.

I'm often told I have no business in the yard and that I should work in the office. I hear that I don't know a woman's place, but I do. I know I'm a human being first and a woman second.

I know I'll never be considered as good as a man and I don't try to be. There's no way I can stack lots of hay or pee on a fence post. But I do have a special place.

I figure it's my job to keep the human element alive out in the yard. It's my job to treat the animals with kindness and respect. After all, they are God's creatures. I'm concerned that the customers leave satisfied with the service they received at the auction. I am organized and I write fast. I get their cattle checked in quickly and I do it with courtesy. I believe they leave with a good feeling about that gal who checked them in and the sale barn in general.

I tried working in a traditional role once. I was a secretary for two divisions of a large institution. Any flicker of humanness was squelched there and a little part of me died every day for a year. I know I'm where I'm supposed to be now.

This life — working with the land and the animals — is a privilege. There are fewer and fewer people who can enjoy the life because our world is changing so much. Living in the country is special and I'm glad you'll be living here with me.

Love, Mom

IDA ANNA HOHM — *Dear Anna, My Great-Granddaughter*

1930s: I was born as Anna and Joshua Hofer's third daughter in 1924 in Beadle County and named Ida Anna. As a child, I never realized that daily dust storms were not normal. Still, my parents never complained. We were poor, but did not know it.

We received free relief food, such as grapefruit, which we had never tasted before — delicious. Once when we opened a can of relief beef, there was a grasshopper on top. We removed the hopper and ate the beef. Sugar being rationed, we ate lots of syrup.

Black Sunday: The day started out calm enough, but by noon it was pitch dark. People lit their kerosene lamps and the chickens sat on high roosts. Our neighbors, who were more religious, were all down on their knees praying; they thought this was the end of the world, a realistic conclusion.

My daily job in summer was to herd the milk cows to the ditches, as there was some vegetation there. I was told to herd them until noon. Since I had little sense of time, I chased the small herd back to the farmstead. My dear father met me and kindly said, "Ida, it is only ten o'clock, just take them back out."

Death: Lightning struck and instantly killed my Uncle John, who was employed by my father; he was in a field cutting thistles with a mower with steel wheels and pulled by two beautiful, look-alike chestnut horses who were also killed. My uncle had a round pocket watch in the bib of his overalls. The only burn he had was behind the watch. My father rushed into the house with muddy shoes, something he never did, for a sheet. My mom knew that something was terribly wrong. Yes, her brother's purple body was then covered with a white bed sheet. Our lives are like beautifully woven tapestry. The threads are light in color amidst dark ones. This is called value in art.

Stormy Death: On a beautiful day in January, 1933, two boys, ages seven and nine, went to visit their neighbors scarcely a mile away. They had so much fun eating peanuts, candy, and leftover Christmas goodies. Suddenly the wind turned to the northwest and those two boys started home kitty-corner across the open field. The wind was ferocious and very cold. These boys never came home. Many people looked all night, but could not find them. The children went with the wind away from their home and were found one mile south of where we live the next morning. The older brother had his jacket pulled over the younger one, who still clutched a nut in his hand.

1930s: Growing up in the Depression, I know what "make do" means. It is a happy challenge for me. Before discarding anything now, I ask myself "Could this be recycled somehow?" I am still shocked by present-day price tags. In a store recently, I saw a T-shirt, all wrinkled as if a big tractor drove over it, marked thirty dollars.

At age nineteen, I taught in a country school for one year. I then married a farmer and have never been sorry.

I'm indeed grateful to God that while in my seventh decade and a grandma, I am able to give back to the community. Call it retired or refired, I'm having a great time. In 1976 I learned oil painting, and now teach seventh and eighth graders. My new hobby is barbershop singing in harmony.

RACHEL C. KLIPPENSTEIN ~~ The Sale

September 29, 1984: Instead of crying, I sit at the typewriter and let my thoughts wander. Getting it down on paper helps.

I've suffered disappointments before, but this time so many thoughts go through my mind that I wish I were an animal that acts from instinct. Kevin can't sleep, and I wake up early.

My greatest sadness is for Kevin, with his tie to the land and cattle. I used to think his world wouldn't end if he did other work. Now I'm not so sure. Time may give perspective, but now we are humiliated, confused, and guilty.

We've pulled so many people down with us — family, friends, our sons. How must they feel now? I don't know what to say to Rob and Ian, to our friends who have stood by us. I don't know what to say to Brad, whose heifer died. I don't even know how much time to give ourselves before we are ready to make decisions.

I do not believe that Kevin and I will give up — but I'm not sure. I'm not even sure how to pray about this fiasco, where to start. So I get up in the morning thankful for dishes to do and clothes to wash. I want to go where I know no one and come back when it's all over. I don't want pity from others.

Twenty years, a pause in life. If we had spent it foolishly, if we had not set goals and worked hard, this would make more sense. We felt the gamble and the effort were worthwhile.

In a way there's been a death in the family; we're going through denial, grief, self-pity, and acceptance.

September 30, 1984: Am I going crazy, like so many plainswomen have?

Kevin and I talked yesterday — mostly it was me talking. I want to know what he is feeling. Maybe we are in an agricultural depression, but part of the American economy is sailing right along. Auto workers ask for job security and more money. How can we in agriculture be so ineffective?

Kevin and I argue over stupid things like whether the report of our sale should be printed in the livestock journal. Kevin's worried about how he's going to get out of this with enough money to start over. I'm worried about how our going under will affect others. I'm tired of worrying.

I woke up this morning dry-eyed — the first day since Thursday. I began to feel better. But tears come unbidden.

Kevin won't tell me how he feels. What can I say to him? What do I want him to say to me? He wanders off. I worry. Will he wander off and never return? I'm scared.

Just now Brent Harrington phoned and asked how the sale went and I told him. How could I make it sound better when it wasn't? I think I will quit answering the phone. I want to tell the truth and yet I don't. Brent is planning a big sale himself, and I wasn't very encouraging.

October 1, 1984: Damn! I'm in tears again. I'm worn out trying to be tough. I keep thinking each day it will not hurt so much. This morning we will load out cattle representing twenty years of our Lazy H 3 genetics. If they had paid their way we would feel better.

I can't say that the buyers stole the cattle because we sat there and gave them away. Please, Kev, talk to me. The banker says our balance owed is $118,000. I will put $7,000 in the bank today, with about $20,000 still to come in. Rob sold one heifer for next to nothing, and Ian sold his Benchmark cow and the yearling for not much more — a great reward for all of their work. Shit.

If Kevin and I tally up everything else we could sell — yearlings, butcher cattle, and a few registered cows — it still won't amount to a hill of beans. Even if we get a decent price for the land and ship all of the rest of the cattle, I doubt we will have anything left.

People tell us, "At least you have your good health," or, "You've raised two fine sons"; it doesn't help. We still owe on Kevin's back surgery, my hysterectomy, rabies shots, Kevin's cyst and his kidney stone. We don't even have enough money to buy a decent vehicle to run away in. Will we run away together? Alone?

October 2, 1984: I feel lonely, different than when I've gone on my long walks once or twice a year when my misery was self-inflicted; I knew then I could work out of my self-pity. Now I'm afraid and empty.

Kevin is a quiet person. Working out solutions quietly in his mind is his way. I'm a yeller and a chest-beater. I've always told Kevin everything; now I feel guilty if I do. And our closest friends have their own difficulties; they need no more burdens.

Kevin has believed that peace is not the absence of conflict, but the ability to cope with conflict. Up till now he has always been able to figure his way out of tough situations.

This morning Kevin was trying to decide whether to drive Rob's pickup, which has gear difficulties, or the car, which has starter troubles, sixty miles to Ruddman. He asked me.

I said, "How would I know? It didn't bother you when I had to take the car on errands never knowing when it would quit."

Kevin replied, "I'm sorry I can't get you a decent car."

It's dumb arguments like that that never used to happen.

I helped Rob load cattle that will be dead meat after a short trip through the livestock auction, but refused to go with him. I looked forward to being here by myself, no demands on me.

Now, when people ask me how I am, I'll say, "Just fine." I couldn't explain all of my emotions, so I'll keep my thoughts to myself.

Rob and Ian offered to stay and help us. Kevin and I agreed they must get on with their lives. Staying would drag them down too; they're young, and full of their own dreams.

I'm not going to write again until I can write on a more positive note.

November 3, 1984: I said I wouldn't add to this until I could write something positive. In truth I must write a little of each; it soothes my soul to let my confusion out on paper.

I sense Kevin's anger, as well as his sadness and disappointment. For the first time, he cannot find a way out.

I don't know how I can support him if I don't know what is bothering him. I have the urge to throw the keys on the table and run away. Perhaps I shall just "be there" for now.

It has been six weeks since the sale, but I can't say I feel better. Finding solutions tires the mind and body. We're only forty-two with half our lives ahead.

I picked up the first livestock magazine I've looked at since the sale. Reading the editorial, I was outraged. The writer said, "it is a way of life we get hooked on," as if to explain why we should be happy to make sacrifices in this business. "To make it," he said, "we would have to quit spending money." Just that simple. And "if interest rates dropped a point or two and the commodity prices came up a little we would be okay."

That's a bunch of bullshit. I sat down and wrote a letter to him. I don't know if it was worth the time. I don't want to stay in this business the way it is. Kevin will have to make that decision; I do feel sorry for everyone who is suffering from this "isolated" agricultural depression.

I want so badly for Kevin and me to share the happiness that till now has been our life. For the first time in my life I feel like it is the two of us against the world. Could we love each other so much that to talk about what has happened makes us feel we are causing more hurt?

One would think a devastating event would pull a couple together, but we seem to keep our thoughts to ourselves. We're sliding apart. God, Kevin, please don't let this happen.

I don't sing anymore. I've been trying to take each day as it comes, but some days are more overwhelming than others.

The boys worry, feeling frustrated they can't help. I've tried while they are home to maintain peace and happiness. I don't want them to get bogged down when they need encouragement for the future. How has this past year affected them?

I think a lot about Providence and that "the Lord's will be done." I am not angry at God, but I would feel much better if I had a clue where all of this is leading. Other people have suffered terrible hurts in their lives and come through, and so I guess we will.

The tears well up as I write, so I'll quit for now.

ELAINE TRAWEEK ~ Dear Grandma

You'll never read this, of course, since you passed away many years ago, but you show up in my memories quite often; today is dark and gloomy anyway, with nothing much to be done outside, so let's set some things straight between us, even if only in my head.

Back then, in the forties and fifties, when we lived on that little 180-acre black dirt farm on the outskirts of Pickwick — Mom, Dad, us six kids, and for the part of each year, you — life seemed so intense and desperate sometimes. We all knew that you had to live four months with us because you had no home of your own, and then you'd move on to Aunt Margaret's and Aunt Ruby's. It could have been fun, but it got a little tough because you never smiled; at least, I can't recall your smile, and you found fault with everything we kids did.

I was too much of a tomboy. It wasn't decent. Girls should be in the house learning to cook, sew, mop floors — proper things like that. They shouldn't be outside, messing around driving teams, cleaning barns, doing "boy things."

But Grandma, those were some of the most fun years of my life. You thought it scandalous that I'd ride one of those big old Belgian draft horses off into the woods and spend hours by myself. You glared and said I acted like a hermit. But those horses didn't care one bit that I was 5'11" and that my hair was already getting gray at the age of eleven. They didn't laugh or make fun like the kids did.

But that was all a long time ago and Minnesota seems so far away now.

Contrary to your expectations that I would remain forever single, I met and married a really nice guy named Mel soon after high school. We have three pretty good kids; Shannon is a legal secretary, Sheila is an artist, and Brian works at a big sports bar.

Anyway, when we'd been married for twenty-three years, Mel passed away when an aneurysm in his brain broke. He was only forty-three.

While I was trying to decide what to do with the rest of my life, Brian asked me one day what I would really *like* to do — not what I thought I should do. It didn't take me too much thought for that answer, but I wasn't sure how they'd take it. "Well-l, I've always wanted to see if I could handle working on a ranch and what Montana is like." Bless their hides, they hardly batted an eye.

"Well, Mother," Brian said, "you'd better get to it 'cause you're not getting any younger."

It took a few months and some ads in a couple of Montana newspapers — to which I received twenty-three replies. In October of 1979 I began working for a widow on a small ranch near Willard. And I could handle most of the work, getting help from her nephew and brothers when mechanical things wouldn't cooperate. The cattle were a bit wild, and, coming from a dairy farm background, I was shocked that cows were moved at a high lope, and that you sorted bulls with a pitchfork in your hand. During the next summer, a job as bookkeeper at a feed pelleting plant in Baker opened up and I took it.

So, that's how I got to Montana, Grandma, and some of what's been going on with some of us since you left us.

While working at the pelleting plant, I met Wayne, the guy who became my second husband. How about that! You thought I'd become a hermit! We live on a small ranch that belongs to his eighty-six-year-old mother about thirty-five miles southeast of Baker; she has an apartment in town.

Because the ranch is fairly small by Montana standards — about three thousand acres — Wayne doesn't have much of a problem doing what needs to be done, but his sixty-five-year-old bones are in a constant battle with arthritis, so his "good, stout young wife" as he jokingly refers to me, gets to help with some of the things that are particularly stressful.

I'm the night checker in our little operation. During calving I pull my snowmobile suit on over my nightgown, poke my bare feet into felt-pack boots, yank a man's winter cap down over my head, grab mittens and a flashlight, and head for the barn, just barely awake.

So, Grandma, I haven't changed much from the tomboy kid you disapproved of. I'm still "messing" with horses every chance I get and now have honky cows to keep track of too. I can hear you snort, "You'll get yourself killed." Possibly, but I try to be reasonably careful. And if that does happen, I'll go out happy with my life, doing something that I thoroughly enjoy. Not too many people can say that.

So you can go back to your straight-backed rocking chair — I'm sure you have one, wherever you are — and be sure to keep that grim scowl on your face so anyone passing who knew you when you were here will be able to pick you out.

FLORENCE F. RENFROW   One Day on the Farm

Never a peaceful moment,
  on that busy summer's day.
The wind upset the chicken feed
  and blew it all away.
The cows got out, broke down the fence,
  and had to be put in.
And, half and hour later,
  had to do it all again.
The shop in town called out to say
  the parts had come, all right.
But two were wrong and two weren't there
  and the price was out of sight.

The biscuits burned, the beans boiled dry,
  the cat was up a tree.
The dogs wouldn't let her come back down.
  She cried so pitifully.
And, finally, when it seemed that there
  might be a little rest,
The thunder rolled and a nasty storm
  developed in the west.
The chicks were out in the flying dirt,
  behind the water can.
She got them into the brooder house
  just as the rain began.

Her husband called — he needed help,
  the tarp was flying wide,
And the seed in the truck was getting wet;
  they finally got it tied.

With knuckles bleeding, hair blown wild,
　　she rescued Anna's pup,
And headed into the wind for home
　　and then the storm let up.
Soaked to the skin and chilled to the bone,
　　she watched the clouds disperse.
Tomorrow would be better.
　　It couldn't be any worse.

NELLIE WESTERSKOW ⚞ **From *Arctic Splendor***
to *Sunset Mountain*

By the time I filed for my homestead, I knew my neighbor Nels was a good, kind gentleman, so when he asked me to marry him, I said I would.

On July 16, 1921, we were married at Preacher Olsen's house. We picked up my trunk and went to Nels's ranch. Nels and his partner, Bill, had moved their shacks together after they proved up on their homesteads. Those two rooms and a little hallway were our first home together.

The first night of our marriage, Nels and I carried our bedroll to a grove of currant bushes about a half-mile south of the house. When we heard horses coming at a gallop, we knew our friends intended to have a good old-fashioned shivaree! The next morning, our back room was full of junk, including the wheels and tongue off the buggy. We sure had a job getting it all out.

The next night we put a note on our door, "Gone to Harding on horseback," and hid our saddles in the manger. We took our bedroll to the same draw and before long we heard horses coming again. Our friends found the saddles in the barn and tied them high on the corral gate. Nels's old-time saddle must have weighed sixty pounds. We found a note on it saying, "Next time, don't ride bareback!"

Nels and I rode horseback a lot that first month of our marriage, along the deep cottonwood draws and up to Lone Mountain and the Short Pine Hills. The fragrant buckbrush blooming in the draws reminded me of the creeping arbutus back in Wisconsin.

At mealtime Nels and I had to share the only fork until Nels found another at an abandoned homestead when he was out riding.

Soon I realized that Nels had depended on Bill to make the decisions and do the hard work. When Nels went to Newell, South Dakota, buying feed for the sheep and potatoes, cabbage, and carrots for our winter food supply, I stayed home alone to watch the sheep and cows.

The first night, after I locked the sheep in our high board corral, I heard an awful racket. I grabbed our double-barreled shotgun and fired two shots in the air on my way down to the corral. Coyotes had gotten in, and in the moonlight I saw a couple of lambs staggering around with blood on their necks. I drove the sheep back over the broken gate and got them bedded down, then fixed the gate. Both injured lambs died.

The next evening I brought the sheep into the corral early and noticed some ducks circling the reservoir. I ran to the house for the shotgun and loaded the last shell. When I peeked over the dam I could see six ducks on the water. I aimed at the middle of the group and fired. Only two flew away.

I took the other four to the house and showed Nels one when he came home. "Oh boy," he said, "now we have some meat to eat. How many times did you have to shoot?"

When I showed him the other three, he said, "Now how in the Sam Hill did you get those? Did you scare them to death?"

He had to believe me when I told him the story. We skinned the ducks and put them in cold saltwater for the night. I fried them in the morning and we had meat for a couple of days.

One spring, I was disking with our horses Buck and Happy on a three-horse disk when our neighbor, Rex Smith, rode by. He offered to let me use his old mare, Beauty; I did a lot of disking before I took her back. Rex also had a light twelve-inch breaking plow two horses could pull. I bought it with a three-dollar cream check and seeded about thirty acres of oats by hand, dragging it in with the two-horse drag. Using my new plow, I broke six acres of land for corn with Buck and Happy.

Once we traded two horses for a fresno, to scrape the manure out of the corrals and to put in dams on our range so the stock would not have to travel so far to water. I drove the three horses while Nels handled the fresno, scraping up the dirt. Then I drove up the embankment and dumped it so Nels would not have to walk so much since he had a bad ankle. My legs would quiver at night when I sat milking the cows; that was my rest period.

Nels and I left the ranch in 1963, and he died in 1966. In the summer of 1972, unable to drive after cataract surgery, I bought a three-wheel bicycle from Sears and Roebuck and rode to visit friends and run errands. It was hard to pedal up hills, so I got off and led it. I rode it to the skating rink during the winter and slid on the ice.

Until 1991 I still skied when there was enough snow, using the skis I bought for our son Norman in 1948. I like to ski in the moonlight and pack a trail. The next day the snow thaws a bit and then freezes to make a good fast run.

But in January 1992, I had an accident that might keep me off the skis. I came home from a meeting after dark. Hurrying to take garbage to the compost pile and food to a stray cat, I slipped and fell, landing on my right knee and right hip. I couldn't get up, but I knew I had to get back into the house or freeze to death. I began to rock my hind end back and forth while inching forward.

I made it into the house, through the kitchen, and to the bedroom. Since I couldn't reach the phone, I prayed that someone would try to call me and realize something was wrong when I didn't answer. With my coat and stocking cap on, I slept on the floor. The pain in my knee was awful, but I could relieve it somewhat by propping it up on a rolled towel.

Eighteen hours later, two friends came by and called the ambulance to take me to the hospital. My knee wasn't broken; it was my hip. When the doctor put a steel pin in my leg bone, it sounded like someone was driving a fence post into hard ground.

I was born in July 1900 in Norway. I've never tired of going to the Short Pine Hills near Buffalo, South Dakota, to camp by the Chickadee Springs to hear the birds sing and to lie back on a carpet of pine needles and watch the clouds. Steaks and coffee taste so much better over a campfire, and sleep is so peaceful on the grassy earth.

MARGARET TRAUTMAN
And the Grasshoppers Came

July 3, 1938: Grasshoppers began to light in the yard. At first the chickens ran everywhere, gobbling, but soon they were so full they wouldn't even look at a 'hopper. Turkeys died from the harsh legs and bodies in their crops, as they couldn't digest the rough fibers.

The 'hoppers came in clouds all afternoon, carried by the wind. The farmyard became a living mass of creatures, crawling on everything and crunching every place. Paul's gloves were eaten full of holes in minutes, as were clothes hanging on the line, especially sheets. The dog dish, the water pans for chickens, the water tank, all were a living mass. The dog crawled under the porch as 'hoppers covered him.

As night came, the 'hoppers began to cover fence posts, gates, the door step; we would hear this crunching, crackling sound. We tried covering garden vegetables, like the lettuce and peas, but they ate through the cloth or crept underneath and chomped away. The carrot tops were eaten off even with the ground. We swept off the screen door as they crawled up and literally covered it.

Finally the wind subsided and the grasshoppers made themselves at home, anywhere and everywhere. The neighbor had a nice field of barley, green and lush, a late seeding. They ate it down until it looked as if it was plowed.

DAWN SENIOR *Never Alone*

My life is about distances, rough landscapes so vast that many whole snow-storms can be watched at once, separated by fair skies. My story is about a human being living in many kinds of wind; the breathtaking perfection of wildflowers so small no one has given them a name; sagebrush hills where hundreds of antelope look like tiny sparkles of reflected sunlight as they migrate through the frozen ghost of an ancient sea.

I grew up here in a log cabin my family built at the foot of Wyoming's Snowy Range. My father taught me the skills to be an artist and a writer, and this place gave me the ideas. Although we own no cattle, I make my living from the land as surely as the neighbor I help on roundups. My art and writing are as dependent on the character of these forests, these cliffed draws and open ranges, as the sheepherder dodging lightning in an alpine meadow or the logger waiting out the spring thaw.

I struggle to describe the velvet-textured scent of wild moss flowers fanned around me by my mare's galloping hooves, or try to draw shadowy mysteries pooled in a sego lily's cup, the way a deer spanks her fawn with a forehoof, or lizards grapple and fling each other from a pinnacle of split boulders. I seek the words of people I know, like the spare, creased rancher who sloshed his cowboy boots up to me at a gathering in town the other day and asked, "You know what we used to do out on the ranch when it'd rain like this?"

"What?"

"We'd let it."

Or the young cowboy with his yodeling laugh: "One time I'm galloping along at a dead run and my horse catches both front hooves in a gopher hole. He turns a complete somersault in the air, and, by golly, when he come down on his feet I'm still in the saddle."

Or the elderly Arapaho leaders who took me to a secret, sacred site where they tested my sense of humor with white man jokes (and Arapaho jokes, Cheyenne jokes, Lakota jokes).

I become part of the stream of memories, the river of stories from this land, beginning with fossil bones I pull from the creek, down through Arapaho elders whose words bring long-dead heroes back to life, visionary warriors and scouts whose courage you can still feel pulsing across the reverberating earth. The stream flows on to me through descendants of the first ranching families, like the old woman who, many years ago, set me on her lap and told me how her granddaddy, one of the early explorers of these mountains, had awakened one morning with his hair and beard frozen to the ground. Had to hack himself free with his knife.

I become one of the gullies carrying these stories down to the children, along with my own rivulet. Sometimes I realize that even though I'm only thirty-five, to the children I am that old pioneer lady with the stories from another time, another world. Once, when I told a classroom of kids about my life at the cabin, how we used chisels and iron dogs and drawknives to build, how we lug water from the hand pump and read by lamplight, I mentioned driving up to the mountains to haul down logs in the pickup. One little boy's eyes widened and he blurted, "You mean you had *cars* back then?"

I tell about the autumn day I sat on the stream bank watching yellow cottonwood leaves fall onto shiny green, blue, and brown reflections to create shifting, mesmerizing designs. I heard loud crunches in the fallen leaves across the stream, and down from the boulders on the draw's wall came the biggest badger I'd ever seen. The huge old fellow yawned and stretched, shook his hair like coarse wild rye, sniffed closer, gave the moist soil a tentative rake with his giant claws. He waddled with his shuffling gait to the opposite bank, lapped water with his tongue, waded across, and came right up to me. Nearsighted, I guess, didn't know I sat there. He lifted a paw to climb over my lap, then froze. He looked into my eyes, his nose inches from mine. I stared back, trying not to blink, and admired the earthen depths of his eyes, the soft gray stripes on his face. Neither of us was afraid. At last, he turned aside and wandered up the draw to hunt.

Although I've been in love more than once, I'm not yet married, partly because I haven't been able to live somewhere else for very long. I like other places — more mellow and green, with people just as charming, more educated and refined. But I keep remembering words that came to me in a dream, perhaps my father's voice, or maybe the thought of an eagle. I remember, and wonder if they're true: "So long as you are with the land, you can never be alone."

BONNIE LARSON STAIGER ⟍ *A Sense of Place*

Given the choice
I would walk
every measured mile
of the contoured prairie

take up a handful of earth
knowing it's time to plant
by the smell of the soil

kick gravel stones
along the section line
and startle a meadowlark
off her grass-covered nest

count redwings in the cattails
unearth a Lakota fire ring
and give thanks to the four winds

Contributors
Acknowledgments
Credits

Contributors

PATRICIA ARCHIE (*page 154*) was born in Minneapolis and grew up on a ranch along Horseshoe Creek near Glendo, Wyoming. Patricia and her husband are both descended from several ranching generations and raised their two children on a ranch five miles farther up the creek. Now a daughter and her husband, with two daughters of their own, have joined the family ranch. A former elementary school teacher, Patricia received a B.A. at the University of Wyoming.

CHERYL ARENDS (*page 159*) lived on her parents' farm near Ponca, Nebraska, until leaving for college in 1964. Both sets of grandparents settled in northeast Nebraska, and Cheryl finds her "spiritual, poetic home in the countryside of Cedar and Dixon counties." An English teacher, she now owns forty acres of cedar-covered river-bluff land southeast of Ponca where she works summers and weekends restoring wildlife habitat. "My father," she says, "knew the name of every wildflower. My mother represents the stability of the land and the people on it."

CRYSTAL SHARPING ASHLEY (*page 246*) of Pukwana, South Dakota, is deputy county auditor of the town where she grew up (population 260), but considers herself first and foremost a rancher, and hopes the economy will allow her to return to ranching full-time. With a B.S. from Dakota Wesleyan, she returned to the family ranch east of town, where with three daughters and her husband she hosts rodeos, raising Corriente cattle for roping and bucking stock.

SUSAN AUSTIN (*page 146*) is a writer and wildlife biologist and does "odd jobs like carpenter's helper and house painter." Growing up in a military family, she didn't understand the expression "a sense of place" until she moved into a cabin in the Teton Valley of Idaho with her husband. "Getting to know a place," she says, "is a meditation, and like meditation the discoveries are never done." After ten years, they are moving into a new house.

JULENE BAIR (*page 281*) is a free-lance writer, teacher, and editor who grew up on a farm in western Kansas, leaving it at eighteen for a sojourn in San Francisco with her then husband. After a divorce eight years later, she moved to a remote cabin in the Mojave Desert. With a two-year-old son, she attended the University of Iowa, receiving an M.A. and an M.F.A. She's managed an audio firm, done accounting, been a park ranger, cowboyed, farmed, taught, and written. She says, "The skies, distances, and aridity of the High Plains form the meaning of home for me."

LUCILLE CRESS BAKER (*page 183*) has lived in the country and small towns in Missouri, Nebraska, and Wyoming. She was sheltered until the age of seven, when her seventy-seven-year-old father died; "then it was work" for room and board through high school, later in the fields with horse-drawn machinery and tractors. She started driving a car at age twelve and still does at ninety-two — "No accident yet." She's worked in offices and done "beauty work" and carpentry, gone on cattle drives, climbed windmills, shot skunks and porcupines. "Laughed, cried, played, worked, loved, been loved, wife, mother of five daughters, grandmother, great, and great-great, failed, got up, saved by love of God, looking forward to Tomorrow."

MARGARET M. BARNHART (*page 148*) grew up in small-town North Dakota with "an inborn appreciation for the subtle beauty of the prairie," discovering the devastating effect of isolation when she moved to Enid, Montana. She is adjunct lecturer of English composition at Dickinson (North Dakota) State University, and executive director of Arts on the Prairie, besides being involved in several state writing projects.

JEANNE M. BARTAK (*page 194*) is a country woman who grew up on a wheat farm in North Dakota. She worked as a secretary until her boss encouraged her to go back to school. She received her B.S. in range management at Montana State University in Bozeman. Now she and her husband, Steve, are raising three sons, Jason, Chris, and Brent, and a daughter, Jessica, on a north central Nebraska farm, raising corn, soybeans, and beef cattle.

VIRGINIA BENNETT (*page 211*) was raised in an agricultural family in New Hampshire and moved to Arizona in 1970, where she barrel-raced for a few years before marrying Pete Bennett. She has worked alongside her husband, co-managing Western cattle ranches, for the last twenty years. At present, they manage the Tice Ranch, a combination hay and cattle operation and corporate retreat in Washington. She started writing cowboy poetry in 1988, and broke colts for seventeen years. Driving a team of Percheron draft horses, she is carrying on the tradition of her teamster father and grandfather. Calling herself "simply a high-school grad," she home-teaches their sixteen-year-old son, Jessie.

FRANCIE M. BERG (*page 265*) was born on her parents' homestead in Garfield County in the Missouri breaks, raised on their ranch in Miles City, and has lived since her marriage in North Dakota. A writer and editor, she publishes a health journal and writes regional history, including *North Dakota: Land of Changing Seasons*, and *South Dakota: Land of Shining Gold*.

VIRGINIA M. BLACKFORD (*page 260*) lists her profession as teacher of "everything except math." She's managed a hotel restaurant, served as a home demonstration agent, appeared on radio programs promoting home economics, catered parties for fraternities, and drawn blueprints for oil and construction companies. Her mother began college at seventeen and became one of the first women to graduate from Gustavus Adolphus College in Minnesota.

VIOLA HAYS BLAIR (*page 219*), born in Oklahoma, attended country schools in South Dakota; her mother died in Whitewood, as she narrates. She was valedictorian of her high school class in Deadwood, and of her class at Black Hills Teachers College (now University) in Spearfish. She now lives in Pleasant Valley, near Sturgis, and writes poetry.

SHIRLEY BLUNT (*page 188*) lists her profession as "ranch person — bookkeeper, cook, and some-time cowboy." Raised on a dryland homestead, she rode horseback to a one-room country school and later received a secretarial degree from Northern Montana College. She married a rancher forty-five years ago and they raised five children on a place purchased from the original homesteaders in 1954. Her writing daughter "pushed" her into writing, her "safety valve." She's disturbed at the current lack of knowledge of the realities of life even a generation ago: "They were tough stock, and the quitters never started west. No wonder we are a boneheaded bunch of individual thinkers, considering the genetics."

SHARON BOEHMER (*page 75*) is a forty-six-year resident of northeastern Nebraska, raised to "work hard, be honest, do whatever you do well, and be proud of who you are." She planned a nursing career until stricken with rheumatoid arthritis. After lengthy hospitalizations, joint replacements, and losing 165 pounds, she is glad to be alive — "Life is good!" She's Candy Cane as a member of Clowns of America International. She and her husband, Richard, have two daughters.

CAROL BOIES (*page 182*) started writing as a South Dakota high school student, graduating from Gregory High School; she's taken college courses in swimming and horsemanship. After high school, she moved to Wyoming, where she fell in love with "the openness of the land and the people," including her husband. In 1982, they moved to Crook County, where she joined the Bear Lodge Writers' Group, learning and receiving encouragement. Five years ago, her family, including two daughters, moved to a farm only three miles from her childhood home.

ETHEL GOUDY BRIGGS (*page 104*) was born in 1910, four years after her father proved up on his claim on Mill Creek Flat near Park City, Montana. In 1931 she married Leo Briggs, whose family land adjoined the Goudy place. Leo bought a small ranch from his uncle where the couple lived. Besides housework and helping with ranch chores, Ethel maintained a large vegetable garden, along with strawberry and potato patches and flower beds. She canned and froze garden produce, and put up dozens of pints of jams and jellies. Donna Gray's interview was published by Smithmark Publishers in Gray's book, *Pioneer Women*.

MAVIS E. BUCHOLZ (*page 40*) has lived in the North Dakota countryside all her life, attending country schools and McClusky High School. Married thirty-nine years, she has two sons, one an attorney and the other a captain in the U.S. Air Force. After her retirement from thirteen years as business manager and secretary of a public school, she and her husband sold their farm and now live in a thirty-foot fifth wheel.

B. J. BUCKLEY (*pages 195, 204*), a Wyoming native, now lives in Montana. She spent seventeen years teaching in artists-in-the-schools programs in several plains states. Her first book of poems, *Artifacts*, was published in 1987 by Willow Bee Publishing, Saratoga, Wyoming. She was the 1994 winner of the Cumberland Poetry Review Robert Penn Warren Narrative Poetry Contest and received a Wyoming Arts Council literature fellowship. She is studying fine arts/education at the University of Montana, Missoula.

EVA POTTS BURTON (*page 191*) spent thirty-two years in Sheridan, Wyoming, raising six "wonderful kids," with intermittent teaching to supplement her income. Born on her parents' homestead fifty miles north of Gillette, she walked two miles to a one-room log school her father built on Little Powder River through eighth grade. After high school in Campbell County, she left college during World War II to marry Ed Wells. She never returned; her parents said, "married women don't belong in college." She hunted and gardened, canning and freezing most of the family's food. After Ed's death four days before their twenty-fifth anniversary, she married Howard Burton in 1986, and lives in Glendo, Wyoming.

LAURIE WAGNER BUYER (*page 275*) was born in Edinburgh, Scotland, and raised on military bases and in suburbs until moving west from Chicago in 1975. She says, "My connection to the land has become a firm foundation on which I base my daily life and my spiritual beliefs. Small mysteries and miracles are the threads that weave our lives together — both to other people and to the land and animals we live with. I am blessed to lead the life I lead." With a B.A. in English from Montana State, she's worked on plains ranches, including on the north fork of the Flathead River near Glacier National Park, and on the O Bar Y and Flying A ranches on the upper Green River near Cora, Wyoming. She and her husband now have a cow/calf operation in Colorado.

ELIZABETH CANFIELD (*pages 90, 206*), a lifelong Wyoming resident and rancher, now lives in Sundance. Retired, she calls herself an "ex-teacher, ex-businesswoman, and ex-rancher." Born in her grandfather's log home south of Upton, she taught in rural schools and worked for the U.S. Department of Agriculture in Denver, Colorado, as well as on newspapers in Torrington and Sundance. After World War II, she ranched with her husband, owned a farm equipment company, and raised three children. She began to write again in 1990 after her husband's death, and has published news, essays, editorials, and poems.

DEB CARPENTER (*page 87*) grew up on a cattle ranch and farm where her dad began raising elk twenty years ago; her husband, Dan, now helps with the cattle/elk operation. She says, "I existed in Illinois during my college years," receiving a B.A. in literature from Wheaton College (Illinois), and an M.A. in education from Chadron State (Nebraska). She teaches at Oglala Lakota College on the Pine Ridge Reservation in South Dakota, and writes poetry, short stories, articles, novels, and songs. In 1995, her first book, *Nature's Beauty Kit*, was published by Fulcrum, Inc., and her first album of original music, *Welcome to the North Star Motel*, was released.

MARGARET CARR (*page 261*) calls herself "another ranch woman." She grew up in Wyoming's Buffalo Basin, married Wick W. Carr in 1928, and they raised four children on ranches near Mona. She served as postmaster, operated the Mona Store, and taught school for twenty-nine years. Widowed after sixty-one years, she lives in Glendo. Besides writing she sews, and paints in oil and watercolors.

BETTY STARKS CASE (*page 280*) was born in Miller, South Dakota, and raised on the Rosebud Reservation on land leased from the Lakota tribe. Granddaughter of a newspaper editor, she had a schoolteacher and a poetic farmer for parents. She attended college before blowing into her husband's life, according to him, on a Dakota tumbleweed. Her diverse background, "along with a passion for Wyoming mountains and wildlife," feeds her writing hunger with materials for her feature stories, newspaper columns, and books, including *Maggie: Set Free in the Wyoming Rockies*.

VIRGINIA A. CASSELLS (*pages 62, 252*) was born and has lived most of her life in Nebraska, attending country schools and completing medical technology training at the University of Colorado. Her love of animals led to raising, training, and showing dogs and horses, and she led 4-H Club dog and light horse projects. She once made her horse rear to discourage a potential buyer. After retirement, she worked with her archaeologist son, walking seventy thousand acres of surveys and helping excavate several sites.

SUE CHAULK (*pages 94, 157, 201, 270*) lives with her husband on the same ranch in western Nebraska where she grew up. For a while they lived in Colorado and drove to the ranch on weekends. After twenty years, they moved "home to find making a living running cows harder than ever, but also better than anything else." Besides being a fourth-generation rancher in Morrill County, she is outreach coordinator at Box Butte General Hospital in Alliance. Asked in grade school to finger-paint her favorite animal, she chose a calf, and during the few times in her life when she didn't own cattle, she felt "like a partial person."

BETH HATHAWAY COLE (*page 294*) is a truck driver for an interstate construction company, working with her husband out-of-state for eight months a year to support their ranch. She's also substituted in grades K–5, and is a certified dental assistant who received a national award for her skills. She's "learned that to be truly successful one must never be afraid to bend his back, learn everything available, and not be stingy with your emotions. Life is like a horse race — never say whoa!" This attitude helped her family as they "struggled together to buy a farm."

GAYDELL COLLIER (*page 3*) has ranched with her husband, Roy, for more than thirty years, raising registered Morgan horses, Hereford and Jersey cattle, and some sheep. In 1977 she established Backpocket Ranch Bookshop in her home, a mail-order business. Doubleday published three horsemanship books that she coauthored and her writing has appeared in many magazines. Since 1985, she's been director of Crook County Library System in Sundance, Wyoming, and was named Wyoming Librarian of the Year in 1990.

BERTIE ROBBINS COX (*page 149*) came from artistic parents — Cleo and Orel Robbins — but worked in a coal mine until she was injured in 1992. Harking to her Cherokee heritage, she has become a writer and artist.

With her sister, Donna Wilson, she opened Western Heritage in Gillette, Wyoming, using antlers and rawhide as materials for their art. Drawing inspiration from Mother Earth, she says, the sisters use ancient art techniques to release life from some of nature's most beautiful resources.

LINDA CRANDALL (*page 224*) is a sixth-generation farmer in Nebraska's Platte River Valley and teaches speech, drama, and creative writing at Holdrege Senior High School. Born in Nebraska, Linda spent her childhood on a homestead near Cody, Wyoming, and moved often as her family followed her engineer father to construction sites around the world. With a B.A. and M.A. from the University of Nebraska at Kearney, she won a 1993 fellowship for study of Swedish immigrant customs and a 1995 award for the pioneer family histories her students wrote while reading Willa Cather.

ROBERTA Z. CROUSE (*page 153*) ranched for forty-five years, living for thirty years at the Ladder Ranch near Cheyenne, and the V Bar east of Centennial, Wyoming, before she and her husband, George, sold it and retired. Born on a farm at Iowa Center, thirteen miles east of Chugwater, Wyoming, she attended grade schools in Iowa Center. She writes three "Barbie-Q's" columns a month for the Cow-Belles, auxiliary to the Wyoming Stockgrowers, and has researched and written regional history, as well as playing piano for her community church for ten years.

NANCY CURTIS (*page 132*) owns and operates a cattle ranch near Glendo, Wyoming, and has operated her business, High Plains Press, since 1985. With thirty books about Wyoming and the West in print, High Plains has won several awards, including 1991 and 1994 Western Heritage Wrangler awards for outstanding poetry book from the National Cowboy Hall of Fame. She's been married to Doug for thirty years and serves as chair of the Wyoming Council for the Arts.

LYN DALEBOUT (*page 135*) studied science, receiving her B.A. in Biology from the University of Utah in Salt Lake City in 1977, but when she returned to the Tetons in 1980, it was to pursue her artistic interests. An educator and astrologer, Lyn seeks to integrate her scientific and artistic interests through writing and has organized regional and community events and performances designed to explore various facets of questions. She is publishing her first chapbook of poems through her own small press.

PATTI DeJONGE (*page 288*) wrote "For a Farmer's Wife" from her own experiences as a farmwife. She raised three children with her husband, Gary, before attending the University of Nebraska at Kearney. She wrote for various publications, serving as farm editor for the *Hastings Tribune* (Nebraska) until her death in 1992, at age forty-two, of breast cancer.

DONNA WILLIAMS DEREEMER (*page 320*) lived in Maryland and California while her husband served with the armed forces, but has spent twenty-five years on a Wyoming ranch raising four children. She graduated with a B.A. in music from the University of Wyoming, and taught elementary music. She remains active in the Laramie County Cow-Belles and Stockgrowers since retiring to the city. Along with writing stories and poems, she composes and arranges music, does needlework and gardening, volunteers at the Old West Museum, and works for the Wyoming state legislature when it's in session.

KELLY REBECCA DEREEMER (*page 306*), Donna's youngest daughter, was born with cystic fibrosis and died at the ranch in June of 1987. She was thirteen years old.

KALLI DESCHAMPS (*page 14*) is a rancher's wife, mother of three, visual artist, writer, and teacher. She moved from Chicago to Montana, from city girl to farmer. In forty years of ranching in western Montana, she worked with dairy cows, yearling steers, on cow/calf and hay and grain operations, and raised purebred Gelbviehs. "Sandwiched among the stalls," she writes, "was the growing stack of paintings and drawings, weaving and batiks I exhibited and sold." Twenty years as a high school art teacher inspired her first published novel, *Color Me Red*, in 1995 and its unpublished sequel, *Shroud Across the Valley*. Now "the nest is empty," but her jewelry design business, Whispering Stones, is growing, and a myriad of stories lurk in her mind.

DIXIE DeTUERK (*page 283*) is a native Nebraskan and a twenty-one-year veteran teacher with two children. She grew up in Mason City, where the population was then 260 and is now about 150. Both sets of grandparents farmed. With few paying jobs for teenagers, Dixie started detasseling corn for seed corn companies at age twelve at a dollar an hour. With a B.A. in English and art and an M.A. in education from Kearney State (now the University of Nebraska at Kearney) she taught one year (for $8,000 in salary) and saved enough money for four months in Europe and Africa. She then moved to Ogallala, where she has taught English and language arts and now teaches eighth grade.

BEULAH G. DONNELL (*page 71*) was born in Crawford, Nebraska, in 1922 and spent her childhood with grandparents, uncles, and aunts until her mother remarried a rancher. Beulah helped with chores and showed registered Herefords at fairs and stock shows. After attending Chadron State College and teaching in a country school, she became deputy county superintendent at Hot Springs, South Dakota. Then she enlisted in the

Marines. After the war, she returned to Hot Springs "and met Art, who had just come home to see his sister. . . . We fell in love, married, and raised six children." An artist, Beulah started Donnell's Mini-Mall in 1966 and teaches classes to children and adults.

MARY DUFFY (*page 206*) writes, "I was lucky enough to grow up in close proximity to my grandparents, spending whole weekends with them often and practically living with them in the summer. It was a relationship that my four children never had the opportunity to develop." Born in a central South Dakota farming community, Mary attended Highmore High School, graduated from South Dakota State University with a B.A. in journalism, and is a newspaper staff writer and columnist.

NORMA NELSON DUPPLER (*page 152*) grew up on the ranch in eastern North Dakota where she now lives. Since she no longer has horses, she uses an ATV to explore ancient burial and religious sites of Native American cultures spanning eight thousand years. She's writing a novel that includes references to actual sites on the ranch overlooking the Sheyenne Valley. She worked five years as a reporter for a large newspaper and interviewed various tribal people in North Dakota. Since 1991 she has been Barnes County emergency manager and works with several public service organizations.

PENNY S. DYE (*page 249*) is a mixed-animal veterinarian in the Black Hills of South Dakota. Growing up on a wheat farm near Chappell, Nebraska, Penny was active in music and Future Farmers of America. With her sister she participated in an F.F.A. project raising 150 ewes, and she was the first Nebraska girl to receive the American Farmer Degree. As an honors agriculture major at the University of Nebraska, Lincoln, she was preaccepted to vet school, receiving her D.V.M. from Ohio State University at Columbus in 1988. With her husband, Jack, of Alliance, she moved to South Dakota.

SHANNON DYER (*page 212*) was a city girl when she saw the Nebraska sandhills for the first time and remarked, "This is a barren wilderness. I'd never live here." That's the last time she said "never." Married in 1982, she moved to ranch country where, with her husband, she runs a feed store. A taste for the sandhills developed over several years and "now I'd never live anywhere else. The rest of the world can scramble after the best image," she writes, "but life out here is *real*." She received a B.A. in Economics from the University of Nebraska, Lincoln.

ROBYN CARMICHAEL EDEN (*page 196*) is a wife, mother, horse-woman, writer, farmer, reporter turned public relations practitioner, and "a confirmed prairie dweller who is never happier than when I can stand on a can of tuna and see thirty miles in all directions." Though she grew up in a farming family and married a farmer's son, they chose not to be farmers. "But once you belong to the land, it never lets you go." So they live on an acreage with apple trees and woods and horse pastures, where cats, a dog, and two growing sons romp.

MARIE ELLENBERGER (*page 253*) moved to Colorado in 1956. Looking back at her first forty years, she says, it's evident her energies "were devoted to children." The death of her first child caused deep depression, and her sixth child and only son was born when she was thirty-seven. After a four-year break, she resumed teaching at the only country school in the area and retired after twenty-two years of elementary classes. She has lived in the same home for thirty-three years.

JACQUELINE S. ELLIOTT (*page 241*) became a rancher's wife who handled cattle and raised and raced quarter horses before she met her first mule. After a divorce, she received a B.S. in criminology from the University of Southern Colorado and an A.A. in criminal justice from Pueblo Community College while raising her children. With her present husband she now raises, trains, and shows mules all over the U.S.

GENEVIEVE EPPICH (*page 34*), now a widow with eight children, lives in the ranch house in Thompson Park near Mancos, Colorado, where she was born in 1919. Her degree, she writes, is "just a hard-working ranch girl" who farmed, ran sheep and cattle and eight hundred laying hens, and drove a school bus for twenty-six years. Her grandparents homesteaded the place in 1887 and her parents bought it in 1946, the same year Genevieve married. Her husband died when their youngest child was nine. It's now a centennial ranch, says Genevieve, "and I intend to stay here."

CORA ESCH (*page 44*) is an innkeeper who operates a bed and breakfast in Spalding, Nebraska. Her forefathers arrived in Blackbird County, now Thurston County, in 1895. Her parents homesteaded unsuccessfully in Grass Range, Montana, before returning to Walthill, Nebraska, where her father traded horses. She grew up on the Omaha Indian Reservation and attended schools in Walthill. With her farmer husband, Cora lived on the Cedar River until moving to the outskirts of Spalding; married fifty-five years, she has ten living children.

PATRICIA MIDGE FARMER (*pages 34, 124*) fell in love with the "outback of America" after marrying and moving to a northeast Wyoming ranch in 1959. Her profession? "Danged if I know. Earth Goddess? I work in investments and write, sometimes house drudge; time flies." She has credits from several Wyoming junior colleges and will graduate "if/when I pick a major. . . . I jealously guard and defend our way of life. Oh yes, I'm very ladylike and demure as I totter off into geezerdom."

FRANCES BURJES FITCH (*page 266*) was born and raised on a homestead in Haakon County, South Dakota, where she now lives with her husband, Ed. After college she worked as part of the farm and ranch operation and taught rural schools for nine terms. A 4-H leader, she also taught Sunday school and still teaches children to dance. An avid sportswoman, she played softball and now takes part in the Senior Olympics. In 1994 she helped build a house with Habitat for Humanity.

RHAE FOSTER (*pages 219, 279*) "grew up restless and eager to escape the desolate prairie [Cheyenne, Wyoming, near where her grandfather homesteaded in 1908] and leave small-town life behind." She returned after eight years, but left again, "convinced there must be a more suitable place for me," in Virginia, Ohio, Pennsylvania, Florida, or North Carolina. In 1992, homesick for the West, searching for "a town that needed me," she tried Colorado Springs before giving in to "an enchantment luring me back to my roots, a spiritual pull," and returned once more to her hometown of Cheyenne.

TERRILL FOSTER (*page 11*) was born during the Great Depression, married a rancher, and has lived in Wyoming all her sixty-three years. After having four daughters, she obtained a teaching degree (with her husband and mother-in-law's approval). A kindergarten teacher for twenty-two years, she hopes to teach into the twenty-first century. With husband Ralph, she plans to retire on their ranch, "now that it's fixed up like we like it," including a movie room and darkroom.

SHARON FRANK (*page 323*) was raised primarily by her grandparents. From her grandfather, an auctioneer and feed salesman in Denver, she learned to love cattle, horses, and rural life, and calls herself a jack of all trades and master of none. Doing a college research paper about the beef cattle industry, she conducted seven interviews with industry people and knew she'd found her calling. She became a farmwife near Greeley, Colorado, in 1991.

CINDY FRENCH (*page 5*) lived on ranches in Washington and Montana until she turned twelve. Later, she recaptured country life by keeping horses, currently a paint filly named Foxy. Cindy works as a legal secretary with a Colorado district attorney's office, has written newspaper columns, and acted as chauffeur for her four sons.

TONI KIM FRENCH (*page 307*) grew up — a wonderful childhood, she says — on an eastern Nebraska farm with her five sisters and one brother. Attending Chadron State College in western Nebraska for a B.S. in education, she met and married her husband. She has taught school in the country system for sixteen years.

ELEANORE GARREAU (*page 162*) is a lifelong resident of the prairie, active in operating her ranch in Dewey County, South Dakota, for the past sixty years. Born and raised on this same property, she left the ranch for only five years, while her husband worked for the Civilian Conservation Corps building dams and roads. In 1941 they came back to the ranch. Eleanore was a director for the Farmers Home Administration, works for the Green Thumb Elderly Program, and serves on the state Advisory Council on Aging.

SUSANNE K. GEORGE (*pages 13, 111, 289*) has become closer to the land through being a farmer's daughter and a farmer's wife. Her son is now farming the land his great-grandfather once tilled, her home place, and she still rides and raises paint horses. Both of her books, *The Adventures of the Woman Homesteader* (1992) and the forthcoming biography, *Kate M. Cleary,* concern Western women and their relation to the land. She is current president of the Western Literature Association, has edited both an atlas of the Big Bend region of the Platte River and *Wellsprings,* a poetry anthology.

BETH GIBBONS (*page 222*) married a farmer who had been her best friend for thirty years. When she lost her husband to a sudden heart attack, she was "really *alone* for the first time in my life." She grew up the third of six children on a ranch in Nebraska and earned a B.A. from Chadron State College in 1988. She has three grown children and five grandchildren, and still lives on the Gibbons family farm. She plans to marry again, after more than four years of widowhood.

TAMMY HANSEN GILBERT (*pages 165, 287*) lives on Storm Lake Ranch, south of Alliance, Nebraska. She writes a weekly humor column and writes and performs two weekly humor segments on KNOP-TV in North Platte. Divorced, with a six-year-old daughter, Sheila, Tammy has lived in Oklahoma, West Germany, and Lincoln, Nebraska, and recently spent two weeks in the rain forests of Peru with other writers. "Curiosity and joy are two of God's greatest gifts," she says, and expects that looking for adventure and mothering will provide plenty of writing material.

JUNE BRANDER GILMAN (*page 150*) spent her teens on a Montana ranch with her older sister, cutting lodgepole pines to build a ranch house, cabins, a dance hall, and a rodeo arena. She also cowgirled and hired out to do ranch and timber work. After WAC service during World War II in Africa and Italy, she worked as a stenographer for a mining company for forty years while building and running her own ranch. She's participated in the Elko (Nevada) and Montana cowboy poetry gatherings since 1986 and published three books of poetry.

PEGGY COOK GODFREY (*pages 107, 123*) has ranched for twenty-three years in the high valleys of northern New Mexico and southern Colorado. Her business card would look like phone booth graffiti: she's done contract hay baling for twelve years, raised cattle and sold freezer beef, and made and sold jerky for twenty years. She welds and does other repairs on her own machinery and has cowboyed for several ranches. Starting with a little bunch of ewes in 1990, she's sold freezer lamb and summer sausage. She's served on the Moffat (Colorado) school board and been a substitute teacher, and is currently raising a foster child.

JEAN GOEDICKE (*page 69*) was honored with a fifty-year retrospective exhibit of her work at the Nicolaysen Art Museum in Casper, Wyoming, in 1993. A Wyoming native, she traveled with the Mobile Arts Symposium, giving workshops throughout Wyoming, but began serious writing recently; her essay is set in a country school in Lenore, now off the map. She received the Governor's Art Award for outstanding service to the community and state in 1993, and is listed in *Who's Who* for American art and the West. In the 1930s she worked for government relief programs, and she spent thirty-seven years at the Wyoming Employment Security Commission.

ANN L. GORZALKA (*page 46*) was born in Wyoming and has lived there all her life, except for six months in Billings, Montana. Retired from social services, she is married to Mike and has published three books and many articles and photos nationally, regionally, and locally. She lives on an acreage near Bighorn, Wyoming.

TENA COOK GOULD (*page 110*) pursued careers in broadcasting and journalism and has been a college admissions recruiter for Chadron State College since 1992. She's been an active advocate for domestic violence victims. The proprietor of a home-based calligraphy business, she has taught both adult and children's classes. She received her B.A. in mass media *summa cum laude* from Chadron State College and has lived on a variety of ranches and farms in Wyoming and Nebraska. Her husband, Pat, is a state fire marshall and volunteer firefighter. They often visit her father's cow/calf operation — Ed Cook lives north of Lusk, Wyoming.

DONNA GRAY (*pages 77, 104*) calls herself a retired ranch woman and fledgling poet; she lives with her husband on a small ranch in Montana's Paradise Valley, between the Absaroka and Gallatin ranges. A Midwesterner by birth, Donna is a Montanan by choice. Recording stories and recollections by ranch women has given her a "deeper love and a stronger sense of place, a place to be forevermore."

MARY ALICE GUNDERSON (*page 77*), a lifelong Wyoming resident, began writing with nonfiction, photojournalism, and public relations writing for the county library, but she always wrote poetry. She's worked in the artists-in-the-schools program and recently taught fiction writing at Casper College. Her books include *Devils Tower* and *Land-Marked: Stories of Peggy Simson Curry.* Her poetry, essays, and short fiction have appeared in various magazines and anthologies.

SHARON GUSTAFSON (*page 137*) says, "I have come full circle." She spent her first seventeen years on a prairie farm — feeding chickens, milking cows, hauling water to wash clothes and water trees. Then she "went out to see the world, got married, had one son, moved fifteen times, and finally returned to the home place." She now gardens on twenty acres of the homestead in summer, lives and works in Rapid City, South Dakota, in winter. "The sunsets are more beautiful than I remember," she writes; "the pheasants and birds more plentiful, and the soil richer. It's good to be home."

LORI HALE (*page 175*) is self-taught and self-employed, working at home with her husband on Mother Mountain Creations. Her children are grown, but she has four dogs and a salamander named Spot. Raised in Minnesota, she married at sixteen, had both her children before she was nineteen, divorced at twenty-one, and remarried at thirty-four. In the next year, she'd like to write a book for women on how to refinish furniture.

VIVIAN HAMBURG (*pages 70, 216*) lived on the 160-acre irrigated family homestead near Longmont, Colorado, until 1949, when she married George R. Hamburg, a civil engineer. At forty-three, after raising four sons and a daughter, she began twenty-three years of teaching kindergarten in Littleton, Colorado. Retirement has allowed her more time for writing, volunteering in classrooms, reading at the library's children's story time, and for her thirteen grandchildren.

MARVELLE HANSEN (*page 142*) has spent her life in Cass County, Nebraska, and for forty-two years she has farmed, grown corn, milo, wheat, and alfalfa, and raised cattle in partnership with her husband. After twelve years of schooling in Louisville, Nebraska, she taught two years in rural schools. "I was a real honest-to-goodness cowgirl," she says, "not nearly as glamorous as portrayed in Western movies. We used to say we hauled hay every day of the year and in every kind of weather: snow, sleet, ice storms, and occasionally in sunny weather."

TWYLA HANSEN (*pages 26, 161, 173, 255*), a horticulturist, has been landscape consultant and arboretum curator at Nebraska Wesleyan University in Lincoln since 1982. She was raised in northeast Nebraska on the land her grandparents, immigrants from Denmark, farmed in the late 1800s. Her parents quit farming in the 1960s and sold the land because her father didn't want any of his children to farm. Twyla's yard is an urban wildlife habitat that drew "weed notices" from the city — and won the Mayor's Landscape Conservation Award in 1994. "It's nice," she writes, "to know the right hand truly does not know what the left hand is doing, at least in this local government."

EVELYN HARD (*pages 245, 311*), at age sixty-six, now lives in an apartment building. "Oh! I miss my old farm homestead!" She used to hunt elk every season, hiked and fished in the high mountains. Having had no formal schooling, she's self-taught. She's divorced with two sons, loves to read, enjoys her friends, has some health problems, but "refuses to quit functioning."

LINDA HASSELSTROM (*page xiii*) dreamed of racing black stallions until age nine, when she moved to a South Dakota ranch where slow horses and waddling cows were the reality. She began writing while learning to ride her first horse bareback, and still finds both jobs slippery. Her first book, *Windbreak* (Barn Owl Books, 1987), convinced her to write about what she knows; her later nonfiction and poetry concern ranching and the environment. Now living in Cheyenne, Wyoming, she owns the family ranch and commutes to care for it.

MARY ANN HAUGEN (*page 167*) left college for an M.R.S. degree and became a company nomad with her IBM engineer husband. Despite a husband and four children used to a full-time home manager, she completed a nursing degree. Returning to their North Dakota origins, the family now lives in a Tudor-style stone house in a prairie grove. Mary Ann does fill-in preaching at area churches, and is "slowly and doggedly trying to write a novel."

EDNA MAE LINK HEHNER (*page 306*) grew up one of ten children on a farm in the Sodtown area of Buffalo County in south central Nebraska. She attended Kearney Normal School (now the University of Nebraska at Kearney) and taught country school for several years before she married. She died in December of 1990, and many people still miss the informative letters she sent to friends and relatives.

LEE HELVEY (*page 35*) was born near New York City and attended twelve schools, including Smith College and the Ecole des Sciences Politiques in Paris. With her husband, Charles, she spent thirty-four years on a ranch in Montana, now operated by her son, the oldest boy of four children. She loved to ride and work with their Hereford and Red Angus cattle, but says she probably should have been born a hundred years earlier, because "I dislike any gasoline-powered contraption and could easily do without a telephone."

MARILYN HENDERSON (*page 245*) was the oldest of four children on her parents' North Dakota farm, where her father, a carpenter, milked cows until they contracted Bang's disease. She writes, "I married a hard-working, goodhearted farmer," and they have four children. Since becoming a farm-wife, she's been a medical receptionist, a teacher, a school board member, a Sunday school teacher, president of the Ladies Aid, and a hospice volunteer, as well as tending a large garden and a menagerie of animals. "My greatest joy is serving the Lord."

TERRY HENDERSON (*page 313*) returned to college after writing about the death of her husband. Eight years later she remarried and moved to a ranch northeast of Douglas, Wyoming. She's also a volunteer rural fire-fighter who had a busy summer in 1996 fighting grass fires. "Since I am a pretty small female," she says, "most people don't think I can do hard ranch work. Just this weekend, I helped my husband haul thirteen ton of hay," handling every bale.

HELEN MOORE HENRY (*page 265*) has lived all her life in Madison County, Nebraska. She began teaching at age seventeen; at twenty-two she married Sam Henry and moved to Madison, where she worked in a drug-store and at the parimutuel race tracks for ten years. Over the summers she took college courses and in winter she taught school — a total of fifteen years teaching in rural schools and twenty-nine years in Madison. Sam died in 1963 at the age of forty, and Helen retired in 1987 to write poems and history. Recently she documented twenty-seven historic buildings.

A. ROSE HILL (*page 59*) and her husband have lived in the same house in Sheridan, Wyoming, for forty years. Born in Missouri, she came to Wyoming with her mother and three sisters in 1947. She kept the books for her husband's radiator repair business and is now bookkeeper for her son in the same business. She is also the mother of three adopted children, grandmother of three, a church historian, and choir member. Near death at two from a ruptured appendix, she survived four surgeries but was unable to have children of her own. "Two desires, to be a mother and to write, have been driving forces in my life, no matter how mutually exclusive," she writes.

MAE HOFFER (page 293) was born and raised in Ohio with five brothers and two sisters. She farmed with her brother and mother until her mother's death in 1982. In June of 1986, after writing to a North Dakota farmer through *Farm Journal* magazine, she met the man for the first time. After three more visits, they were married on November 14, 1986. She writes, "Been here ever since. I love the Land and all that goes with it. I am country thru and thru."

JOAN HOFFMAN (page 178) says, "I'm a Nebraska woman — born August 22, 1923. Books are as important to me as the next breath. Writing is something I believe, something I believe in. It is almost what I am, rather than what I do. (And I say this even knowing I have no claim to renown.)" Her poems are in *Graining the Mare,* a collection of ranch women's poems edited by Teresa Jordan, and she's working on a chapbook of poems with Up the Creek Publishing of Hamilton, Montana. Her column "Over the Corral Fence" is published in the *Clearwater Record.*

IDA ANNA HOHM (page 325) appreciates her growing-up years. "There was no junk food," she writes. "I knew no overweight child. There was no push-button machine and no air conditioning — not even a fan. I know the value of money and how to handle it." She has lived in Beadle County, in east central South Dakota, all her life. A retired public school teacher, she is an artist and barbershop singer who believes retired citizens should be active in their communities. She's a fifty-year member of her Mennonite Brethren choir; married to her husband, Jimmy, for fifty-two years, she's raised four children.

BERTHA HOLSINGER (page 46) was born while her parents were visiting in North Dakota, but lived all her life in Montana. Her father died when she was four years old and her mother married a widower with five children. Together they had six more and Bertha, the eldest of all fifteen, helped care for the younger ones. She attended country school through the eighth grade near Billings, and worked for many years as a cook or a waitress. She had a special love of reading and writing poetry, and wanted to do something for which she would be remembered. She died in 1994.

DECK HUNTER (*page 30*) is a retired physical education teacher and librarian, a New Jersey native, who started backpacking and climbing in the Wyoming mountains in 1970. She led Girl and Boy Scout groups as well as adults on trips before she and her husband, Bob, retired to Wyoming in 1984. Since then, she's written five books on the history of Big Horn, Wyoming, and contributes articles to the local newspaper. She is president of the Board of Trustees of the Museum of the American Cowboy, to be completed in Sheridan by the year 2000.

JENNIE SENRUD HUTTON (*page 70*) lived in rural Montana most of her married life, and now lives in the small town of Ekalaka. Married, she has eight children, thirty grandchildren, and six great-grands. She wrote a column for the *Dakota Farmer* for eight years, and her fourth book — poetry — is forthcoming. She taught school for six years and worked at the local hospital. "Love it here," she writes; "wouldn't want to live elsewhere."

MAXINE BRIDGMAN ISACKSON (*page 66*) was born on an Oklahoma ranch in 1933, but has spent most of her life in the sandhills of Nebraska, the fifth generation of her family to do so. With her husband, Richard, she has lived thirty-five years on a combination farm/ranch in Wild Horse Valley north of Brady, raising two sons. She's published numerous short stories and articles, and a book, *The Sandhills Beckon*.

JANEEN JACKSON (*page 40*), born in 1946 in New Orleans, Louisiana, lived with her stepfather and mother in Arizona until her teens. Working as a waitress in The Chatterbox Café in Cottonwood, she met her husband, Jimmy; they married in 1963. After a 1968 vacation in Montana, they were determined to move north. For eighteen years they worked toward the move, eventually buying a ranch in the Bull Mountains between Billings and Roundup, Montana. Janeen is a free-lance photographer and artist and writes for several publications.

MAEANN B. JASA (*page 82*) spent most of her childhood dreaming of travel. Born and raised on a farm near Wahoo in eastern Nebraska, she attended a one-room school through eight grades, graduated from Wahoo High in 1960, and in 1987 took an associate's degree with honors in hotel/restaurant management. As a business consultant, she is living out her dreams. "I've learned the importance of flexibility from traveling through thirteen foreign countries."

BARBARA JESSING (*page 105*) calls herself a "reverse urban homesteader"; she left California to pioneer in Nebraska twenty-five years ago. Growing up in a large family with a great storytelling tradition, she learned about her ancestors' Nebraska roots before moving, and later visited her great-grandmother's eastern Colorado homestead. Family stories sparked her interest in writing, and she was encouraged by the Feminist Writers Group in Omaha. With her husband, Timothy Butz, she has two daughters.

CAROLYN JOHNSEN (*pages 217, 251*) says her childhood on a dryland Nebraska farm in the 1950s has been the major formative element in her life. She was a high school English teacher for twelve years, including a year as a Fulbright teacher in England. After ten years as a self-employed writing coach, she is now a broadcast journalist and accompanies her fiddling husband on piano and spoons.

JEAN KEEZER-CLAYTON (*page 207*) is rooted in south central Nebraska, and says the anthology title "sums me up. I married young — same week I graduated from high school — and had three sons in short order. When my oldest was fifteen, he was severely brain-injured. Six weeks after that, my husband was killed in a car accident. I've been leaning into the wind since. . . . While living with loss I determined to live life with zest." She attended college, and is remarried to a dairy farmer, and they co-parent a blended family of seven.

AUDREY A. KEITH (*pages 24, 101*) has been married forty-five years and looks forward to the day when her son will take over the farm so she can spend more time writing, painting, and exploring local history. Except for her husband's stint in the army, she has lived on a farm all her life, and done most of the work. Her daughter teaches and writes music.

KATHRYN E. KELLEY (*page 257*) was raised on stories of her pioneer ancestors and writes that she's been a "closet writer *until now!*" Pure Midwesterner, she attended a one-room country school, a small-town high school, and a Catholic girls' college before graduating from the University of South Dakota with a degree in medical technology.

DIANNE ROOD KIESZ (*pages 43, 223*) grew up on the South Dakota prairie and wandered out to seek her fortune. She came home twenty years later, glad to have tasted other lifestyles, but also glad to be home. A pastor in the United Church of Christ, she was formerly a college speech and theater instructor and owned a thrift shop. "When I applied for my first teaching job," she writes, "I described my favorite smells: rain, new-mown hay, and fresh bread from the oven. That pretty well sums me up."

RACHEL C. KLIPPENSTEIN (*page 326*), "a writing rancher," left the paved streets of Pittsburgh for the graveled roads of South Dakota. The Klippensteins, including husband, Marc, and two sons, raised Polled Hereford cattle until they, like thousands of others, lost their land and home during the 1980s' farm crisis. Forced to leave the prairie land, Rachel began writing. Her second book is *Do You, Rachel, Take Ranching for Better or for Worse?*

SANDRA C. KNOX (*page 14*) lives with her husband, Bill, on the Colorado ranch her grandfather settled in the 1880s and where she was born and raised. "Ranch life is my love," she says. "Riding horseback through the timber is my way of putting my life in the proper perspective." She has received awards for her photography, cowboy poetry, and artwork, and has operated a gift shop, The Cottage, in Walden, Colorado, for eleven years.

BERNIE KOLLER (*page 59*) lives with her husband, Dennis, on the South Dakota prairie land of her birth, where her German forebears homesteaded, and attends their original church. On several trips to Russia, she has investigated her ancestors' lives, forging new alliances with modern Hutterites through their shared religious heritage. She speaks on history at Schmeckfest, the annual German-Russian ethnic feast, and directs the public library in Freeman.

DIANA ALLEN KOURIS (*page 116*) has spent much of her life as a working cowgirl, riding beside expert cowhands, pushing cattle along the rugged trails once ridden by Butch Cassidy and the Wild Bunch. Her family owned the historic Brown's Park Livestock and Red Creek ranches on the Outlaw Trail near the "three corners" of Utah, Colorado, and Wyoming. A longing to honestly portray the stories of those days drives her work as a free-lance writer.

ROSE KREMERS (*epigraph*) was a farmgirl and a teacher in Colorado and the Southwest and is now a ranch woman in Niobrara County, Wyoming, as well as a writer and a poet. She began writing at a young age and currently has a novel under consideration by a major publisher.

LAURIE KUTCHINS (*page 199*) was born in Casper, Wyoming. "The strong winds there," she says, "crept into my ear and my imagination at an early age and indelibly shaped them." She is a professor of creative writing and literature of American landscapes at the University of New Mexico at Albuquerque. Her first book, *Between Towns*, pays homage to the Western landscape; *The Night Path* is forthcoming from BOA Editions. Her poem "Weather" was written during a residency at Ucross Foundation in Wyoming and forecasts her third volume, *Weather Stories*, an interdisciplinary, multigenre work including oral histories and weather stories.

GRACE E. KYHN (*page 264*) received her GED at age fifty-one and is still attending college. Besides having the responsibilities of a large family, she volunteered as an EMT for twelve years, taught Sunday school, and worked to promote better education. She has studied painting and writing and enjoys sewing, cooking, horseback riding, and helping others.

PAGE LAMBERT (*page 17*) has lived for the last eight years on a small ranch in the Wyoming Black Hills with her husband, Mark (a fifth-generation rancher), and their two children. Her essays have appeared in both regional and national publications, including a *Reader's Digest* excerpt from her first book, *In Search of Kinship: Modern Pioneering on the Western Landscape*. A Colorado native, she is a founding member of Women Writing the West. Her first novel, *Shifting Stars*, set in 1850s Wyoming, was published in 1997 by Forge/Tor.

PHYLLIS M. LETELLIER (*pages 15, 306*) wrote farm and ranch humor for more than twenty years, never realizing she had a specialty until the farm was foreclosed in the 1980s' farm depression. She lost her inspiration, and many of her farm magazine markets. She still lives in the country, where her husband and son run a farm equipment repair business. She grew up a farmer's daughter, riding, breaking, and showing horses, and became a newspaper reporter, photographer, and editor. She has a ten-year record of perfect attendance at school board meetings in Greybull, Wyoming.

DELCIE DANROTH LIGHT (*pages 20, 126*) has been married for thirty-five years to the same man and has three grown children. She and her husband built their own home in an oak forest near Devil's Lake, North Dakota. Retired from twenty-eight years of teaching high school English, Delcie says her life is just beginning. "I love being a crone! I love the vastness and mutability of the sky, the land, the epochs revealed in the geology. I love the reliability, resourcefulness, resilience of the people." She's looking forward to raking leaves, writing, and meeting friends and family at the coffee shop.

SHIRLEY D. LILLEY (*page 255*) has spent most of her life on the Chimney Rock Ranch, 57,000 acres crossing the Wyoming-Colorado state lines southwest of Laramie, Wyoming. With her husband, Frank, manager of the ranch through several owners, Shirley has raised three children. She rode a horse before she could walk, and is still most confident with work she can do on horseback. She owns her own cow herd, "though I feel it's like an addiction. I just have to see that next calf crop."

TAMMI LITTREL (*pages 22, 208*) lists her profession as "rancher," but keeps her teaching certificate current, just in case. She started ranching so she could work and still be with her small children, and admits that at times all three — cows, kids, and woman — were bawling. Now she's using her education in anthropology to study medicinal uses of prairie plants, and is grateful for a supportive husband who keeps her haying equipment running, though he has never professed to like cows. Ranching is a genderless job, she says; the pay is the same no matter who's in charge.

PATTY LITZEL (*page 303*) grew up between prairie and small town in northwestern South Dakota, where great distances and time led her to find pleasure in writing and music. A summer baby-sitting job on a Harding County ranch turned into ranch work as the children grew. Chores lent themselves to thought, and the children's wonder prompted her to keep a journal; the job paid for her college tuition. At night she learned to play a banjo on the bunkhouse steps. Following her family roots, she's begun a genealogical search while working as master control operator at KELO-TV in Sioux Falls, South Dakota, "more job than profession."

ANITA LORENTZEN-WELLS (*pages 20, 39*) is in her second year of a doctoral program at the University of Alberta, Canada, but says, "My whole life has been affected by the farm." With her brother and sister, she worked in her family's corn and soybean fields, irrigating and driving machinery. She married a farmer from her hometown, where they still live, and they have three children. She teaches at a university near her husband's and parents' farms.

BARBARA LOVE (*page 210*) is a third-generation Wyomingite, living on the LU Ranch her husband, Danny, manages, with their two children and various horses, sheep, cats, and dogs. She has studied biology, worked on a dude ranch and for the Bureau of Land Management, enjoys art, sheep, and being a 4-H leader.

BETTY L. LYE (*page 301*) and her husband, John, will celebrate their fiftieth wedding anniversary in 1997, and she has been a farmwife, sheepherder, and tractor driver for thirty-five years. They lived on a farm twenty-five miles west of Riverton, Wyoming, until they sold it in 1985. She's been state secretary for the Wyoming State Grange for twenty years and treasurer for the United Methodist Women for ten, a state PTA officer, a 4-H leader, a Sunday school teacher, and she sings in the choir.

FREYA MANFRED (*page 141*) has been a writer since she was sixteen and has published three books of poetry: *A Goldenrod Will Grow*, *Yellow Squash Woman*, and *American Roads*. A memoir, *Love, Dad*, about her father, Frederick Manfred, a well-known Midwestern author, is currently with her agent. She's writing movie scripts and poems about water and death. Her thirty-minute documentary poem, "The Madwoman and the Mask," was presented on KTCA-TV in Minneapolis, Minnesota, in 1991.

JANELLE MASTERS (*page 17*), daughter of a railroad worker, was born and raised in Niobe, North Dakota. After ten years in Southeast Asia and Florida, she returned out of homesickness. She now lives in a century-old house in Mandan with three cats and thirty bats. She's an amateur astronomer and birdwatcher with an M.A. from Rollins College in Winter Park, Florida, and a Ph.D. from the University of North Dakota. She writes, "I continually think, write, and dream about the house I grew up in."

NOREEN McCONNELL (*page 32*) raises elk with her husband in the same area of Colorado where her great-grandparents on both sides homesteaded. With her husband, she runs a custom wheat harvest crew from Texas to Montana. She's worked as a well-site geologist and on cattle ranches, and now runs a bed and breakfast. Establishing the ranch and building a log home required 2.5 miles of new road, 2.5 miles of electric and telephone lines, and 12 miles of elk fence.

PHYLLIS LUMAN METAL (*pages 49, 115*) was raised on a ranch in Wyoming, the granddaughter of the "Cattle King of the Green River Valley." She has worked on Lakota reservations in South Dakota, and with Mother Teresa, and as a nighttime crisis counselor at a San Francisco, California, suicide prevention center. She says she's "the mother of four remarkable, creative women, and grandmother and great-grandmother to two more." She is now blind, but says, "I have so much to write."

LUCY C. MEYRING (*page 163*) grew up on a ranch in southeastern New Mexico. After leaving college, she worked in journalism and broadcasting. Then she "returned to the love of my life — ranching," in the mountains of northern Colorado. She and her husband, Danny, are partners in an old family cow/calf/yearling operation near Walden, where they put up hay and feed with Percheron teams. Lucy trains all the ranch saddle horses and keeps the books; in her "spare" time, she promotes ranching.

ROSALEE M. MICKELSEN (*page 226*), a poet, writer, singer, mother, grandmother, and fast-food restaurant employee, was born in Kearney, Nebraska, and has lived for thirty-eight years on a farm near there. She wrote her first poem — about her little sister — in high school, and has continued to write steadily. She has always been an avid reader, encouraged by teachers who insisted she read books and newspapers and give reports.

EDNA BOMGARDNER MILLER (*page 248*) was born in 1913 in Box Butte County, Nebraska, and spent her childhood on the Bullock Ranch in

Wyoming, which her parents bought in 1917. She taught for two years at Fishcreek, a rural Platte County school, before she married Robert Miller, owner of the old Thompson Ranch on the Laramie River. During ten years there, they had three children. In 1950 they moved to Montana, where they ranched and raised a family while Edna taught school. In 1967 they returned to Guernsey, Wyoming, moved to Casper in 1974, and to Cedaredge, Colorado, in 1978. Robert died in 1987, a year short of their fiftieth anniversary.

JOYCE M. MILLER (*page 228*) began writing professionally ten years ago in addition to her work as a nurse in public health, family practice, and family planning. Born and raised in western Pennsylvania, she came home to Wyoming twenty-six years ago. She enjoys hiking, photography, needlework, and gardening. "However, writing about Wyoming, her people, and the land we all share is what I cherish."

KAY MOON (*page 195*), who wrote about the Wyoming landmark Elk Mountain while living in Cheyenne, considers herself a "Wyomingite" though she has lived in several Western states and in Europe. With a B.A. and an M.A. in German literature from the University of Wyoming, she says her work with non-English-speaking students has given her an even greater love of words and writing. She is studying linguistics and plans to continue writing.

LOIS J. MOORE (*pages 21, 68*) grew up on a farm in northern Nebraska, completing grade school in six years and high school in three. At age fifteen she began teaching with a twelve-hour certificate. Her interest has always been in working with children, and she's been an elementary school teacher for thirteen years. She spent eight years teaching at Nebraska Center for Women, a state prison, where she was coordinator of children's visits to their mothers. She has three children of her own and four foster children and lives on a northern Nebraska ranch.

SUE A. MORRELL (*page 158*) is a South Dakota native living and writing just north of the Missouri River near Springfield. Sue teaches language arts at Bon Homme High School in Tyndall. She writes, "I have twenty-five years of experience as a wife, twenty-two years as a mother. . . . This is essential to me: that somewhere in the course of a day filled with hectic family schedules and a demanding job, I can walk out my door and find prairie earth and boundless sky."

CANDY VYVEY MOULTON (*page 185*) was raised, as her essay indicates, on the ranch her grandparents homesteaded and her parents owned and later sold. Since age eighteen she has made her living as a journalist, writer, and photographer. Her nonfiction books include *Steamboat: Legendary Bucking Horse; Legacy of the Tetons;* roadside histories of both Wyoming and Nebraska; and *Wagon Wheels: A Contemporary Journey on the Oregon Trail.*

FLORENCE M. NEWSOM (*page 169*) was born on her grandfather's North Dakota place in 1903 and has farmed it since 1914. She took care of her mother and siblings after her father died in 1943, making a living by raising cattle and poultry, caring for a milk herd, and gardening. Always interested in writing, nature, and music, she reports that she "had cancer and stroke in 1990; recovered, now garden, write, work with kids."

DONNA NIEDERWERDER (*page 193*) grew up on a farm/ranch in western South Dakota, and she and her husband have always wanted the same great childhood for their two boys. Unable to farm and ranch full-time, they work other jobs to support their farming "habit." Donna is a teacher's aide at the school their children attend.

BONNIE RAE NORDBERG (*page 73*) was born in Basin, Wyoming, and raised on her parents' ranch near Burlington. She met her husband, John, at Northwest Community College in Powell, and moved to Montana, where they have lived ever since. Bonnie enjoys watercolor painting, cooking, and her flower garden.

NELLIE A. O'BRIEN (*page 57*) was born, one of eight, in a log cabin on Pole Creek Ranch between Boulder and Pinedale, Wyoming. Retired from the Missouri Division of Employment Security after twenty-five years, she is now a free-lance writer who has published a book and sold poems, short fiction, and articles. She writes, "A Wyoming-bred woman does not give up, even when faced with old age and incredible heartache." She is primary caregiver to her husband, John, who was stricken with Alzheimer's disease in 1983.

KAREN OBRIGEWITCH (*pages 95, 181*) is the granddaughter of homesteaders, born in Montana and ranch-raised. Two of her grown children help operate the family ranch, the fifth generation to ranch in the same county. Karen lists her profession as jack-of-all-trades and believes a good book to read at the end of the day is better than dessert. "I've loved good men and rode good horses," she says.

PAMELA J. OCHSNER (*page 319*) is a farmwife from South Dakota who raises hogs, cattle, and kids (in descending order by quantity), and works with the developmentally disabled. Since her father was a truck driver, her family moved often. She finally settled down seventeen miles from the family's permanent stop when she married Del. She began writing at age nine, and when her work filled a hutch, her banker insisted she begin sharing her work with others, she says, adding, "Thanks, Roger!"

LAURA M. OSADCHY (*page 166*) lived with her husband, Paul, on their ranch near Max, North Dakota, for thirty-eight years. A ranch wife, she drove all the trucks and tractors and wrote many articles for regional magazines. Her husband says, "Laura did not think about herself but for others." She died of liver cancer on October 20, 1994.

ELAINE M. OSTER (*page 123*) was born in Colorado and has lived there all her life — on the same farm for the past twenty-three years. She lives with her husband, Ted.

LINDA HOUGHTALING OYAMA (*page 113*) loves country living and has always lived close to the earth, running a trap line, hunting, fishing, and cooking in hunting camps. Her home is an old log cabin with no running water and a woodstove. She was reared at the south edge of the Gallatin Valley, poor and without much education. Her writings are mostly from personal experience, and her heroes are Charlie Russell and Will James.

ELSIE PANKOWSKI (*page 232*) has lived in Montana for nearly forty years, but was born and raised on a western North Dakota farm. More than two hundred of her poems and short prose pieces have been published. She is a retired partner in an excavating company. Her writing "reflects the open landscapes of the plains, the good people who live here, and the details of a life spent where vision falls on distant horizons."

THOMASINA PARKER (*page 258*) walked and rode horseback to a one-room school. She married South Dakota rancher Johnny Parker in 1942. "With Johnny, I've done it all," she writes. "Mowed hay, repaired windmills, fed cattle, pulled calves, doctored sick animals, set a calf's broken hind leg." They've reared four sons on their ranch. She's a certified lay speaker, writes for a church and senior center newsletter, helps in a local school, and does volunteer work.

DONNA PARKS (*page 307*) is an artist, free-lance writer, homemaker, student of computers, world traveler, promoter of creativity in general, and all-around straw-spinner. She says, "The open spaces of the West have etched themselves into my vision so that whatever I see in my travels is measured against them." Born and reared in western South Dakota, she then married and moved to the shale hills of Wyoming, then back, circling the hills on her personal raceway.

GARNET GERING PERMAN (*page 120*) lives on Rock Hills Ranch near Lowry, South Dakota, population: 10. A native, she was born and grew up in Freeman, a largely Mennonite community, and met her husband, Lyle, in college. She taught school for a couple of years and is a perpetual volunteer in 4-H and the local library. Mother of two, she's been "head chore girl and dishwasher" for the ranch for twenty years.

MARIAN D. PETERS (*page 234*) spent most of her working years employed in South Dakota's state government and now considers herself a writer. Her poem was modeled after a newspaper account and some of her other work has been published in *Prairie Winds*, the Vermillion literary project, *South Dakota Magazine*, and *Pasque Petals*. President of South Dakota's State Poetry Society, she has received awards in several literary contests.

GWEN PETERSEN (*page 179*) says she "eats, sleeps and worries," but she's also written six books — humorous looks at country life — directed plays and melodramas, and is a syndicated columnist. "We're all going to be dead one day," she says, "but before we leave this coil, it's important to tell the country stories. Absolutely everybody's story is important." Her most popular titles include *The Ranch Woman's Manual* and *The Greenhorn's Guide to the Woolly West*. Her performances as a speaker leave audiences gasping with laughter.

NORMA F. PLANT (*page 256*) was her husband's business partner and helpmate on a dairy farm until dust storms and the Great Depression drove them to Pueblo, Colorado, where James supervised the Dairy Improvement Association for thirteen years. They managed and then bought a dairy herd in Rocky Ford, Colorado, but were driven from the business — "the good life," she says — by government regulations. For fifteen years they owned a drive-in restaurant, selling it because of her husband's illness. Her high school sweetheart, James died in 1979.

JANN HIRSCHY POTTER (*page 312*) has lived in Wisdom, Montana, all her life. A great-great-uncle and aunt homesteaded there in 1892, and her great-grandparents in 1894. With her husband and two children, Jann raises commercial cattle, feeding with a horse team in winter; "we don't hire help." The whole family competes in team roping and rodeos, and sponsors rodeos in their own indoor-outdoor arena. Jann produced an all-girl rodeo for thirteen years and manages the Beaverhead County Fairgrounds in Dillon, sixty miles away, the closest big town — population: 4,500.

JOAN L. POTTS (*page 271*) says, "The land feeds me in more ways than raising food. . . . If I don't get to see a sunset at night, I feel like I missed something. I feel a part of me has been unfed for the day." Living in the rolling hills of northeast Nebraska, Joani is a farmwife and a development director.

ROSE POTULNY (*page 248*), a homemaker, has lived on a North Dakota farm all her life and loves it. Born and raised four miles south of Lankin, she married at nineteen and moved twelve miles away to a farm where she and her husband still live after fifty-nine years of marriage.

C. L. PRATER (*page 190*) grew up on the Rosebud Sioux Indian Reservation of south central South Dakota. "Buttes, canyons, rolling hills, and lots of sky provided scenic diversity," she writes, "while the people around me provided the cultural richness that feeds a budding writer." Now she gardens and raises children, "my most beloved areas of interest," and often travels back to the reservation to visit. Three of her works have been published.

C. J. PRINCE (*page 27*) has lived in many places, from California to Maine, but settled on a small farm in Colorado's outback in 1972. An actress and writer, C.J. follows a busy schedule, but is always balanced when she returns to the animals and the land. She raises Karakul and Lincoln sheep and Nubian goats. A columnist, she is working on a book titled *Confessions of a Greenhorn Shepherdess*. She is also executive director of Berge Prince Comedy Theatre Company and executive producer of Gunter Goose Productions, as well as a co-producer and actress on KWGN, Denver.

OLIVE M. RABEN (*page 253*) is officially retired, but loves working as a Green Thumb volunteer for the Chadron, Nebraska, library. Born and raised on farms, she has lived near Harrison and Crawford most of her life. She worked for Nash Finch Company until she married a farmer and raised six children. Widowed, and an only child, she moved to Chadron to care for her parents.

LINDA M. RACE (*page 236*) loved her childhood on a Colorado dairy farm and knew she wanted to marry a farmer, so she attended college in Kansas, heart of the Midwest. Ironically, she was placed in a secretarial job in Detroit, Michigan. But, she remarks, "God's way was sure more direct than mine." Two years later, she was married to a farmer and had moved near her family. After twelve years, 1995 brought their best crop ever, "a gorgeous little farm daughter!"

JUNE WILLSON READ (*page 273*) learned rich lessons in survival and resourcefulness growing up on a cattle ranch in eastern Wyoming during the years after the Great Depression. This strong foundation carried her through marriage at nineteen, raising a family, and earning a Ph.D. from Texas Tech. As a psychotherapist, she worked from 1981 until 1991 in a community mental health agency in the Big Horn basin.

LUCY REBENITSCH (*page 190*) was one of twelve children on the family farm; at sixteen she attended college by hard work and going hungry. She taught in rural areas and small towns, on Indian reservations and in special education programs. She's been married fifty years and has had five children. Now living on a ranch near Fort Rice, North Dakota, she home-schools her grandchildren.

ELLA SCHLATER REICHART (*page 260*) was born the fifth of six children on an eighty-acre farm in Platte River, Nebraska. The farm was sold in 1931 and the money banked; in the fall of 1932, the bank failed. "I have learned to do without many luxuries," she says. Married in 1934, she reared three boys and worked for twenty-three years in the Clarkson Hospital food service. She has nine grandchildren and eight great-grandchildren.

FLORENCE F. RENFROW (*page 331*) has lived near Turtle Lake, North Dakota, all her life, a farmer's wife for fifty years. She attended Turtle Lake High School. After a summer of training, she taught for three years in rural schools.

JAN RIPPEL (*page 202*) grew up on a Kansas farm and says one of the saddest moments of her life was seeing the prairie pasture destroyed there. A graduate of Southwestern College in Winfield, Kansas, she married in 1968 and traveled for twenty years while her husband served in the air force. She's the mother of three grown daughters, and her hobby for several years has been learning about wild plants in the Black Hills.

SHELLY RITTHALER (*page 96*) and her husband, Reuben, a third-generation rancher, own and operate a northeastern Wyoming ranch. A self-taught author, Shelly won the Western Writers of America Spur Award for her book *The Ginger Jar*. Her children's book, *Dinosaurs Alive*, was named a Children's Choice Book by the International Reading Association and the Children's Book Council. A lifelong Wyoming resident, she serves on the University of Wyoming Board of Trustees.

GAIL RIXEN (*pages 103, 310*) has been writing most of her life, no matter what she did for a living: self-employed finish carpenter, substitute teacher, part-timer at a group home for the developmentally disabled. Her poetry has appeared in many small magazines; in *Pictures of Three Seasons*, a collection; and in a chapbook, *Chicken Logic*. Raised on a northern Minnesota farm, she lived for twenty-three years on prairie farms near the South Dakota border, and now co-owns a farm near Bemidji, Minnesota.

JEANNE ROGERS (*page 23*) has lived in Wyoming since age seven and considers herself a "near-native." Following in the bootsteps of her mother, a rodeo trick rider, Jeanne dreamed of horses and married a cowboy. Though the couple has no ranch, they have a small cow herd, a few horses, a couple of dogs, and four children. They did custom haying for several years, help ranching friends with chores, and take packhorse trips into the Wyoming wilderness. "My family and my church keep me strong and sound."

NANCY HEYL RUSKOWSKY (*page 290*) writes that, like "any woman in getting to this place, tragedy has struck in enough forms to provide me with a little more depth and reflection as well as more appreciation for the celebrations." Mother of four daughters, grandmother of five, and shepherd of a thirty-ewe flock of natural-colored sheep, this thirty-year Wyoming resident need not search for stories.

MARJORIE SAISER (*page 268*) grew up in a small-town café (with living quarters in the back) along the Niobrara and Keya Paha rivers. She says, "I had no idea how poor I was. That's a very good way to grow up," adding that her grandmother gave her connection with the land and belief in herself. She often writes at a café table with other women, using free-writing to begin poetry.

AURIEL J. SANDSTEAD (*page 239*) celebrated the golden anniversary of her marriage to husband, Willard, in February 1996. She writes, "Harvest ended on July 28, 1947; our beautiful daughter was born July 29." A retired teacher and social worker, Auriel farmed with her husband on the high plains of northeastern Colorado, near Willard in Logan County. She attended the University of Denver and the University of Northern Colorado in Greeley.

BOBBIE SAUNDERS (*page 168*), born in Cincinnati, Ohio, is a housing management assistant for the army. She finished college in Atlanta, Georgia, and worked in Savannah briefly before transferring to Denver, Colorado. Her poems have appeared in various small magazines, and a collection of poems, *Illusions*, was published by Wyndham Hall in 1990; she does calligraphy and collage and enjoys dogs, jazz, and baseball.

TERRY L. SCHIFFERNS (*page 127*) lives with her three children in a cabin on the south bank of the Platte River in Nebraska. She writes, "We cohabit this space with the sandhill cranes, white-tail deer, eagles, and other assorted creatures that enrich our lives." She teaches writing at Central Community College in Grand Island, Nebraska, where her students "both delight me and enlighten me."

RUTH SCHUBARTH (*page 160*) left her native Colorado to roam the world before returning home. She sees herself as an eclectic Renaissance Christian who believes in Jesus and the Bible, but not always in religion. Her sixth child, Mercy Spring, was born in early 1996. Among her many interests are Lakota beadwork, clay working, mothering, writing, gardening, music, midwifery, and creative cookery. She's thirty-six, recovering from rheumatoid arthritis and chronic fatigue syndrome with alternative health care.

DAWN SENIOR (*page 335*) lives mostly in her family's hand-hewn log cabin in the foothills of Wyoming's Snowy Range. As a teenager, she spent five winters on a Navajo reservation in Arizona. She's an artist-in-schools for arts councils in several states, and has been an editor for her family's small press. Her bronze sculptures, multicolor woodcuts, and oil paintings have been shown regionally. Recent publications include her own poems and essays as well as illustrations for other books.

MARLAINE RUSTAD SLAAEN (*page 122*) writes of herself, "farmgirl-artist; student-artist; mother-artist; university teacher-artist; European traveler-artist; grandmother-artist." She was the first of the eight children in her family to be born in a hospital instead of at home on the farm in Bonetraill Township near Grenora, North Dakota. After college, she married the gray-eyed, handsome farmer/rancher of her poem. Traveling in seventeen countries, she never left the place of her heart, the prairie, and explores in her work "the movement of its tectonic plates in quietness."

LINDA SLATER (*page 80*) has never had enough time to do all she wants to do. Growing up on a cattle and hay ranch in western Montana, she raised 4-H steers, won blue ribbons for her pies and breads, and collected a few scholarships. She makes soaps from her garden herbs, as well as gardening, restoring quilts, and making pottery. Working in Montana bars, one of her thirty past jobs, she heard stories from all kinds of patrons. She loves the sense of community in her Unitarian church.

BARBARA M. SMITH (*pages 6, 135*) writes poetry and fiction about living in the boom-and-bust West, finding many parallels between her ancestors' lives and those of modern women. She was born in North Dakota, granddaughter of Norwegian homesteaders, daughter of Great Depression parents, all of whom kept moving West, looking for better lives. She's lived mostly in Rock Springs, Wyoming, "a friendly immigrant mining community," teaching college English as well as life-story writing classes for senior citizens.

CLARA L. SMITH (*page 100*) was born in South Dakota ninety-five years ago and has lived in her home state for ninety-three of those years. While watching the transition from horse power to atomic energy, she has been a farmer's daughter, country school teacher, farmer's wife, and mother of four daughters. "We have gained much," she says, "and lost something in moral values. My early life was never prosperous, but we were rich in a home with a mother who sang and read to us, told us bedtime stories, and played word games."

MARGARET E. SMITH (*page 233*) raised cattle, horses, and boys in her forty-year marriage to a Broken Bow, Nebraska, rancher. She grew up on a farm in Custer County and taught school one year before her marriage. Besides four sons and a permanent foster daughter, the family hosted exchange students, other foster children, and nieces and nephews during the summers.

JONITA SOMMERS (*page 84*) has been riding horses since she climbed on with her father when she was six months old. She says, "Nothing is more satisfying than riding a well-broke cow horse you have trained." Raised on a cattle ranch in the upper Green River valley of Wyoming, she's taught school for fifteen years, currently at Big Piney Middle School. Her love of history led her to work with a local museum and to write *Green River Drift*.

MORGAN SONGI (*page 92*) discovered five years ago that her father was a mixed-blood Chippewa. Enrolled with the Red Cliff band in northern Wisconsin, she traced the family history on Lake Superior back to the 1700s and her great-great-great-great-grandfather, Chief Gaibiash. Learning and telling these stories for Denver, Colorado, public schools and libraries, folk festivals and storytellers' conferences has inspired her to write a novel. She grew up on a farm in western Nebraska, married, and has two sons.

BONNIE LARSON STAIGER (*pages 75, 336*) lived in Minnesota just long enough to "know it was time to come home." Her ancestors homesteaded in both Dakotas, and she is the first woman in her family to receive a college degree. "Our values and spirit are formed by the place we live," she writes. "Having started to write poetry at age forty-two, I'm just beginning to feel like a grownup . . . to get my taproot down so I could flourish." She owns a small business specializing in the management of nonprofit groups.

CORA MADSEN STEFFES (*page 64*) was born in Snohomish, Washington, but grew up on her parents' homesteads in eastern Montana. Later she married and reared two sons on a ranch forty miles from town, north of Baker. She and her husband now live in Bozeman, where she completed a degree as an "older-than-average" student. Her essays have appeared in newspapers, magazines, and the anthology *Montana Sketchbook*.

LOUISE STENECK (*pages 36, 143*) says, "I am a peasant — a woman of the land." She's a hog farmer and a librarian who has lived in cities but was always "tuned to the works of nature, rather than the works of man." A wife and mother, she was once a VISTA volunteer in Lame Deer, Montana; a magazine writer in Denver; a newspaper feature editor in Nyack, New York; and a marina owner in Charlestown, Rhode Island.

MARY KATHRYN STILLWELL (*pages 38, 303*) left Nebraska years ago, headed east in the 1960s version of the Conestoga wagon — a yellow VW convertible with four cats and a color TV. She intended to live a Bohemian life in Greenwich Village and write the great American novel. For free tuition, she worked at New York University, where she took poetry writing with Bill Packard, Erica Jong, Stephen Dobyns, and Marilyn Hacker. *Moving to Malibu*, a book of poems, was published in 1988 by Sandhills Press. In 1990 she returned with her family to Nebraska, a wanderer come full circle.

DEIRDRE STOELZLE (*page 296*) specializes in firsthand accounts, making herself a vehicle her subjects can use for communication. She's lived in New Orleans, New York City, Washington, D.C., Boston, San Francisco, and New Jersey, and is now an editor for the *Casper Star-Tribune* in Casper, Wyoming.

LINDA KNOUSE STOTTS (*page 85*), born and reared on a small farm near Chadron, spent most of her life in rural northwestern Nebraska. "My heart is a captive of a rural lifestyle," she writes, "My family and my rural values are my soul." In her mid-thirties, she moved to Kansas City, Missouri, to attend college and research her family's roots.

JODY STRAND (*page 237*) has been her husband's "hired man" for years on cattle ranches in North and South Dakota and Colorado. He now works on the 101 Ranch in Montana. She can ride, work cattle, brand, feed, calve, and break colts, but she doesn't castrate or do AI (artificial insemination); "Ya gotta draw the line somewhere." Feedlot work is her favorite. "Just give me a vaccine gun in each hand and stand back!" She also edits the *Fallon County Times* in Baker.

JEAN McKENZIE SWEEM (*page 61*) says that since her father bought a home and a ranch just before the Great Depression, "I am a product (*not* a victim)" of it and World War II. James McKenzie, an emigrant from Scotland, "didn't have a dime, but through hard work sent all of us to Scotland on visits more than once." Born and raised near Gillette, Wyoming, Jean and her husband raised three children in Sheridan; she is now "very retired" and lives in Fort Collins, Colorado.

PEGGY R. SYMONDS (*page 271*), born at Eagle Butte, South Dakota, moved with her family to Crook County, Wyoming, in 1953. With her husband, Tom, and their five children, she ranched and farmed in South Dakota from 1959 to 1987, raising horses and Hereford cattle, trying sheep, pigs, and goats. A 4-H leader for twenty-five years, Peggy likes to write about things that "seemed tragic but have brought us a million laughs." In 1987 the family moved back to Wyoming, where Peggy is custodian for the Crook County courthouse.

ANITA TANNER (*pages 92, 242*) moved to Colorado eleven years ago and helped start a writers' group. "Seeing others develop their writing and sharing my own helps fill my insatiable thirst for books and words." Born and raised on a small farm in Star Valley, Wyoming, she learned to love nature, "the value of simplicity, and the gift of abundance"; education helped her "hone the love into words." The mother of six, she's a homemaker.

URMA DeLONG TAYLOR (*page 77*) was born in North Dakota in 1911 and spent her childhood on the move as her parents searched for ways to make a living on the land. Donna Gray, who interviewed her, says she spoke of days of poverty with sadness, but also with triumph. She was severely crippled with arthritis at the time of the interview, published in Gray's book, *Pioneer Women*.

MARTHA THOMPSON (*page 7*) is a housewife and newspaper reporter. Born in New Mexico, she moved to Wyoming in 1927 with her family. She has done exhaustive research into the history of southeastern Wyoming and written hundreds of newspaper articles. An archive area was named in her honor after she donated historical materials to the Pine Bluffs Texas Trail Museum. She's written three books about the region, but finds it hard to write without her "dearly beloved" husband, Gerald, who died in early 1996.

JULIA BROWN TOBIAS (*page 54*) was born in 1902 and raised in rural Nebraska, where her family farmed, raised trotting horses, and ranched. She married Ralph Tobias in 1919 and moved to Omaha, where she opened a custom clothing design shop. Sewing on a machine at age four, by the age of eight she dreamed of designing clothes. In 1954 she opened a design shop in Cherry Creek, Denver, Colorado. She retired in 1972 and published her first book in 1996.

DIANNA TORSON (*pages 53, 240*) grew up on the back of a horse on the family farm in northeast Iowa. She has always lived in rural areas, closely associating with animals, and respects their intelligence and emotions. After raising her children, she returned to college and taught at Sinte Gleska University, Rosebud Reservation, South Dakota. In college she began writing poetry centered around her love of the earth. In 1996 she moved back to her acreage near Brookings, South Dakota.

MARGARET TRAUTMAN (*pages 48, 334*) has always lived on a North Dakota farm, except when she attended college for a teaching degree. Her parents moved to the state from West Virginia in 1910. With her husband, she operated the family farm, taught school for more than twenty years, and reared three children.

ELAINE TRAWEEK (*page 329*) grew up on a Minnesota farm, married a city boy fresh out of high school, and raised three children before she was widowed in her early forties. She then married a Montana rancher, and when she was widowed again in 1994 and her husband's brothers opted to sell the family ranch, she realized she would never live on a ranch again. "I miss it all, grand and not so grand," she says. She works at a ranch store in Baker. "I try to content myself with the . . . training of my yearling colts" and riding for the landlord; "It could be worse."

JUANITA KILLOUGH URBACH (*page 60*) was born in 1922 and raised in the Woodrow community. She married J. Max Holt in 1939. Retired from Colorado's revenue department, she took up travel, sewing, and free-lance writing — she sold more than two hundred short items. Her book, *Quest of the Shepherd's Son,* was published by Capper's Press, and she was named Writer of the Year by the American Christian Writers Association. Juanita died suddenly on October 12, 1996.

TONI VANCE (*page 84*) has been writing since she can remember, "which is getting shorter each day." A lifelong South Dakota resident, she lives with her husband, Scott, field man for Faith Livestock Sales, and their two children on a ranch along Flintrock Creek. She's a school counselor and says, "I just don't think I could live in town," but she loves competition so much that she plays softball or volleyball weekly in Spearfish and Sturgis, towns a hundred miles away.

GLORIA VAN DYKE (*page 283*) has been farming with her husband for forty years; "I've always been here for my husband when he needed help . . . We've never had children to help so it was always up to me . . . I could not have done this without the Lord's help." They expect to keep farming "as long as we are able." She loves to paint, draw, write poetry and children's stories, and she reads a lot.

MARILYNN J. VAN WELL (*page 321*) has lived on the South Dakota prairies all her life. Born and raised on a farm in Hyde County, she met her husband in Hoven, where she worked as secretary in a bank. Married in 1963, they've raised three sons. She loves to write short stories and poetry, and she does calligraphy, creating her own greeting cards. She is involved in church work and retreats, and writes, "I have a strong relationship with our Lord."

LINDA VELDER (*page 273*) is curator of the Newell Museum in South Dakota as well as a housewife and mother. She has spent most of her life in northwestern South Dakota, raising five children. Adverse conditions, she writes, along with her "experiences, vivid imagination, strengths, and appreciation for hard work," give her excellent story topics. A history buff and amateur archaeologist, she enjoys visiting with older citizens to learn more about early settlers and Native Americans.

JANICE M. VIERK (*page 143*) grew up on a central Nebraska farm in the '50s and '60s, attending the same country school her father attended, and inheriting his love of the country. She helped with both inside and outside chores, including milking cows, slopping hogs, and haying. She teaches in several Omaha area colleges and is pursuing a Ph.D. in English composition and women's studies. A single parent, she has two sons, also in college.

ROSALIE VIGIL (*page 305*) has always enjoyed the outdoors and creating crafts from natural materials, as does her father. Her mother read to her four daughters and encouraged them to create stories to banish boredom. Rosalie keeps a journal, recording memorable events to share with her sons when they are grown. Born in New Mexico, she works as a librarian and high school Spanish/French facilitator. She lives in Baggs, Wyoming.

ANN KOSTENKO VONTZ (*page 42*) has been busy all her life, working her way through school and teaching for four years in North Dakota. In Powell, Wyoming, where her husband worked for Amoco for thirty years, she raised three daughters, did volunteer work for her church and for 4-H groups, and studied and taught Russian, oil painting, and sculpture.

MARY LYNN VOSEN (*pages 200, 237*) says she's "a fourth-generation Montanan in love with the plains and the creatures who live here. I shall always make sacrifices to keep my relationship with the land." Describing herself as "a student *and* teacher of horses and other animals," she lives with her fifteen-year-old daughter near Great Falls, "flat broke and unwilling to give up; one of God's greatest examples of the human condition." She recently rehabilitated a great horned owl, who is now hunting on his own, but drops by to chatter from huge cottonwood trees.

DONNA WALBERG (*page 108*) lived on her family farm near Ipswich, South Dakota, with two brothers and a sister. Until she married, she helped her father and brothers in the fields, enjoying farm work. She has two children and she enjoys crafts and being a wife and mother. "God has given us a beautiful world to enjoy," she writes. "We need to make each day count."

REBECCA WAMPLER (*pages 216, 319*) lists her profession as "unknown." Though she has worked as a lobbyist, camp cook, bookstore manager, plumber, and cleaning lady, she's always been a writer. She "would like to continue documenting Western culture and its wholesomeness to newcomers so they might reconsider, or at least introduce their changes slowly and kindly." She has written magazine articles, the minutes of the Jackson Hole Outfitters, and wildlife and hunting movies, and she was always a closet poet, "fourth-generation Wyoming working class," who has lived in ten counties of her home state.

TRUDY Z. WARDWELL (*pages 131, 151*) lives on a small ranch at 8,500 feet in Wet Mountain Valley near Westcliffe, Colorado, with her "darling cowboy, Mike." A rancher, she's also a newspaper columnist and a graphic artist; Mike is county appraiser and dispatcher for the sheriff's office and "We *work* at making ends meet." Trudy was married at sixteen, later widowed, and courted by fortune hunters for her widow's mite ("Got some of it, too," she reports). She taught kindergarten for eleven years and sold real estate, but "hated it."

ERLA K. WERNER (*page 76*) has been a North Dakota farm and ranch gal all her life, from birth as the oldest of eleven children. She attended rural schools in Grant County, Carson-Roosevelt public school, and Leith High School. She loves cattle, riding horseback (especially on trail rides), reading, fishing, gardening, and raising flowers. She's a 4-H leader and enjoys woodworking and crafts. For thirty-five years she's been married to Mark, and they have four children.

KATHLEENE WEST (*page 170*), born on a farm near Genoa, Nebraska, has written seven books of prose and poetry, two of which are currently in print: *Water Witching* (Copper Canyon Press) and *The Farmer's Daughter* (Sandhills). On a Fulbright fellowship she studied language and Old Norse literature at the University of Reykjavik, Iceland, for two years. An associate professor in English at New Mexico State University, she was a delegate at the U.S./China Joint Conference on the Status of Women, held in Beijing in 1995.

NELLIE WESTERSKOW (*page 332*) is retired from ranching and farming at age ninety-six. "Now I scribble for a hobby," she says. Born in Norway on July 1, 1900, she came to America on July 5, 1905 with her mother and five siblings to join their father and brother. In Rice Lake, Wisconsin, at a logging camp where their father sawed logs for $15 a month, she learned English and Chippewa. When she was twenty, Nellie moved to South Dakota to work and homestead. Her life story is told in *From Arctic Splendor to Sunset Mountain*, cowritten and published in 1991 by her daughter, Joanne Simmons.

AGNES WICH (*page 150*), a registered nurse, spent her childhood in Iowa, moving to Colorado while in high school. A "self-acknowledged city-girl," she married a farmer twenty years ago and has developed "a very keen appreciation for this vanishing way of life and for all those who came before us to pave the way through hardships and hard work." She says she would "never again return to the city." With two boys, the family now lives on part of the land her children's great-great-grandfather bought from the railroad more than one hundred years ago.

JOANNE WILKE (*pages 82, 193*), reared in urban California and rural Iowa, moved to Montana in 1978 on a trade scholarship. In 1980 she and her husband moved a house to Trail Creek Road, fifteen miles outside Bozeman. For fifteen years — beginning without power, plumbing, or phone — they rebuilt the house from the inside out. Her poems included in this collection were written during that time. She and her husband later moved to town with their two-year-old son.

ARLYS M. WINKLER (*page 74*) spent her first few years on a farm and worked as a bank teller in North Dakota most of her adult life. When her husband retired from his job as a postmaster, she quit her job to write — "I love to write!" She is now writing children's books for the National Children's Reading Foundation. She and her husband spend winters in Florida and the rest of the year in North Dakota.

SHELAGH WULFF WISDOM (*page 9*) helped her father on the family's Wyoming ranch as a little girl and continues to operate it and care for her mother. With her husband, George, she raises sheep and Hereford cattle, and raises and trains horses; she also teaches dance classes. In rodeo, she team ropes, barrel races, and competes in breakaway roping, pole bending, and steer stopping. She's also taken correspondence courses in writing, photography, and animal husbandry, and does ad layout and typesetting at the local newspaper.

JANE ELKINGTON WOHL (*page 322*) began writing after she moved to Sheridan, Wyoming, in 1978. She's known her husband, Barry, since they were both thirteen years old; they have three children. She has taught every age level from nursery school to college, facilitates a high school writers' group, and co-directs the Sheridan YMCA young writers' summer camp.

KATHERINE WOOD (*page 197*) found her voice on blue paper in second grade, writing five-page mystery novels. Soon she developed a love for poetry and has been writing it ever since. When she's not teaching high school English in Colorado, she's traveling through "the wonders of nature, listening for whispered poems," accompanied by her golden Lab, Tosca. Old buildings attract her — especially train depots — and Nebraska back roads. She paints, quilts, camps, fishes, enjoys music, dancing, and spending time with family and friends.

CAROLE D. WORKMAN-ALLEN (*page 175*) finds herself "in the middle years of life, old enough to have grown children, but young enough to experience giddy excitement at any given moment and for almost any reason." Her spiritual connection to earth and wildlife are, she says, "a significant part of who I am." She lives on the edge of the plains with her husband, a dog, and two cats, belongs to an animal rescue group, reads, works with medicinal herbs, and bakes bread.

Acknowledgments

Like a quilt, this book was shaped by the contributions of many women. We are indebted to all those who freely shared their stories with us. Some of those voices speak in these pages. However, we also wish to clearly acknowledge the women who wrote pieces that fit outside the final pattern of the book. We thank *all* of the women who allowed us to read their stories and who sent other material for their patience, trust, and generosity. Among the patchwork of stories and letters we found the gifts of friendship, wisdom, humor, and faith for which we will always be grateful.

We relied on a network of friends, acquaintances, librarians, and newspapers to help us reach women with stories to tell. We thank those who sent us lists, prodded their mothers and neighbors to write, and supported our vision. We thank the Wyoming Council on the Arts and the Custer Area Arts Council in South Dakota for providing funding that helped us with start-up expenses and gave us confidence.

We thank women who came before us for establishing a solid framework of literature about the women's West. If this book encourages more women to express themselves, we will feel gratified.

Our appreciation goes to Tracy Eller and to Lisa Sacks for their care in preserving the character of the writing. To Marc Jaffe and Mindy Keskinen we confer the status of honorary citizens of the High Plains. The honor has been earned.

CREDITS